# *The Puritans:*
## *Their Origins and Successors*

# *The Puritans: Their Origins and Successors*

Addresses delivered at the
Puritan and Westminster Conferences
1959–1978

D. M. LLOYD-JONES

THE BANNER OF TRUTH TRUST

THE BANNER OF TRUTH TRUST

*Head Office*
3 Murrayfield Road
Edinburgh, EH12 6EL
UK

*North America Office*
610 Alexander Spring Road
Carlisle, PA 17015
USA

banneroftruth.org



First published 1978
Reprinted (retypeset) 2024
with the addition of an Appendix: '1662–1962: From Puritanism to Nonconformity' © The Evangelical Library, London.

*

ISBN
Print: 978 1 80040 486 1
Epub: 978 1 80040 487 8

*

Typeset in 11/13 pt Adobe Garamond Pro at
The Banner of Truth Trust, Edinburgh

Printed in the USA by
Versa Press, Inc.,
East Peoria, IL

# *Contents*

# *Introduction*

This volume brings together for the first time the nineteen addresses which Dr Lloyd-Jones gave at the Puritan and Westminster Conferences, from 1959 to 1978. It is convenient to remember that, as his birthday was on December 20, 1899, Dr Lloyd-Jones' age coincided with the years of this century and so he was on the eve of his sixtieth birthday when the first of these addresses was given on December 16, 1959, and almost seventy-nine at the time of the last.

The Puritan Conference met annually on the Tuesday and the Wednesday of the week before Christmas at Westminster Chapel, London, being convened for the first time on December 19, 1950. It originated in an upsurge of interest in the writings of the English Puritans among a small group of students who were members of the Oxford Inter-Collegiate Christian Union (a branch of the InterVarsity Fellowship) in the late 1940s. This interest was surprising for virtually no Puritan books were then in print and the evangelicalism to which they belonged was commonly occupied with other concerns. As these undergraduates took up such hard-to-find authors as John Owen and Richard Baxter they felt as though they had wandered into some forgotten El Dorado.

It was as their paths crossed with those of the minister of Westminster Chapel, London, that the idea for a conference was born. They met him either at Inter-Varsity meetings and conferences, where he was speaking, or through his daughter, Elizabeth, herself an undergraduate at Oxford at this period and a member of OICCU. In Dr Lloyd-Jones' preaching they heard, for the first time, a minister of God whose teaching was clearly harmonious with their newly discovered reading. He advocated and urged the biblical view both of sin and of divine grace. In his presentation of the gospel he put God first and the need for holiness before any promise of happiness. Instead of sharing in the kind of evangelism which concentrated upon special efforts and modern methods, he called people to a God-centred way of life in which Christian witness would become a spontaneous part of every-day behaviour. In these priorities it was clear to them that here was a modern preacher whose spiritual affinities belonged to a tradition much older than the evangelicalism of the late 19th century.

James I. Packer, one of the Oxford students, came up to London in 1948 to tutor students for a year at Oak Hill College. He was regularly at Westminster Chapel on Sunday evenings. It was probably his friend Raymond Johnston, supported by Elizabeth Lloyd-Jones, who first appealed to 'the Doctor' to lead another conference under the auspices of the Tyndale Fellowship (the theological wing of IVF). Various Tyndale Fellowship conferences already existed, but the idea of one which would concentrate upon the Puritans was novel and unlikely to command general acceptance. Dr Lloyd-Jones readily agreed, however, and *The Christian Graduate* for June 1950 contained the brief note: 'December 19–20, Tyndale Fellowship Conference at Westminster Chapel, "The Distinctive Theological Contribution of the English Puritans." Speakers include the Rev Dr D. Martyn Lloyd-Jones.' No other speakers were named and the truth was that, for a two-day conference, it was not easy to find speakers who shared this new enthusiasm for Puritan authors.

The first Conference was one of small beginnings. Only about 20 gathered in the church parlour at Westminster Chapel and Dr Packer recalls that he gave three of the addresses while Dr Lloyd-Jones spoke on the Puritans and assurance. Lloyd-Jones' contribution was, however, far larger than any single address. He chaired the sessions and the discussion periods which followed the six addresses were very often as valuable as the papers themselves. From the outset the Conference represented far more than a mere intellectual interest in the Puritans. Each session began and ended with prayer (an example of which can be read on pp. 52-3) and notwithstanding the sometimes strong debate which followed the addresses, the ethos was more akin to a service of worship than to a lecture room. 'The interests of the Conference,' Packer wrote, 'are practical and constructive, not merely academic. We look on the Puritans as our fellow-Christians, now enabled to share with us, through the medium of their books, the good things which God gave them three centuries ago. We study their teaching on the topics which took first place in their own thoughts and writings...We study the history of their doings as a commentary upon their convictions. And the question which we ask is not simply the historical one: what did they do and teach? (though, of course, that is where we start); our questions are rather these: how far is their exposition of the Scriptures a right one? and what biblical principles does it yield for the guiding of our faith and life today? The second half of each session of the Conference is devoted to discussing the contents of the paper that has been read, from the standpoint of these two questions.'[1]

Unnoticed by the religious world at large, something of far-reaching consequence had begun in the Conference of 1950. Speaking on another occasion of his part in that first Conference, Dr Packer says: 'I simply wanted to share what my own reading had taught me, and was quite happy with the 20 or so folk who came on that first occasion. The Doctor, however, with whom as Conference organiser I was now conversing for the first time, made no secret of his belief that what we were doing was of great potential importance for the church: which struck me, for really I had never thought of it that way.'

During the 1950s interest in the Puritans grew markedly and, as the result of a whole combination of influences, James I. Packer, Raymond Johnston, and others who were formerly students together at Oxford, produced articles in *Inter-Varsity* and *The Christian Graduate;* the Evangelical Library provided ready access to the rarest books; Ernest F. Kevan, Principal of the London Bible College, gave his testimony to the worth of the old authors; the *Banner of Truth* magazine commenced in 1955 (the full-scale republishing of books following in 1957); and closely related to all these

[1] Foreword to *A Goodly Heritage,* papers read at the Puritan Studies Conference, 1958.

endeavours was the leadership and week-by-week ministry of Dr Lloyd-Jones. In his Address at the Annual Meeting of the Evangelical Library in 1955 he said:

'There is another remarkable thing to which I must refer; I feel that we are witnessing a true revival of interest in the Puritans, and a number of young men are studying their literature constantly. There is held annually a Puritan Conference which is attended by some sixty people, and this library has played a very central part in it.'[2]

By the end of the 1950s the numbers attending the Conference – with a large proportion of students for the ministry and mission field – were well over one hundred and the meetings had assumed the settled pattern which was maintained until 1969. The Conference now met in the much larger Institute Hall of Westminster Chapel; instead of the platform normally used for meetings in that Hall, a small table and desk was placed on the side of the room, at floor level, so that speaker and chairman were surrounded on three sides. This arrangement served the exchanges at 'close-quarters' in the discussion periods which invariably began with questions addressed to the speaker and these were followed by far-ranging debate. Beginning at about 10.45 am, each day of the conference was divided into three periods. After a first address it was often hard to end the intense discussion in time for lunch, prepared, year by year, by a band of willing ladies belonging to Westminster Chapel. There was time, perhaps, for a brief walk in St James' Park before the second address at 2 pm, this session being divided by a break for tea from the final meeting at 5 pm.

From 1959 it became the custom for Dr Lloyd-Jones to give the final address on the second day. It was the only session which was not followed by discussion. The reason for this was certainly not because the speaker did not wish to have his views debated. The whole Conference was a witness to the fact that no man's beliefs were to be regarded as above criticism. The Puritans themselves differed at various, and sometimes important, points. Similar differences would often emerge in the Puritan Conference and

[2] *The Annual Meeting of the Evangelical Library*, 1955, p. 14.

the whole arrangement of speakers and discussion was against any supposition that the meetings were designed to produce a stereotyped modern 'Puritan.' As Dr Lloyd-Jones says in these pages with reference to John Knox: 'He thought things out for himself. I am emphasizing this because it is a very important matter. We must not swallow automatically everything we read in books, even from the greatest men. We must examine everything.'

Similarly, the Conference was geared to the idea that the object of studying the Puritans was practical rather than theoretical. The second address in this volume is a very powerful warning on that point and in Dr Lloyd-Jones' 1978 address on John Bunyan he was to assert, for the last time, that he was interested in 'these seventeenth-century men,' mainly, 'that we may learn from them, and watch them, as they battled with the same problems and difficulties which confront us.' For this reason he generally chose to speak on a subject which he believed to be of particular contemporary relevance and most of his addresses are related to major issues which he was convinced the churches needed to face.

Comparatively few of his addresses are largely doctrinal in content. This was not because he disapproved of doctrinal studies linked with the Puritans. On the contrary, with the Conference organiser, Dr Packer, he was always looking for speakers competent to undertake such addresses and many valuable ones were given in the course of the years. But in these Conferences he personally took something of a rest from his usual work of biblical exposition and doctrinal instruction, and concentrated upon lessons arising out of biographical and historical themes.

Another factor should also be borne in mind by those who read these addresses. Dr Lloyd-Jones believed that it is very often detrimental to a conference if lectures are *designed* for publication, because there is then a temptation for the speaker to fail to concentrate upon the needs of his actual hearers. In a conference the needs of those gathered must be foremost. It was certainly on this principle that he prepared the addresses of this book: he knew he was speaking to people who were enthusiastic – sometimes too enthusiastic! – readers of the Puritans. There was no need for him, in such a setting, to do what he did elsewhere, namely, urge upon his hearers the great values of Puritan literature. Nor was there any need for him to counter criticism of the Puritans; on the contrary the need was to see that his hearers were not uncritical. Had Dr Lloyd-Jones prepared a book for the Christian world at large on the Puritans and their successors it would probably have differed in a number of ways from the following pages; nonetheless, the wider usefulness of this material cannot be doubted.

From the mid-1950s reports of the Puritan Conference addresses were issued, first in duplicated form, then, as interest mounted, the 1958 Conference papers appeared in print. As Dr Lloyd-Jones never spoke from a manuscript, but used only an outline of notes and a few books from which he would take quotations, his material, as subsequently published in the annual Puritan Conference reports, was a transcript of his addresses as recorded on tape. To this transcript he gave only brief revision; he never re-wrote for publication. In this volume no further editing has been attempted. To have done so might have achieved greater accuracy on some points of detail but it would no longer have been the text which Dr Lloyd-Jones himself approved for publication.

To the thousands who only heard Dr Lloyd-Jones preach, and never attended a Puritan Conference, the extent and variety of his knowledge of church history as revealed in these pages may be a surprise. Certainly his colleagues in the ministry were often astonished at his researches in this particular field. Both for leisure and for personal profit he read constantly in church history and Christian biography, rarely taking any notes, yet able, with his phenomenal memory, to recall all salient facts at a much later date. The brevity of the outline notes from which he spoke is indication enough of his rare gift. The reader may sometimes wish that for purposes of further research he knew more about the sources upon which Dr Lloyd-Jones was dependent or why he should take one view against another, but it should be remembered that these addresses were not intended as definitive statements. They are primarily a stimulus to further thought with the guidance of his own convictions clearly indicated.

The initial concern that the Puritan Conference should be related to the contemporary state of the church finally led to its demise in 1970. Dr Lloyd-Jones believed that the sheer confusion in the church scene in England, and the ecumenical drive for visible unity, provided a great opportunity for evangelicals to stand together and to give their first allegiance to evangelical truth rather than to denominational alignments. Accordingly in 1966 at a Conference of the Evangelical Alliance he indicated his own conviction concerning the doctrinal compromise characteristic of the major denominations and appealed to ministers in those denominations to re-assess their positions.

Although Dr Packer's re-assessment led him to the conclusion that he should stay in the Church of England, the Puritan Conference continued as usual after 1966 and it was not until 1970, upon the publication of the ecumenical volume, *Growing into Union*,[3] that the three non-Anglican members of the Puritan Conference Committee (John Caiger, David Fountain, and Dr Lloyd-Jones) decided that it was impossible for the Conference to continue without the introduction of serious controversy. Dr Lloyd-Jones' withdrawal meant that no conference met in 1970. Again, in order to avoid public controversy, no public statement was made; the Conference had simply ended. In fact, the title for the 1969 papers, By Schisms Rent Asunder (which did not appear until late 1970), bore little relevance to the subject matter.

At a meeting of the Westminster Ministers' Fraternal in November 1970 it was urged by members that another conference be started which would continue the work of the Puritan Conference. It was this proposal which bore fruit in December 1971 and apart from a change of name (now 'The Westminster Conference') and the absence of the annual paper by Dr Packer, it was to all intents and purposes the old conference resumed. Anglicans were not excluded from the Westminster Conference (as has been suggested) but in his addresses for 1971 and 1972 it can be seen why Dr Lloyd-Jones believed that an ecumenical approach to church

[3] *Growing into Union, Proposals for forming a united Church in England,* C. O. Buchanan, E. L. Mascall, J. I. Packer, The Bishop of Willesden, S.P.C.K. 1970.

unity is fundamentally at variance with Puritan convictions. He has shown elsewhere why he also believed it is at variance with evangelical Christianity.

This may be said to be a volume on the Puritans only if the word is interpreted in its widest sense. As is clear from the first address in this volume, Dr Lloyd-Jones never intended to confine himself to the seventeenth-century and a number of his addresses are on themes outside the Puritan era. It is, however, the same underlying theme of doctrinal, reformed Christianity – the faith for which he lived and preached and prayed. The era in which these addresses were given was one both of encouragement and difficulty. Despite the difficulties, and the burden of responsibility which he bore as a leader, we never knew Dr Lloyd-Jones to speak as a man who was either anxious or depressed. 'Do not waste too much of your time in worrying about the future of the Christian church,' he says, characteristically, in one of these addresses.

The revived interest in Puritan and reformed theology of the early 1950s has today reached the ends of the earth. It is too early to know how this will eventually be assessed by later generations, but of one thing we can be sure, the author of these addresses will be remembered as one who stood fast for forgotten truths and who encouraged generations to come to believe in God and in his mighty works.

The Publisher
April 1986

# 1959

# *Revival: An Historical and Theological Survey*

WE are dealing with this subject because this year is the exact centenary of the Revival of 1859 which took place, as you know, in various countries. But, still more important, we are calling attention to it because of the present state of the world. It is a good thing that at this end of our conference we should be looking at a subject such as this, because the ultimate object of this conference is not mere intellectual stimulation, it is that we may have a true and deep concern about the state of the church. If that is not our main object, then our study becomes just a sort of Puritan scholasticism, a mere barren intellectualism which, though interesting and entertaining, will finally prove to be of no value at all.

Let me make it clear before I go any further that I am not going to give what may be regarded as a formal address on 'revival' as such. For twenty-six Sunday mornings this year I have tried to preach on 'revival.' I am not going to do that this evening. I am speaking primarily to ministers and ministerial students, and my purpose is not to give an address on 'revival,' but to attempt to face some of the problems and difficulties which seem to surround this whole subject.

## I

There is no need to take any time in giving a definition of what is meant by revival. It is an experience in the life of the church when the Holy Spirit does an unusual work. He does that work, primarily, amongst the members of the church; it is a reviving of the believers. You cannot revive something that has never had life, so revival, by definition, is first of all an enlivening and quickening and awakening of lethargic, sleeping, almost moribund church members. Suddenly the power of the Spirit comes upon them and they are brought into a new and more profound awareness of the truths that they had previously held intellectually, and perhaps at a deeper level too. They are humbled, they are convicted of sin, they are terrified at themselves. Many of them feel that they have never been Christians. And then they come to see the great salvation of God in all its glory and to feel its power. Then, as the result of their quickening and enlivening, they begin to pray. New power comes into the preaching of the ministers, and the result of this is that large numbers who were previously outside the church are converted and brought in. So the two main characteristics of revival are, first, this extraordinary enlivening of the members of the church, and, second, the conversion of masses of people who hitherto have been outside in indifference and in sin. (There are many other consequences which I do not stay to mention, such as the needed provision of larger church buildings, the establishing of new causes, large numbers of men offering themselves for the ministry and beginning to train, and so on.) Here, then, in its essence is a definition of what we mean by revival.

## II

Having said that, our best approach perhaps is to start with the actual historical survey. And the first thing I would mention is this. There has never been a revival in the Roman Catholic Church. That is a significant fact as a starting point. Individuals in that church have known and experienced what can be called revival, but the church as such has never known revival. Why? I would say that the main explanation is this – it is a direct consequence of their whole doctrine of the Holy Spirit. They confine the Holy Spirit to the church and the priesthood, and particularly to the sacraments, and more particularly still to that of baptism. So, dealing with the Holy Spirit and his operations in that way, they leave no room for revival at all, and the result is that they never have revival.

In the same way there has never been revival in the Unitarian Church. I am simply stating facts.

The next observation I would make – and here I would be very careful to indicate that I am in no sense concerned to offer criticisms, I am simply trying to face facts – is that on the whole it is true to say that the Anglican church has not known much about revival. There have been occasions when men in her ministry have undoubtedly been part and parcel of a revival, and greatly used, as we shall see, but, looking at her history, there has been no such thing as a general revival in the Anglican church. That again is surely a fact of great significance. There was a little experience of revival in the Anglican body in Ireland a hundred years ago, but very little as far as I can find out anywhere else in the Anglican communion. Now why is this? Is it possible that there is something in her form of service that militates against the freedom of the operation of the Spirit? Is it also possible, perhaps, that her association with the State operates in the same direction, and that the whole character of the church and her view of herself and her parochial system tend to discourage the phenomenon of revival within her ranks? There, at any rate, is a big fact which stands out in the history of the Anglican church.

Looking at it now a little more in terms of the centuries, and leaving the Reformation out of account for a moment because I shall come back to it in a later section, we find that in the seventeenth century there was a remarkable revival, or, indeed, series of revivals in Northern Ireland. This was in the 1620s. There were similar sporadic revivals in different churches in Scotland under the ministry of people like Welsh and Bruce and Livingstone and David Dickson and Rutherford and Blair. And surely we must agree that in England in the case of Rogers of Dedham, and Baxter at Kidderminster, we are entitled to speak of revival. Then when you come to the eighteenth century there was that remarkable revival that took place about 1727 in the Moravian community at Herrnhut in Germany. That amazing movement of the Spirit is graphically described in the early part of the Journals of John Wesley, and of course in many manuals on the history of the

Moravian Brethren. Then in the United States of America you have Jonathan Edwards and the 'Great Awakening,' in which George Whitefield also took such a prominent part. In England under the ministry of Whitefield, again, and of the Wesleys and various other men, almost right up to 1790, there were clear outpourings of the Spirit in revival. Indeed, this whole period, in a sense, and looked at broadly, can be described as an age of revival.

Exactly the same thing was true of Wales from 1735 onwards. Both Howell Harris and Daniel Rowland received their 'baptism of power,' as they would put it, and a great revival broke out. It lasted a number of years, then it began to wane, then it came back again. There was a succession of revival after revival; it came in several waves right up to the end of the life of Rowland and even beyond that. There were periodic revivals right through to the end of the century. The same thing, of course, was true of Scotland. All who know the story of the eighteenth century have heard about Cambuslang and what happened there on the occasion of that famous communion service, and later at Kilsyth and various other places.

Then when we come to the nineteenth century we find that a notable revival broke out in Northern Ireland in 1858 (though it is generally called the '59 Revival), and this spread later to Scotland. There was a similar movement of revival in Wales lasting right throughout that year. And the same thing had happened, as you know, in America, starting in 1857.

It would be very interesting to stop with these revivals and to give an account of them. There is, however, no need to do so, as excellent books giving an account of them have appeared recently. Two, for instance, have been published on the revival in Ireland, and one has just come off the press about the revival in Wales in 1859.[1] There are various other older books covering the same ground, but in all cases they are simply accounts of the happenings and events. They do not, therefore, deal with our particular

[1] Ian R. K. Paisley, *The 'Fifty-Nine' Revival;* John T. Carson, *God's River in Spate*; Eifion Evans, *When He Is Come.*

difficulties. Even a book like Sprague's *Lectures on Revivals,*[1] is too general in its treatment to do that. However, there is the history, right up until 1860. It is a story of over a century of recurrent revival. I cannot but be interested in this fact, that between 1760 and 1860 there were at least fifteen major revivals in Wales alone.

We now come to the striking fact that there seems to have been a great change in people's outlook on this whole matter after about 1860, or 1870. There seems to be a kind of dividing line at that historical juncture. Before that, we find that people thought in terms of revival, and we hear of frequent revivals in the history of the church; but after that, revivals become rather exceptional phenomena. By now, I believe, we have reached an age in which the vast majority of church members have almost ceased to think in terms of revival at all. Up until 1860 it was the instinctive thing to think in terms of revival. If there had been a period of spiritual drought, if things were not going well in the church, the first thing they thought of was this – 'Should not we have a time of confession and humiliation and prayer to God to visit us again?' They did it almost instinctively. But we do not do that. Why not? What is the explanation of this change that seems to have come into the thinking of the church? I think I can suggest some of the factors.

The first factor, beyond any doubt, is the decline in Reformed theology. The whole Modernist movement that had started in the forties of the last century gained great momentum in the sixties. It increased at an alarming speed and the Reformed theology in particular fell into the background. Until that date – speaking at any rate for nonconformity – the prevailing theology was almost entirely Calvinistic, apart from that of the Methodist bodies. But there was a very sad decline and sudden waning of all that. The change took place very rapidly, and those who are familiar with the life of Charles Haddon Spurgeon will know how he not only saw the fact but deeply regretted it and bemoaned it.

Secondly, there was the influence of the writings of Charles G. Finney. Because of the numerical success of his campaigns and his meetings, his work attracted great attention, and his volume of

[1] Re-published by the Banner of Truth Trust.

lectures, *Revivals of Religion,* soon became very popular and almost a best-seller. Finney's whole outlook and teaching seems to have become a governing factor in the outlook of the church. It has led to the notion of what we call 'evangelistic campaigns.' Finney is the man of all men who is responsible for the current confusion with regard to this matter. Our American brethren even get confused about the very terms. They talk about 'holding a revival meeting'; they mean, of course, an evangelistic campaign. That is the result of Finney's influence, and it has really befogged the whole situation. The influence of Finney's teaching upon the outlook of the church has been quite extraordinary. People now, instead of thinking instinctively about turning to God and praying for revival when they see that the church is languishing, decide rather to call a committee, to organise an evangelistic campaign, and work out and plan an advertising programme to 'launch' it, as they say. The whole outlook and mentality has entirely changed.

Thirdly, we come to a matter which is a little controversial. I am not certain about it myself – but increasingly I feel that this is a very important factor. I am still dealing, remember, with the change that took place round about 1860, and I cannot but feel that theological seminaries have been an important factor in the change. Here is an attempt to explain how it worked. Up until, say, the 1830s the position was something like this. At first the preaching was done by clergy and ministers who had themselves been revived. Numbers of men who had been converted then began to feel a call to preach, or it was suggested to them by some of these leaders that they had a preaching gift. They had manifested it in prayer or in taking part in a class meeting or in a discussion, and now they were encouraged to preach. These men were farmers, workers, manual workers and so on. They had not been to a theological seminary. They were men who had a living experience of God in their hearts, who read and studied their Bibles and books about the Bible. They were men of strong natural talents and were very largely self-taught. This was the class of men who largely became the preachers after the death of the first great leaders. But then, the idea came in that as education had spread among the masses and the congregations were now more sophisticated and more learned, the ministry of these simple ordinary men was no longer adequate. (I am not criticising that attitude; I am trying to put the actual facts before you.) It was felt that there was a need for training and that you must have learned men in the ministry. This started with an undoubtedly good and right motive. Nor is there any *a priori* reason why spirituality and learning should be incompatible; but nevertheless it does seem to be the case in practice that as men become more and more learned they tend to pay less and less attention to the spiritual side of things. Now this is almost inevitable, of course, for we are yet in the flesh, and are still imperfect. Whether a man wants to or not, he gradually finds himself becoming more and more interested in things in a purely intellectual manner. I have known this very thing in my own life. Unconsciously one can become so interested in the purely intellectual aspect of Christianity, and in learning and understanding and knowledge, as to forget the Spirit. I am therefore putting it simply as a possibility for consideration that perhaps the increase in theological seminaries may have been a factor in discouraging people from thinking about revival. The more learned we become, the more respectable we tend to become. As we become 'men of weight' and important, we feel that we have to be very careful as to what we do or allow to happen to us. It is extremely difficult for such men to maintain that 'simplicity which is in Christ Jesus'; certainly more difficult than for the other type of man whom I have just been describing. I do not want to exaggerate this, but I am suggesting that it may very well have been a serious factor.

Whatever the explanation, we have come now to this extraordinary position that, unless I am greatly mistaken, there is a lack of interest today in this question of revival. I am speaking out of knowledge. I am interested in discussions, and I frequent certain circles where men meet for discussion. I suggest on the basis of such experience that there is not only a lack of interest in revival but also an antagonism to the idea. I am told by the publishers that the book on the subject which I commended, Sprague's *Lectures on Revival,* has not been selling too well. I am amazed at this, but it is a fact. Why is there this lack of interest in revival? Why has the subject dropped out of the minds of people? And this is the interesting thing: what I am saying is not only true of the Arminian brethren, it is equally true of the Calvinistic brethren. Let us be clear about this. If you examine the books on the Holy Spirit published during the past fifty years by men of all schools you will find that they do not even mention revival at all. One is not surprised at this in some instances, because the writers' particular outlook is one which, though it pays lip service to the work of the Holy Spirit, really pins its faith on what man does himself, on what man organises. That whole outlook expresses itself through evangelistic campaigns and their appendages. You first of all get your men to go to the evangelistic campaign to get them saved. Then you take them to another place where they get a further desired blessing. That is the outlook. I am not poking fun at it, I am simply describing what is actually the controlling thought: that you take them to the right places and the results can be expected to follow. 'What more do you need?' say such people. 'Why are you talking about revival? Things are going well. Look at the crowds, look at the masses of people who are coming; isn't this enough? Why go any further?' Their attitude is perfectly logical if you grant its initial premise.

But that the same thing should be true of Reformed people – this is to me not only surprising but tragic. It is not only the books by Arminians which omit all reference to revival, the same is true of those by Calvinists. Dr Lewis Sperry Chafer, for instance, in his great volume on Pneumatology, does not mention revivals at all. Here is an example of a Calvinist who had on this point become infected by this general climate of opinion. But here is a still more tragic fact. As I was preparing this lecture, I turned to Charles Hodge, but I got no help. Charles Hodge does not seem to have been interested in revival. Why not? I would say it is for the reasons I have already been giving. A man like Charles Hodge becomes a theologian and he tends therefore not to think as he should in terms of the church in its local concrete situation, but in terms of great abstract systems of truth. He lives in that realm of comparisons and arguments and contrasts, of systems and especially of philosophy, and almost inevitably he ceases to think as he should about revival and the immediate operations of the Spirit.

There is one very interesting point just here. I would say that this change of outlook on the part of Calvinists came in the U.S.A. somewhere between Archibald Alexander and Charles Hodge. Charles Hodge, as you know, was the successor of Archibald Alexander in the theological seminary at Princeton. Now Archibald Alexander had had experience of revival in his early days. Charles Hodge knew something about it, but not to the same extent as Alexander, who was an older man and who belonged partly to the previous century. It is just there that this change seems to me to have taken place.

Another interesting point to observe is that if you want any help at all on the subject of revival you are more or less driven back to books on the Holy Spirit and his work that were written before 1860. There are, for instance, *The Doctrine of the Holy Spirit,* by George Smeaton, and also *The Office and Work of the Holy Spirit,* by James Buchanan. They both have a section on revival, but you will observe that they are both prior to the date I mentioned. Is not that an interesting fact? They belonged, you see, to the period when the church instinctively thought in the way I have described.

## III

Let us now try to analyse this. Why is it that men belonging to the Reformed tradition, of all traditions, have apparently lost interest in this question of revival? I have already given you one reason, which is the danger of becoming theoretical and intellectual in one's approach. A minister of the gospel is a man who is always fighting on two fronts. He first of all has to urge people to become interested in doctrine and theology, but he will not have been long at that before he will find that he has to open up a second front, and to tell people that it is not enough to be interested only in doctrine and theology, that there is a danger of becoming a mere orthodox intellectualist and of growing negligent about your own spiritual life and the life of the church. This is the besetting danger of people who hold the Reformed position. They are the only people who are really interested in theology, so the devil comes to them and drives them too far along the line of that interest and they tend to become pure theologians and interested in truth only intellectually.

Secondly, I am sure that this phenomenon was due to the fact that so much energy in the last century had to be given to the fight against Modernism. The enemy was attacking along that particular line and all the energy of the orthodox was bent to quell him and to hold him back and to defeat him. Yes, but unconsciously they allowed this conflict to control their entire thinking, and apologetics became the chief thing with them instead of a positive message. The same thing had happened in the early part of the eighteenth century. Rationalism and Deism had come in and the church became concerned about it. What did they do? They set up the Boyle Lectures, Butler wrote his *Analogy,* and so on. They tried to stem the tide by answering the objections and dealing with the intellectual position. Do not misunderstand me; I am not arguing against the value of apologetics altogether, but I am saying this, that a church which becomes governed by the apologetic interest is a church that is ceasing to function positively. The devil has got her, and she tends to be negative only and to fail to recognise the positive activity of the Holy Spirit. History shows that what the Boyle lecturers and Bishop Butler and others failed to do, God did by pouring out his Spirit upon men like Whitefield and Wesley.

The third reason, I would say, is a natural dislike of too much emotion. The theological thinker tends to be distrustful of emotion. After all, he argues, other people can and do display emotion; but we are different. In a most subtle manner such a man develops a dislike of emotion that becomes unhealthy and wrong; he loses his balance, and becomes guilty of quenching the Spirit.

Another closely related reason, which I think operates in particular today, is that there has been an excessive reaction against Pentecostalism and its phenomena. Many are so afraid of Pentecostalism and its excesses and aberrations that they are quenching the

Spirit. There is always a danger of such extremes, of over-reacting against something and so losing the balance of the Scripture.

There is another factor worthy of careful consideration. I have known a number of men belonging to the Reformed constituency who really seem to be controlled by some such thoughts as this. After all, they say, a man like John Wesley had a prominent part in the revival of the eighteenth century. From that they seem to deduce that there is something undesirable and wrong about revival. 'Can any good come from such a quarter? If men like Wesley and Finney and other Arminians can be involved in revival and used in it, well, we ought to be suspicious of revival.' The mistake here is that we all tend to think in terms of labels and parties, not realising that God displays his sovereignty often in this way, that though a man may be muddled in his thinking, as John Wesley was at certain points, God may nevertheless bless him and use him. And if he cannot do this, then there is no such thing as the sovereignty of God, and his omnipotence. Thus because of party spirit we can go wrong in our thinking and be guilty of quenching the Spirit of God.

But perhaps the most important and most serious matter is this. The Puritans themselves do not seem to teach us anything about revival. Oh, that I could have quoted copiously and extensively out of the Puritans! But I cannot do so. As far as I can find, they did not write on the subject. Did they even recognise it? John Owen's volumes on the work of the Holy Spirit do not deal with it. Try to discover what John Owen has to say on John 7, verses 37 to 39, or what he has to tell us on Peter's sermon in Acts 2: 'This is that which was spoken by the prophet Joel,' or on Acts 3:19, 'that times of refreshing may come from the presence of the Lord.' He just does not deal with the subject of these verses; neither do the others. This undoubtedly creates a very real difficulty for many people. 'The Puritans did not deal with revival,' they say; 'they never talked about it. Can it therefore be right? Is there not something inherently dubious about this whole matter?'

We must address ourselves directly to this question. Why did the Puritans not deal with revival? I would like to suggest some reasons for your consideration. Was it not partly the fact that they lived in a particular age and had to meet a particular need? The Puritans in their day were up-to-date; they were modern men; they lived in their own century and faced realistically the actual conditions which confronted them. They had to fight on many fronts themselves. They had to fight not only the old Roman teaching, and the High Church teaching of Laud and his friends, but also the views of some of the 'wilder men' amongst themselves, and of the sects. I do not like this epithet 'wilder men,' but there were among the Puritans men like Walter Craddock and Morgan Llwyd, who differed in a radical way from men like John Owen and Thomas Goodwin. They were much more directly experimental in the pneumatic sense, and had leanings toward mysticism. This was certainly true of Morgan Llwyd and, of course, the Quakers. The leading Puritans, whose works we have, were fighting such men; they were gravely concerned about these excesses and afraid of them. The result was that much of their writing on the Holy Spirit was determined by this polemical interest, and hence very often they are too negative in their approach. I believe that is a partial explanation.

Dare I also hazard the opinion that the fact that some of these leading Puritans were brought up in a certain communion and carried over certain ideas and traditions which may have had an inhibiting effect upon them? At any rate they were very concerned about order – perhaps too much so. So anxious were they that everything should be done 'decently and in order' that I find it very difficult at times to acquit them of the charge of quenching the Spirit.

I am tempted to add another note. I wonder whether even temperament enters into this matter? I announced that I would speak on revival from an historical and theological standpoint. I very nearly added the word 'geographical,' and even a further word, 'ethnological'! I am not sure whether this comes in, but I think it does. Every man has a fight to wage; we are all temperamentally different, and we all have particular weaknesses of temperament to fight against. I wonder whether it is not true to say that the

Englishman has a particular fight just here, and that he should be aware of it? Is it just an accident that these revivals in the history of the church have generally been outside England? Not, of course, entirely. The eighteenth century stands out, as I have reminded you, and there were those odd sporadic instances in the seventeenth century. But is there not a real danger that unconsciously, because of temperament and make-up, one man may be more prone to the sin of quenching the Spirit than others of different temperaments?

Whatever may be the true explanation, we can certainly agree about this as regards the Puritans – their primary interest was pastoral and experiential in a personal sense. That was their genius; and it was this that fitted them for the peculiar work that they were called upon to do – the analysis of cases of conscience, the resolution of doubts and helping people who were in trouble. They excelled at that, and there can be no doubt that this was the thing that was needed particularly in their day and generation.

There, then, are some, at any rate, of the reasons as I see things for the lack of interest in revival amongst those who belong to the Reformed tradition.

## IV

Let us come now to another section – difficulties, and objections to the idea of revival. An obvious general objection (with which I unfortunately have not the time to deal at length) is the dislike of phenomena. Some people are so appalled and alarmed at the phenomena that sometimes occur in revival that they dismiss the whole subject. The answer is, of course, that you can have, and have had, revivals where there have been no such phenomena at all. Revivals differ greatly from time to time and from age to age and from place to place. I leave it at that.

Here is another particular difficulty. I do not know exactly what is believed by present-day Plymouth Brethren but I do know that the early Brethren taught, and taught very strongly, that it was wrong to pray for revival because, they said, the Holy Ghost had been given once for all on the Day of Pentecost: In view of that, what right have you to ask him to come now? That was their teaching, and I believe it has had a very pervasive effect and has influenced large numbers who do not belong to that section of the church. The argument is, 'Why do you pray for the coming of the Spirit, for an outpouring of the Spirit? He was outpoured on the Day of Pentecost. How can he be poured out again?' Such teaching actively discourages prayer for revival.

Another objection sometimes alleged is that nowhere in the New Testament are we taught to pray for revival. Here we come to a subject which might well occupy the whole of our time. There is an abundant answer to this objection. The main point of it is this – that the New Testament church was not exhorted to pray for revival because it was in the midst of a revival. What we read about the church in the New Testament is an account of revival. The New Testament church was full of the power of the Spirit. When you read the history of revivals, are you not reminded at once of the book of the Acts of the Apostles? The church always looks like the church in the New Testament when she is in the midst of revival. The New Testament period was a period of revival; the great outpouring on the Day of Pentecost was continued. The church of the New Testament was a pneumatic church, filled with the Spirit. I have often put the argument like this. Take 1 Corinthians 14, where Paul has to write to the church about speaking in tongues and speaking one at a time, and how, if a man is prophesying and sees another wanting to speak, he should stop and so on. Would you need to write that chapter to the church today? Of course not! Why? Because the church today is not in this pneumatic condition. The New Testament church was a church that was filled and baptized with the Spirit. Let me add here another controversial remark. It seems to me that the societies that were started in England and Wales by the Methodist Fathers of both schools of thought in the eighteenth century were much nearer to the New Testament church than were the Puritan churches of the seventeenth century. There was more of the freedom of the Spirit, more spontaneity, more taking part by the mass of the people. I think that is something which is worthy of our consideration.

That, then, provides a part of the answer to the objection that we are not told to pray for revival in the New Testament. But there is much more along the same line. I know that the exegesis of Acts 3:19 is somewhat doubtful. Buchanan and Smeaton, however, seem to be in no doubt as to the exegesis; they say it refers to revival, and I tend to agree with them. These 'times of refreshing … from the presence of the Lord,' they say, are periods of revival, as if Peter's message was this: 'Well now, here you have had the first great sample of the Spirit's power and blessing. This is going to keep on recurring until the time of the restitution of all things.' Again, in order to prove that the New Testament church was a church in revival, look at this further evidence. In 1 Thessalonians 1:5, Paul says, 'Our gospel came unto you not only in word, but in power and in the Holy Ghost, and with much assurance.' What was it that turned the ancient world upside down? Was it just theological teaching? Was it mere enunciation of correct doctrine? Over and above that there was this mighty 'demonstration of the Spirit and of power.' How did those people turn the world upside down? The answer is that in the book of Acts we have an account of a great revival, of the Spirit outpoured. What happened could not have happened otherwise. How did all these churches come into being? Was it merely that the apostles taught correct doctrine? Of course not! It was the Spirit's demonstration and power which accompanied the correct doctrine. Correct doctrine can leave the church dead; you can have dead orthodoxy, you can have a church that is perfectly orthodox but perfectly useless. Over and above, there was this demonstration, this unction, this authority, this outpouring of the Spirit's power. It is the only explanation of the astonishing things that happened.

That brings us to the next difficulty, about which we are hearing a good deal at the present time. We are told that we must not talk about revival because we need reformation first. You cannot have revival, it is said, without prior reformation. You must be right with respect to your doctrine before you have a right to pray for revival. So we must concentrate on reformation alone. I grant that the relationship between these two things is an extremely difficult question, but I hold that the line is not quite as clear-cut as some would have us think. What happened in the Reformation of the sixteenth century? To start with, of course, there was this unique factor, that not only was the teaching of the Church of Rome wrong; her entire church system was wrong too. We called what happened 'the Reformation' largely because of the revolution that took place in men's thoughts about the nature of the church and consequently in its organisation. It was not only a change in doctrine. And let us never forget this, that there was a great revival in the period of the Reformation. You cannot read the account of a man like Latimer without realising that obviously the man was being used as a revival preacher. Is it a feasible suggestion that the common people of England were influenced by a mere change of doctrinal teaching? Could that ever lead to such results? Can any examples of that be found? Of course not! No, no, there was a genuine revival then, the presence and the power of the Spirit were undoubtedly there. It is the only adequate explanation of what really took place in the sixteenth century.

Now let me say this on the other side. It is a fact of history that in Northern Ireland, before the Revival of 1859, there had been a great period of doctrinal controversy. The Presbyterian Church had become very largely Arian, and the great and famous Henry Cooke had fought and won the great battle against Arianism well before the revival came: actually, about thirty years before. That time interval is not without significance. To be fair, however, I have to recall these facts.

But now I want to put a fact on the other side again. There are people who say, 'You have no right to talk about revival, you have no right to expect revival until people become Reformed in their doctrine.' The simple answer to that is that George Whitefield received his baptism of power in 1737, but did not become a Calvinist in his theology until about 1739, when he was out in America. Revival had come to him, and through him to many others, before his doctrine became right. Exactly the same thing is true of Howell Harris in Wales. He had his great baptism of power in 1735, and it was only two or three years later that he came to see the truth doctrinally. Once more, therefore, I would use this argument. If you say that God cannot give revival until first of all we have had a reformation, you are speaking like an Arminian, you are saying that God cannot do this until we ourselves have first done something. That is to put a limit upon God. It is to lapse into Arminian terminology and thinking, and to deny the fundamental tenet of the Reformed position. If you truly believe in the sovereignty of God, you must believe that whatever the state of the church, God can send revival. As a sheer matter of fact, that is what God did in the eighteenth century. There was the church under the blight of Deism and Rationalism, and generally dissolute in her living. That was true of the clergy and the leaders; and among the nonconformists there was a deadness resulting from the Arianism that had even infected such a man as Isaac Watts. In the midst of such conditions God did this amazing and astonishing thing, even while some of the men he used were still confused in their doctrinal views. It is amazing that any man holding the Reformed position can be guilty of such a contradiction as to say that you cannot have revival unless you have reformation first. Such a man should never speak like that; he has no right to put in conditions. Revival is something that is wrought by God in sovereign freedom, often in spite of men.

## V

Let me now attempt to summarise and assess the position. The result of all this confusion is that the church seems to be divided at the present time into two main groups. There is a group of people that always talk about revival and only about revival. They are only interested in the exceptional and unusual, and they tend to 'despise the days of small things,' the regular work of the church and the regular work of the Spirit in the church. The other group so emphasise the ordinary, regular work of the church and of the Spirit in the church, that they distrust the whole notion of the unusual and exceptional. The answer is, of course, that both are wrong. Let me quote from Buchanan on *The Office and Work of the*

*Holy Spirit.* Buchanan was a professor in the Free Church College in Edinburgh and this is what he wrote in 1856:

'The Holy Spirit is not limited to any one mode of operation in the execution of his glorious work; and his sovereignty ought ever to be remembered when we are considering a subject of this nature. It has, unfortunately, been too much overlooked, when, on the one hand, some have insisted, as we think, with undue partiality and confidence, on a general and remarkable revival, as being in itself the best manifestation of the Spirit's grace, and as being, in all cases, a matter of promise to believing prayer; and when, on the other hand, not a few have looked to the quiet and gradual success of the gospel ministry, to the exclusion, or at least disparagement, of any more sudden and remarkable work of grace. [Do you not know the two groups today?] The former have given a too exclusive preference to what is extraordinary and striking; while the latter have fallen into the opposite error, of preferring what is more usual and quiet. We think it were better to admit of both methods of conversion, and to leave the choice to the sovereign wisdom and grace of the Spirit. It is equally possible for him to convert souls successively or simultaneously; and in adopting either course doubtless he has wise ends in view. We have no sympathy with those who, overlooking the steady progress of the great work of conversion under a stated ministry, make no account of the multitudes who are added, one by one, to the church of the living God, merely because their conversion has not been attended with the outward manifestations of a great religious revival; nor can we agree with them in thinking, that the church has any sure warrant to expect that the Spirit will be bestowed, in every instance, in that particular way. But as little have we any sympathy with those who, rejecting all revivals as unscriptural delusions, profess to look exclusively to the gradual progress of divine truth, and the slow advance of individual conversion under a stated ministry. Both methods – the simultaneous and the successive conversion of souls, are equally within the power of the Spirit; and there may exist wise reasons why, in certain cases, the first should be chosen, while, in other cases, the second is preferred.'[1]

[1] pp. 229-30.

There, I believe, you have a remarkable statement synthesising the characteristic experiences of the seventeenth and eighteenth centuries, and God forbid that we should ever pit the one way of divine working against the other. Both happen, in the providence and wisdom of God.

What then is my final answer to all this? Once more, I can do nothing better than quote to you out of Buchanan:

'We have been so much accustomed to look to the more slow, and quiet, and gradual method of maintaining and extending the kingdom of Christ, that we are apt to be startled, and even to listen with some degree of incredulous surprise, when we hear of any sudden and general work of the Spirit of God; nay, we cease even to expect and to pray for any more remarkable or more rapid change in the state of the church and world, than what is usually observed under her regular ministry. [I wonder how many are guilty of that today?] But God's "ways are not as our ways, neither are his thoughts as our thoughts"; and often, in the history of his church, he has been pleased, for wise reasons, to manifest his grace and power in a very extraordinary and remarkable manner; partly to awaken and arouse a slumbering church; partly also, to alarm and convince gainsayers; and most of all, to teach them at once the sovereignty and the power of that grace which they are too prone to despise.'[1]

Then listen to a quotation from Jonathan Edwards in Smeaton's book where the same point is made again in a remarkable manner: 'It may be observed that from the fall of man to our day, the work of Redemption in its effect has mainly been carried on by remarkable communications of the Spirit of God.' Notice that. He continues: 'Though there be a more constant influence of God's Spirit always in some degree attending his ordinances, yet the way in which the greatest things have been done towards carrying on this work always has been by remarkable effusions at special seasons of mercy.' Any impartial reading of church history must surely lead us to substantiate and to agree with the dictum of Jonathan Edwards. Surely the history of the progress and development of the

[1] p. 220.

church is largely a history of revivals, of these mighty exceptional effusions of the Spirit of God. There is no question that God has really kept his work alive and has advanced it most of all by these unusual, exceptional, signal manifestations of his glory and of his power. I am asserting that history alone proves that beyond any peradventure.

## VI

I close by putting this question: Why should Reformed people above everybody else be interested in the subject of revival? Surely, for the following reasons. First, nothing so proves that the church is the church of God. The graph of the church's history is one of up and down, up and down. That in itself proves that the church is not a human institution. If it were it would long since have perished and disappeared. It is the church of the living God. It is solely due to the fact that she is his and that he has graciously intervened from time to time for her preservation that she is alive.

Secondly, I would say this – that this history above everything shows man's impotence when left to himself. However great a defender of the faith he may be, however doughty a champion of orthodoxy, he can fight and sweat and pray and write and do all things, but he is of no avail, he is impotent, he cannot stem the tide. We persist in thinking that we can set the situation right. We start a new society, we write a book, we organise a campaign, and we are convinced that we are going to hold back the tide. But we cannot. When the enemy comes in like a flood, it is the Lord who will raise, and does raise the banner. The fact of revival proves, I say, so clearly again and again the impotence and the smallness of man left to himself.

Here is another important point. What so proves that the work of salvation is the work of the Holy Spirit, and not a mere matter of moral suasion or argumentation, as revival? How? Well, by the very suddenness of revival. If salvation is the result of argumentation and moral suasion, then you need to engage in it for some time. That was the whole fallacy in the thinking of a man like

Charles G. Finney. Though he pays lip service to the Holy Spirit he virtually excludes the Spirit. The work of conversion is achieved by a rational argument. That has always been the position of Arminianism, ultimately. But the Reformed man says – 'No, no, it is the work of the Holy Spirit, the direct operation of the Spirit upon the man in his mind and heart and will, in illumination and renewing.' And when and where is that seen more clearly than in a revival? Look at the suddenness of the conversions; yes, look especially at the fact which is found so abundantly in the history of revivals, that many people have been converted even before they reached the meeting or heard the preacher. They were converted on the road; conviction suddenly came upon them. You cannot say that is moral suasion. They had not even heard the sermon, there had been no preliminary argumentation whatsoever. Revival thus establishes and proves the great point which was in a sense *the* point of contention at the Synod of Dort – in conversion where does the Holy Spirit come in? The ultimate defect and error in the Arminian argument and all that has emanated from it is that it excludes the Holy Spirit from the real decision, and asserts that man is able to convert himself. Revival demonstrates the contrary contention that this is always and invariably the work of the Holy Spirit. In revivals you see that on a big and dramatic scale, and so attention is called to that truth.

In the fourth place, I would ask: Is there anything that so demonstrates the sovereignty of God as revival? Think of it in terms of the timing of revival. When does revival come? The answer is not that it is when we have produced certain preliminary conditions, as Finney taught. No, God does it at most unexpected times. You never know when he is going to do it; there is always a suddenness and unexpectedness about it. It is Arminian thinking that teaches in some shape or form, 'If only we do certain things, then …' No, the history of revivals proves the exact opposite, both as regards the beginning, and equally with respect to the ending. This is something which is most glorious. Man not only cannot start a revival, he cannot stop it either. Nor can he keep it going when it has stopped. Men have tried to do all these things but they have never succeeded. The sovereignty of God appears in the timing. Yes, and also the sovereignty of God appears in the place where revival starts. I do not understand Christian people who are not thrilled by the whole idea of revival. If there is one respect in which God confounds the wisdom of the wise more than in any other it is in revival. Look at the places in which he starts revival – little villages, hamlets, places you have never heard of. It is men who start their movements in London, in St Paul's Cathedral or in some great hotel. But God does not do that, he ridicules the wisdom of man and the cleverness and the importance of man both in the matter of time and in the matter of place, and also in the matter of the men used. Look at the men he has used. If you want a perfect exposition of 1 Corinthians 1:25-31, read books on revival. 'Not many wise men after the flesh, not many noble,' but the foolish, the nobodies, the unwise – God ridiculing, turning upside down the wisdom of men and exposing it. The sovereignty of God is seen in revival above everything.

Lastly, nothing so shows the irresistible character of grace as revival. This is seen, of course, in every true conversion, but it is in revival that it is seen on the grand scale, and unmistakably. Men who went to the meetings to upset them and to destroy them are suddenly struck, thrown down, their eyes are opened, and they are given life. There is nothing that is so obvious in a revival as just this irresistibility of the grace of God. Not only 'the fools who came to scoff,' but the enemies, the arrogant, are humbled, subdued, converted, and born again. Revival thus underlines and emphasises this particular biblical doctrine in a striking manner.

The conclusion of the whole matter is this: that we are called at this moment above everything else to pray for revival. God forbid that we should become a body of people who just denounce activism and do nothing! That is what is said about some of us. God forbid it should be true! Are we to be merely negative, merely to point at the faults of others, to point out the holes in their system and to be always denouncing negatively and ridiculing them? Of course not! What then are we called upon to do? We are called upon to go on with our regular work of preaching the gospel in all its fullness, in all its wholeness, after the manner of Puritan preaching. Let us do everything we can by every biblical and legitimate means to propagate and to defend the faith. Let us use our apologetics in their right sphere. Let us do all that, and let us go on with the work of reformation in which we are engaged; but let us at the same time maintain the balance of which we were reminded by Buchanan. Let us pray for revival, because nothing else will avail us in the fight in which we are engaged. Thank God our efforts are producing results, and far be it from any of us to despise them or underestimate them; but it is not enough. The age in which we are living and the condition of the church, not to mention the world, call for a mighty conviction of the sovereignty of God, the absolute necessity of the work of the Spirit, and these various other points I have been trying to emphasise. And that means that nothing less than revival is needed.

## VII

Very well then; let us pledge ourselves to pray for an outpouring of the Spirit of God, and let me put the appeal to you to do so first of all in these words taken from Smeaton. 'As to the peculiar mode of praying, we may say that in every season of general awakening the Christian community waits just as they waited for the effusion of the Spirit, with one accord in prayer and supplication in the interval between the Ascension and Pentecost. No other course has been prescribed; and the church of the present has all the warrant she ever had to wait, expect, and pray. The first disciples waited in the youthfulness of simple hope, not for a spirit which they had not, but for more of the Spirit which they had; and Christianity has not outlived itself. Ten days they waited with one accord in prayer, when of a sudden the Spirit came to give them spiritual eyes to apprehend divine things as they never knew them before, and to impart a joy which no man could take from them. It was prayer in the Spirit (Eph. 6:18) and prayer for the Spirit, the great "promise of the Father." But the prayer which brought down the Holy Ghost was not that style of petition which ceases if it is not heard at once, or if the heart is out of tune. The prayer which prevails with him who gives the Spirit is that which will not let him go without the blessing. When the spirit of extraordinary supplication is poured out from on high – when an urgent desire is cherished for the Holy Ghost, when the church asks according to God's riches in glory, and expects such great things as God's promises warrant and Christ's merits can procure, the time to favour Zion, the set time, is come (Psa. 102:16-18). When we look at the prayers in Scripture, we find that God's glory, the church's growth and welfare, her holiness and progress, were ever higher in the thoughts and breathings of the saints than personal considerations. And if we are animated with any other frame of mind, it is not prayer taught by the Spirit, nor offered up in the name of Christ. The prayer attitude of the church in the first days after the Ascension, when the disciples waited for the Spirit, should be the church's attitude still. I need not refer to the copious references of the apostles to the urgent duty of praying "in the Spirit" and praying "for the Spirit," nor shall I refer at large to the habits of all true labourers, such as Luther, Welsh, Whitefield, and others, in proof of the great truth that prayer is the main work of the ministry. And no more mischievous and misleading theory could be propounded, nor any one more dishonouring to the Holy Spirit, than the principle adopted by the Plymouth Brethren, that because the Spirit was poured out at Pentecost, the church has no need, and no warrant, to pray any more for the effusion of the Spirit of God. On the contrary, the more the church asks the Spirit and waits for his communication, the more she receives. The prayer of faith in one incessant cry comes up from the earth in support of the efforts put forth for the conversion of a people ready to perish. This prayer goes before and follows after all the calls to repentance.'

There is nothing better that one can do, therefore, in the light of that, than to suggest that the urgent call that comes to us at this moment is to offer unceasingly the prayer that was offered up by Isaiah in the terrible day in which he found himself living. Listen: 'Look down from heaven, and behold from the habitation of thy holiness and of thy glory: where is thy zeal and thy strength, the sounding of thy bowels and of thy mercies towards me? Are they restrained? Doubtless thou art our father, though Abraham be ignorant of us, and Israel acknowledge us not: thou, O Lord, art our father, our redeemer, thy name is from everlasting. O Lord, why hast thou made us to err from thy ways, and hardened our heart from thy fear? Return for thy servants' sake, the tribes of thine inheritance. The people of thy holiness have possessed it but a little while: our adversaries have trodden down thy sanctuary. We are thine: thou never barest rule over them; they were not called by thy name.'

And then, having asked God to look down, he goes further – 'Oh that thou wouldest rend the heavens, that thou wouldest come down, that the mountains might flow down at thy presence. As when the melting fire burneth, the fire causeth the waters to boil, to make thy name known to thine adversaries, that the nations may tremble at thy presence! When thou didst terrible things which we looked not for, thou camest down, the mountains flowed down at thy presence. For since the beginning of the world men have not heard, nor perceived by the ear, neither hath the eye seen, O God, beside thee, what he hath prepared for him that waiteth for him. Thou meetest him that rejoiceth and worketh righteousness, those that remember thee in thy ways: behold thou art wroth; for we have sinned: in those is continuance, and we shall be saved. But we are all as an unclean thing, and all our righteousnesses are as filthy rags; and we all do fade as a leaf; and our iniquities, like the wind, have taken us away. There is none that calleth upon thy name, that stirreth up himself to take hold of thee; for thou hast hid thy face from us, and hast consumed us, because of our iniquities. But now, O Lord, thou art our father; we are the clay, and thou our potter; and we all are the work of thy hand' (Isa. 63:15–64:8).

How many of us have stirred ourselves up to take hold of God? How many? This is typical biblical teaching, this was also the teaching of our fathers. They waited upon God and cried and cried until he did rend the heavens and come down. Let us lay hold upon him and plead with him to vindicate his own truth and the doctrines which are so dear to our hearts, that the church may be revived and masses of people may be saved.

# 1960

# *Knowledge – False and True*

## A STUDY OF 1 CORINTHIANS 8:1-3

As we come to the end of our conference it is essential that we should attempt to apply what we have been considering together, and perhaps not only that, but to take a general view of what we have been doing and to comment on it. There is no need to apologise for doing this. It is something the Puritans themselves invariably did; they were first and foremost pastoral, and therefore we must of necessity be pastoral. If the conference ends without this pastoral note, which means the application of what we have been considering together, it will have failed in its purpose. The very title and name of our conference demands our doing it. But that is not our only reason for doing so. It is not a sufficient reason; indeed, as I am hoping to show you, it can even be a dangerous one. I have very much stronger reasons for doing this than a mere desire to perpetuate what the Puritans did in their day and generation.

What are these stronger reasons? The first is, that it would be extremely dangerous for us not to do this. That is much more important than simply the desire to be Puritan in our method and scheme of things. We are compelled to do this because of the terrible danger of not doing it. Another reason we might adduce would be this: that there could be nothing quite so ridiculous as to turn the teaching of the Puritans, of all people, into a kind of new scholasticism and to spend our time in merely quoting texts, repeating phrases, and displaying our theoretical knowledge. That would be to do what the great opponents of the Puritans did. I mean the Caroline divines, and people like them, whose sermons consisted very largely of strings of classical allusions.

Here, then, are our main reasons for spending our time together in this way at the end of the conference.

## I

The dangers confronting Christian people are not uniform and always the same. There are different types of personality and different emphases in the life of the Christian church and in the gospel. We who gather here, for example, are very well aware of the particular dangers that confront the activist – that type of person who is so common amongst us in evangelical circles – the man who lives on his energy and on what he does, who is always busy, organising meetings and attending them, etc., and who says that you must always be 'doing' something. We have realised very clearly the terrible danger that is inherent in that kind of activism, and we are never tired of protesting against it and of showing the danger of an almost exclusive emphasis on life, living, and activity at the expense of doctrine, understanding, and a growth in knowledge. But while we see that so clearly, there is a real possibility of our being unaware of the entirely different type of danger that confronts us, and which is something that applies to a different kind of individual. The first thing we always have to do is to know ourselves, to note the particular group to which we belong, and to realise that there are dangers inherent in every type and in every group. To come immediately to the point, there can be no question at all, it seems to me, that the peculiar danger that threatens those of us who meet annually in this conference, is the danger of pride of intellect and pride of knowledge.

I have put that quite bluntly. I am not saying that we are actually guilty of it. My whole object is to show that there is a very real danger of it. I do not say that my discernment and diagnostic capacity, such as it is, is able actually to detect the presence of this disease. But, if I may be allowed to use a medical illustration, I am not at all sure that I have not noticed some of its prodromal symptoms. Let me expound my illustration. In the field of medicine and diseases of the body, there are what are known as infectious fevers. For instance, take a condition like measles. You think of this, do you not, in terms of a little child covered with a rash, who also has a cough, and is feverish, etc. Those are certainly manifestations of measles. But – and this is the interesting thing – the rash in measles, if I remember rightly, does not come out until about the fourth day of the disease. Before that you have an ill and a sick child who is feverish, complains of headaches, is off its food, may vomit, and so on. In addition, on the inside of the cheeks there may be white spots. Now what are these? They are quite clearly symptoms. Yes, but they are not actually those of measles as such; they are what are called 'prodromal' symptoms, and the really good physician is a man who can recognise them and does not have to wait until the rash appears. He is so experienced, and he has so cultivated the art of medicine that when he recognises a certain group or complex of prodromal symptoms he says, 'It looks to me as if this child is sickening for measles.'

That is what is meant by prodromal symptoms, and I am suggesting that while I cannot make a true or a full diagnosis of this horrible condition of pride of intellect and of knowledge, I think that I have occasionally, in certain instances, seen certain of the prodromal symptoms. I propose, therefore, to consider this whole subject with you, and I do so in terms of what we find in 1 Corinthians 8:1-3: 'Now as touching things offered unto idols, we know that we all have knowledge. Knowledge puffeth up, but charity edifieth. And if any man think that he knoweth anything, he knoweth nothing yet as he ought to know. But if any man love God, the same is known of him.' I want to consider this with you, in order that we may apply it to ourselves. We need take no time in dealing with the particular context and the state of affairs in the church at Corinth. The apostle is dealing here with the question of the meats offered to idols because it was a cause of division in the church. There were the more enlightened, the stronger brethren, and there were the weak brethren. They did not see alike on this matter. The strong brother said that there was no such thing as another God, that there was but one God. Everybody should know that, any man who knows anything at all knows that; therefore the idea that you should not eat meat offered to idols was just nonsense, and was virtually a going back to idolatry. A Christian was free to eat any meat he liked. Some of them went so far as to say that, if asked, they could even go to the heathen festivals. 'Why not,' they asked, 'as "these gods" are really non-existent?' So they went. And thus they were becoming a stumbling-block to the weaker brethren, whom they despised, of course, because of their weakness of intellect and grasp and understanding. There was grievous trouble in the church of Corinth because of this conflict between the enlightened men of knowledge, and those who were weaker and lacking in knowledge.

The exact context is most interesting. But we are concerned with the way, the most interesting way, in which the apostle deals with it. As is his custom he does not deal with the thing just in and of itself and directly; he lifts it up; he finds a great principle. And the principle he finds is this whole question of knowledge. The real trouble in Corinth, in a sense, was not at all the question of meats offered to idols, but simply men's view of their own knowledge. So he discusses the matter primarily in terms of their attitude towards knowledge. Our theme therefore, and the principle which we extract from our text, is the danger of a false view of knowledge.

To be accurate in our exegesis let me indicate that the 'knowledge' Paul speaks of here is not the same as that referred to in 1 Timothy 6:20, where he talks about some who have gone astray and made shipwreck of the faith because of – as it is translated there – 'science falsely so-called.' 'Science' there means knowledge, 'Knowledge falsely so-called.' But that is not the same 'knowledge' as we have here in 1 Corinthians 8. There, the problem has reference to a kind of mystical knowledge, and to people claiming that they were receiving some direct knowledge by inspiration; it was the danger of a false mysticism. But here, it is 'knowledge' in the sense in which we normally use the term and in which, certainly, it applies to us who are members of this conference.

## II

There is no need, of course, to emphasise the fact that knowledge is all-important. We can never know too much. Knowledge is essential, doctrine is vital. The Bible is full of doctrine, and the New Testament particularly so. The epistles are mighty, glorious expositions of doctrine and of truth. The apostles not only preached the truth but they emphasised the all-importance of a knowledge of the truth. Ultimately most of the troubles in the church, according to the teaching of the epistles, stem somewhere or another from a lack of knowledge and of understanding. Knowledge, therefore, is in and of itself absolutely essential; indeed we must give it priority, and see to it that it always comes first. We were reminded of that in the paper which gave an exposition of Dr John Owen's teaching on the question of apostasy. Truth came first, you remember, then godliness, and then worship. We are all agreed about that. It is no problem to us. But – and this is where our theme comes in – it is possible for us to develop a false notion of knowledge. It is possible for this gift of knowledge and understanding, which is in many ways God's most precious gift to us next to the gift of his Son and our salvation, to become a snare to us and a very real danger in our spiritual life. Such was the position in Corinth. It is good for us therefore at the end of this conference, in which we have been spending so many hours in the pursuit of knowledge and understanding – it is good for us that we should face this possible danger which may be confronting us. I suggest the following treatment of the subject.

## III

First, we must consider *the causes of this false view of knowledge*. We cannot go into these in detail, but we may divide them into *general and particular*. Obviously at the back of everything is the adversary. The devil having failed to keep us out of the faith and in a state of ignorance and darkness of the mind, and having seen that we have discovered the danger of a busy activism that may be nothing but a man revolving round himself, suddenly completely changes his tactics. Transforming himself into an angel of light, he drives us to such an extreme in this matter of knowledge as eventually to ensnare us quite as successfully as he ensnares the activist. In other words we are back to a phenomenon with which we are all so familiar – the danger of going violently from one extreme to the other, the danger of over-correction. It seems to be the besetting sin of mankind and one of the most terrible results of the Fall, that there is nothing so difficult as to maintain a balance. In correcting one thing we go to such an extreme as to find ourselves in an equally dangerous position. We are always confronted by the devil, who is ever ready to take the best things and turn them into his own instruments of unrighteousness and to produce the shipwreck of our souls.

A second general cause is, as a well-known proverb reminds us, 'a little learning.' 'A little learning is a dangerous thing.' That does not mean, of course, that there is no danger in much knowledge. There is. But I am not sure that in this respect there is not a greater danger in a little, because it always means that the element of the tyro or novice who imagines that his little knowledge is all knowledge comes in. Is it not notorious that first-year students always know much more than final-year students? I leave it at that – the danger that arises from a little learning.

But we must give more attention to the third cause which may be a little more controversial. To me, there is a very special danger at this point and in this matter which we are discussing, in reading as against preaching. Perhaps in the age in which we live this is one of the greatest dangers of all. I am asserting that reading is much more dangerous than listening to preaching, and I suggest that a very real danger arises in this connection if a man just spends his time reading and does not come under the power of preaching. What do I mean? I mean something like this. While a man is reading a book there is a sense in which he is in entire control. It depends partly on the book, I know, and if it is beginning to make him feel uncomfortable he can shut it up and go for a walk and – he can do many things. But you cannot do all that when listening to preaching. Of course, you may be rude enough to get up and go out, and some people do so, but on the whole that is not the custom.

Preaching in a sense, therefore, safeguards us from these peculiar dangers that arise from reading only, provided of course that it is true preaching. For when a man is listening to true preaching he comes under the 'power' of the truth in a way that he does not when he is only reading. You may or may not like Phillips Brooks' definition of preaching as 'truth mediated through personality,' but there is a great deal to be said for it; and the Scriptures give us many illustrations of that. God does use the human personality. Not only that, a preacher not only expounds but also applies the Scriptures, and thereby makes sure that application takes place. When a man reads a book, however, he may never come to application. He can decide to shut the book and stop whenever he likes; there is no insistence upon the application. I fear that in this present age, when people are tending to listen less and less to preaching, and preaching becomes shorter and shorter, and our reliance upon reading becomes correspondingly greater, we are therefore more exposed to the danger than our forefathers were. I am not of course denouncing reading, and saying that there should be a ban on all publications! Of course not! I am simply trying to show the dangerous tendency that arises, and asserting the priority and primacy, and the superiority of preaching. We need to be brought under the *power* of the truth. We do not like that, but it is the business of the preacher to do that, and if he fails to do so, he is a very poor preacher. We always try to evade these conclusions and applications, but the preacher brings them home. He holds us, and makes us face them, and therefore he safeguards us against certain dangers. An age which attaches greater importance to reading than to the preaching of the word is already in a dangerous position.

## IV

But let us pass to particular causes. One is, to take a purely theoretical and academic interest in truth and knowledge, to make knowledge an end in and of itself – the purely theoretical and academic approach. This is an obvious and well-known danger. I therefore take the general principle for granted, and mention only certain particular illustrations of it here.

I have always felt that it is wrong to hold examinations on scriptural knowledge, for the reason that it tends to develop this theoretical interest in it. It makes a subject of it, something which you have to learn in order to pass your examination or to get a certain number of marks. It may not happen, I grant, but I am suggesting that the moment you have an examination you have already started this tendency to regard biblical knowledge as a subject in and of itself, like any other subject. I remember lecturing at a certain conference in America in 1932. The conference had been started by a saintly bishop in 1874 for religious people, but it had degenerated, not so much in numbers but in its theology and approach to truth. I found there that the great claim for this conference (and this is how it was advertised) was that it taught any subject in which anybody could be conceivably interested. I also found that item number sixteen on the list of advertised subjects was 'Religion.' There is an example of this purely academic and theoretical interest in truth – you take it up as a subject: chemistry, history, art, religion, theology – knowledge about these matters. And if you have an examination in addition, the whole thing is greatly aggravated.

It is also, and I say this with very real regret, one of the dangers inherent in a study of religious history. I have known three men who have been expert historians on the history of Christianity, the history of the church, and the history of its great men and movements. They have given their whole lives to this, and all three were particularly interested in the eighteenth century. But what has always amazed me is that though they spent their lives in reading about those glorious revivals of religion and those mighty men of God, it had not touched them at all. To them it was just a subject, a matter of academic and historical interest. They knew all the details, but as for the spirit of the thing, it was as if they had never read about it at all. That, I suggest, is a danger that is always inherent in the historical approach, and is an illustration of this purely theoretical approach.

The same thing can apply also even in the process of studying theology. It can become just a subject set for an examination, or a subject essential to obtaining a certain degree or diploma. And the very fact that this is the system may result in a man viewing the knowledge of God entirely in this way. But even without examinations this is still a possibility. A man can take a purely academic and theoretical interest in theology. I have known many such men. They happen to have had that as their hobby, whereas others turned to crossword puzzles. It was essentially the same approach – there was no question about that at all. It was purely theoretical, and thus it had become this false type of 'knowledge.' Are we entirely free from this danger?

The second particular cause is that we approach truth purely in terms of intellect – intellect only. There is nothing so dangerous as to isolate the intellect. We are all agreed about the priority of intellect. But there is all the difference in the world between our asserting its priority and talking only about intellect and regarding man as if he were nothing but an intellect. There is nothing that is so calculated to lead a man directly to this 'false knowledge,' about which the apostle is speaking, as a purely intellectual interest in truth, in which the heart is never engaged at all and the power of the truth is not felt, indeed in which feeling does not enter at all. The man is merely concerned to absorb knowledge with his mind. And it is precisely the same when the will is not engaged. If the interest does not lead to any action, or 'move' the will, it is equally bad. We need not stay with this. The text for all this is, of course, Romans 6:17: 'But God be thanked,' says the apostle, 'that ye have obeyed' – will! – 'from the heart' – heart! – 'the form of (sound) doctrine delivered to you' – to the mind. There you have them together. If you isolate the intellect and leave out the heart and the will, it is certain that you will end in this position of having a false view of knowledge, and indeed as I want to show, with false 'knowledge' also.

To vary the expression, this danger is one of knowing 'about' a subject rather than knowing it. 'Knowing about!' What a vital distinction this is. What a difference there is between preaching about the gospel and preaching the gospel! It is possible to preach round the gospel and say things about it without ever presenting it. That is quite useless – indeed it can be very dangerous. It may be true of us that we know 'about' these things, but do not really know them. And this, of course, becomes all-important when we realise that the whole end and object of theology is to know God! A person! Not a collection of abstract truths, nor a number of philosophical propositions, but God! A person! To know him! – 'the only true God, and Jesus Christ, whom thou hast sent!'

There we have what I would regard as the main causes of this trouble. I would add just one further practical one for the preacher – the preacher only. This is very germane to the matter under consideration in this kind of conference. There are men who seem to me to be using the Puritans and their writings as a substitute for thought. Let me expound that. A man once came to me after listening to an attempt of mine to preach a sermon in which, as I am doing now, I had made a detailed analysis of a certain condition and had given the reply to it in a number of propositions. He was a preacher himself and he asked me: 'Did you find that list of questions and answers in one of the Puritans?' He revealed to me thereby that that was what he did himself! I must confess that I was rather amazed and alarmed at the thing, but I can see the possibility. Now if you do that, you are using the Puritans as a substitute for thought. You are not working the thing out yourself and putting yourself through the process and discipline of thought, but you are just taking ready-made divisions and thoughts. The moment you do that you are undoubtedly guilty of having this 'false knowledge.' It is something purely for the mind. God deliver us from this danger of 'preaching the Puritans' or of using them as a substitute for honest thinking and travail of soul. This applies equally, of course, to the misuse of any other writers.

## V

We come now to the second general heading, *the signs and indications of this condition*. There are certain general signs of this possession of a false knowledge and a false view of knowledge. For instance in such cases, there is always a lack of balance. It is the bit of knowledge that the man happens to have that he is always interested in, and he knows nothing else. So there is lack of balance at once. He has been suddenly attracted by a type or aspect of knowledge, and goes after it. He acquaints himself with this; but he knows nothing else and is lop-sided and lacking in balance. That in turn expresses itself in the use of slogans, clichés, tabloid expressions and phrases which always characterises this condition. These phrases keep tripping off the tongue; the same catch phrases and slogans always. That is unfailingly indicative of a little knowledge, a lack of true knowledge, and above all of this lack of balance of knowledge.

The apostle uses the term 'puffed up' – 'Knowledge puffeth up.' What an expression! What does he mean? He is describing a proud man, is he not? Here is a man who thinks he really 'knows it all'; he is not like those other people, he knows; he is a man of knowledge and understanding. He knows it all! He is not like those others who never read; he is a great reader. And, of course, as the result of this he has arrived, and he is proud of it. 'Puffed up!' How do we know that he is proud of his knowledge? Well, he is always parading it. The heavy, important, Puritan gait! The way of speaking and so on! That is a part of the parading that is inevitably one of the manifestations of being 'puffed up.' How difficult it is to stand erect with all this great weight of knowledge!

It manifests itself also in an impatience of any restraint and any correction; and still more in an impatience with any opposing view. It is intolerant of anything else. It 'knows,' and nothing else must even be suggested. No opposing view has a right to exist, and must not even be considered. In other words it is a part of this being 'puffed up.' It means 'arrogance.' The apostle James knew certain people of this type, so he says 'Be not many masters, my brethren' (James 3:1). What a terrible thing it must be to have a church with nothing but masters in it. All are authorities, all know everything and 'all about it.' 'Be not many masters, my brethren.' But there is always this tendency to feel that you do know, and understand, and, of course, to let it be known. So men arrogate unto themselves positions – and thereby betray themselves.

But still more serious is the way in which this manifests itself in its attitude to others. That was the trouble in the church at Corinth where these men who were enlightened said, 'We have knowledge, we know.' The apostle's reply was, 'We know that we all have knowledge.' Now he was there, according to some of the commentators, repeating their own phrase, 'We have knowledge.' The result was that their attitude to others was one of superiority. They tended to despise others, they were like the Pharisees. They did not boast so much of the good works they did as of their knowledge and their understanding. These others who did not understand, who were not clear about idols – why, they were almost beneath contempt. So they looked down upon them, were inconsiderate towards them and said they were hardly worthy to be considered at all. It may show itself like that. Or it may show itself by just ignoring these others altogether. You ignore them to such an extent that you do not even feel contemptuous toward them, because in a sense they are not there at all! You are so much up in the air and in the clouds yourself that you do not even see them. It is as if they were not there. Then another way in which it manifests itself is in feeling that these other people who are so slow to learn are a hindrance to us. Why should the preacher still be dealing with such simple matters? These men who know so much would like to go on to the great things, but the preacher is always staying there with some preliminaries. There he is, preaching evangelistic sermons every Sunday night, and on Sunday mornings he seems to be thinking that he has many people in his congregation to whom everything has to be explained in great detail. Because of that they are being held back and cannot go on to the great heights. They have long scaled the Alps, why does the preacher not take them to Mount Everest? These other people are just a nuisance and a hindrance with their slowness. Now that was the case in Corinth, and it is the case in many churches today. These men of knowledge want to go on, but they are being held back by these others whom they therefore despise. There it is, displayed in the attitude towards others.

The last sign that I am going to mention, in order that I may pass on to something else, is that in some cases this wrong view of knowledge, and this possession of what is not true knowledge, manifests itself by its victim just doing nothing at all; he simply enjoys his 'knowledge.' He does not seem to be aware of the fact that there is a lost soul anywhere in the world. He spends the whole of his time in reading, and if he meets people, in letting them know what he has been reading and in having discussions about truth. There are sections of the church today, with the world as it is, which never have any contact with the world at all. You never hear of them having a single convert; they do not seem to be aware of the existence of the problems of mankind and the ravages of sin. Why not? Because they spend the whole of their time within that circle of theirs, dotting their i's and crossing the t's, arguing about their great knowledge, and displaying it to one another. They are thus completely useless and entirely cut off from any kind of activity. We may not know this in its extreme form; but I would ask everyone present to examine himself or herself. Have you not found that it is a very easy thing indeed to spend the whole of your time in just reading and adding to your knowledge and building up your understanding, and forgetting all about the sinful world in which you live? It is the peculiar temptation that comes to people of intellect and ability who have realised the importance of knowledge. You can spend the whole of your life in merely adding to your own knowledge or in comparing notes with others who are like yourself.

## VI

But let us come to the third section which is the uselessness of such supposed knowledge. Look at the way in which the apostle puts it in the second verse: 'if any man think that he knoweth anything.' Well, he says, there is only one thing to say about him – 'he knoweth nothing yet as he ought to know'; which means partly, that this man, who is proud of the knowledge that he thinks is his, has not really got any knowledge at all. Is this not obvious? The argument is that if this man has a true knowledge of God he simply could not be like that. So the apostle says, this man who thinks he knows, in fact 'knows nothing yet as he ought to know,' because if he did know as he ought to know he could not possibly be behaving as he is. This does not need any demonstration; it is a sheer impossibility; he has no true knowledge. He thinks that he has a knowledge of God, but all he has is some kind of knowledge 'about' God; it is not a knowledge of God, otherwise he could not possibly be what he is.

Let me put this in the words of the great George Whitefield. He is talking about the Bible: 'This is my rock, this is my foundation. It is now about thirty-five years since I have begun to read the Bible upon my pillow. I love to read this Book, but the Book is nothing but an account of the promises which it contains, and almost every word from the beginning to the end of it speaks of a spiritual dispensation, and the Holy Ghost that unites our souls to God and helps a believer to say, "My Lord and my God." If you content yourselves with that – [now he means by that, the Bible itself, remember] – if you content yourselves with that, the devil will let you talk of doctrines enough. You shall turn from Arminianism to Calvinism; you shall be orthodox enough, if you will be content to live without Christ's living in you.'[1]

Note what Whitefield says. If you just go in for that sort of theoretical intellectual knowledge, the devil will let you talk of doctrine enough; you will turn from Arminianism to Calvinism, you shall be orthodox enough, if you will be content to live without Christ's living in you. The devil does not care at all whether you change from being an Arminian to being a Calvinist if you do not know Christ and if you do not know God. One is as bad as the other. A theoretical Calvinism is of no more value than a theoretical Arminianism – not the slightest. That is what Whitefield is saying. He therefore warns against this because he is concerned about our having the Spirit. And he goes on to say, 'Now when you have got the Spirit, then you may say "God is mine."' His point is that any knowledge which falls short of that does not interest the devil at all, because it is not really the true knowledge which is

[1] Sermon on Isaiah 60:19, 'God a Believer's Glory.'

going to make a difference to you. That is how Whitefield puts it, who was himself a Calvinist and one of the greatest evangelists the world has ever known.

But let me adduce another reason. Why is this such a ridiculous position to be in – this feeling that we really do know and that we have knowledge, this pride in ourselves and this despising of those activities, those busy people who do not know any theology or doctrine, those people of whom we speak in a derogatory manner and whom we more or less dismiss? Why is this so utterly ridiculous? And why is it not a real knowledge at all? The answer is – because of the vastness of the knowledge! What do I mean? The knowledge about which we are speaking is *a knowledge of God!* All these doctrines are about God! The moment you realise that, you see how impossible it is that a man should be proud of his knowledge. The moment he realises the endlessness, the vastness of the knowledge, he is bound to realise that he is but a pigmy, a mere beginner, a little child paddling at the edge of the ocean. He thought he was out in the great depths. Great depths! He knows nothing about them, he has been thinking in purely theoretical terms. But when you realise that all this knowledge, everything in the Bible, is meant to bring us to know God, the Everlasting and the Eternal in the glory and the majesty and the holiness of his being – how can a man be proud of his knowledge when he realises that that is the knowledge about which we are speaking? Or take the way the apostle puts it in writing to the Ephesians. He is praying for these Ephesians and he 'bows his knees unto God the Father.' What for? Well this, he says: 'That they, together with all other saints, may come to know the breadth, and the length, and the depth, and the height; and to know the love of God, which *passeth* knowledge' (Eph. 3:18, 19). Think of a little man strutting about because he knows so much, because he has read the Puritans, and has read theology and is not like these other people who are ignorant. 'Puffed up!' Poor fool, who is not aware of his ignorance – 'he knoweth nothing yet as he ought to know.' If he really had a true knowledge of God he could not be like that. The thing is a sheer impossibility. The endlessness, the vastness of it all!

In order to emphasise this great truth I felt I could do nothing better than remind you of the experiences of certain men who knew just a little about this knowledge of which I am speaking. Let me start with Charles Haddon Spurgeon, who puts it like this: 'All ye that think that you know and have a knowledge of the truth, may the Holy Spirit grant that we may not say a word which is not strictly verified by our experience. But I hope we can say we have had converse with the divine Father. We have not seen him at any time, nor have we beheld his shape. It has not been given to us, like Moses, to be put in the cleft of the rock, and to see the back parts, or the train of the invisible Jehovah. But yet we have spoken to him, we have said to him, "Abba, Father." We have saluted him in that title which came from our very heart, "Our Father, which art in heaven." We have had access to him in such a way that we cannot have been deceived. We have found him, and through the precious blood of Christ we have come even to his feet. We have ordered our cause before him, and we have filled our mouth with arguments. Nor has the speaking been all on our side, for he has been pleased to shed abroad by his Spirit his love in our hearts. While we have felt the Spirit of adoption he, on the other hand, has showed us the loving-kindness of a tender Father. We have felt, though no sound was ever heard; we have known, though no angelic messenger gave us witness, that his Spirit did bear witness with our spirit that we were born of God. We were embraced of him – no more at a distance. We were brought nigh by the blood of Christ.'[1]

That is real true knowledge of God! Well, there is one example. But let us come to some others.

Isaac Watts tells us that when John Howe, the Puritan, died, it was found that he had written the following on the blank leaf of his own Bible: 'But what I sensibly felt through the admirable bounty of my God and the most pleasant, comforting influence of his Spirit on October 22nd 1704, far surpassed the most expressive words my thought can suggest. I then experienced an inexpressibly pleasant melting of heart, tears gushing out of mine eyes for joy

[1] Sermon on 1 John 1:3, September 15, 1861.

that God had shed abroad his love abundantly through the hearts of men; and that, for this very purpose, mine own heart should be so signally possessed of and by his blessed Spirit.'[1]

Watts also quotes the case of John Flavel. Flavel was on a journey when suddenly God began to deal with him in this intimate manner: 'There going on his way his thoughts began to swell and rise higher and higher like the waters in Ezekiel's vision, till at last they became an overwhelming flood. Such was the intention of his mind, such the ravishing tastes of heavenly joys, and such the full assurance of his interest therein, that he utterly lost all sight and sense of the world and all the concerns thereof, and for some hours he knew no more where he was than if he had been in a deep sleep upon his bed. Arriving in great exhaustion at a certain spring he sat down and washed, earnestly desiring, if it was God's good pleasure, that this might be his parting place from the world. Death had the most amiable face in his eye that ever he beheld, except the face of Jesus Christ which made it so, and he does not remember, though he believed himself dying, that he even thought of his dear wife and children or any earthly concernment. On reaching his inn the influence still continued, banishing sleep – still, still the joy of the Lord overflowed him and he seemed to be an inhabitant of the other world. He many years after called that day one of the days of heaven, and professed that he understood more of the life of heaven by it than by all the books he ever read or discourses he ever entertained about it.'[2]

That is the great John Flavel bearing his testimony. But let Jonathan Edwards also speak to us about this: 'As I rode out into the woods for my health in 1737, having alighted from my horse in a retired place as my manner commonly has been, to walk for divine contemplation and prayer, I had a view that was for me extraordinary of the glory of the Son of God as mediator between God and men, and his wonderful, great, full, pure, and sweet grace and love, and meek and gentle condescension. The grace that appeared so calm and sweet appeared also great above the heavens. The

[1] Isaac Watts, *Evangelical Discourses,* 1746.

[2] John Flavel, *Treatise of the Soul of Man.*

person of Christ appeared ineffably excellent, with an excellency great enough to swallow up all thoughts and conceptions, which continued, as near as I can judge, about an hour, which kept me a greater part of the time in a flood of tears and weeping aloud. I felt an ardency of soul to be what I know not otherwise how to express, emptied and annihilated, to lie in the dust and be full of Christ alone, to love him with a holy and pure love, to trust in him, to live upon him, and to be perfectly sanctified and made pure with a divine and heavenly purity.'[1]

Let me give one more. It is from a book published in 1635 by Robert Bolton, a Puritan, in which he relates the experience of a man named John Holland. This is what he says: 'Hear how another blessed saint of God ended his days. Having the day before he died continued his meditation and exposition upon Romans 8 for the space of two hours or more, on the sudden he said, "Oh stay your reading! What brightness is this I see? Have you lit up my candles?" To which I answered, "No, it is the sunshine" for it was about five o'clock in a clear summer's evening. "Sunshine" said he, "Nay, my Saviour-shine!" "Now farewell world, welcome heaven! The day star from on high hath visited my heart. Oh speak it when I am gone and preach it at my funeral, God dealeth familiarly with men." [That is what he wanted them to preach after his death, "God dealeth familiarly with men."] "I feel his mercies, I see his majesty; whether in the body or out of the body I cannot tell. God he knoweth, but I see things that are unutterable." So, ravished in spirit he roamed towards heaven with a cheerful look and soft sweet voice, but what he said we could not conceive. With the sun in the morning following, raising himself as Jacob did upon his staff, he shut up his blessed life with these blessed words: "Oh, what a happy change shall I make; from night to day, from darkness to light, from death to life, from sorrow to consolation, from a factious world to a heavenly being. And oh my dear brethren, sisters and friends, it pitieth me to leave you behind, yet remember my death when I am gone and what I now feel I hope you shall find ere you die, that God dealeth familiarly with men. And now

[1] Jonathan Edwards, *Personal Narrative*.

thou fiery chariot, that came down to fetch up Elijah, carry me to my happy home, and all ye blessed angels who attended the soul of Lazarus to bring it up into heaven, bear me, O bear me, into the bosom of my Best Beloved. Amen. Amen. Come Lord Jesus, Come quickly." And so he fell asleep.'[1]

That is true knowledge. That is what we should understand by knowledge. My argument is this, that when we realise that that is the knowledge to which the Bible is meant to bring us and that that is the whole end of theology and the whole purpose of all teaching concerning these matters – when we realise that that is 'knowledge,' can we possibly feel that we have knowledge and be 'puffed up' and boast of 'our knowledge' and 'our learning' in these matters? The thing is a sheer impossibility.

But let us consider the tests which show whether we have this true knowledge. First and foremost, obviously, is love of God. As the apostle puts it in verse 3 (1 Cor. 8:3): 'If any man love God.' That, he says in effect, 'is knowledge.' In other words, here is the argument. To know God, of necessity, is to love him. You cannot know God without loving him. It is impossible. Why? Because God is love, because of the glory of his being, because God is who and what he is. If any man really knows God he will be 'lost in wonder, love, and praise'; he will love God. True knowledge always leads to a love of God. If therefore we cannot say that we love God, have we any right to claim any knowledge of God? We can have a great deal of knowledge about him and concerning him, we can even apprehend with our minds the full scheme of salvation, but we still may be ignorant of 'knowledge of God.' 'This is life eternal, that they might know thee, the only true God, and Jesus Christ whom thou hast sent.' That knowledge has been defined in the above quotations from the writings of godly men.

Secondly, another way to test knowledge is by the character it produces. 'Knowledge puffeth up' says the apostle, 'but charity edifieth,' – builds up. What kind of character does it build up? It is described perfectly in 1 Corinthians 13: 'Charity suffereth long, and is kind; charity envieth not, charity vaunteth not itself, is not

[1] Robert Bolton, *Comforting Afflicted Consciences.*

puffed up, doth not behave itself unseemly, seeketh not her own, is not easily provoked, thinketh no evil; rejoiceth not in iniquity, but rejoiceth in the truth; beareth all things, believeth all things, hopeth all things, endureth all things. Love never faileth: but whether there be prophecies, they shall fail; whether there be tongues, they shall cease; whether there be knowledge, it shall vanish away. For we know in part, and we prophesy in part. But when that which is perfect is come, then that which is in part shall be done away.' That is the character! What are its characteristics? First and foremost, humility. Look at those men in the Bible who have had a glimpse of God. They fall down as 'dead.' They say with Isaiah, 'Woe is me, for I am undone!' Proud of their knowledge and their learning and their superiority? No! – they feel that they are unclean and not fit to be there at all, that they are not in a position to criticise anybody because they are so aware of their utter unworthiness. True knowledge invariably leads to humility, and also to holiness and godliness.

What about the attitude to the neighbour? It has been stated perfectly there in 1 Corinthians 13 we will love our neighbour. Our Lord himself said that it is the second great commandment: 'Love thy neighbour as thyself.' And, of course, especially so if he is weak and ignorant. What if he is an Arminian? What if he does not understand the doctrines of grace? How are we to treat him? Are we to despise him, are we to dismiss him as a fool, or as a nonentity, or as a man who knows nothing – is that to be the attitude? Let me again quote Whitefield to you: 'Believers consider Christ's property in them. He says "My sheep." Oh, blessed be God for that little, dear, great word "My!" We are his by eternal election, "the sheep which thou hast given me" says Christ. They were given by God the Father to Christ Jesus in the covenant made between the Father and the Son from all eternity.' What a noble, wonderful statement of the great doctrine of election, one of the doctrines of grace! But Whitefield goes on: 'They that are not led to see this, I wish them better heads, though I believe numbers that are against it have got better hearts. The Lord help us to bear with one another where there is an honest heart!' There is nothing to be added to that. It is the right way to look at it. 'I wish they had better heads,' says Whitefield, and, of course, we must say that with him. We believe these people are wrong and that they are mistaken; but the trouble is in their heads. They have not seen it. Do not despise nor deride them, do not dismiss them, do not walk on the other side of the street when you see them coming, do not feel that they are not fit to have converse with you or that you would be wasting your time if you even discussed anything with them. No, no! Let us rather say with Whitefield, that their hearts are better than their heads. And as long as a man's heart is right, though his head may be wrong, let us be patient with him, let us try to help him. We should not spend our time just proving that we are right and everybody else is wrong. If you believe that you are right and the other wrong, well, it is your bounden duty to try to put him right, and you do so by loving him, by being patient with him, by understanding. You do not browbeat him, you do not knock him down; still less do you dismiss him. You try to understand him and put things to him, and reason with him. You do not hurl slogans at him; you expound the Scriptures in as loving a manner as you can, and try thus to lead him to a better understanding with his head. Oh yes, when a man has this true knowledge he must 'love his neighbour as himself.'

In other words, to sum it up, what is the result of true knowledge? First, it is that we rejoice in the Lord. My friends, we do not only believe in the Lord when we know him, we rejoice in him. 'Rejoice in the Lord alway: and again I say, rejoice.' The happiest people in the church ought to be those who know the doctrines of grace. They should not be 'puffed up' with their little knowledge, they should be men filled with joy because they know God and something about his love.

Likewise they should have a holy zeal for God's name, and resulting from that they should be filled with compassion for the lost. The greatest evangelists the world has ever known have been men who have held the doctrines of grace. Why? Because they have had the greatest knowledge of God. Did you know that this was a fact, that every single person who was involved in the beginning of the great missionary enterprise in the 1790s was what is called a Calvinist? I dislike the use of these labels and extra-biblical terms, but that is a simple fact of history. There is a notion abroad today that a man who holds these doctrines of grace is a man who does nothing, and that he does not believe in evangelism. Why is that notion abroad? Why have people got that notion? Is there something in it? If there is, it means this, that the knowledge we think we have is no knowledge at all. We have got this theoretical, useless knowledge, and it is not a knowledge of God. If a man knows God he will above all others have a zeal for the glory of God and the name of God. He will want the whole world to come to God, he will be the most active preacher and evangelist of all. He *must* be because his knowledge of God is greater and his compassion for the lost is greater. And, as we know, there was no man in the eighteenth century who was so active, none who laboured so indefatigably as that great George Whitefield from whom I have been quoting.

The man who has true knowledge will be full of compassion for the lost and of zeal for the glory of God. There is no need to prove this, the thing demonstrates itself. If only we knew him! That is why the Son came from heaven, to let the world know something about the glory of the Father. He even came into the world and died to do this. And we should know them – God the Father, God the Son, and God the Holy Spirit. And as we do so we shall in our little measure produce our Lord's life and shall be patient, as he was patient: 'A bruised reed shall he not break, and the smoking flax shall he not quench.' God have mercy upon us for the intolerance that often results from our false knowledge, and for the arrogance which is so often displayed! 'Let this mind be in you, which was also in Christ Jesus.' The lowly Jesus! Let us show that we know God by not only loving God but by loving our neighbour, and especially the lost and those who are weak and feeble and who have fallen by the way, the children in the faith, the beginners, and those who are slow to learn. Let us be patient with them, even as he has been patient with us.

My last word – how are we to get this knowledge? I give you but the bare headings. Bible study! Obviously you start there. But in addition, self-examination. How vital that is! Reading the Bible is not enough. Self-examination! How do you examine yourself? If you read your Bible correctly, you will soon discover. Ask yourself questions, apply what you are reading to yourself. Say: 'This was spoken to a Pharisee, is it true of me?' – and so on. But if you want further help as regards self-examination, read the diaries of men who have truly known God. Jonathan Edwards drew up a list of questions for people to ask themselves. John Fletcher of Madeley did exactly the same thing. You can use them if you like. But however you do it, be sure that you do it. Examine yourself!

Then another thing – and I want to emphasise this – balanced reading! I am concerned about this. I know of nothing that has such a tendency to produce false knowledge, and to make men victims of this false knowledge, as reading which lacks balance. If a man reads nothing but theology, he is exposing himself to this danger. I would therefore advise that we should always balance our reading as we balance our material diet. You should not eat only one kind of food. If you eat nothing but proteins you will soon be ill. You should always have a balanced diet. That principle is equally essential here. 'What do you mean?' asks someone. Well, if I may say so with humility, the thing that has been of the greatest help to me has been to balance theological reading with the reading of biographies. That is the best advice I can give. I have always done this: I have always done it on holiday and I have tried to do it day by day. But on holiday in particular I used always to give my mornings to reading some theological work, but I was also careful to read some biography at night. It worked like this. Having read for three or four hours in the morning I felt before lunch that I was quite a considerable man, and that I had a great deal of knowledge which I would be able to display to others. There I was! But I remember very well when I first 'stumbled' – and I am speaking the truth literally – when I first stumbled across Jonathan Edwards in 1928. I had never heard of him before but I began to read him and I soon discovered that you cannot read a page of Jonathan Edwards without feeling very small indeed. It completely corrected what had been happening in the morning. The best antidote to the poison of false knowledge is to read a biography like that of Jonathan Edwards or Whitefield or Fletcher of Madeley.

I have generally tried to do the same thing on Sunday night. Sunday is a very dangerous day for a preacher. If you want to keep yourself in order, when you get home on Sunday night and have had a cup of tea or a very light meal, pick up one of these men – Whitefield, Edwards, etc., or one of those great Puritans and their experiences. I don't care which of them it is. And if you have gone home foolishly thinking that you had had a wonderful day, and that you were a great preacher and had preached mighty sermons, you will not have read them for long without being brought back to earth. Indeed you will soon begin to feel that you have never preached in your life. Have we, I wonder, have we ever really preached? How many times? How often have we had Whitefield's experiences? There he is on one occasion preaching, when suddenly he stops and says to the congregation, 'Oh, I would that you were feeling now what I feel!' What about it, preachers? How monstrous, how ridiculous, how foolish it is to think that we know these things, that we have a knowledge of God simply because we have garnered a certain amount of intellectual and theoretical and academic information! 'Grow in grace and in the knowledge of the Lord.' Can we say with Spurgeon that we know what it is to be 'embraced' by him? Have we ever really been there in his presence in a 'sensible' way – using the term 'sensible' as the Puritans used it?

To 'know and feel' that God is near! What is the value of all the knowledge we may have if we are ignorant of that! 'Though I have the gift of prophecy, and understand all mysteries, and all knowledge; and though I have all faith, so that I could remove mountains, and have not charity, I am nothing' (1 Cor. 13:2). May God preserve us from this 'false knowledge' which is not knowledge but a counterfeit, and which is finally useless!

# 1961

## *Summing-Up: Knowing and Doing*

It is not my intention to deliver an address at this session but simply to say a few words before we turn to God in prayer. A number of friends expressed a desire that we should have a session of prayer, and as mine was the only session for which no subject had been announced and as in any case it is the last session, it was the obvious choice for this purpose. It is right and fitting that we should do this – although we are not quite clear about adopting this as a regular part of each conference. There are those who feel that as we are all praying men and women who belong to churches which pray, and as it is very difficult to get together to a conference such as this for two days, the primary object of this gathering should be to discuss these great matters together so that we may pray more efficiently when we go home. I am quite sure that that is right.

It must not be assumed, therefore, that this will always be the character of the last meeting. But we must be fluid in these matters, and not become set. If therefore we have the feeling, as I certainly have had on this occasion, that we should give this session to prayer, you will understand the reason for it and perhaps it is a good thing that on this one occasion we should remind ourselves that there should be an 'end' to all we do here.

In order to direct attention to that 'end' I would like to consider with you briefly the words of our Lord, 'If ye know these things, happy are ye if ye do them' (John 13:17). In many ways the greatest danger confronting all of us, is the danger of being content with a merely intellectual knowledge and apprehension of spiritual things. Such knowledge is most valuable, but if it stops at that it can be quite useless and, indeed, positively harmful, because it may drug us into a condition in which we feel that nothing further is necessary.

There was nothing that was more characteristic of the Puritan method of preaching than the way in which they always came to the 'application.' They were always very insistent upon that. I have sometimes wondered whether the trouble with many of us is our tendency to forget the application. There are many reasons for this. The chief one, I believe, is the danger of reaction, and of an over-violent reaction, against something else. It is a very subtle thing, but quite unconsciously we allow other people, and other positions, and other ideas, and other movements to determine ours. That, surely, must always be wrong. We should always be in control, we should always be positive, we should not merely be a 'reaction' against something. This is a principle, you will agree, which can be worked out along many lines. I feel that we are always in danger of allowing an opponent, or somebody who is obviously wrong, to determine the grounds of argument and the matter to be argued about. Now up to a point that is inevitable, but it is merely the negative part of our work, and it is essential that we should be positive. We are all in a bad state when we are just 'reactions' against various things, because that means that having reacted against them we stop, and so our witness is nullified and becomes quite ineffective. Now if it is true to say of us, as has been suggested once or twice in this conference, that we are a people who seem to be lacking in an active urgent concern for souls and in activity and action, it is a very serious matter. I am not admitting the charge for a moment, but if there is some suspicion of truth here, this conference should have made us examine ourselves very seriously. In fact, I feel that this is the way in which one can sum up this year's conference. It seems to have been a repeated challenge along that particular line. Are we always a little liable to be content with just knowing? And having known, to stop at that and to do nothing? The first challenge came to us with respect to missionary activity. We must examine ourselves very seriously about that. We of all people should have a concern for the glory of God, and therefore for the salvation of men's souls. Have we got that as we should have it? Does our understanding of Bible doctrines lead us to a great compassion for the lost? Have we real zeal for the glory of God? Not in theory, not in statement only, but in actual practice?

Then take the second session where we were dealing with the vital matter of communion with God. To what extent is our communion with God real? We are all clear about what is bad, what is false, and what is wrong, but what of this matter positively? What is the condition of our praying, our 'prayer life'? How much time do we spend in prayer? What kind of prayer is it? What do we really know about praying in the Spirit, which is surely the essence of real communion with God? 'If ye know these things, happy are ye if ye do them.' If we merely feel upbraided and searched and condemned, and stop at that, we shall simply become miserable. We shall probably analyse ourselves and the situation still more and then become introspective and morbid and spend our time in utter discouragement, just thinking about ourselves and our own failure. That, of course, is utterly hopeless and useless. Surely, the effect it should have upon us is to make us realise what is possible and to be concerned about arriving at it. If we really have grasped what is possible for us in this whole matter of communion with God, we must go on, and we must give ourselves neither peace or rest until this has become a living reality to us in our experience. And so with all the other themes that have been put before us.

In the last session we faced the duty of rejoicing in the Lord, and of always rejoicing in the Lord. Now of all people, surely, we should be rejoicing most of all in the Lord, because the more you know about him, the more you delight in him and the more you rejoice in him. There is something wrong somewhere, otherwise these charges, these suspicions about our position spoken about this afternoon, would never arise at all. We were reminded that people normally think of the Puritan as a miserable person. It is wrong, of course, but why have they got that impression? It would be foolish and untrue to say that there is no foundation for it at all. There is a misunderstanding of Puritanism that does lead to misery.

There are some people who are so much afraid of false joy that they are only really happy when they are more or less unhappy. There is no doubt about this. I once listened to a man preaching a sermon on 'The rainbow in the cloud'; but the whole of the sermon was devoted to warnings against false joy, so instead of going out of the service filled with thoughts about the rainbow we were sent out with thoughts about the cloud, for the good man was obsessed by this fear of the false.

The Puritans were always warning against the false, but they did not stop at that. And we must not stop at that. Otherwise, as I have said already, we just become reactions, we are merely and only against the false. But that is of no value, it does not lead anywhere. Surely we ought, if we understand these things at all, to have such a knowledge of God, and such access to God through the Lord Jesus Christ by the one Spirit, that we should be increasingly men and women who come out of his presence in such a way that people will know that we have been in his presence.

What is needed today above everything in the church is the type of knowledge of God which is seen in such a man as Robert Murray M'Cheyne. When that saintly man entered his pulpit on Sunday morning people began to weep at the mere sight of him, before he had uttered a sound. Like Moses, having spent time on the mountain with God, it was evident to the people when he came down that he had done so. There was a radiance about him. Do we know anything about that? Is it going to be obvious to our families and our friends and fellow church members, as the result of these two days of conference, that we really have been with God? That is the object of our gathering together. Otherwise it becomes a kind of scholasticism, it becomes a coterie. God forbid that we should ever degenerate into that! The end and object of all this, and all we have done, is to bring us to a knowledge of God. And if it does not do that we shall merely have been turning round in circles, giving a good deal of satisfaction to the flesh. We shall go away proud of our knowledge and our understanding, but it will be no help to anybody at all. No, there is always an end, a purpose, to be kept in view. Take the New Testament Epistles, take the great Pauline

Epistles with their great doctrines – every single one of them was written with a pastoral intent. We tend to forget that! They all have a pastoral intent and object. All our knowledge must be applied. It is sinful not to do so. 'If ye know these things, happy are ye if ye do them.'

There is just one other word I want to say. I am not sure but that the danger confronting some of us, our greatest danger at the moment – and there have been indications of it in this conference – is the danger of our estimating and judging aspects of doctrine in terms of our own experience and thereby 'limiting the Holy One of Israel.' There is a great deal of that at the present time. Take for instance what was said in passing by several about people's reactions to the Journals of George Whitefield. You noticed the tendency to say about them, 'Ah, excess of youth,' etc.! How many of us are in danger of having that charge brought against us? Thank God, I say, for a man who is subject or exposed to that charge! Or let us put it like this. To how many churches today do you think it would be necessary to write the First Epistle to the Corinthians? How many of our churches are so thrilling with spiritual life that you have to tell them about control and of being aware of excesses? I do not know of one. That is because there is no life. When you have life and vitality there is always a danger of excess. I would not venture to suggest that Whitefield had no failings, but I cannot understand the type of person who can read those Journals of Whitefield and simply feel that this was just a young man who was carried away by animal excitement. We were actually given a quotation, which proved that he was not. We thank God for the way in which Whitefield was kept by the Spirit from losing his head, or losing himself in any respect, in spite of the phenomenal success that attended his ministry. No man was more humble, no man was more aware of the dangers. But what I am afraid is happening is this, that we read of a man like Whitefield lying on his bed, badly in need of physical rest in the midst of strenuous preaching, but finding sleep quite impossible because God was pouring his love upon him; and having read that we simply say, 'Ah, this is ecstasy, this is excess, this is enthusiasm!'

Why do we say that? I am afraid there is but one reason for it. It is that we know nothing whatsoever about such experience. And because we do not know it we criticise it in Whitefield. In other words, we are reducing what is offered us, and promised us, in the New Testament to the level of our own experience. Because there are so few Christian people today who know this 'real' joy of the Lord, these 'real' manifestations of the Son of God, these overwhelming experiences of the Spirit being poured out – because that is such a rare experience today our tendency is to criticise, to query and to doubt its spiritual character. We are defining doctrine in terms of our experience and of our understanding. We must come back to the New Testament itself and see how then the people of God knew what it was to pray in the Spirit. Look at them in the book of the Acts of the Apostles, and look at the teaching given in the Epistles. What do we know about the Spirit coming down? What do we know about being lost in wonder and amazement? What do we know of being in prayer-meetings when you forget time altogether? Now that happened in the early church, and it has happened in the subsequent history of the Christian church. What right have we to express our criticisms and to say, 'Ah, this is just youthful effervescence, something which a man outgrows'? The fact was that those men never outgrew such experiences. Whitefield and others were aware of the fact and ready to admit that they used certain unguarded expressions in their preaching and in their writing, but the whole glory of that period is – I am referring particularly to the eighteenth century – the way in which the amazing spiritual experiences persisted. And we know something of the way in which these people died. Exalted spiritual experience was not something that applied to their youth only; some of them had their greatest experiences during their last days on earth. Thank God you cannot explain these things psychologically or in terms of age or of anything else. Let us be careful lest we become guilty of 'quenching the Spirit.' We can easily become guilty of this sin. In our fear of certain things we can become so careful and so wary and so cautious and so afraid, that nothing at all will ever happen to us, and nothing will ever happen to our churches. And so the position will continue as one of utter discouragement and may even go from bad to worse.

I feel that we have to be careful about these things and that we must come back again to the New Testament and see what is possible and open to God's children, to Christian people, while here on earth. Is this kind of 'pneumatic' element as prominent amongst us as it should be? That seems to me to be the great question. Doctrine after all is a foundation, and no more. It is not an end, it is only a beginning. It is the means. We must never stop at it. It is always designed to bring us, by faith, into that knowledge, that intimacy, that deep experience of the living God, in which we really meet with him, know that he is present, and are conscious of the energies of the Spirit in us and amongst us. Do let us, therefore, examine ourselves very seriously about these things. It is very wonderful and enjoyable to have fellowship of kindred minds. How delightful to discuss and to talk about these things. What is more enjoyable than this? But it can lead to nothing – nothing at all – if we are not ever mindful of the fact that it is merely the means provided by God to bring us to a knowledge of himself.

With that word let us turn to God together. Let us worship him, let us praise him, let us thank him. But above all let us plead with him to have mercy upon us and to visit us. Let us take the phrase of Isaiah, and 'lay hold upon God.' How many are there that stir themselves up to lay hold upon God? That is the call to us, it seems to me, at a time like this. Here is the truth. Yes, but why is it so ineffective? It needs this power to come upon it, the Spirit and the word, the Spirit upon the word, the Spirit using the word, the Spirit through the word. Let us pray to God to give us this 'demonstration of the Spirit and of power,' this power and unction that can take a word that often sounds so dead, a mere letter, and turn it into a living flame that will do its saving and transforming work in the minds and the hearts of men and women.

Let us pray:

> *O Lord our God, we come into thy holy presence and we come, O Lord, to worship thee; we come to praise thy name. Great God of wonders, all thy ways are Godlike, matchless,*

*and divine. We thank thee for the opportunity we have had together to remind ourselves of this. O help us, we pray thee, at this hour to realise that thou art the living God, and that thou art looking down upon us in this room. O Lord, we come in the name of thy dear Son. We recognise we have nothing else to plead, we have nothing which we can present before thee. We are all by nature the children of wrath, even as others, and we have sinned against thee deliberately and spurned the voice divine so often, followed our own wills, been proud of ourselves, of what we are, not even recognising that what we are is the result of thy gracious gifts to us. O God, we see how poor and sinful and vile we all have become as the result of man's original disobedience and sin and fall, and our own misdeeds and transgressions. So we come and we plead only the name and the blood of thy dear Son, and we do thank thee that in him we know that we have this access. Lord, make us all sure of it. Forgive us if we ever come into thy presence in his name, yet uncertainly. Grant us all the full assurance of faith that we may know our acceptance, that we may rejoice in thy presence and praise thy name. We thank thee together for the energies of thy blessed Spirit. We thank thee that he does work within us both to will and to do of thy good pleasure. We know that we would not be here even this afternoon were it not for this. We thank thee that he brings us back to thee, that suddenly he visits us and causes us to read thy word and to turn unto thee in prayer. O Lord, we have never seen and known so clearly that, were not this salvation thine from beginning to end, we would still be undone. We know it is thy work and that thou art continuing it within us, and we humbly thank thee for his disturbing us, for his convictions, for his drawings, for all his movements within us. O God, we thank thee for this and our prayer is that we may know this in a greater, a mightier manner. O Lord, enable us to pray in the Spirit. O come, we pray thee therefore, upon us in this very gathering and enable us so to pray. Lord, thou knowest our desire is that thy great name may be magnified, that men and women may be humbled before thee; yea, that the very nations be humbled before thee. O God, authenticate thy word, grant power by thy Spirit unto those who preach it in sincerity and truth. Revive thy work, O Lord, in the midst of these evil days. Hear us in our prayer, and lead us on now by thy Spirit that we may pray truly unto thee. We ask it in Christ Jesus' name. Amen.*

# 1962

## *Puritan Perplexities – Some Lessons from 1640–1662*

### I

THE subject on which I propose to speak is, 'Some lessons from 1640–1662.' I have four main reasons for calling attention to this subject. The first is, of course, that this does happen to be 1962, and it would be a terrible thing if this conference, of all conferences, did not give some time and attention to the consideration of the notable events of 1662.

Having already tried to say something about it from the more purely historical standpoint in a lecture I gave under the auspices of the Evangelical Library,[1] I am going to take it for granted on this occasion that we are most of us familiar with the salient facts of that great story. I am concerned rather to draw certain lessons from what happened, not only in 1662 but also during the whole period of 1640 to 1662.

My second reason for dealing with this subject is, that as we have been rightly reminded more than once in this conference already,[2] there was nothing more remarkable about the Puritans than their emphasis upon the conscience. 'The Puritan conscience!' There was nothing more characteristic of them. They were scrupulous in their desire to know exactly what the truth was, not simply that

[1] *1662–1962, From Puritanism to Non-Conformity, The Annual Lecture of the Evangelical Library, 1962.* See Appendix.

[2] *The addresses for this year's Conference were published under the title, 'Faith and a Good Conscience.'*

they might have a theoretical knowledge of it, but in order that they might carry it out, and put it into practice whatever might be the cost. That has been emphasised already in this conference, and therefore it is essential that one session at any rate, and perhaps most appropriately the last session, should be given to the application of what we have been considering. This is particularly appropriate this year, for the message of 1662 is one which places emphasis upon the conscience and the importance of translating what we have already understood in theory, and intellectually, into actual practice.

The third reason is already implied by what I have just said – anyone who knows anything at all about Puritan preachers knows that they had never finished until they came to 'application.' It is vital, therefore, that we should do this year by year. These men with their pastoral and experimental interest were essentially concerned with application. There is nothing that they more deplored than a mere academic, intellectual, theoretical view of the truth. It was one of their criticisms of the Caroline preachers, that they contented themselves with that, giving their learned disquisitions with their classical allusions and so on, and were more or less indifferent to the practical application in the lives of the people. The Puritans always put great emphasis upon application. So we must try to apply to our own contemporary situation something of what we have learned of their whole attitude to the Christian faith, and to the church, and to practical Christian living, and to conscience.

My last reason is this, that concerned as we all are, or at any rate should be, with a true revival of religion, with a manifestation of the power of Almighty God amongst us, with a shaking and a bringing together of the 'dry bones,' with a demonstration of the power of God and an authentication of his most holy word – concerned as we are about that, we must realise that there is nothing more urgently important than that we should examine ourselves. Some kind of reformation generally precedes revival. There are certain conditions in this matter of revival, and God has so ordained it, as history shows us clearly, that before he pours forth his Spirit upon a people, or upon an individual, he first prepares that people or that individual. It is inconceivable that great blessing should be given to a Laodicean, backsliding, or apostate church without a preliminary work of repentance. It is vital, therefore that we should address ourselves to this whole problem of the condition and state of the church in order that we may obey the leading and prompting of the Spirit of God and prepare ourselves for the much longed-for and looked-for out-pouring of his Holy Spirit.

Those are my four reasons for dealing with this subject. It would have been wrong of us, as I say, to allow this year to pass without trying to garner for ourselves some fruit from that great and notable event of 1662. That it was a crucial episode in the religious history of this country is something about which all, I think, will agree. It was a turning-point at which the history and the pattern of religion in this country was more or less determined for nearly three hundred years. There is a sense in which the period 1640 to 1662 is almost as important as the Protestant Reformation itself, because a final decision was taken at that point with regard to the nature of the Anglican church.

## II

It is vital that we should remind ourselves that from the very beginning of the Protestant Reformation in this country there had not been complete satisfaction in the church. The group that became known as Puritan was dissatisfied from the very beginning; they had a feeling that the reformation was incomplete. If we do not lay hold on that we cannot possibly understand this history. There was never a period when they were satisfied. Some have been trying to say recently that, from about the time of the setting aside of the Cartwright and Marprelate episodes to the arrival of Laud upon the scene, the Puritans and Anglicans 'differed very little.' That is a statement that simply will not hold water when tested by the facts. The book of the American Professor George and his wife which it is claimed 'demonstrates' this, seems to me to be based upon a fallacy – and that is, that they rely almost exclusively upon the sermons of that period and not upon the actual historical facts. It is true that there were not perhaps the same number of references in the sermons to the dispute during that period, but this was to be explained by the utter discouragement which the Puritans felt as the result of the disappointment of the Hampton Court Conference of 1604, and also of certain repressive measures introduced by James I and Archbishop Bancroft. The result was that the Puritans just went on preaching quietly and positively and were not as active in their protest as they were before, and as they were after. But there are facts, and I have tried to state some of them in my lecture delivered at the Evangelical Library, which make it abundantly clear that there was a continuous and persistent sense of dissatisfaction. At no period from the time of the Reformation to 1662 were the Puritans satisfied with the state of affairs in the church. As for the early part of the reign of James I, the conclusion arrived at by Dr S. Barton Babbage in his book *Puritanism and Richard Bancroft* (S.P.C.K. 1962) is undoubtedly correct: 'His achievements were solid and substantial; however, it is not unfair to say that, in relation to the challenge of Puritanism, the peace which reigned was more apparent than real; the conflict was only postponed and not concluded.' But our immediate concern now is that all this came to a head and to a climax in 1662, for then a final decision was really taken.

It is a most remarkable phenomenon. How often have we contemplated this fact – the extraordinary change which took place almost within a matter of a year? I mean this. Look at the period of the Civil Wars and the Interregnum and the Commonwealth under Cromwell. By 1644 the bishops and the various other offices had been abolished, the Prayer Book had been prohibited, and the Westminster Directory had been brought in. The Church of England as she had been known for nearly one hundred years, seemed to be almost entirely defunct; many of her own people, her greatest supporters, thought she was. She seemed to have gone and to have gone for ever, and the Puritans of various schools were in control. And yet by 1662 you find a complete transformation; indeed you already see the beginnings of it in 1660. Here in this nation which had beheaded Charles I, and had dealt in a drastic manner with the whole Anglican conception of the Christian church, you see the transformation that produced the crowds in London acclaiming the return of Charles II on May 29, 1660, and the Presbyterians having a prominent place in the procession of that monarch into the City of London and into Westminster. The thing is a phenomenon, the change truly extraordinary. And it must be examined by us.

I assert again that what happened in 1662 was really a definite turning-point in the history of the Church in England. Let me put this point in the words of Dr Robert S. Bosher in his book *The Making of the Restoration Settlement* (first edition 1952, second edition 1958). He says that, '1662 marks the final refusal to come to terms with the Continental Reformation.' This statement by Bosher is interesting because he writes from the Anglican standpoint, and his book has been recommended in a Foreword to it by the late Dr Norman Sykes, a historian and professor of church history in Cambridge at one time and later Dean of Winchester in the Church of England. Dr Norman Sykes says that he feels that Dr Bosher has established his thesis; and the thesis is that 1662 was a complete victory for the Laudian party in the Anglican church. It is for that reason that it can be regarded as the final refusal of the Anglican church to come to terms with the Continental Reformation. The Puritans had hoped throughout the century that the Church of England would be brought into conformity with the Reformation as it had worked itself out on the continent. They hoped against hope that this could be done. But after 1662 there was no longer any hope. The Laudian view of the church, according to Dr Bosher, was something that was finally established; it was a complete victory for that point of view.

This is something, therefore, that we must consider, and consider very seriously. Dr Bosher says again, 'The ecclesiastical settlement which thus took effect has been rightly regarded as a major landmark in English Church history and remains as a permanent achievement of the Laudian party. The Church of England would continue to be a meeting place of divers traditions, but, broadly speaking, its essential position, and the limits of its comprehensiveness, were finally established by the decision made in 1662. If, a century before, Anglicans had solemnly affirmed that the Church of Rome hath erred, the Laudian triumph resulted in a judgment of equal moment – that the Ecclesia Anglicana was of another spirit than Geneva.' 'In the Elizabethan settlement,' he goes on, 'the Reformation had been given a peculiarly English expression, and we may interpret the settlement of 1662 as an equally characteristic version of the counter-Reformation.' What happened in 1662 was, therefore, a most important event; it was a very real turning-point. The hope of the Puritans was finally dashed to the ground. It was their final defeat, and the exploding of all their longings.

## III

Why is it important that we should look at this matter and examine it? I suggest that it is important for this reason – that is, if I am not guilty of entirely misreading and misunderstanding the signs of the times – that we are today in a position that is more closely similar to the whole state of affairs from 1640 to 1662 than has ever been the case during the intervening three hundred years. What I mean is this. During the period we are examining (1640–1662) everything was in the melting-pot, as it were; the possibilities were tremendous, it was difficult to prophesy which way they were going to turn. Many of the Puritans believed at one or two points that they really had succeeded at last, and that they had got everything they had wanted; but in the end it all proved to be in vain, and everything was in the melting-pot again.

Surely today everything is in the melting-pot once more. The whole question of the nature of the church is being raised acutely again. Men are now prepared to think in a more loose and detached manner of their denominational attachments than they have been for three hundred years. Until comparatively recently they have fought for their denomination, the particular denomination to which they belong, with great tenacity, and there has often been much bitterness. All that has practically gone and men are now apparently prepared to throw the whole situation into the melting-pot again, and are talking about the emergence of something new.

Well, here is my question: are we ready for that? Where do we come in at this point? What is our attitude to these possibilities? For I believe they are very real, and I think we shall witness something quite new probably in the lifetime of most of us. So it seems to me that here we have brought before us, as it were providentially, by this tercentenary of 1662, the very thing that we need to give us some guidance. Alas, unfortunately, the lesson, as I see it, of this period is mainly one of warning. God grant that we may turn even that into a source and a means of blessing and of encouragement. We are in a situation in which we must all examine ourselves, and do so very honestly. I predict that we are going to pass through a period in which probably every one of us in this room will have to make as vital and as drastic a decision as did those men of 1662. We shall be forced to decide one way or the other – indeed that is already upon us. It is for that reason, therefore, that I invite you to turn to a consideration of this most extraordinary period.

## IV

So I start by asking a question: what went wrong? What was it that produced this amazing change from the apparent utter defeat of Laud to the triumph of his cause? You remember that he was impeached and put to death and that all that belonged to that side seemed lost, especially when Charles I was beheaded. It seemed to be in utter defeat; and yet in 1662 here they are victorious. The Laudian party that had seemed to be almost exterminated is back in control again and celebrating a notable victory. What went wrong? What went wrong especially with the Puritans who had been in the ascendancy during most of this period? What were the causes of failure?

I can simply put before you my own analysis of the period, my own idea as to what it was that went wrong. The first cause, I would say, was the admixture of religion and politics. That was the thing that seems to me to bedevil most of Puritan history. It was unfortunate that Laud, in addition to being archbishop, was a most important political person who as chief adviser to the king had a great deal to do with politics. The result was that it was impossible to disentangle the political grievances and the religious grievances. There were many people who were not very religious but who had political grievances. Finding that the Puritans also had grievances they naturally gravitated together, with the result that you had this – I had almost said unholy – alliance between those who were purely political in their motives and those who were essentially religious, because they seemed to be fighting a common enemy. This meant, of course, that the real issue tended to be confused and men made compromises for the sake of gaining a victory over the common enemy.

The records make it quite clear that there were those on the Puritan side, such as Baxter, who did not really believe in the Solemn League and Covenant, but in order to have the help of the Scots many of them subscribed to it. Thus, the motives became mixed, as they always will become mixed if we begin to confuse and admix politics with our religion.

It is a fact also that about 1640 there were even Royalists who heartily disliked and hated Laud and all his practices. Men who in 1660 and 1662 were nothing but pure Royalists and supporters of the bishops had been anti-bishop, because of the excesses of Laud, twenty years earlier. Their dislike of Laud had driven them to work with the Puritans, whose interest was more purely religious, and the result was that there was a great deal of confusion.

I do not want to stop with this, but I put it first because I have always felt that it is the first key to the understanding of the tragedy of what happened in 1662. This is always a danger, this admixture of politics and religion. Surely we need to face it at the present time. I feel certain that every nonconformist or free churchman in this conference will agree with me when I say that the main cause of the present condition of nonconformity is to be found in the action of the leaders at the end of the last century and the beginning of this century who were more politicians than religious leaders! If you object to bishops in the House of Lords, I hope you object equally to the preacher-politician who was the curse of the nonconformist churches during the second half of the reign of Queen Victoria and indeed right up to 1914. The fire and the zeal and enthusiasm went into social reform and political action and there was real justification for the saying that nonconformity was the Liberal Party at prayer as the Church of England was the Tory Party at prayer.

To mix politics with religion in the church is always a danger. May we learn the lesson of 1640 to 1662 and keep clear of any such worldly entanglements! Let us fight the battle of the Lord with spiritual weapons. That is the first explanation.

The second is a much more tragic one. It is the unfortunate and most regrettable divisions in the ranks of the Puritans. This is what makes the story a real tragedy. Fundamentally these men were all agreed about doctrine. What is the difference between the Savoy Declaration and the Westminster Confession? It is negligible. They were fundamentally agreed about the great essentials of the faith, of their approach to it, and all it contained. Yet the picture that is presented is one of division, endless divisions almost, in the ranks of the Puritans. They divided chiefly, of course, on the question of church government; but there were other matters which also caused division. No one can read the biography of Oliver Cromwell without seeing the way in which that righteous man's soul was vexed by these endless divisions amongst the Puritans. There is something pathetic in the way in which he wrote in a letter from Bristol on September 14th 1645, 'Presbyterians, Independents all have here the same spirit of faith and prayer: the same presence and answer; they agree here, have no names of difference; pity it is it should be otherwise anywhere! All that believe have the real unity, which is most glorious, because inward and spiritual, in the body, and to the head' (Letter xxvi).

I do not want to be unfair to any section, or any one group amongst them, but I am compelled to say that, taking a detached historical view – and especially for one who has been brought up as a Presbyterian – the really guilty party in all this was the Presbyterian party.

On what grounds do I say that? I do so for this reason, that they were the most intransigent. Not only that, they were always ready to make agreements with the king, whether it was Charles I or Charles II. It is almost incredible, but actually in 1650 the Presbyterians in Scotland came to an agreement with Prince Charles, afterwards Charles II, and brought him over from France. There was that brief war, which fortunately ended in disaster for the Royalist party and their Presbyterian supporters in the Battle of Worcester. But is it not a tragic thing that the Presbyterians should be found in such company, and fighting against the men who on the vitals of the Christian faith were in such entire agreement with them?

And then, later, at the end of the Interregnum or Commonwealth, and the early part of 1660 you come across that character, General Monck. What can one say about him? He was the man in many ways who 'sold the pass' and made possible the return of Charles II and his Laudian entourage; and it was very largely because of this Presbyterian interest that he did so.

Divisions arose among the Puritans, and, as I say, they were almost endless. You had the Presbyterians, the Independents, the Fifth Monarchy Men, the Quakers, the Diggers and the Levellers, and others. You see the Puritan party divided, almost splintered. And, of course, the Anglicans not only knew this, but they played upon it and took advantage of it. Their policy was as it has always been the policy of people who stand for any kind of Establishment, 'divide and conquer.' And it worked out most successfully! The result was that you had eventually the disaster of 1662. While the Puritans were divided and quarrelling among themselves, that brilliant group of Laudians, men who believed in the teaching of Laud, and most of whom escaped to the continent, were planning and scheming for the restoration of all they held dear.

Bosher brings this out and establishes this fact very clearly. His great thesis, which Professor Norman Sykes, as I say, asserts he has proved to the hilt, is that it was this brilliant Laudian party in exile which produced the extraordinary victory of that party in 1662. They had the aid of the most brilliant politician of the century in many ways, Edward Hyde, afterwards the Earl of Clarendon. They were all there together, and they were the people who immediately surrounded the person of the prince, who eventually became King Charles II. They just went on preparing and scheming and plotting, and in the meantime kept in touch with their agents in this country. While the others were quarrelling amongst themselves and poor Oliver Cromwell was driven to say that 'the new presbyter was as bad as the old priest,' here was this party with its cohesion standing together, fighting together, though everything seemed to be hopeless. The result was, in the end, that because of the divisions among the Puritans and their successful exploiting of those divisions, they obtained this their most notable victory in 1662.

That brings us to the third point I would establish – the main cause of the division. And that is none other than the whole question of the state church idea. Now let us be clear about this: they all really believed in that idea. The Presbyterians believed in a state church quite as much as the Anglicans. There is a sense in which it is perfectly true to say that the same thing applies even to Oliver Cromwell! We need not be surprised at this. After all, this was the situation and the position which they had inherited; they had never known any other situation at all. The church had always been the state church. So they started with the position as they found it. They were all essentially Erastian in their standpoint.

The position of Cromwell in this matter is to me particularly interesting. There is a sense in which he was Erastian but it was, as Bosher says, 'an Erastianism with a difference.' Let me quote Bosher again. He is talking about the anarchy in the national church during the Interregnum, or during the Commonwealth, and he says: 'Nonetheless, beneath the anarchy of a national church based on the merely negative principles of tolerance, a coherent policy can be observed radically different from the old. The clue to the Cromwellian church is to be found in the vehement "religiousness" of the new regime, in its profound conviction of the religious character of the state, its endless legislation upon matters of private and public morality. Unlike previous governments, it was utterly non-ecclesiastical and non-clerical in its attitude toward the state church. The questions of ordination, sacramental administration, liturgy, and ceremonial, which, as the symbols of church order and unity, had been bones of contention in the past, were now ignored. Every attempt to elaborate a doctrinal basis for the church beyond the simple requirements of "faith in God by Jesus Christ" was resolutely opposed by the Protector. To a recalcitrant Parliament he declared that "whoever hath this faith, let its form be what it will: he walking peaceably, without the prejudicing of others under another form" would be guaranteed full liberty of worship.' I repeat what I said in my lecture at the Evangelical Library – here is the father and the pioneer of toleration and of religious liberty in England. Let us go on with the quotation: 'The new conception was unashamedly Erastian, but Erastian with a novel twist.' Now comes the important point: 'The authority of the state was to be exercised not for regulating religious doctrine and practice, but for preventing any such regulation.' That is the exact opposite of the view held before. Previously it had been 'to regulate religious doctrine and practice'; as is still the case. But Cromwell was opposed to that. What he wanted the state to do was to put an end to such regulation, and thereby to guarantee toleration and liberty. To go on with the quotation: 'To make the Establishment the instrument for enforcing an almost unlimited tolerance of opinion, and for uniting the warring groups in a common zeal for godliness was Cromwell's ideal.' Thank God for Oliver Cromwell! 'Hence,' Dr Bosher continues, 'he could regard with equanimity the crazy patchwork of the Commonwealth church at the parish level – a spectacle that to Anglican and Presbyterian alike seemed an intolerable nightmare.'

We say and quote all that in defence of and to the glory of Oliver Cromwell. Though he took, in a sense, the Erastian view of a state church and held it and practised it, his idea was to use the power of the state to guarantee tolerance and variety and liberty, not to enforce particular points of view.

What, then, is our criticism of the other idea? I do not mean the Cromwellian, but the idea that largely controlled thinking both on the Anglican and the Presbyterian side. Is it not that it was too much governed by the existing conditions, instead of stopping and asking, 'What does the New Testament say about this?' Instead of taking the present position as it was and saying, 'What can we do to this?' they should rather have said, 'Well now, here is an opportunity for a new start; let us go back and look at the church as depicted in the New Testament, and start from that.' But they did not do so in reality, though both claimed to be scriptural. They started, as if it were beyond any need of demonstration or proof, with the fact of a state church; and the whole point then resolved itself to this – should it be Episcopal, or should it be Presbyterian?

Secondly, were they not too much influenced by the analogy of the Old Testament and of Israel? Here, it seems to me, was the source of the trouble, that they would persist in taking the analogy of Israel in the Old Testament and applying it to England. Was not that the real error? In the Old Testament and under that Dispensation the state (of Israel) was the church (Acts 7:38), but the state of England in the sixteenth century was not the church. In the Old Testament the two were one and identical. But surely in the New Testament we have the exact opposite. The church consists of the 'called out' ones, not the total state. The state and the church are not coterminous, but the church consists of those who are 'called out' of the world, out of the state, into this peculiar and separate body. Nowhere in the New Testament is a direct connection between church and state taught. To conceive of the church of the New Testament in its relationship to the pagan Roman Empire in any other way is just impossible. Moreover the Christians are those who are 'delivered out of this present evil world' and who are told, 'Be ye not unequally yoked together with unbelievers,' and exhorted to 'come out from among them, and be ye separate' (Gal. 1:4; 2 Cor. 6:14, 17). The called out ones are of all nations, 'whether Jews or Gentiles, Barbarians or Scythians, bond or free.' So, there, it seems to me, is a large part of the explanation of what led to this ultimate tragedy.

But, furthermore, holding the view they did of the state-church connection, quite naturally they believed that their particular view should be 'enforced.' Now let us be perfectly fair to the Anglicans, who were most responsible for that Act of Uniformity in 1662;

the others did exactly the same thing when they had the power, and would have done so in 1660–62. The Presbyterians believed, quite as much as the Anglicans, that people should be compelled by Act of Parliament and the power of the state to submit to their particular view of the church, and in 1644 they enforced their view by the power of the state and by the enactments of Parliament.

This view means that ultimately these matters depend upon and are determined by the fickleness of the crowd. The result is that the same London crowd that had acclaimed Cromwell is to be seen in 1660 in its gaiety and its buffoonery welcoming back Charles II. The same people! That is what follows when you give this power to legislate and to enforce doctrine to the state. You are left ultimately with the fickleness of the crowd, without stopping to mention the inherent inability and incapacity of the crowd, the irreligious crowd in particular, to have any opinion that is of any value concerning these matters. If we are told in 1 Corinthians 6 that members of the Christian church should not take even matters of private personal disputes to the public law courts, how much less should we take matters of doctrine?

It seems clear that both sides were starting with the given position and did not trouble to examine it in the light of the New Testament teaching. In addition to all this, as we have already seen, they also believed that you could enforce a kind of 'strict religious behaviour' upon the populace by Acts of Parliament; hence those various Acts they passed with regard to sports and entertainments and certain other things. I am bringing this forward quite deliberately because it is more than likely that there will be a fight about all this in the immediate future, and you and I will be expected to have some kind of attitude with respect to it.

I venture to assert that once more we are dealing with a standpoint which is based upon a fallacy, which is Old Testament thinking again rather than New Testament; and it always leads to trouble. Take that crowd, the London crowd, that had been compelled to live in a given way, and according to a given pattern, during the Commonwealth. It had never believed in what was being forced on it, and had never understood the principles on which it was being enforced. Consequently it got very tired and weary of it. This was one of the main factors in turning people back to royalty, and to saying that they must have the king back, and that they must get rid of those wretched Puritans who were spoiling life, and so on. That kind of 'enforcing' of morals by Act of Parliament instead of by moral and spiritual suasion, it seems to me, is bound to produce a reaction against itself. I believe we are witnessing just that at the present time. We are witnessing a reaction against Victorianism, which was so similar to what was in force during the period of the Commonwealth. This has been described in many books. During the time of Queen Victoria, and even before, as the result of the work of Wilberforce and others, what is called 'Victorianism,' came into being and people were compelled by Act of Parliament, as it were, to live a certain kind of life. But that always produces a reaction against itself as it did towards the end of the Commonwealth and in 1660–1662.

I am suggesting that if only all these different divisions and factions had stood together when they had a wonderful opportunity, and especially at the return of Charles II – if they had only stood together for a general religious toleration, the whole situation would have been entirely different. But the Presbyterians would not agree to that; it had to be Presbyterianism. And so the forces were divided; and the Anglicans, as I say, with their ability and astuteness and cohesion, and with what is generally described as the astounding 'political finesse' of Sheldon, the Bishop of London, afterwards archbishop, were entirely and completely successful. If the Puritans had but stood together for religious toleration in general rather than any one system, the history at that time and during the subsequent three hundred years would have been very different.

Now that was all that the Independents asked for. The Sectarians, the Independents, simply asked for toleration. They did not go into the discussions at the Savoy and various other places. They were not interested in this 'either – or,' Presbyterianism or Anglicanism. All they wanted was liberty to worship God in the way they understood the Bible to teach. But, that, unfortunately, was not the view held by all Puritans and because of their divisions about these secondary matters, the whole position was lost. Of course, it was not lost in the sense that these men did not go on preaching. Alas, too late, many of them were forced to see the truth of the position taken by Dr John Owen and Dr Thomas Goodwin and others, and they were driven to that position. But by then the damage had been done, and a glorious possibility and opportunity had been missed.

## V

There, then, is a kind of analysis of the causes of failure. Let me now attempt in a final section to draw some lessons for ourselves today. The first is this: what is it, according to our Reformed and Puritan view, that really matters? I have tried to show that this central all-important point became obscured for the various reasons I have adduced – the political admixture, and the concern about matters which are not, surely, of primary importance. Well, then, we must ask ourselves the question – what do we regard as of supreme importance? What are we going to put in the centre? What are we going to say matters above all else, and which we must never lose sight of? Surely there can be no disagreement among us with regard to the answer. It is the gospel of salvation which is also 'the gospel of the glory of God.' It is the thing about which all those Puritans were agreed – the nature, the essence of the gospel. We have looked at it so many times in these conferences that I need say no more.

Coupled with that, there was their emphasis upon the necessity of having able and good ministers, and the primacy and the centrality of preaching. These were the things about which they were all agreed, and about which, surely, we must also all agree as being the first, the primary, and the most essential things.

What is the gospel? Must we not put this first – that there can be no uncertainty about this? Our consciences must compel us to say this; that we cannot allow any vagueness or uncertainty or indefiniteness about this. Surely our whole position is based upon this, that we say the gospel can be defined, can be stated in propositions. We *do* believe in confessions of faith, we *do* believe in creeds. It is just there that we are differentiated from the majority of people in the Christian church at the present time. Surely, then, that is something which we must assert and proclaim and defend at all costs – this pure gospel, this pure word of the gospel. And we will tolerate no compromise with respect to this.

Then secondly, we are surely compelled by all this to face again our whole view of the church. That was a question about which the Puritans – and, indeed, for that matter the Anglicans as well at that period – were all agreed as being central. We must praise and commend them all in that respect: they were all concerned about the church. They did not try to solve their problems by forming movements; every one of them was concerned about the state of the church. The Anglicans were contending for their view of the church. The Presbyterians were not content to be just a movement within the church, they wanted the whole church to be Presbyterian. The point I am making is, that they did not meet the position by just saying, 'Well, all right, we will remain Anglicans, but we will have a movement of our own within the church, and we will meet together and have fellowship and carry out activities from time to time' – leaving the church untouched as it were. That was not their view at all. The same is true of the Independents also. Every one of them was contending for a view of the church. They were not content to allow the condition of the church to be chaotic as long as they could meet together in fellowship in their movements. Every one of them was concerned about the state and condition of the church. The doctrine of the church was central with all of them.

We need to be reminded of that. Is it not the case that for far too long we as Evangelicals have been divided, and are rendered ineffective, because we do not think in terms of the church? We have formed movements, and we have not applied what we believe to the church situation – hence the chaos and the anarchy of our time in almost every department of our life and activity.

That, then, raises the question: what is our view of the church? What is the New Testament view of the church? What has the

New Testament to say about this whole question of a state church, and as to the way in which doctrine and practice are to be determined? Surely this question ought to be one of our priorities. These people of 1662 compel us to face that. The movements around us today, the Ecumenical Movement in particular, and other factors, I believe, are forcing us to ask this question: what is our view of the church? And surely at this point we need to learn this great lesson from the Puritans – the all-importance of the purity of the church, especially in the matter of doctrine. Implicit in that, of course, is the necessity for discipline. Is it right to tolerate in the same church people whose views on the essentials of the faith are diametrically opposed? Is it right that we belong to the same company, calling itself a church, as men who deny almost everything we stand for – the deity of our Lord, the virgin birth, his miracles, his atoning sacrificial death, the punitive and substitutionary elements in the atonement, our Lord's literal physical resurrection, the person of the Holy Spirit, regeneration, justification by faith only, the 'blessed hope' of our Lord's return? Is it right in the light of New Testament teaching that we regard such people as 'brethren,' that we should refer to people who never darken the doors of a place of worship as 'lapsed Christians' simply because they were baptized when infants? Is that compatible with the New Testament teaching with regard to the church, and her purity, and her discipline, and her life? Such questions have got to be matters of prior and primary consideration for us if we really take these Puritans seriously, if we pay any serious regard to their teaching about the conscience, and of the need of being scrupulous, and of honestly carrying out what we believe to be the truth whatever the consequences.

Another urgent question surely is the freedom of the church to determine her own affairs. Is there any suggestion anywhere in the New Testament that any body, the state and monarch included, has any right in that respect save the church herself? Do we not need to remind ourselves again of 'the crown rights of the Redeemer'?

I go on to put a practical question: can we who are agreed about the vital, fundamental, first things allow anything of lesser importance to divide us? We have a great lesson in the history of 1640 to 1662 which shows us what happens if we do so. As Evangelicals we are divided among the various denominations, and our efforts are made negatory and nullified; and in the end we count for very little. But is it right, I ask, for us to allow ourselves to be separated and divided by anything which falls short of the great central things we have mentioned? Is it right that we should be more associated in general, and in our total life as Christians in the church, with people with whom we do not agree, than with people with whom we do agree about these central vital matters?

The next lesson we learn from 1640–1662 is the importance of fighting this battle in a spiritual manner, and not with carnal weapons. If 1640 to 1662 teaches us nothing else it teaches us this: that in that kind of ecclesiastical fighting, the ecclesiastics will win every time. They are past masters at it. It is the thing in which they really believe. While you and I are concerned about doctrine, and the culture and the nurture of the soul, their whole attention is given to practicalities and to the politics of the situation. So the moment we begin to fight with a semi-political, ecclesiastical outlook, the moment we develop a party spirit and begin to think in terms of party advantage, and regard people who really agree with us about the centralities as enemies almost, and in opposition, the cause is already lost.

There is nothing, it seems to me, that is more offensive, or more removed from the spirit of the New Testament than a party spirit that puts the interests of its own particular point of view upon matters that are not of primary and central importance before those matters that are of primary and central importance. Not only is it wrong but, as I say, the ecclesiastics will always succeed best at that kind of thing. They always have succeeded; they always will succeed. Our only comment upon them is this – 'Verily, they have their reward.' They are past masters at manipulation, at lobbying, at meeting behind the scenes, and at organising. And they will stoop to almost anything. Fancy the Presbyterians, during this period we are examining, actually co-operating with Henrietta Maria, the widow of Charles I! They co-operated with her though she was a

Roman Catholic who really hated everything for which they stood. They did so in order to get an advantage over the Anglicans. Shame on them!

'The weapons of our warfare are not carnal, but mighty through God to the pulling down of strongholds' (2 Cor. 10:5). But the moment men become animated by a party spirit they will stoop to almost anything to get their ends and to ensure the success of their party; and so you get these unholy alliances. They are a blot upon the Presbyterian record during that whole period. Thank God, the men whose names are most frequently mentioned in this Conference – John Owen and Thomas Goodwin – cannot be charged with that! They had this other view of church government to which I have already referred. They did not look to the state connection; they but wanted liberty to worship as they understood God to teach in the New Testament, and therefore they never resorted to these shameful practices and subterfuges. May God preserve us from developing a narrow party spirit that is more interested in the success of its point of view than in the glory of God and the purity and the welfare of the church! If that does not come as a lesson to us from 1660 to 1662, well then, I say, God help us – our cause is already lost.

## VI

My final word is this and it is a still more practical one. A great lesson that comes to us from this period is to be alert to the danger of being ensnared and bought by the subtlety and the craftiness and the wiliness of men. All this was practised upon the Puritans, and especially on the Presbyterian party, from 1660 to 1662. The principle on which the Laudians acted was the principle on which such people always act; it is the principle on which they are acting today. It can be seen in ecumenical circles at the present time. The Roman Catholics, and the present Pope in particular, are acting on it. The principle is this – stand inflexible on the essentials, but having done that, be affable, be ready to concede on the irrelevancies, the matters that really do not matter at all. Speak kindly to, fraternise with, and flatter members of the opposing group. It was a deliberate part of the policy of the Laudian party to bribe some of the Puritans. Richard Baxter was offered the bishopric of Hereford, Calamy was offered the bishopric of Lichfield, Reynolds was offered the bishopric of Norwich, and Thomas Manton was offered the deanery of Rochester. Bates was offered the deanery of Lichfield, Bowles was offered the deanery of York. The only one who accepted was Reynolds, who actually became the Bishop of Norwich.

I do not want to say anything about Reynolds, but I do say this about the others: there is the Puritan conscience in action! It cannot be bribed, it is not 'taken in' by the affability and the niceness and the flattery of men. It does not say, 'You know, some of these other men are much nicer than our people.' It sees through all that, and it sees beyond it. Attempts were made in that way to divide the Puritan party by offering preference to some of their leaders; but it was rigidly and sternly and conscientiously rejected and refused. These men could not compromise on these matters, their consciences could not be bought. They preferred to go out into the wilderness, and to the suffering that followed to so many and in such a terrible manner. That, I say, is the Puritan conscience in action; the scrupulosity, the carefulness, and particularly the carefulness not only to have the right view, but to act upon it whatever the consequences might be.

In other words, the ultimate lesson to be learned from this period, is this: 'The arm of flesh will fail you, ye dare not trust your own.' We must 'trust in the Lord, and in the power of his might.' We must be 'strong in the Lord, and in the power of his might.' We must indeed realise that 'the weapons of our warfare are not carnal, but mighty through God to the pulling down of strongholds.' It does not matter what they are, nor who they are; it does not matter how small we may be. If we see what the truth is, well then, I say, we must hold to it and fight for it, and refuse to compromise about it, whatever it may cost us. We must refuse every enticement, every offer, every form of flattery, and of honour; we must be wise to detect the devices that will be used against us – the offering of offices, preferments, positions of honour, places in our denomination, or whatever else it may be – we must reject it all as these men rejected it all, in order that we may fight for the faith and the purity of the church, the honour of God and of his Christ.

We thank God for the memory of these men, who, having seen the position clearly, acted upon it at all costs. May God give us grace to follow in their train!

# 1963

# *John Owen on Schism*

## I

I AM going to speak, as you have been told, on 'John Owen on the subject of Schism.' Why am I dealing with this? I have a number of reasons for doing so. One is, and I make no apology for this, that it is a kind of postscript to what I was trying to say last year about 1640–1662. I have not finished with that in my mind yet, and I do not think any of us should, because, as I tried to indicate then it has a great deal to say to us at the present time. We are again in a stage of transition, in an age when these great fundamental questions are thrust before us once more; and I believe that we can obtain real guidance and help from these men of three hundred years ago who had to face a similar situation. The term 'Schism' was, obviously, one that was bandied about a great deal three hundred years ago. That is not at all surprising, and the term was used by all sorts of people. The Roman Catholic Church, of course, used it with respect to all Protestants, the Church of England included. Then, the Church of England began to use it with respect to the Presbyterians. And then both the Church of England and the Presbyterians used it with respect to the Independents. In other words, this is a term that is almost invariably used by any church or body from whom a number go out to form a new church. It is a term that is bandied about freely and loosely, and it was because of that that John Owen took up the subject.

I call attention to it because it is already being bandied about, and we can be quite certain that if the Ecumenical Movement ever develops 'the great World Church' that they so delight to talk about, well then this is the term that will be hurled against everybody who refuses to be part and parcel of that mammoth organisation. I feel therefore that it is our duty to prepare our own minds beforehand. Whatever may be the truth now, it will certainly be the case then that we shall be charged with schism, and it is right that we should be clear about it, and that we should instruct the people to whom we are privileged to minister concerning this all-important matter. Schism is a very great sin, it is a very serious matter. Nobody should be guilty of the sin of schism, and it is vital therefore that we should be clear in our minds as to what exactly it is.

John Owen dealt with this subject many times. I propose to deal with the main treatises in which he did so. There is one which is just called, *Of Schism*. Then he had to defend that – *A Review of the true nature of Schism*. Then he had to answer various people who attacked him very bitterly on this subject. There is also a very interesting treatise of his called, *A Brief Vindication of the Nonconformists from the Charge of Schism*. That was Owen's reply to a sermon preached by Dr Stillingfleet, who was at that time Dean of St Paul's and later became the Bishop of Worcester. Stillingfleet charged nonconformists with being guilty of schism in a sermon which he preached on Philippians 3:15 and 16. Owen, having here a foeman worthy of his steel, and not merely a carping critic like a certain Mr Cawdrey, a Presbyterian, who simply abused him and vilified him, produced this most interesting treatise in answer to that sermon. But then, in addition to that, there is one called, *A Discourse Concerning Evangelical Love, Church Peace and Unity*. Another has the title, *An Inquiry into the Original, Nature, Institution, Power, Order, and Communion of Evangelical Churches*. Again, there is *An Answer to Dr Stillingfleet's Book of the Unreasonableness of Separation*. And finally – and greater, perhaps, than all of them – was his treatise on *The Nature of a Gospel or a New Testament Church*. John Owen, you see, was very concerned about this matter because he regarded schism as being a most serious charge in view of the character of the sin involved in it.

His main object was to defend himself and the Independents from this particular charge, and as he does so, he incidentally helps to clear the Presbyterians also from the charges of the Church of England, and the Church of England in turn from the charges of the Roman Catholics. But he had a deeper motive than that; he was concerned about the truth concerning the nature of the church. That was the thing that, ultimately, was his great concern. And that, I suggest, should be our great concern also at the present time.

I have decided that Owen himself should do the speaking, and if I can succeed somehow in conveying the spirit and the method of John Owen to you I shall be more than satisfied. With such a wealth of material, selection has been difficult, but I have tried to distil the essence of his teaching.

## II

We start with Owen's method, his whole approach; and I am really more concerned about this than about any particular thing that he said. Owen never dealt with a problem, as it were, immediately and directly, he always put it into its context. He did not 'rush' at a question that was put to him, or at a charge that was brought against him, and just answer immediately and directly with a kind of 'quid pro quo.' He was not interested in polemics as such, his whole nature indeed rebelled against that.

In dealing with any problem his first question always seems to have been – 'Well now, what is the principle involved here? Where does this come in, in the whole doctrine and teaching of the Bible? Let us settle that first.' So Owen did not meet this charge of schism directly and merely in and of itself. He could hear people hurling this charge against one another, bandying it about, and each one feeling that he was right in doing so. But it was obvious on the surface that they could not all be right, because they were all bringing the charge against one another. There was something wrong, therefore, and Owen came to the conclusion that it was all due to the fact that none of them had really stopped to ask the question – 'How do we decide what schism is? What is our authority and what are our terms of reference?' So he turns to the Scriptures and he sees at once that certain great questions are involved.

But even before we examine his particular method let us look at the spirit in which he approached the question. Here is no bitter partisan or narrow-minded sectarian or dry-as-dust academic theologian. Out of his heart he writes:

'I confess I would rather, much rather, spend all my time and days in making up and healing the breaches and schisms that are amongst Christians than one hour in justifying our divisions, even therein wherein, on the one side, they are capable of a fair defence. But who is sufficient for such an attempt? The closing of differences, amongst Christians is like opening the book in the Revelation – there is none able or worthy to do it, in heaven or in earth, but the Lamb: when he will put forth the greatness of his power for it, it shall be accomplished, and not before. In the meantime, a reconciliation amongst all Protestants is our duty, and practicable, and had perhaps ere this been in some forwardness of accomplishment had men rightly understood wherein such a reconciliation, according to the mind of God, doth consist. When men have laboured as much in the improvement of the principle of forbearance as they have done to subdue other men to their opinions, religion will have another appearance in the world.'

Let us say, 'Amen.'

Now that is the sort of thing I am anxious to convey to you. Many people think of this man as a dry-as-dust theologian. It is a foul aspersion upon him. Listen to this further quotation in which Owen shows us how he ever became an Independent. For John Owen was not born an Independent, he was born into the Church of England. He says about his father, interestingly enough:

'As I was bred up from my infancy under the care of my father, who was a nonconformist all his days [that does not mean that he was an Independent, remember] and a painful labourer in the vineyard of the Lord, so ever since I came to have any distinct knowledge of the things belonging to the worship of God I have been fixed in judgment against that which I am calumniated withal, etc.'

Owen, in his younger days, had once published a book on

the whole question of the nature of the church and in it he was favourable to the Presbyterian point of view. When he published this treatise on schism therefore, a certain Mr Cawdrey, a Presbyterian from Northampton, attacked him violently saying that he was contradicting entirely what he had said in that previous book. Owen felt this charge very deeply. He does not however reply in any spirit of bitterness, but he does take the trouble, in replying to Cawdrey, to tell us how he ever became an Independent. In looking at this we shall see something of the greatness of this man. The trouble, as he points out repeatedly, over the whole question of schism is that people will defend the position that they are in. They shut their minds, they are not ready to listen, to be instructed, and to change. Owen was big enough to change his opinion and to move from one position to another. This is his account of how it came about:

'Indeed, not long after, I set myself seriously to inquire into the controversies then warmly agitated in these nations. Of the congregational way I was not acquainted with any one person, minister or other; nor had I, to my knowledge, seen any more than one in my life. My acquaintance lay wholly with ministers and people of the presbyterian way. But sundry books being published on either side, I perused and compared them with the Scripture and one another, according as I received ability from God.'

What an excellent way that is! You read right round the subject and compare it with the Scripture. Owen continues,

'After a general view of them, as was my manner in other controversies, I fixed on one to take under peculiar consideration and examination, which seemed most methodically and strongly to maintain that which was contrary, as I thought, to my present persuasion.'

Of the multiplicity of books he picks out one which he regards as the best, to see what it has to say to him. 'This was Mr Cotton's book of the Keys,' he tells us. That is a reference to the famous John Cotton, a Church of England clergyman and a godly man. For many years Cotton was vicar of Boston in Lincolnshire and then moved over, about 1634 if I remember rightly, to Boston in

Massachusetts. As the result of his thinking and meditation and reading in this country – and still more after his arrival in New England – he became a convinced Independent, and so wrote his book – *The Keys*. This is how John Owen describes the effect that the reading of this book had upon him:

'The examination and confutation hereof, merely for my own particular satisfaction, with what diligence and sincerity I was able, I engaged in. What progress I made in that undertaking I can manifest unto any by the discourse on that subject and animadversions on that book, yet abiding by me. In the pursuit and management of this work, quite beside and contrary to my expectation, at a time and season wherein I could expect nothing on that account but ruin in this world, without the knowledge or advice of, or conference with, any one person of that judgment, I was prevailed on to receive that and those principles which I had thought to have set myself in an opposition unto. And, indeed, this way of impartial examining all things by the word, comparing causes with causes and things with things, laying aside all prejudicate respects unto persons or present traditions, is a course that I would admonish all to beware of who would avoid the danger of being made Independents.'

I trust that we get the full implication of that. If you approach this subject quite honestly, comparing and contrasting all teaching with the Scriptures and especially 'laying aside all prejudicate respects unto persons or present traditions,' you will find it very difficult to avoid becoming an Independent, says Owen. However, that is the way in which he approached it. He set out to read this book in order that he might answer it, but he was so honest that, comparing it with the Scripture, he was persuaded. The result was that he became a convinced Independent.

Now that is surely one of the great lessons we learn from this man. Whatever else we may think, whatever our disagreements, surely we must all agree with this spirit and with this method. Most of our differences, I think, arise from the fact that we all of us, in one way or another, are unprepared to do that. The first thing you must do is to bring everything to the bar of Scripture. Here,

Owen lays down the rule with respect to Scripture that we have been reminded of several times already in this conference. He says, 'And by the Scripture as our rule, we understand both the express words of it, and whatever may, by just and lawful consequence, be deduced from them.'

In other words he says that the whole trouble, in a sense, arises in this way, that men start from fixed positions, from things as they are, and then regard any departure from that as schism: and so hurl that charge at any who disagrees with them. We must not do that, says Owen, but go back to the fount and to the origin. We must start with Scripture itself – which is the rule we find taught in the Scripture. When we thus go to the Scripture what do we find? How do they define what is meant by 'schism'? This how he puts it:

'The thing whereof we treat being a disorder in the instituted worship of God, and that which is of pure revelation, I suppose it a modest request, to desire that we may abide solely by that discovery and description which is made of it in Scripture, – that that alone shall be esteemed schism which is there so called, or which hath the entire nature of that which is so called. Other things may be other crimes; schism they are not, if in the Scripture they have neither the name nor nature of it attributed to them.'

Having arrived at it in that way, this is now Owen's definition of schism.

He points out that this is really only dealt with actually in 1 Corinthians. It is very interesting to observe how he works. He gives a good general bird's-eye view of the whole subject as it is dealt with there, and then points out that the other document dealing with more or less exactly the same subject, that comes down to us from the early ages, is an epistle from Rome to the church at Corinth by Clement at a later date. But to continue:

'The schism, then, here described by the apostle, and blamed by him, consists (and here is the vital definition) in causeless differences and contentions amongst the members of a particular church, contrary to that exercise of love, prudence, and forbearance, which are required of them to be exercised amongst themselves, and towards one another.'

His whole point is this: that the only schism that is described in the New Testament is division, causeless divisions, within the church. The people guilty of schism in the church of Corinth had not left the church of Corinth. The New Testament definition of schism is 'causeless divisions' within the body of a particular church. Having laid that down he then goes on to indicate in various ways what is meant by schism. But listen to this:

'But now this foundation having been laid, that schism is a causeless difference or division amongst the members of any particular church that meet together, or ought so to do, for the worship of God and the celebration of the same numerical ordinances, to the disturbance of the order appointed by Jesus Christ, and contrary to that exercise of love in wisdom and mutual forbearance which is required of them, it will be easy to see wherein the iniquity of it doth consist, and upon what considerations its aggravations do arise.'

Schism, then, means this: 'Despising of the authority of Jesus Christ. It is an offence against his wisdom, whereby he hath ordered all things in the church on set purpose that schism and divisions may be prevented.' They despised that. Thirdly: 'The grace and goodness of Christ are also ignored and are offended.'

That, then, leads him to say this:

'Let, then, the general demand be granted, that schism is "the breach of union," which I shall attend with one reasonable postulatum – namely, that this union be a union of the appointment of Jesus Christ.' He keeps on repeating that – it must be the breaking of a union appointed by the Lord Jesus Christ. 'The consideration, then, of what or what sort of union in reference to the worship of God, according to the gospel, is instituted and appointed by Jesus Christ, is the proper foundation of what I have farther to offer in this business. Let the breach of this, if you please, be accounted schism; for being an evil, I shall not contend by what name or title it be distinguished. It is not pleaded that any kind of relinquishment or desertion of any church or churches is presently schism, but only such a separation as breaks the bond of union instituted by Christ.

'Now, this union being instituted in the church, according to the various acceptations of that word, so it is distinguished. Therefore, for a discovery of the nature of that which is particularly to be spoken to, and also its contrary, I must show –

'1. The several considerations of the church wherein and with which union is to be preserved.

'2. What that union is, and wherein it doth consist, which, according to the mind of Christ, we are to keep and observe with the church, under the several notions of it respectively.

'3. And how that union is broken, and what is that sin whereby it is done.'

You notice that he approaches his subject in such a way, that you come at once to the great doctrine of the nature of the church. You cannot decide what schism is until you have decided what the church is. That must be the first great question. Roman Catholics say that 'All Protestants are schismatics.' Why? 'Because they have left us.' But then the question to ask them is, 'Who are you?,' 'What are you?,' 'Are you a church?' – and this question must always be asked. You cannot define schism unless you are clear about your doctrine of the nature of the church; and Owen, of course, gives the definition of the church that we would expect of him as an Independent. In this connection he says a very interesting thing which some of us need to remember at this present time: 'Let none mistake themselves herein; believers are not made for churches, but churches are appointed for believers.' That is reminiscent, is it not, of what our Lord said about the Sabbath? There are many people, it seems to me, who think that believers are made for churches. They are not. Churches are made for believers. 'Their edification, their guidance and direction in the profession of the faith and performance of divine worship in assemblies, according to the mind of God, is their use and end; without which they are of no signification. The end of Christ in the constitution of his churches was, not the moulding of his disciples into such ecclesiastical shapes as might be subservient unto the power, interest, advantage, and dignity, of them that may in any season come to be over them, but to constitute a way and order of giving such officers unto them as might be in all things useful and subservient unto their edification; as is expressly affirmed in Ephesians 4:11 to 16.' The church was made for us, not we for the church.

Now there he lays down a great postulate. Again, his whole point is, that that is the church which was instituted by the Lord Jesus Christ himself, and by him alone. Owen brings out this point:

'There is, indeed, by some pleaded a subordination of officers in this church, tending towards a union on that account; as that ordinary ministers should be subjected to diocesan bishops, they to archbishops or metropolitans, they again to patriarchs, where some would bound the process, though a parity of reason would call for a pope: nor will the arguments pleaded for such a subordination rest until they come to be centred in some such thing.' The logical end of that argument, he says, is to have a pope of some sort or kind. 'But first, before this plea be admitted, it must be proved that all these officers are appointed by Jesus Christ, or it will not concern us, who are inquiring solely after his will, and the settling of conscience therein. To do this with such an evidence as that the consciences of all those who are bound to yield obedience to Jesus Christ may appear to be therein concerned, will be a difficult task, as I suppose. And, to settle this once for all, I am not dealing with the men of that lazy persuasion that such affairs are to be ordered by the prudence of our civil superiors and governors; and so seeking to justify a nonsubmission to any of their constitutions in the things of this nature, or to evidence that the so doing is not schism. Nor do I concern myself in the order and appointment of ancient times, by men assembled in synods and councils; wherein, whatever was the force of their determinations in their own seasons, we are not at all concerned, knowing of nothing that is obligatory to us, not pleading from sovereign authority or our own consent: but it is after things of pure institution that I am inquiring. With them who say there is no such thing in these matters, we must proceed to other principles than any yet laid down.'

The great point is that we are only to be concerned about that which is instituted by the Lord Jesus Christ himself. In this connection we have got to look for a moment at what he says about the general councils, because they have come so much into this argument. Owen says that we must be concerned about nothing but that which we can establish has been instituted by the Lord Jesus Christ himself. But then the argument comes in – What about the authority of the general council? Owen takes that up and this is what he says:

'The Church of England, as it is called (that is the people thereof) separated herself from the Church of Rome. To free herself from the imputation of schism in so doing, as she (that is, the learned men of the nation) pleaded the errors and corruptions of that church, under this especial consideration of their being imposed by tyrants; so also by professing her design to do nothing but to reduce religion and the worship of God to its original purity, from which it has fallen. And we all jointly justify both her and all other reformed churches in this plea.

'In her design to reduce religion to its primitive purity, she always professed [this is the Church of England] that she did not take her direction from the Scripture only, but also from the councils and examples of the first four or five centuries; to which she laboured to conform her reformation. Let the question now be, whether there be not corruptions in this Church of England, supposing such a national church-state to be instituted? What, I beseech you, shall bind my conscience to acquiesce in what is pleaded from the first four or five centuries, consisting of men that could and did err, more than that did hers which was pleaded from the nine or ten centuries following? Have not I liberty to call for reformation according to the Scripture only? or at least to profess that my conscience cannot be bound by any other? The sum is – the business of schism from the Church of England is a thing built purely and simply on political considerations, so interwoven with them, so influenced from them, as not to be separated.'

That is his attitude towards the general councils; but he has something still more drastic to say about them, and as we are likely to hear a good deal about this sort of thing in the coming years I think we must pay heed to what he says:

'But a general council is pleaded with the best colour and

pretence for a bond of union to this general and visible church. In consideration hereof I shall not divert to the handling of the rise, right use, authority, necessity, of such councils; about all which somewhat in due time towards satisfaction may be offered to those who are not in bondage to names and traditions – nor shall I remark what hath been the management of the things of God in all ages in those assemblies; many of which have been the stains and ulcers of Christian religion – nor yet shall I say with what little disadvantage to the religion of Jesus Christ I suppose a loss of all the canons of all councils that ever were in the world since the apostles' days, with their acts and contests might be undergone – nor yet shall I digress to the usefulness of the assemblies of several churches in their representatives, to consider and determine about things of common concernment to them, with their tendency to the preservation of that communion which ought to be amongst them – but as to the present instance only offer –

'1. That such general councils, being things purely extraordinary and occasional, as is confessed, cannot be an ordinary standing bond of union to the catholic church. And if any one shall reply, that though in themselves and in their own continuance they cannot be so, yet in the authority, laws, and canons they may; I must say, that besides the very many reasons I have to call into question the power of law-making for the whole society of Christians in the world, in all the general councils that have been or possibly can be on the earth, the disputes about the title of those assemblies which pretend to this honour, which are to be admitted, which excluded, are so endless; the rules of judging them so dark, lubricous,[1] and uncertain, framed to the interest of all contenders on all hands; the laws of them, which "de facto" have gone under that title and name, so innumerable, burdensome, uncertain, and frivolous, in a great part so grossly contradictory to one another, that I cannot suppose that any man upon second thoughts can abide in such an assertion. If any shall, I must be bold to declare my affection to the doctrine of the

[1] Slippery, oily, elusive

gospel maintained in some of those assemblies for some hundreds of years, and then to desire him to prove that any general council, since the apostles fell asleep, hath been so convened and managed as to be enabled to claim that authority to itself which is or would be due to such an assembly instituted according to the mind of Christ.'

He is challenging the whole authority of these general councils, but he admits with his customary honesty, his intellectual honesty and his largeness of heart:

'That it hath been of advantage to the truth of the gospel that godly learned men, bishops of churches, have convened and witnessed a good confession in reference to the doctrine thereof, and declared their abhorrence of the errors that are contrary thereunto, is confessed. That any man or men is, are, or ever were, intrusted by Christ with authority so to convene them, as that thereupon and by virtue thereof they should be invested with a new authority, power, and jurisdiction, at such a convention, and thence should take upon them to make laws and canons that should be ecclesiastically binding to any persons or churches, as theirs, is not as yet, to me, attended with any convincing evidence of truth. And seeing at length it must be spoken, I shall do it with submission to the thoughts of good men that are in any way acquainted with these things, and in sincerity therein commend my conscience to God, that I do not know anything that is extant bearing clearer witness to the sad degeneracy of Christian religion in the profession thereof nor more evidently discovering the efficacy of another spirit than that which was poured out by Christ at his ascension, nor containing more hay and stubble, that is to be burned and consumed, than the stories of the acts and laws of the councils and synods that have been in the world.'

He continues with his denunciation of these general councils, and especially of the claim that they had authority and power to legislate with regard to these various additions in the matter of offices and forms of worship in connection with the life of the church. Owen rejects all these claims and having done so, he makes the following positive statement:

'I now descend to the last consideration of a church, in the most usual acceptation of that in the New Testament – that is, of a particular instituted church. A church in this sense I take to be a society of men called by the word to the obedience of faith in Christ, and joint performance of the worship of God in the same individual ordinances, according to the order by Christ prescribed. This general description of it exhibits its nature so far as is necessary to clear the subject of our present disquisition.'

But he not only contends that the general councils are not to be authoritative in this matter, he goes further. He says:

'We deny that the apostles made or gave any such rules to the churches present in their days, or for the use of the churches in future ages, as should appoint and determine outward modes of worship, with ceremonies in their observation, stated feasts and fasts, beyond what is of divine institution, liturgies or forms of prayer, or discipline to be exercised in law courts, subservient unto a national ecclesiastical government. What use, then, they are or may be of, what benefit or advantage may come to the church by them, what is the authority of the superior magistrate about them, we do not now inquire or determine. Only we say, that no rule unto these ends was ever prescribed by the apostles; for –

'1. There is not the least intimation of any such rule to be given by them in the Scripture.

'2. The first churches after their times knew nothing of any such rule given by them; and, therefore, after they began to depart from the simplicity of the gospel in any things, as unto worship, order, and rule, or discipline, they fell into a great variety of outward observances, orders, and ceremonies, every church almost differing in some thing or other from others, in some such observations, yet all "keeping the unity of the faith in the bond of peace." This they would not have done if the apostles had prescribed any one certain rule of such things that all must conform unto, especially considering how scrupulously they did adhere unto every thing that was reported to be done or spoken by any of the apostles, were the report true or false.'

Then he goes on to say something that is most interesting at the present time, because of the proposal to fix Easter. His third argument is this:

'3. In particular, when a difference fell out amongst them in a business of this nature, namely, in a thing of outward order, nowhere appointed by the authority of Christ – namely, about the observation of Easter – the parties at variance appealed on the one side to the practice of Peter, and on the other to the practice of John (both vainly enough): yet was it never pretended by any of them on either side that the apostles had constituted any rule in the case; and therefore it is not probable that they esteemed them to have done so in things of an alike nature, seeing they laid more weight on this than on any other instance of the like kind.

'4. It is expressly denied, by good and sufficient testimony among them, that the apostles made any law or rule about outward rites, ceremonies, times, and the like.'

Now there again is something that is of importance for us to bear in mind. But I must hurry on, and leaving out much interesting material, let me quote Owen on the nature of the union. The church he defines in terms of that which is clearly instituted by Christ, which is this particular church that meets together for the ends and the objects that he has been indicating. Now he comes to deal with the nature of the union that should obtain in these churches, and how this union is to be maintained. His great point is that it is always a spiritual union, it is a union in the Spirit. He quotes, to that end, the familiar passage in Ephesians 4, and he works it out and shows how this is the controlling principle. Let me just give you his headings.

'First, that unity which is recommended unto us in the gospel is spiritual.

'Secondly, unto this foundation of gospel unity among believers, for and unto the due improvement of it, there is required a unity of faith' – [It is a spiritual union; secondly, it is a unity of faith] – 'or of the belief and profession of the same divine truth; for as there is one Lord; so also there is one faith and one baptism unto believers.' So he emphasises these two.

'Thirdly, there is a unity of love' – and,

'Fourthly, the Lord Christ, by his kingly authority, hath instituted orders for rule, and ordinances for worship, Matthew 28:19, 20, Ephesians 4:8-13 to be observed in all his churches.'

That is the nature of the union. Next the question arises: How is this union to be preserved? Here he has some excellent things to say.

'Now, that this union be preserved, it is required that all those grand and necessary truths of the gospel, without the knowledge whereof no man can be saved by Jesus Christ, be so far believed as to be outwardly and visibly professed, in that variety of ways wherein they are or may be called out thereunto.'

There is no union unless there is agreement about the truths of the Gospel. It is a spiritual union, but it is also a union of faith. If there is disagreement about the faith, there is no union. There can be no union, therefore, between the evangelical and a man who denies the essentials of the evangelical faith. It is impossible.

'Secondly, that no other internal principle of the mind, that hath an utter inconsistency with the real belief of the truths necessary to be professed, be manifested by professors.'

Not only must there be no open, explicit disagreement, there must be no implicit disagreement either.

'Thirdly, that no thing, opinion, error, or false doctrine, everting or overthrowing any of the necessary saving truths professed as above, be added in and with that profession, or deliberately be professed also. This principle the apostle lays down and proves, Galatians 5:3 and 4. Notwithstanding the profession of the gospel, he tells the Galatians that if they were bewitched to profess also the necessity of circumcision and keeping of the law for justification, Christ or the profession of him would not profit them.'

In that way Owen lays down his great cardinal principles as to the nature of the union and how it is to be preserved. Then, he proceeds to deal with the question of how this union can be broken. Here, in a very wonderful way he quite conclusively proves without any difficulty at all, that on these principles, the first church to be guilty of schism was the Roman Catholic Church. By additions, and innovations, and contradictions of basic New Testament teaching involved in, and implied by, teaching concerning the sacraments and other matters the Roman Catholic Church has been more guilty of the sin of schism than any other church that the world has ever known.

Owen has some very wonderful things to say on this whole subject of the preservation of union. Here is something of what he has to say:

'We do confess, that because the best of men in this life do not know but in part, all the members of this church are in many things liable to error, mistakes, and miscarriages; and hence it is that, although they are all internally acted and guided by the same Spirit in all things absolutely necessary to their eternal salvation, and do all attend unto the same rule of the word, according as they apprehend the mind of God in it and concerning it, have all, for the nature and substance of it, the same divine faith and love, and are all equally united unto their Head, yet, in the profession which they make of the conceptions and persuasions of their minds about the things revealed in the Scripture, there are, and always have been, many differences among them. Neither is it morally possible it should be otherwise, whilst in their judgment and profession they are left unto the ability of their own minds and liberty of their wills, under that great variety of the means of light and truth, with other circumstances, whereinto they are disposed by the holy, wise providence of God. Nor hath the Lord Christ absolutely promised that it shall be otherwise with them; but securing them all by his Spirit in the foundations of eternal salvation, he leaves them in other things to the exercise of mutual love and forbearance, with a charge of duty after a continual endeavour to grow up unto a perfect union, by the improvement of the blessed aids and assistances which he is pleased to afford them. And those who, by ways of force, would drive them into any other union or agreement than their own light and duty will lead them into, do what in them lies to oppose the whole design of the Lord Christ towards them and his rule over them. In the meantime, it is granted that they may fall into divisions, and schisms, and mutual exasperations among themselves, through the remainders of darkness in their minds and the infirmity of the flesh.'

This is most important. It explains the differences even among us in this very conference. That is a perfect account of it. Our Lord, he says, as it were makes provision for this, anticipates that it is going to happen: 'In the meantime, it is granted that they may fall into divisions, and schisms, and mutual exasperations among themselves, through the remainders of darkness in their minds and the infirmity of the flesh, Romans 14:3; and in such cases mutual judgings and despisings are apt to ensue, and that to the prejudice and great disadvantage of that common faith which they do profess. And yet, notwithstanding all this (such cross-entangled wheels are there in the course of our nature), they all of them really value and esteem the things wherein they agree incomparably above those wherein they differ.' [Thank God we can still say that!] 'But their valuation of the matter of their union and agreement is purely spiritual, whereas their differences are usually influenced by carnal and secular considerations, which have, for the most part, a sensible impression on the minds of poor mortals.'

Let every man examine himself! That is my interjection. But you notice what Owen says: 'Their valuation of the matter of their union and agreement is purely spiritual, whereas their differences are usually influenced by carnal' – What church were we born in? where were we brought up? – 'and secular considerations' – What happens to me if I make a change? – 'and secular considerations, which have, for the most part, a sensible impression on the minds of poor mortals.' We are all guilty! That is also my comment, not John Owen's. We are all guilty. He proceeds:

'But so far as their divisions and differences are unto them unavoidable, the remedy of further evils proceeding from them is plainly and frequently expressed in the Scripture. It is love, meekness, forbearance, bowels of compassion, with those other graces of the Spirit wherein our conformity unto Christ doth consist, with a true understanding and the due valuation of the "unity of faith," and the common hope of believers, which are the ways prescribed unto us for the prevention of those evils which, without them, our unavoidable differences will occasion. And this excellent way of the gospel, together with a rejection of evil surmises, and a watchfulness over ourselves against irregular judging and censuring of others, together with a peaceable walking in consent and unity so far as we have attained, is so fully and clearly proposed unto us therein, that they must have their eyes blinded by prejudices and carnal interests; or some effectual working of the god of this world on their minds, into whose understandings the light of it doth not shine with uncontrollable evidence and conviction.'

Then in another place he points out how Paul in Philippians 3, says: 'Nevertheless, whereto we have already attained, let us walk by the same rule.' 'And if,' he says (in Phil. 3:15) 'in anything ye be otherwise minded, God shall reveal even this unto you.' They were not to quarrel or part over minor matters. 'Go on together,' he says, 'and pray together, and God will reveal the truth concerning those matters also.' Paul teaches that that is the way in which this union is to be maintained.

## III

Now there is one other aspect of the subject that we must just notice. Owen draws a distinction between schism and separation, and teaches quite definitely that at times separation is demanded of us, that it is indeed a duty at such times:

'What may regularly, on the other hand, be deduced from the commands given to "turn away from them who have only a form of godliness," 2 Timothy 3:5; to "withdraw from them that walk disorderly," 2 Thessalonians 3:6; not to bear nor endure in communion men of corrupt principles and wicked lives, Revelation 2:14; but positively to separate from an apostate church, Revelation 18:4, that in all things we may worship Christ according to his mind and appointment; that is the force of these commands.'

Then he gives these commands. In so doing he gives a very good account of the reasons which led the Church of England to leave the Church of Rome. Here he again has a command with regard to this question:

'I deal, as I said, with them who own reformation; and I now suppose the congregation, whereof a man is supposed to be a member on any account whatever, not to be reformed – in this case, I ask whether it be schism or no for any number of men to reform themselves, by reducing the practice of worship to its original institution, though they be the minor part lying within the parochial precincts, or for any of them to join themselves with others for that end and purpose not living within those precincts? I shall boldly say this schism is commanded by the Holy Ghost, 1 Timothy 6:5; 2 Timothy 3:5; Hosea 4:15. Is this yoke laid upon me by Christ, that, to go along with the multitude where I live, that hate to be reformed, I must forsake my duty and despise the privileges that he hath purchased for me with his own precious blood? Is this a unity of Christ's institution, that I must for ever associate myself with wicked and profane men in the worship of God, to the unspeakable detriment and disadvantage of my own soul?

'I suppose nothing can be more unreasonable than once to imagine any such thing.'

He continues his argument along those same lines.

'It is usually objected about the church of Corinth, that there was in it many disorders and enormous miscarriages, divisions, and breaches of love; miscarriages through drink at their meetings, gross sins, the incestuous person tolerated, false doctrine broached, the resurrection denied; – and yet Paul advises no man to separate from it, but all to perform their duty in it. But how little our present plea and defensative is concerned in this instance, supposed to lie against it, very few considerations will evince:

'First, the church of Corinth was undoubtedly a true church, lately instituted according to the mind of Christ, and was not fallen from that privilege by any miscarriage, nor had suffered anything destructive to its being; which wholly differences between the case proposed in respect of many particulars, and the instance produced. We confess the abuses and evils mentioned had crept into the church; and do thence grant that many abuses may do so into any of the best of the churches of God.'

An argument is often brought forward at this point in these terms, that if you do act on these principles, how long would it last? We cannot guarantee absolute purity even if we separate, and then even the new church may go wrong. According to Owen you must not expect anything different:

'Nor did it ever enter into the heart of any man to think that so soon as any disorders fall out or abuses creep into it, it is instantly the duty of any to fly out of it, like Paul's mariners out of the ship when the storm grew hazardous; it being the duty of all the members of such a church, untainted with the evils and corruptions of it, upon many accounts, to attempt and labour the remedy of those disorders, and rejection of those abuses to the uttermost; which was that which Paul advised the Corinthians and some others unto; in obedience whereunto they were recovered. But yet this I say, had the church of Corinth continued in the condition before described – that notorious, scandalous sins had gone unpunished, unreproved, drunkenness continued and practised in the assemblies, men abiding by the denial of the resurrection, so overturning the whole gospel, and the church refusing to do her duty, and exercise her authority to cast all those disorderly persons, upon their obstinacy, out of her communion – it had been the duty of every saint of God in that church to have withdrawn from it, to come out from among them, and not to have been partaker of their sins, unless they were willing to partake of their plague also, which on such an apostasy would certainly ensue.'

Now, there, he points out that in certain conditions and circumstances separation is actually a duty, and he goes on in this immediate context to point out that this has reference to the reason why the Church of England left the Church of Rome.

We turn now to a very interesting point, the relevance of which will be obvious:

'It may be some will yet say (because it hath been said often), "There is a difference between reforming of churches already gathered and raised, and raising of churches, out of mere materials. The first may be allowed, but the latter tends to all manner of confusion."' In other words, he imagines a possible objection might be made to this effect: It is all right to reform an existing church, but that does not justify you in forming, as it were, a new church, as he puts it, 'out of mere materials.'

'I have at present not much to say to this objection, because, as I conceive, it concerns not the business we have in hand; nor would I have mentioned it at all, but that it is insisted on by some on every turn, whether suited for the particular cause for which it is produced, or no. In brief, then –

'1. I know no other reformation of any church, or any thing in a church, but the reducing of it to its primitive institution, and the order allotted to it by Jesus Christ. If any plead for any other reformation of churches, they are, in my judgment, to blame.

'And when any society or combination of men (whatever hitherto it hath been esteemed) is not capable of such a reduction and renovation, I suppose I shall not provoke any wise and sober person if I profess I cannot look on such a society as a church of Christ.' Let me repeat that – 'And when any society or combination of men is not capable of such a reduction' (that is to say, to the primitive institution) 'and renovation, I suppose I shall not provoke any wise and sober person if I profess I cannot look on such a society as a church of Christ.' A church that cannot reform itself in that way is not a church of Christ. He goes on, 'and thereupon advise those therein who have a due right to the privileges purchased for them by Christ, as to Gospel administrations, to take some other peaceable course to make themselves partakers of them.'

'2. Were I fully to handle the things pointed to in this objection I must manage principles which, in this discourse, I have not been occasioned to draw forth at all or to improve. Many things of great weight and importance must come under debate and consideration before a clear account can be given of the case stated in this objection, such as:

'(1) The true nature of an instituted church under the gospel, as to the matter, form, and all other necessary constitutive causes, is to be investigated and found out.

'(2) The nature and form of such a church is to be exemplified from the Scripture and the stories of the first churches, before sensibly infected with the poison of that apostasy which ensued.

'I urgently commend the consideration of those words at this present time. We must study the Scriptures and also the history of the first three centuries of the Christian church.

'(3) The extent of the apostasy under Antichrist, as to the ruining of instituted churches, making them to be Babylon, and their worship fornication, is duly and carefully to be examined. Here lie our disorder and division; hence is our darkness and pollution of our garments, which is not an easy thing to free ourselves of: though we may arise, yet we shall not speedily shake ourselves out of the dust.' That is the chief difficulty for every one of us; we are all bound by what has gone before us.

'(4) By what way and means God begat anew and kept alive his elect in their several generations, when antichristian darkness covered the earth and thick darkness the nations, supposing an intercision of instituted ordinances, so far as to make a nullity in them as to what was of simple and pure institution; what way might be used for the fixing of the tabernacle of God again with men, and the setting up of church worship according to his mind and will.

'(5) What was the way of the first Reformation in this nation, and what principles that godly learned men of those days proceeded on; how far what they did may be satisfactory to our consciences at the present, as to our concurrence in them, who from thence have the truth of the Gospel derived down to us; whether ordinary officers be before or after the church, and so whether a church-state is preserved in the preservation of officers, by a foreign power to that church whereof they are so, or the office be preserved, and consequently the officers inclusively, in the preservation and constitution of a church – these, I say, with sundry other things of the like importance, with inferences from them, are to be considered to the bottom before a full resolution can be given to the inquiry couched in this objection, which, as I said, to do is not my present business.'

All that means this: Before you rush off to start a new church, consider all these subjects very seriously and very deeply. It is not a matter to be rushed into, it is all to be examined in the light of Scripture and the early history of the Christian church.

What then is the conclusion of all this? Owen sums it up himself in these words:

'Let us now see the sum of the whole matter, and what it is that we plead for our discharge as to this crime of schism, allowing the term to pass in its large and usual acceptation, receding, for the sake of the truth's further ventilation, from the precise propriety of the word annexed to it in the Scripture. The sum is, we have broken no bond of unity, no order instituted or appointed by Jesus Christ – have causelessly deserted no station that ever we were in, according to his mind; which alone can give countenance to an accusation of this nature. That on pure grounds of conscience we have withdrawn, or do withhold ourselves from partaking in some ways, engaged into upon mere grounds of prudence, we acknowledge.

'And thus, from what hath been said, it appears in what a fair capacity, notwithstanding any principle or practice owned by us, we are in to live peaceably, and to exercise all fruits of love towards those who are otherwise minded.'

He feels that he has thus clearly absolved himself from the charge of schism.

## IV

Finally, let me put before you the great appeal which, it seems to me, Owen addresses to us who are here gathered at this present time as reformed evangelical Christians. Let us listen to his moving words:

'The truth is, if God would be pleased to help us, on all hands, to lay aside prejudices, passions, secular interests, fears, and every other distempered affection, which obstruct our minds in passing a right judgment on things of the nature treated on, we should find in the text and context spoken unto a sacred truth divinely directive of such a practice as would give peace and rest unto us all; for it is supposed that men, in a sincere endeavour after acquaintance with the truths and mysteries of the gospel, with an enjoyment of the good things represented and exhibited in them, may fall, in some things, into different apprehensions about what belongs unto faith and practice in religion. But whilst they are such as do not destroy or overthrow the foundation nor hinder men from pressing "toward the mark for the prize of the high calling of God in Christ Jesus," that which the apostle directs unto them who are supposed to be ignorant of or to mistake in the things wherein they do differ from others, is only that they wait for divine instruction in the use of the means appointed for that end, practising in the meantime according to what they have received. And as unto both parties, the advice he gives them is, that "whereunto they have attained," wherein they do agree – which were all those principles of faith and obedience which were necessary unto their acceptance with God – they should "walk by the same rule, and mind the same thing;" that is, "forbearing one another" in the things wherein they differ: which is the substance of what is pleaded for by the nonconformists.'

But consider further:

'It is not impossible that some may, from what hath been spoken, begin to apprehend that they have been too hasty in judging other men. Indeed, none are more ready to charge highly than those who, when they have so done, are most unable to make good their charge. What real schisms in a moral sense have ensued among brethren, by their causeless mutual imputation of schism in things of institution, is known. And when men are in one fault, and are charged with another wherein they are not, it is a ready way to confirm them in that wherein they are. There is more darkness and difficulty in the whole matter of instituted worship than some men are aware of; not that it was so from the beginning, whilst Christianity continued in its naked simplicity, but it is come occasionally upon us by the customs, darkness, and invincible prejudices that have taken hold on the minds of men by a secret diffusion of the poison of that grand apostasy. It were well, then, that men would not be so confident, nor easily persuaded that they presently know how all things ought to be, because they know how they would have some things to be, which suit their temper and interest. Men may easily perhaps see, or think they see, what they do not like, and cry out schism! and separation! but if they would a little consider what ought to be in this whole matter, according to the mind of God, and what evidences they have of the grounds and principles whereon they condemn others, it might make them yet swift to hear, but slow to speak, and take off from the number of teachers among us. Some are ready to think that all that join not with them are schismatics, and they are so because they go not with them; and other reason they have none, being unable to give any solid foundation of what they profess. What the cause of unity among the people of God hath suffered from this sort of men is not easily to be expressed.

In all differences about religion, to drive them to their rise and spring, and to consider them as stated originally, will ease us of much trouble and labour.'

We have to go back beyond the seventeenth century, beyond the sixteenth century; we have got to go back to the beginning. Now that is an exhortation we all need. We all suffer from the tendency to defend inherited positions and our own particular history. We must go back to the very beginning, to the rise and spring of it all in the first century. He then goes on to say:

'Perhaps many of them (i.e., the differences) will not appear so formidable as they are represented. He that sees a great river is not instantly to conclude that all the water in it comes from its first rise and spring; the addition of many brooks, showers, and land-floods have perhaps swelled it to the condition wherein it is. Every difference in religion is not to be thought to be as big at its rise as it appears to be when it hath passed through many generations, and hath received additions and aggravations from the disputings and contendings of men, on the one hand and on the other engaged. What a flood of abominations doth this business of schism seem to be, as rolling down to us through the writings of Cyprian, Austin [Augustine], and Optatus, of old, the schoolmen, decrees of popish councils, with the contrivances of some among ourselves, concerned to keep up the swelled notion of it! Go to its rise, and you will find it to be, though bad enough, yet quite another thing than what, by the prejudices accruing by the addition of so many generations, it is now generally represented to be.

'The great maxim, "To the law and to the testimony," truly improved, would quickly cure all our distempers.'

May I be allowed to say that this is my profound belief also. I believe our present-day distempers also could be cured if only we obeyed this injunction. Owen felt that. He proceeds:

'In the meantime, let us bless God that though our outward man may possibly be disposed of according to the apprehension that others have of what we do or are, our consciences are concerned only in what he hath appointed. How some men may prevail against us, before whom we must stand or fall according to their corrupt notion of schism, we know not. The rule of our consciences in this, as in all other things, is eternal and unchangeable. Whilst I have an uncontrollable faithful witness that I transgress no limits prescribed to me in the word, that I do not willingly break or dissolve any unity of the institution of Jesus Christ, my mind as to this thing is filled with perfect peace. Blessed be God, that hath reserved the sole sovereignty of our consciences in his hand, and not in the least parcelled it out to any of the sons of men, whose tender mercies being oftentimes cruelty itself, they would perhaps destroy the soul also, when they do so to the body, seeing they stay there, as our Saviour witnesseth, because they can proceed no further! Here, then, I profess to rest, in this doth my conscience acquiesce: Whilst I have any comfortable persuasion on grounds infallible, that I hold the head, and that I am by faith a member of the mystical body of Christ; whilst I make profession of all the necessary saving truths of the gospel; whilst I disturb not the peace of that particular church thereof by my own consent I am a member, nor do raise up nor continue in any causeless differences with them or any of them, with whom I walk in the fellowship and order of the gospel; whilst I labour to exercise faith towards the Lord Jesus Christ, and love towards all the saints – I do keep the unity which is of the appointment of Christ. And let men say, from principles utterly foreign to the gospel, what they please or can to the contrary, I am no schismatic.

'Perhaps the discovery which hath been made, how little we are many of us concerned in that which, having mutually charged it on one another, hath been the greatest ball of strife and most effectual engine of difference and distance between us, may be a means to reconcile in love them that truly fear God, though engaged in several ways, as to some particulars. I confess I have not any great hope of much success on this account; for let principles and ways be made as evident as if he that wrote them carried the sun in his hand, yet whilst men are forestalled by prejudices, and have their affections and spirits engaged suitably thereunto, no great alteration in their minds and ways, on the clearest conviction whatever, is to be expected. All our hearts are in the hand of God; and our expectations of what he hath promised are to be proportioned to what he can effect, not to what of outward means we see to be used.'

Last of all here is a very beautiful passage from Owen's treatise on Christian love and peace:

'Herein, therefore, lies the fundamental cause of our divisions; which will not be healed until it be removed and taken out of the way. Leave believers or professors of the gospel unto their duty in seeking after evangelical unity in the use of other means instituted and blessed unto that end – impose nothing on their consciences or practice under that name, which indeed belongs not thereunto; and although, upon the reasons and causes afterward to be mentioned, there may for a season remain some divisions among them, yet there will be a way of healing continually ready for them, and agreed upon by them as such.'

Oh, that we might all give that a hearing and our careful attention! 'Where, indeed, men propose unto themselves different ends, though under the same name, the use of the same means for the compassing of them will but increase their variance: as where some aim at evangelical union and others at an external uniformity.' There is our exact position at the present time. Some of us are aiming at evangelical union; others are aiming at 'external uniformity': '... both under the name of unity and peace, in the use of the same means for these ends, they will be more divided among themselves.' [If the aim is different we are only going to increase the division.] 'But where the same end is aimed at, even the debate of the means for the attaining of it will insensibly bring the parties into a coalition, and work out in the issue a complete reconciliation.'

If we all as evangelicals are out to defend the faith, and to show men clearly the way of salvation, then, Owen says that we shall be brought together. If that is our real objective!

'... In the meantime, were Christians duly instructed how many lesser differences, in mind, and judgment, and practice, are really consistent with the nature, ends, and genuine fruit, of the unity that Christ requires among them, it would undoubtedly prevail with them so to manage themselves in their differences, by mutual forbearance and condescension in love, as not to contract the guilt of being disturbers or breakers of it; for suppose the minds of any of them to be invincibly prepossessed with the principles wherein they differ from others, yet all who are sincere in their profession cannot but rejoice to be directed unto such a managery of them as to be preserved from the guilt of dissolving the unity appointed by Christ to be observed. And, to speak plainly, among all the churches in the world which are free from idolatry and persecution, it is not different opinions, or a difference in judgment about revealed truths, nor a different practice in sacred administration, but pride, self-interest, love of honour, reputation, and dominion, with the influence of civil or political intrigues and considerations, that are the true cause of that defect of evangelical unity that is at this day amongst them: for set them aside, and the real differences which would remain may be so managed, in love, gentleness, and meekness, as not to interfere with that unity which Christ requireth them to preserve. Nothing will from thence follow which shall impeach their common interest in one Lord, one faith, one love, one Spirit, and the administration of the same ordinances according to their light and ability. But if we shall cast away this evangelical union among the disciples and churches of Christ – if we shall break up the bounds and limits fixed unto it, and set up in its place a compliance with, or an agreement in, the commands and appointments of men, making their observations the rule and measure of our ecclesiastical concord – it cannot be but that innumerable and endless divisions will ensue thereon. If we will not be contented with the union that Christ hath appointed, it is certain that we shall have none in this world ...'

I believe that evangelicalism is being challenged in these days along that very line. If we do not face the challenge of the ecumenical movement at the present time and achieve this evangelical union, I prophesy that we shall never have it. Our divisions will only be greatly increased:

'If we will not be contented with the union that Christ hath appointed, it is certain that we shall have none in this world; for concerning that which is of men's finding out, there have been, and will be, contentions and divisions, whilst there are any on the one side who will endeavour its imposition, and on the other who desire to preserve their consciences entire unto the authority of Christ in his laws and appointments.

'There is none who can be such a stranger in our Israel as not to know that these things have been the great occasion and cause of the divisions and contentions that have been among us near a hundred years, and which at this day make our breaches wide like the sea, that they cannot be healed. Let, therefore, those who have power and ability be instrumental to restore to the minds of men the true notion and knowledge of the unity which the Lord Christ requireth among his churches and disciples; and let them be left unto that liberty which he hath purchased for them, in the pursuit of that unity which he hath prescribed unto them; and let us all labour to stir up those gracious principles of love and peace which ought to guide us in the use of our liberty, and will enable us to preserve gospel unity – and there will be a greater progress made towards peace, reconciliation, and concord, amongst all sorts of Christians, than the spoiling of the goods or imprisoning the persons of dissenters will ever effect. But it may be, such things are required hereunto as the world is yet scarce able to comply withal; for whilst men do hardly believe that there is an efficacy and power accompanying the institutions of Christ, for the compassing of that whole end which he aimeth at and intended – whilst they are unwilling to be brought unto the constant exercise of that spiritual diligence, patience, meekness, condescension, self-denial, renunciation of the world and conformity thereunto, which are indispensably necessary in church guides and church members, according to their measure, unto the attaining and preservation of gospel unity, but do satisfy themselves in the disposal of an ecclesiastical union into a subordination unto their own secular interests, by external force and power – we have very small expectation of success in the way proposed. In the meantime, we are herewith satisfied: Take the churches of Christ in the world that are not infected with idolatry or persecution, and restore their unity unto the terms and conditions left unto them by Christ and his apostles, and if in any thing we are found uncompliant therewithal, we shall without repining bear the reproach of it, and hasten an amendment.'

May God grant unto us, every one of us, the spirit of John Owen in this matter.

I trust that I have been able to show that John Owen speaks very directly and immediately to our situation at this very moment. May God give us grace to ponder these things. But above all may he give us great wisdom, and beyond everything, may he give us great love and charity in our hearts, and patience with one another, so that as men professing the same faith we may present it together to an apostate church, though she be 'a world church,' and to lost men and women everywhere.

# 1964

# *John Calvin and George Whitefield*

## I

Before I deal with the subject which has just been announced I should like to read a few verses to you from the book of Judges, chapter two, verses 8, 9, and 10:

'And Joshua the son of Nun, the servant of the Lord, died, being an hundred and ten years old. And they buried him in the border of his inheritance in Timnath-heres, in the mount of Ephraim, on the north side of the hill Gaash. And also all that generation were gathered unto their fathers: and there arose another generation after them, which knew not the Lord, nor yet the works which he had done for Israel.'

The title of my address needs a little explanation because as announced it sounds so pretentious. Those of us who have been in this conference for the last two days will already have heard five addresses on John Calvin and different aspects of his work, so it looks at first sight as if I am claiming to be one who can not only deal with John Calvin but also throw in Whitefield into the bargain! I want to disabuse your minds of any such notion.

The second misconception into which you may have fallen I also want to dismiss. Some of you may think that, realising that five men would already have spoken on John Calvin, I came to the conclusion that they would have said everything that could be said, so that little being left for me, I decided to talk about George Whitefield.

That, again, is entirely wrong. The subject of John Calvin and his work, and what he has left to us as a rich heritage, is so great and so vast that it would not have been at all difficult for me to continue the theme of the 400th anniversary of the death of John Calvin. The explanation of why I am going to speak on George Whitefield is much more interesting. We had planned that the whole of the conference this year should be devoted to the memory of John Calvin, and this meeting was to take that form like all the others. But I received a letter from Mr Hilton Day, who was then the minister of the Whitefield Memorial (Presbyterian) Church in Gloucester, pointing out how this year, being the two hundred and fiftieth anniversary of the birth of George Whitefield, they there felt that something must be done to celebrate this. So he invited me to go down to Gloucester on Wednesday evening, December 16th, to speak on the subject of George Whitefield. Why did they choose December 16th, which is today? Well, they chose it because Whitefield was born on December 16th two hundred and fifty years ago. I wrote back and said I was extremely sorry, that I could imagine no greater privilege than to speak on George Whitefield, and especially in Gloucester, but, alas, I was committed to this meeting in connection with this conference. But they very kindly changed their date, and I had the great privilege on Tuesday, December 8th, of speaking in the Whitefield Memorial Church in Gloucester on George Whitefield.

But it did not stop at that. All this immediately put into my mind the suggestion that we should devote this meeting tonight to commemorate George Whitefield and his great and glorious services in the eighteenth century, and Dr Packer and others were very ready to agree with this suggestion. We felt that it would be very wrong, much as we revere the memory of Calvin, to allow this year, and this night of all nights in the year 1964, to pass without saying something about this great and mighty man George Whitefield. The difficulty was to discover how to put this on the programme. The subject of all the other papers was to be John Calvin. Suddenly to introduce Whitefield would seem odd to people. So we decided on this compromise, and to announce it as 'John Calvin and George Whitefield.'

The connection is not quite as remote as some might imagine. There are many good reasons why these two men should be put together, though they were two very different men in many ways. John Calvin was an extremely thin man, almost cadaverous. Whitefield on the other hand was rather stout and portly. John Calvin was what is called a typical introvert. Whitefield, I would say, on the whole, was an extrovert. And there are many other differences. But the thing that connects them is the similarities. It is not some chance association based on dates that determines that these two men should be put together.

Here is one point which they have in common, if one may use such an expression – they were both Calvinists. We will leave it like that. What we mean is that they were both Paulinists. But it has become customary to use the term Calvinist. Anybody who knows anything about the eighteenth century will know that the Methodists of that century divided into two groups, into two camps, around the persons of George Whitefield and John Wesley. They did so largely in terms, at the beginning at any rate, of this difference in point of view theologically. George Whitefield was a follower of the teaching of Calvin. He was a truly Reformed man in his doctrine, whereas Wesley was Arminian. So this division came in. Now this clearly links Whitefield with Calvin. Whitefield remained more loyal to the Thirty-nine Articles of the Church of England than did John Wesley. Those Articles have a Calvinistic emphasis, and Whitefield adhered to that, whereas John Wesley departed from that and therefore was mainly responsible for the division. So Calvin and Whitefield had that in common.

But they had other things in common. We heard last night from Dr Packer about the zeal of John Calvin, and about the stupendous amount of work which he did. It was quite phenomenal: all those Commentaries and the *Institutes* and all the letters and the tracts and all the rest that he produced! How one man was able to do it all, and to preach so regularly in addition, is very amazing for us to contemplate. Exactly the same thing is true of Whitefield. There is no man who has laboured with greater zeal in God's kingdom than George Whitefield. They are very similar in that respect also.

Another thing they have in common is that they both ended their earthly course round about the age of fifty-five. This is a remarkable thing. John Calvin died just short of fifty-five, and Whitefield died just short of fifty-six. These two men who did such stupendous work both died in their middle fifties.

Another thing they share in common – and I do want to emphasise this – is that they were both men who longed, perhaps more than any of their contemporaries, for unity amongst evangelicals. In this conference we have considered that point in connection with Calvin. Calvin was tremendously concerned that all reformed and evangelical people should come together in unity. He bemoaned the divisions and the differences that had arisen, and he was prepared to do anything he could – he said he was ready to cross, if necessary, ten seas in order to attend a conference which would help to promote this unity amongst reformed evangelical people. Not unity with Rome, of course, but unity among reformed evangelical people.

The same thing is very true of George Whitefield. He had to stand on his principles, his doctrine, as against the two brothers Wesley, but at the same time he bemoaned the division, and he did almost everything a man could do in order to bring the parties together. And towards the end of his life they had come at any rate to the position in which they were preaching in one another's pulpits, and, by Whitefield's own request, John Wesley was the man who preached his funeral sermon. That is most interesting, that these two men, Calvin and Whitefield, have this again in common, this great concern about the unity of those who are united in the preaching of the gospel of salvation.

Lastly, they are similar in the matter of their tremendous influence upon their contemporaries and subsequent generations. I turn now to that. Somebody may ask, 'Why are you commemorating the 250th anniversary of the birth of George Whitefield?' There are many answers to that question. One is that he was, as our chairman has rightly pointed out, the greatest son of the city of Gloucester. Bishop John Hooper of the sixteenth century was Bishop of Gloucester, Robert Raikes was a Gloucester man, and

Tyndale came from that shire. But I was glad to hear Dr Packer saying that beyond any question the greatest of them all was George Whitefield. But we are calling attention to him tonight, not for that reason, but because he is, beyond any question, the greatest English preacher who has ever lived. You notice my emphasis! I say the greatest 'English' preacher. I am not saying the greatest preacher in the world. There was a contemporary of his two hundred years ago who, I am glad to note, even Bishop Ryle, himself an Englishman, has to grant and to admit was the equal of Whitefield. I am referring to a man called Daniel Rowland who lived and ministered in Wales in that same eighteenth century. However, it is generally agreed that George Whitefield is beyond any question the greatest English preacher of all time. Let us be accurate. If you say that, and if you put Rowland in with him, well then I think there are good grounds for saying that these two men were probably the greatest preachers since the days of the apostles. That is not an overstatement, as Ryle would agree.

Whitefield was not only the greatest English preacher of all time, we commemorate his memory because of his profound influence upon the course of history. Dr Packer said that very thing last night of John Calvin. And it is, of course, true. It is equally true of Whitefield. His influence in England, his influence in Wales, his influence in Scotland, and his influence in America, in particular, is beyond calculation. If the historian Lecky is right in saying what is so often quoted – that it was undoubtedly the Evangelical Awakening that saved this country from a revolution such as that which was experienced in France in 1789 and following – if that is true, well then, George Whitefield more than anybody else is responsible for that fact. That, again, is why we believe it is right to call to mind the memory of this great man, this great preacher.

## II

There is one remarkable fact about this man Whitefield to which I must turn for a moment, and that is the amazing neglect which he has suffered. It would be very interesting to discover what the result would be if I asked everyone present now to write an essay on George Whitefield. How much would you have to say? I venture to assert that he is the most neglected man in the whole of church history. The ignorance concerning him is appalling. One is constantly discovering this in reading and in listening to people. It has become the habit to refer to the great awakening and revival of two hundred years ago as the 'Wesleyan' Revival. It is spoken of always in terms of what John Wesley, in particular, did – even Charles has had to suffer. People seem to have the idea that all that happened in the eighteenth century was the sole result of the activity of John Wesley.

I came across an instance of this in a new book on Charles Wesley by Frederick C. Gill. It is called *Charles Wesley, the First Methodist*. In it there is a typical example of how Whitefield is depreciated. In dealing with the difference of opinion that arose about the doctrine of election and predestination and the parting that took place, he says about Charles Wesley, 'It was with sorrow that he departed from the convert of his Oxford days.' In other words, Whitefield is referred to as a convert of Charles Wesley! Thus throughout the years Whitefield has been either forgotten or depreciated. I am glad to be able to say that the best and most distinguished Methodists are very ready to acknowledge this. The late Dr J. Ernest Rattenbury was very ready to say that Methodism had never given its due place to the memory of George Whitefield. And Dr Skevington Wood, a Methodist historian of today, is equally ready to say the same thing.

But the question is, why has Whitefield been neglected like this? Most people know something about John Wesley – I do not think they know much even about him, but they know something – whereas Whitefield is an unknown man, and the great story concerning him is something that people never seem to have heard. Why is this? The explanation is most important; that is why I read those verses from the second chapter of the book of Judges. You notice the point which is made: not only did Joshua die but 'that generation was gathered unto their fathers' – the contemporaries of Joshua. And then we are told 'there arose another generation after them, which knew not the Lord, nor yet the works which he had done for Israel.' That is a most interesting and significant statement. It always seems to me to cast great light upon our present position. When people do not know the Lord, they very soon become ignorant of church history. Once you lose the knowledge of the Lord you lose an interest in his works.

That, I think, is what has happened during the last hundred years. Knowledge of the Lord always leads to, and stimulates, an interest in church history. May I suggest in passing tonight that there is something wrong with an evangelicalism that is not interested in church history? There is something surely wrong with an evangelicalism that seems to think that evangelical history began with the first visit to this country of D. L. Moody about 1873. There is a defect somewhere in our knowledge of the Lord; for once a man has a true knowledge of the Lord he has a lively interest in all the works of the Lord, in all the known and recorded events in the long history of the Christian church. I think that this is something that should cause us to examine ourselves very seriously. These two things, according to the text, are indissolubly linked together: loss of knowledge of the Lord, loss of knowledge of his servants and his great works through them. Let us examine ourselves at our leisure in the light of that proposition.

But there is a second reason why people are so ignorant about Whitefield, and that is because of his humility. He was, like Calvin, a most humble man. He said, 'Let the name of George Whitefield be forgotten and blotted out as long as the name of the Lord Jesus Christ is known.' Again may I throw out, especially for the members of the conference, a theological question here? Is there something in the idea that those who tend to follow the teaching of John Calvin are less interested in advertising than those who follow the Arminian teaching espoused by John Wesley? I just put it to you. I just ask you to keep your eyes on the religious journals and papers and see whether there is not something in this suggestion. The teaching of John Calvin humbles man in the first instance; it glorifies God. It makes man feel that he is insignificant, that he is nobody; and however much a man may be privileged or enabled to do, he knows that it is God who does it. That is the thing in which he is interested. Is that true, I wonder, of the other emphasis and teaching? The fact remains that we know so much less about George Whitefield than we do about John Wesley.

But the main explanation, I have no doubt, of the neglect of Whitefield is this, that he never founded or established a denomination. He may have felt a little towards the end of his life that he was wrong here. It is said that he said before the end that John Wesley was wiser than he had been, that he had 'penned his sheep' whereas he had not. However, the fact is that he was not concerned to found or to leave behind him a religious denomination. He was content to preach the gospel, to fertilize every conceivable religious body. So he did not leave behind him a denomination. But John Wesley left a denomination behind him, and he left a denomination with a particular theological outlook, and great attention has been paid to his memory. Books have poured out on John Wesley without ceasing throughout the intervening years; but in the case of Whitefield there was no religious denomination to do so. That is, I think, the main explanation of why he has been so sadly neglected.

## III

But why should we take this trouble then to bring to memory again this man, and to put him before ourselves and the religious public? My answer is: because of the phenomenon of the eighteenth-century revival of religion, one of the most amazing episodes in the long history of the Christian church. I am very ready to agree with those who say that this was probably the greatest manifestation of the power of the Holy Spirit since apostolic days. A very good case can be made out for saying that. If you want to know what I mean you can look at it like this. Consider the state of this country before that evangelical awakening and revival. It was deplorable. I must not go into it, I have not the time. There is a book which deals with it thoroughly. Note the title, *England Before and After Wesley*. How significant it is! Of course it was written by a Wesleyan Methodist – Wesley only counts. But the facts that the author adduces are true. He was a good historian in that sense, but a bad theologian and lacking in understanding of what truly happened. But he was a very good collector of facts. Read that book by J. Wesley Bready and you will see that in almost every conceivable respect this country had sunk to one of the lowest depths that it had ever reached. The Church of England was dead; you know about the pluralities of livings, you know about the drunkenness and the fox-hunting – it has all been described so often. But the other denominations were not much better. They may have been a bit better on the moral side, but the Presbyterian Church of those days had fallen into the heresy of Arianism and eventually disappeared altogether. And the other nonconformist bodies were in a state of lethargy, holding to a dead orthodoxy.

Attempts had been made by certain people to stem this tide of degeneration. A man called Boyle established a lectureship, Bishop Butler produced his *Analogy* in defence of the gospel, and various others wrote, but they were of no avail whatsoever. Then this great revival came, and the whole face of England was entirely changed. The Church of England, in many respects, was revived; nonconformity was revived; a new body came into being called Methodist Societies, and the repercussions in a wider area were really quite amazing and astonishing. The case has often been made out, and it can be proved, it seems to me, that the Trades Union movement in this country rose indirectly out of that revival. It was because men, who had formerly been ignorant and had been living a drunken besotted life, were changed and born again, that they began to realise their dignity as men and to demand education and better working conditions, and so on – that is where the Trades Union movement came from. We know the connection between the abolition of slavery movement led mainly by William Wilberforce and this revival. He was one of the results of this revival, and indeed a case is made by some for saying that we would never have had the Reform Bill of 1832 were it not for this great Evangelical Awakening.

Now this is my point: those were some of the profound changes produced by the Evangelical Awakening. Very well; in all that, George Whitefield was the leader, he was the first. This is where the neglect of this man and the corresponding over-prominence of John Wesley is so scandalous. Do not misunderstand me. I am not just indulging in a kind of controversy. This is a matter of sheer justice, and of honesty, and of truth. This is where the neglect of Whitefield is so wrong, and so deplorable; because in all the following instances I am going to give George Whitefield was the first.

He was actually the first to be converted. The author of the book I have just quoted refers to Whitefield as 'Charles Wesley's convert in Oxford.' The facts are these – that George Whitefield was converted in 1735, whereas Charles Wesley was not converted until 1738. Of course what the man means is that when Whitefield went to Oxford Charles Wesley and some others had already started the Holy Club and Whitefield was invited to go to the meetings. But that was not his conversion, as I shall show. The first of them to be converted in England was George Whitefield in 1735, the same year in which Howell Harris and Daniel Rowland were converted in Wales. So he is first even there.

But then he was the first of them to start preaching the true gospel in an awakening manner. Whitefield began to do this in 1736 and one of his greatest years was 1737; whereas we all know that the Wesley brothers only began to preach in an evangelical sense at all after the month of May 1738. So that Whitefield is ahead of them all along the line. In 1737 he was gathering great crowds here even in the city of London, and astonishing results were following.

Then everybody knows that one of the great characteristics of that revival was open-air preaching. These men preached to vast crowds in the open air, twenty thousand and more very often. Who was the first to preach in the open air? The answer is always the same – George Whitefield. George Whitefield was the first to preach in the open air, and he had very great difficulty in persuading both John and Charles Wesley to do the same. They were both much more conservative than Whitefield. He preceded them by several months in this respect and brought great pressure to bear upon them to persuade them to follow him. So you see he is the leader, the pioneer, the first in all these respects.

He was the first of them, also, to order societies – religious societies. He was also the first in works of charity. There is a very famous Methodist school called the Kingswood School, to which many Methodist ministers send their boys to be educated. It was started as a school for the poor children of miners and others. Who founded the Kingswood School? George Whitefield. It was always George Whitefield in the van, he was the leader. I trust that by now I have convinced you that my protest against this disgraceful neglect of this man is more than justified.

But in addition to all this he was the fructifier of the religious revival in Wales. He was actually the first moderator of what is now known as the Welsh Presbyterian Church. It used to be known as the Welsh Calvinistic Methodist Church. Whitefield became the first moderator of this church in 1743. We must be accurate. I believe he became moderator for this reason. There were those two great men and great preachers in Wales – Daniel Rowland and Howell Harris – and the problem was which of the two should be made first moderator. Well, Englishmen have many uses but on this occasion one of them became very useful! They solved the problem by agreeing that neither of the two Welshmen should be made first moderator, and by putting the Englishman in the position. The two Welshmen were delighted to bow to him as moderator of this first Presbyterian Association in Wales.

He also had tremendous influence in Scotland. Anyone who has ever read about that communion season at Cambuslang, which is now a part of Glasgow, will know exactly what I mean. His influence in America, again, is something that really baffles description. All the writers, including those who are concerned at the present time to reproduce the writings and the works of Jonathan Edwards, are all careful and honest enough to say that the influence of Whitefield in America about 1740 and onwards was simply overwhelming. There was a second 'great awakening,' greater, even, than the first that had taken place in 1735.

These are some of the reasons why we are calling attention to this man. He visited America seven times. Some of us find it difficult to cross the Atlantic now, but imagine doing so two hundred years ago! And Whitefield crossed the Atlantic thirteen times. He died there on his last, his seventh visit, so he actually crossed the Atlantic thirteen times. He visited Scotland fourteen times. It is computed that he probably preached eighteen thousand sermons in the thirty-four years of his preaching life.

## IV

That is why, I say, it is right that we should commemorate the memory of this man. This man was simply a phenomenon. There was no man who was better known in London two hundred years ago than this man George Whitefield. What are the facts about him? Let me give a brief summary in order to try to give some conception of the phenomenon known as George Whitefield. He was born, as I have reminded you, in Gloucester at the Bell Inn on December 16th, 1714. Many of his ancestors had been clergymen in the Church of England, but his father was not. His father was the keeper of this inn, the Bell Inn in Gloucester, and there he was brought up as a boy. His father died when he was very young and he tells us in his Journal that he fell into many sins, most of the sins that young men tend to fall into. But he was never really happy, he had a tender conscience always. He left school for a while but then he began to feel that this was wrong. During the time when he left school he was just serving, drawing drink in the ordinary way in that public-house, in Gloucester. But his conscience was still troubling him, and he went back to school, and eventually was able to gain an entrance into a college in Oxford. There, as I say, he came under the influence of this Holy Club that had been formed by Charles Wesley and some others and which later was joined by John Wesley. Having finished his course in Oxford, he was ordained by Bishop Benson, the Bishop of Gloucester at that time, on June 20th, 1736, at the age of twenty-one. Now Bishop Benson had made a rule that he would not ordain anybody under the age of twenty-three, but having heard what he had heard about this remarkable young man, and having met him for himself, he decided to break his own rule, and so ordained him though he was only twenty-one.

On June 27th, a week after his ordination, he preached for the first time in Gloucester in the Church of St Mary le Crypt, where he had been baptized as a child and where he had taken his first communion. Naturally this was an event which caused a great deal of interest, and perhaps some excitement. His mother was well-known as the keeper of the inn and so on, and all the relatives and friends and others came to the service, with the result that the church was full. Now this is the interesting thing; immediately in this first sermon he showed that he was a man apart, that there was something quite unusual about him. The effect upon the congregation was tremendous. It was said afterwards, and even reported to the bishop, that fifteen people had been driven mad by this sermon. Bishop Benson was a very wise man and his reported comment was this: 'All he wished and hoped was that the madness might not be forgotten before next Sunday.' However, he was a wise man, and he realised that here there was a most unusual preacher. Whitefield's very first sermon marked him out as an entirely exceptional preacher at the age, remember, of twenty-one.

I must not weary you with all the details. He came first to London in the following August, of 1736. His first sermon in London was preached in Bishopsgate. The post he came to was to act as a locum to the chaplain in the Tower of London, but he was given opportunities of preaching elsewhere, and again the moment he began to preach he attracted attention, and he attracted crowds. People had never heard preaching like this. Instead of reading a most prosaic kind of essay which was supposed to do duty as a sermon, here was a man preaching with the whole of his being, with authority and power and conviction – and, immediately, every time he preached the churches were always full, were always packed.

Then after spending about two months here in London he went down to do a locum for a friend of his in a curacy in Hampshire. There it was exactly the same. As the result of this, of course, he was offered many curacies, and various possibilities and prospects of success and advancement in the Church of England were placed before him. But under the influence of his friends John and Charles Wesley, who were out in Georgia trying to do a bit of missionary work, he felt a call to go to Georgia, and so he decided definitely that this was the one thing he must do. There was not a ship available immediately and there were various arrangements to be made, so he was enabled to go back to Gloucester to say farewell to his mother and friends and relatives. He preached there, and again it was remarkable. In a sense this proved to be the real turning-point in his life and career. He had some relatives in the neighbouring city of Bristol, and he wanted to bid farewell before he left for Georgia. So he went there. Whenever he heard that there was any kind of lecture or preaching in a church on a weekday he always attended. So, in Bristol he went to a certain church and there he was sitting in the congregation when the man who was due to preach recognised him and went down to him and asked him if he would preach instead. Whitefield says, 'I happened to have notes of a sermon in my pocket so I agreed to preach.' And he did so. That was the beginning, in a sense, of the real phenomenon of George Whitefield. The whole congregation was electrified. He preached in other churches and they were also crowded. People came from everywhere, and in the churches they would be holding on to the lamps, holding on to the loft, to the gallery – anything in order to be in the building to hear him. Now this is astounding. He preached in Bristol for the first time in January 1737. Delays occurred, he was still not able to go to Georgia, so he was able to pay a return visit to Bristol in May 1737 and arrived there on May 23rd. Here is something that will help you to realise what a phenomenon this man was. Remember, he was only a young curate of twenty-two years of age, but this is what he says about his return visit to Bristol: 'Multitudes came on foot to meet me, and many in coaches a mile without the city, and almost all saluted and blessed me as I went along the street.' Can you picture this? A young man of twenty-two! People walking out a mile, travelling in coaches in order to meet him. It was a kind of 'royal procession' and all was entirely the result of his amazing and astonishing preaching. And it continued like that – back he went to Gloucester, then to Oxford, and then to London. It is said that between August and Christmas 1737 he preached one hundred times, and he preached on each occasion to crowded audiences. He became one of the most famous men in the whole of London, and the whole of the country. There was a very popular magazine in those days called *The Gentleman's Magazine,* and to get your name in it was quite an achievement. Well, in November 1737 there was a poem on George Whitefield in *The Gentleman's Magazine* and he was still only twenty-two years of age. Nine sermons of his were published in 1737 and they had a very great sale indeed.

Then at long last he was able to go to America, and he spent most of 1738 in America. Now this year 1738, remember, is the year in which the two Wesley brothers were converted during the month of May. But Whitefield came back to this country at the end of 1738 for various reasons. Now this brings us to the great year 1739. Going back again to his old haunts – Gloucester, Bristol, and so on – he began to hear about the terrible condition of the miners living in that village of Kingswood then on the outskirts of Bristol. They were living a most depraved kind of life. Whitefield felt concerned about them. They never went near a place of worship so he began to feel that he must go to them, and he went one day and preached to just about a hundred of them. But the effect again was so tremendous that from there on he began to preach to at least five thousand of them at a time. These men would come up from the pit, they had no time to wash; they just stood and listened, and there he would preach to them. It is said that he was soon preaching to twenty thousand people, all of them standing in the open air and listening to him. And after that, as I have told you, he influenced the brothers Wesley to do the same thing.

But when Whitefield came back from America he found that a great change had taken place here in London in the attitude of the clergy and ministers to him. He had left on the crest of a wave of popularity, but when he came back he found that many doors were closed to him. Why?

Well, there were many reasons for this. Some of his converts had been a bit unwise, and they had acted in a way that was not becoming to the gospel, and had antagonised their own clergy and ministers. Moreover, some of the clergy had never really liked his preaching on the absolute necessity of the new birth. Above all, parts of the Journal which he had begun to keep had been published, and they felt that this was exhibitionism, and that he was saying things that he should not say. These things no doubt, plus a great deal of jealousy, meant that many churches were closed to him. So he was driven to the open air still more. He was refused to be allowed to preach in St Mary's Church in Islington; just as he was about to enter the pulpit they stopped him. But he then decided that he would quietly close that service. He then led the people out, and preached to them in the churchyard. All this aggravated the situation, and the attacks that were made upon him became really quite unbelievable. Attacks were made upon his moral character, and they were even offensive to his personal appearance. Whitefield had the misfortune of having what is called a squint in one eye, and so he was known by the crowd, the popular crowd in London, as 'Doctor Squintum.' However it did not make any difference. The point was that he was this well-known preacher, and that is how his life went on. He would preach on Moorfields Common, he would preach in Marylebone Fields – just north of the present Marylebone Road. He would preach in what was then called May Fair, which we now call 'Mayfair.' He used to preach on Kennington Common. He used to preach on Blackheath. Indeed, in any place where there was a great open space Whitefield had but to get up and to preach and thousands crowded to listen to him. His average congregation was somewhere in the neighbourhood of twenty thousand people at a time, and, remember, they all had to stand. But they stood willingly.

He just went on doing this for the rest of his life. He did this all over England, he did it in Wales as I have told you, he did it in Scotland, he did it in America. Thus this phenomenon continued. When it was heard that he was in the neighbourhood and about to preach, shopkeepers shut their shops at once, for they must hear him; business men forgot their business, farmers put down their tools. He could get a congregation of thousands any time of day or night; he could get them and hold them in snow, sleet, frost, rain – it did not matter what the conditions were. In America in one very cold winter they used to stand by the thousand listening to this man preaching the gospel, and they would travel endless distances in order to get this great opportunity and privilege.

I can sum up the rest of his life by just telling you this – that from that beginning in the open air in that way in 1739 he just went on and on doing this in all these countries until at last in the early morning of September 30th 1770 he breathed his last breath and went on to be with that Lord whom he had longed to see from his earliest days as a young preacher. His end is very characteristic of him. He was not well by now. The amazing thing is that he lived as long as he did. For this man used to preach five or six times a day. That was quite ordinary for him, and thus he put his body under a tremendous strain. There he was; he had promised to preach in a place called Newbury Port in New England, on Sunday, September 30th 1770, and he was travelling in that direction. He had to go through a place called Exeter, and when they heard he was there they all came crowding out. He must preach to them, and at last they persuaded him to do so. At first he could scarcely speak at all. He was in such a weak physical condition that he really could not articulate. He began slowly, and gradually he began to revive. He ended by preaching to them for two hours. That was George Whitefield. He became filled with power and strength, and the congregation, as usual, was deeply affected. Then he arrived at the place where he was to stay that Saturday night at Newbury Port and at last he said he was going to bed. They handed him a candlestick with a candle, but the place was crowded with people. Wherever he went people crowded round him, asking questions, wanting to have a word from him. This last picture of him is a most wonderful, idyllic picture. He was trying to break away from them, and began mounting the stairs holding the lighted candle in his hand. Then he turned round and spoke to them again, and gave them another exhortation. And he went on doing so until the candle had burnt right out in the socket and he had just got the candlestick in his hand. At last he got into his bedroom and into his bed. He had a very severe attack of what we would now call cardiac asthma and he died. He just went on, as I say, to be with the Lord whom he loved so much. When you read his wonderful Journals, keep your eye when you do so on the way in which be longed to go to be with the Lord. It was not mere talk; he meant it; he was reprimanded sometimes for saying this, but it was his greatest desire, and at last it was granted. Well, there is the phenomenon that is covered by the name of George Whitefield, and that is why it is good that we remind ourselves of all this.

Here was a man who could preach in that way to all classes. He had a great following amongst the aristocracy here in London. The Countess of Huntingdon thought there was no man like him as a preacher, and she used to open the rooms in her great house and invite all the leading aristocracy of the age to listen to him; and they all delighted in listening to Whitefield. He was the greatest of these preachers to the aristocracy, but as I reminded you, he was also the greatest preacher to the miners, the greatest preacher to the crowd in Moorfields, Kennington Common or wherever he happened to be. He could preach to children equally well in the orphanage. What an astounding and amazing man he was!

He was also supreme in the matter of collecting money. He founded an orphanage in Georgia and it cost a great deal to keep it going. So it became a custom with him to preach a sermon, and at the end of the sermon to take up a collection. He used to get enormous collections of money, and with this money he would also help anybody who was in need, any poor person, anybody in difficulties. The whole of England was talking about him. It was always known when he was in London, and he could attract people of every class or stratum in society.

## V

What is the explanation of this phenomenon? It is very difficult for us to conceive it, is it not? We are living in very poor days. What a century that eighteenth century was! Here is the phenomenon; what is the explanation? Let me attempt some kind of analysis.

Let us start with the man himself. The natural man was very interesting. As a boy he is said to have been alert and able and very lovable. But the most outstanding thing about him was his gift of oratory. He showed that when he was quite a boy. He would imitate preachers in the Inn. He was a born actor, and he had wonderful elocution. A man is born an orator. You cannot make orators. You are either an orator or you are not. And this man was a born orator. He could not help it. He was always good at declaiming portions of Shakespearian drama. In school he was generally given a part, or if an address was to be delivered to the notabilities of the city of Gloucester he was the boy who was chosen because of his amazing elocution and the ease and the grace with which he did it all. He was a born orator, and like all orators, he was characterised by the great freedom and appropriateness of his gestures. The pedantic John Wesley was not an orator, and he sometimes tended to be a bit critical of George Whitefield in this respect. I remember reading in Wesley's *Journal* of how once they both happened to be in Dublin at the same time and how John Wesley went to listen to Whitefield. In his account of the service, Wesley refers to his gestures, and says that it seemed to him that Whitefield was a little bit too much like a Frenchman in a box. He means that Whitefield tended to speak with his hands as much as with his lips and mouth. But that is oratory. One of the greatest orators of all time was Demosthenes. Somebody asked Demosthenes one day, 'What is the first great rule of oratory?' And Demosthenes answered, 'The first great rule of oratory is – action; and the second great rule of oratory is – action; and the third great rule of oratory is – action.' An orator is not just a man who moves his lips and his tongue, his whole body is involved. 'Action!' We are living in evil days; we know nothing about oratory. George Whitefield was a born orator. Have you heard what David Garrick is reported to have said? David Garrick was the leading actor in London in those times and whenever he had an opportunity he always went to listen to Whitefield. He was not so much interested in the gospel as in the speaking and in the gestures and so on. Garrick is reported to have said that he would give a hundred guineas if he could only say 'Oh!' as George Whitefield said it. And somebody else said that if he could only utter the word 'Mesopotamia' like Whitefield he would be completely happy.

I have a still greater authority to quote. One of the great men of the mid-eighteenth century was Bolingbroke. He was an able, cultured man, a man of the world, a very wise man, and again one who was interested in oratory and in speaking. Bolingbroke said of Whitefield, whom he heard many times, that he had a greater 'commanding eloquence than any man he had ever heard.' He had heard all the greatest statesmen and political orators and other types of orator also. He put Whitefield's at the top of the list, as the greatest 'commanding eloquence' that he had ever heard. In addition to all this, Whitefield had a warm, sympathetic, outgoing nature. There is the natural man.

But that does not explain the phenomenon of George Whitefield. Turn now to the spiritual. Here is the explanation. May I put it in a crude and almost ridiculous manner. God knows what he is doing, and when he chose this man George Whitefield, to whom he had given these natural gifts, he knew what he was doing. George Whitefield underwent a remarkable conversion. It was a long, painful process. There were many steps in it. As I have reminded you, his conscience troubled him as a boy, as a young man, and when he went to Oxford he would not join in the various parties to which he was invited. He would not do so; he was too serious. Then he went to the Holy Club meetings, and they made him still more serious. They did their good works, they had their fast days, and they visited the prisons … But none of it really helped him. Then he read a book, a famous book written by a Scotsman of the name of Henry Scougal who had lived toward the end of the seventeenth century. The title of the book was, *The Life of God in the Soul of Man*. This had a profound effect upon him. It convinced him that he needed to be born again, that to be a Christian means not that you live a good life, or do this or that, but that you have the life of God in your soul. He realised that he had not got it; and this drove him to the depth of despair. He went through agonies. He used to lie prostrate on the ground in prayer, he would go out and pray in the open air; there was nothing he would not do. He went through this terrible process of conviction of sin; but eventually God graciously smiled upon him. In other words the conversion of George Whitefield was not a question of 'making a decision.' It was not sudden. No, he went through this tremendous agony of conviction, and then the light broke upon him. In addition to this he was given what he called 'the sealing of the Spirit' upon the fact that God had forgiven his sins. The Spirit sealed it. There is no question but that this man received a 'baptism of the Spirit.' That is what explains the extraordinary character of his preaching from the very beginning.

But let us remember this. Though that is the beginning, he continued throughout his life to be characterised by a most amazing piety. The prayer-life of this man puts us all to shame, and has often made me feel that I know nothing about these matters at all. I have already referred to his humility and saintliness. Nothing shows that more clearly than the way in which he was terrified at the thought of preaching. Though he had been trained for the ministry, and the time had come for him to be ordained, he was terrified of preaching. He felt it was such a sacred task; and who was he to enter into a pulpit and to preach? He felt he would run a thousand miles away in order not to preach. Such was his view of it all, and such was his view of himself and his own unworthiness, that it took a great deal to persuade George Whitefield to enter a pulpit and to preach.

Brethren, is there not a lesson there for some of us? He also hated press notices, and was always annoyed when he received them. He was, in other words, an extraordinarily humble and saintly man. John Wesley pays him the tribute of saying that there was only one man whom he thought he had ever known who was the equal of Whitefield in saintliness – and conceivably he thought this other man was a little higher, he was not sure – and that man was John Fletcher of Madeley. But for John Wesley to say that at the end of Whitefield's life, and in view of all that had happened between them, is a tremendous tribute to Whitefield's saintliness and godliness.

I have already emphasised his zeal. I want also to emphasise his brotherly spirit and the element of catholicity that characterised him. I reminded you at the beginning that he, like Calvin, was very concerned about true evangelical unity. There was nothing small about this man; there was nothing narrow about him. He had his strong views. He was ready to differ with his great friends John and Charles Wesley on doctrinal matters and to resist them. But that did not make him rigid and narrow; it did not make a small party man of him. No! I can prove this. In Scotland, for instance, the two brothers Erskine, Ralph and Ebenezer, who had gone out in the first Secession – and who had very good grounds for doing so – tried to persuade Whitefield to preach only for them in Scotland. But he would not do it. He said, if there are men in the Church of Scotland who believe the gospel, and who are ready to open their doors to my preaching of the gospel, I will do so. He would not be tied down by the Erskines. And he preached for Church of Scotland ministers, as I have reminded you, in Glasgow, in Cambuslang, Edinburgh, and various other places. Now this was all the result of the Spirit of God in him – the love and the brotherliness, the large-heartedness, the desire that all who really have an evangelical gospel to preach should be one and should be working together.

## VI

There then is the man. Let me say just a word about his message. He described it as 'honest,' he described it as 'plain.' He was always direct. What did he preach about? One of his great themes was original sin. No man could expose the condition of the natural unregenerate heart more powerfully than George Whitefield.

Then another great theme was regeneration. He says himself that his sermon on 'the nature and necessity of the new birth in Christ' began the awakening in London, Bristol, Gloucester, and Gloucestershire. He was himself convinced that it was his famous sermon on this theme that really led to the Great Awakening. It was his leading theme.

Another theme that was prominent in his preaching was this. He believed in the direct, immediate, inward impressions of the Holy Spirit upon a man. Now Jonathan Edwards took him to task about this. There is a very interesting story in the Memoirs of Jonathan Edwards of how Edwards and others once talked to Whitefield about this. Edwards says, 'I tried to deal with him on this question of the emphasis that he places on inward impressions.' Whitefield placed great emphasis upon the direct leadings of the Spirit. He believed the Spirit was speaking to him directly, and he acted upon it. Edwards was a much abler man and a much greater genius in an intellectual sense. Edwards was unhappy about this; and it is most interesting, and almost amusing, to notice how Edwards records that it was quite clear that Whitefield was really not listening to what he, Edwards, was saying. However, that was something which Whitefield did preach and did emphasise a great deal.

Then the next great theme, of course, was justification by faith. Some may wonder why I put regeneration before justification by faith. I did so for this reason – that Whitefield preached regeneration before he preached justification by faith. It is most interesting to observe that he underwent a change in this respect. At first his preaching was almost entirely on the corruption of the natural unregenerate heart and the need for the new birth. This was undoubtedly the effect of Scougal's teaching. In the nine sermons of his that were published in 1737 there is no mention of justification by faith. In his Journals – (you will find it on page 81 of the latest edition of his Journals) – in referring to the theme of justification by faith, he states significantly, 'though I was not so clear in it as afterwards.' He admitted himself that he was not as clear on justification by faith in 1737 as he should have been. If you also read pages 193-94 in his Journals, you will find that the two men who had to put him right on that particular aspect of truth were John and Charles Wesley. They preached justification by faith from the very beginning; Whitefield did not. And they helped him to come to a better balance in this respect. We must be honest. I have said that Whitefield was not a party man; and I must not be a party man. All honour to John and Charles Wesley for helping Whitefield to see the importance and the place of justification by faith in the preacher's message.

I have already reminded you of the Calvinistic emphasis in his preaching. He was clear and unequivocal on this.

Another thing that characterised his preaching, especially at the beginning, was his strictures on unconverted preachers. Jonathan Edwards ventured to pull him up on that also; but Whitefield did not listen to him. Whitefield used to denounce an unconverted ministry, and he would do so even when large numbers of ministers were listening to him. Another way in which he put that was to say that, to him, for a man to preach what he called an 'unfelt Christ' was a most terrible thing – to preach about Christ without feeling the Christ within. He would denounce without measure men who were guilty of that.

## VII

I have said something about the man, I have said something about the message, I end with what was the most characteristic thing of all about this man, namely, his preaching. Do you recognise that distinction and division? I ask the question for this reason. There is nothing that has so often discouraged me, if I may make a personal reference as a preacher, as the failure of people to differentiate between the message and the preaching. There is a tremendous difference between uttering truths and preaching. You may have a correct and an orthodox message but it does not follow that you are preaching it. The thing that puts Whitefield in a class apart with Rowland is the preaching.

What do I mean? I mean the way in which the message is presented and conveyed. There were other men at that time, as there have been since, who preached the same message, but it was not the preaching of George Whitefield. How can one describe *his* preaching? You can only describe it as apostolic and seraphic. I like the remark of an American preacher who heard him a lot and who was responsible for publishing some of his sermons. Commenting upon his style of preaching, he said, 'A noble negligence ran through his style.' What does he mean? He means that Whitefield did not sit down and write wonderful literary masterpieces of sermons, with every sentence perfectly balanced, and always finished, and polished and so on. No, he did not do that. He had not got the time to write sermons. He was an extemporary preacher, and there was what this man calls 'a noble negligence' in his preaching. He broke the rules of grammar now and again, he did not remember to finish his sentences always, but to those who know anything about preaching that is nothing. 'Noble negligence!' – oh that we had a little more of it, and a little less of the polished essays that pass for sermons in this our degenerate age! But the thing that characterised the preaching was the zeal, the fire, the passion, the flame. He was a most convicting and alarming preacher. You remember what was said about the first sermon in Gloucester. The effect he continued to produce was like that. He could so expose the darkness and the sinfulness of the natural human heart that men were terrified and amazed and in agonies of soul as they listened to him. But that would be followed by a pathos, a love, and a melting quality that were irresistible.

That is preaching! I like Whitefield's own comment about this matter of preaching. He was asked one day for a copy of the sermon he had preached in order that it might be published, and this was his reply. He said, 'I have no objection, if you will print the lightning, thunder, and rainbow with it.' You cannot put preaching into cold print; it is impossible. You can put the contents of the sermon, but you cannot put the preaching; you cannot put the 'lightning,' you cannot put the 'thunder' – the roar of the thunder, the flash of the lightning – you cannot capture the 'rainbow.' All that is in the spoken word, in the action, in everything about the preacher. You cannot put that in print. That is why people, when they have read the sermons of Whitefield, often say, 'I cannot understand this. How could the man who produced sermons like this be such a phenomenon, such a wonderful preacher?' If you have ever said that, you are just displaying your ignorance of what is meant by preaching. You cannot put preaching on paper. I hold the view that that has been one of our great troubles since about the middle of the last century or even before. The printing of sermons, the printing of everything that is spoken can have a devastating effect on preaching as such. Men have their eye upon the people who are going to read it rather than on those to whom they are preaching at the time. Concern about reputation and what the literary and pedantic critics will say, alas, comes in. Let us then remember the words of Whitefield on that matter.

The effect of such preaching, of course, was simply overwhelming. He tells us himself about what he observed in the past of the poor colliers at Kingswood. These poor men had just come up out of the mines and their faces were quite black with the coal-dust as they stood listening to Whitefield. He says, 'As I was preaching to them I suddenly began to observe white furrows in their black faces.' What was it? Oh, the tears were streaming down their faces and making furrows in the coal-dust and grime. That is preaching! These poor men who knew nothing about doctrine, who knew nothing about anything but sin, who were just living in drunkenness and even in debauchery, listening to this amazing preaching of the word of God were weeping copious tears. Or take the way in which it is described by the author of the great hymn which begins with the words:

*Great God of wonders, all Thy ways*
*Are matchless, godlike, and divine.*

Samuel Davies himself was an astonishing preacher and a great intellect also. He had been in a revival in America in that same century. He was made principal of a college. Samuel Davies and Gilbert Tennent were sent over to this country to collect money for that college. They arrived after a terrible voyage, during which they thought they were going to be shipwrecked many times over. They at last arrived in London on a Saturday morning, and the first question they asked was – 'Is Mr Whitefield in town?' To their delight they were told that he was, and that he was due to preach the next morning, I think it was in Moorfields. So they made certain that they would be there in very good time to listen to him. Samuel

Davies writes the account of the service and this is what he says. He says, 'It became clear to me quite soon in the service that Mr Whitefield must have had an exceptionally busy week; obviously he had not had time to prepare his sermon properly.' He adds, 'From the standpoint of construction and ordering of thought it was very deficient and defective; it was a poor sermon. But,' said Samuel Davies, 'the unction that attended it was such that I would gladly risk the rigours of shipwreck in the Atlantic many times over in order to be there just to come under its gracious influence.' That is preaching, my friends. Poor sermon, but tremendous preaching!

What do we know about this? Why do we talk about preaching as 'giving an address' or 'saying a word'? Preaching! That is the thing that produced that tremendous revival under God. You can read the accounts of what Jonathan Edwards and Mrs Edwards felt under Whitefield's preaching. Let me tell you what the great Lord Chesterfield said. Chesterfield was a humanist, a typical eighteenth-century man, a 'man about town' who wrote a famous book of advice to his son. He used to delight in listening to Whitefield, and he, like others, came under the power of the preaching. You remember the famous story: Whitefield, one afternoon was using an illustration to show the perilous danger of the sinner's position, how the sinner was walking in the direction of hell without realising it, and he introduced this picture. He compared the sinner to a blind man being led along by a dog. He had a staff in his hand, and he was being led along by the dog. The dog unfortunately broke loose and ran away, and left the man to grope along with his stick as best he could on his own. Unconsciously, said Whitefield, the poor man wanders to the edge of a precipice, his staff drops from his hand down the abyss, too far to send back even an echo. The blind man reaches forward, cautiously, to recover it; for a moment he poises on vacancy and … At that moment Lord Chesterfield sprang to his feet shouting, 'Good God! Stop him!' and sprang forward involuntarily to try to stop the blind man from falling over the abyss. That is not only oratory, that is also preaching; and it can affect even a man like Lord Chesterfield in that extraordinary manner.

But the story I like best of all is the story about Benjamin Franklin listening to George Whitefield. Now here was another genius. Benjamin Franklin is famous as a scientist, famous as a man of letters, as one of the leaders in the American Revolution, as the first ambassador sent by the United States, as it became, to represent them in France. He often came here to London. This able, cultured man called himself a Quaker; he was nothing at all from the Christian standpoint. Now Benjamin Franklin used to live in Philadelphia, and at the time of Whitefield's visits he was a printer. He was an astute business man and he used to print Whitefield's sermons and sell them. He never missed an opportunity of listening to Whitefield, and this is what he says concerning one of those occasions. I have reminded you that Whitefield invariably at the end of a sermon took up a collection for his orphanage in Georgia, and Franklin knew this very well. He had seen it happen many times, and he had often put something into the collection; but he was getting a little tired of doing this. He thought that Whitefield was taking too much of his money. So he says that on this particular occasion as he went to listen to him he had solemnly decided that he would not give anything at all in the collection at the end. He says, 'I had got in my pocket gold, silver, and copper; but I decided I would give nothing at all, I had given so often.' But this is what he goes on to say, 'As the preacher proceeded I began to soften, and concluded to give the copper. Another stroke of his oratory determined me to give the silver. And he finished so admirably that I emptied my pocket wholly into the collector's dish – gold and all.' Now that is preaching! This is beyond oratory, this is inspired oratory – oratory inspired by the Holy Ghost, conveying the message of the word of God and its glorious gospel.

## VIII

Can I in a few headings indicate what I regard as some of the lessons that George Whitefield has to teach us today? I wish I had time to develop them. The first lesson he teaches us is this: that the position is never hopeless – never! Things could not have been worse than they were in the period leading up to 1736–37 – absolutely hopeless, apparently. It was just at that point that God placed his hand on this unknown boy from the Bell Inn, Gloucester – George Whitefield. The sovereignty of God! Do not waste too much of your time in worrying about the future of the Christian church. Do not listen too much to the mere analysts at the present time who simply describe the position confronting us. It is never hopeless. This was one of the most surprising things that God has ever done.

Secondly, let us, I hope, once and forever put an end to that lie which says that Calvinism and an interest in evangelism are not compatible. (I do not like these labels, but as they are used I must use them.) Here is the greatest evangelist England has ever produced and he was a Calvinist. Charles Haddon Spurgeon, the greatest evangelist of last century, confesses that he had modelled himself – as far as he had modelled himself on anybody – on George Whitefield. And he was a Calvinist. The objection which some of us have to certain aspects of modern evangelism has nothing to do with Calvinism at all. I am certain that John Wesley would object to the things that we object to in modern evangelistic methods quite as much as we do. The objection is not based on Calvinism. That doctrine which emphasises the glory of God and the total depravity of man and God's eternal plan and purpose of redemption in the Lord Jesus Christ has always urged and driven its true adherents to evangelism. Whitefield alone is enough to establish that; yet he is but an outstanding shining star in a great galaxy.

The third lesson, is the absolute necessity of an orthodox faith. This man preached the gospel as it had been preached by the apostles, the Reformers, the Puritans. He lived in the Puritans and their writings. He sometimes even preached their sermons when hard-pressed! Wesley says more than once that he found Whitefield clearly preaching Matthew Henry. But there it is! It was the same message, and there it was ready-made in Matthew Henry! But what I am emphasising is the absolute necessity of orthodoxy, of a belief of the truth – the truth that we were reminded of so excellently in Dr Packer's address.

But – and, to me, this is the thing that Whitefield tells us more than anything else – orthodoxy is not enough. There were orthodox men in his time, but they were comparatively useless. You can have a dead orthodoxy. Orthodoxy is essential, but orthodoxy alone has never produced a revival, and it never will. I say, as I end, that my main justification for speaking on Calvin and Whitefield is this, that in a sense John Calvin always needs George Whitefield. What I mean is this. The danger of those who follow the teachings of Calvin, and do so rightly, is that they tend to become intellectualists, or they tend to sink into what I would describe as an 'ossified orthodoxy.' And that is of no value, my friends. You need the power of the Spirit upon it. To state the truth is not enough, it must be stated 'in demonstration of the Spirit and of power.' And that is what this mighty man so gloriously illustrates. He was orthodox, but the thing that produced the phenomenon was the power of the Spirit upon him. He says that he felt something even at his ordination, as if he had received a commission from the Spirit himself. He was always conscious of this – wave after wave of the Spirit would come upon him. No man ever knew more of the love of Christ than this man. It sometimes overwhelmed him, almost crushing him physically. He would be bathed in tears because of it.

This power of the Spirit is essential. We must be orthodox, but God forbid us to rest even on orthodoxy. We must seek the power of the Spirit that was given to George Whitefield. That will give us a sorrow for souls and a concern for souls, and give us the zeal, and enable us to preach with power and conviction to all classes and kinds of men.

Another thing – and this is very important today – he was a great believer in the value of religious societies. There were a number of religious societies in Whitefield's early days which had been started in the previous century, and he was greatly helped by them. His first sermon on that Sunday, June 27th 1736, in Gloucester was actually on 'the value of religious society.' I say that for the encouragement of little groups of evangelical people, for whom I thank God, and whom I know in different parts of this country today, who are meeting together, some of them every week, some of them every month, to study the Scriptures and to pray and to talk together about the things of God. Whitefield believed in the inestimable value of religious societies.

But, chiefly, and I must end with this in the light of what I have been saying and for every other reason. Whitefield, I believe, is calling us back to preaching. I hope that I am not going to be misunderstood, but nothing can be a substitute for preaching. I am a great believer in reading; I get much of my greatest enjoyment in reading. But reading is no substitute for preaching; and to read a sermon and to listen to it being preached are not the same thing. Thank God the Spirit can use a written sermon, but it does not compare with a preached sermon. There is a real danger today that people may think that reading alone will do, or perhaps listening to a wireless or a television sermonette. No, you need the freedom of the Spirit; you need 'the lightning and the thunder and the rainbow.' You cannot get them in books, and you do not get them on your controlled, time-limited programmes provided by these modern agencies. No, when the Spirit comes the programmes will be forgotten, time will be forgotten, everything will be forgotten except God in his glory, and my soul, and this blessed Saviour.

What does Whitefield teach us about the theme of preaching? The theme was, 'By grace ye are saved through faith; and that not of yourselves: it is the gift of God.' That was the glorious message of the eighteenth-century preaching.

May God call us back to preaching! Not a mere mechanical statement of correct beliefs, but let us pray God so to grant us his Spirit, that though we may never become, and never shall become it is certain, preachers in the sense that George Whitefield was – well, that at any rate we may be able to preach 'in demonstration of the Spirit and of power.' We are not meant to be imitators, but let us listen to this man as he calls upon us so to a living realisation of this truth, and so to be filled with the living Spirit of God, that with all we are we may tell forth the riches and the glories of his grace. We all, I am certain, thank God for the memory of such a man. May he grant unto us grace to examine ourselves, to examine our ministry, and may he create within us all a longing and a desire to see the manifestation of the right hand of God again in this country in a mighty revival of religion!

# 1965

## *'Ecclesiola in Ecclesia'*

THE subject allotted to me is one that comes in a logical sequence as well as in a chronological sequence to what we have already heard in this Conference. It is in a sense a kind of postscript, or critique of the approaches to reformation which we have been considering, and may, therefore, legitimately come under the general heading, although in and of itself it cannot properly be defined as 'an approach' to reformation.[1]

In other words what I am going to put before you is something which, I trust I shall be able to demonstrate, throws light upon those various points of view towards, and efforts at reformation which were carried through in the sixteenth century. But in addition, and this is why it is so important for us, I think I will be able to show that it has a very real relevance to the pastoral position in which most of us who are pastors here today find ourselves, having as members of churches many, unfortunately, whom we can at best only regard as nominal Christians. The subject before us will inevitably raise the question as to what our attitude should be to these people who are in the church, but concerning whom as evangelical pastors we may have serious reservations.

### I

First of all let us define the term 'Ecclesiola in Ecclesia.' It is very important that we should be clear as to the precise definition, because the whole argument turns on this precision. What

[1] 'Approaches to the Reformation of the Church' was the conference theme in 1965.

does it mean? It really means 'little church in the church' or 'little churches within a church.' In other words the idea of those who formed these little churches was not to form a new church. That is basic. They were not concerned at all about separation; indeed they were bitterly and violently opposed to it. They were not out to change the doctrine of the church. The early Reformers in this country, like Thomas Bilney and others, were out to do that; but the people who believed in forming 'ecclesiolae' had no such intention whatsoever.

What were they concerned about? Well, their position was that they were not so much dissatisfied with the nature as with the functioning of the church. They were not concerned about the church's doctrine, but were very concerned about its spiritual life and condition.

This is quite basic to our whole outlook upon this subject. The people who believed in the idea of the 'ecclesiola' were not out to change the whole church, but to form a church within a church which would form a nucleus of true believers inside the general church. Their object in the formation of this nucleus was that it might act as a leaven and influence the life of the whole church for the better. That is the definition. It was thought of in terms of the local church and local churches. It was not a movement, but something that was to happen in individual local churches.

That being our definition, we have to understand further – and this was true, I think we can say, of all the men who became interested in this and tried to put it into practice – that for these people this was only a second best. The argument seems to be that if the attempt to reform the whole church fails, well then, all you can do, and the thing that you should do, is to form this nucleus within the church which you trust will permeate the life of the whole and eventually reform it.

The subject is in some ways a little difficult to handle because it was attempted by a number of different men in different countries and in different centuries. I must not weary you with a detailed description of all these. Indeed I deliberately refrain from this because to do so might only end in confusion. I am much more concerned about the principle involved in the idea. That, it seems to me, is the important thing for us.

But we must give some general indication as to how this idea was put into operation. There are certain things which were common to practically all of them. For instance, they were all animated by that same fundamental idea. They all likewise stressed the voluntary membership of these nuclei. People could either join this inner church, this little nucleus, or not; it was left entirely to their own volition. But the moment you did join you had to submit to a very strict discipline. They kept a list of members and observed their attendances very closely, and if a man or a woman failed to turn up with regularity he or she would be excluded, excommunicated. Sometimes indeed, a fine was imposed.

What did they do in these societies? Actually there was a good deal of variation about this, but the central idea in all of them was that the meetings should be an occasion for instruction which could not be given in the open preaching. Most of them held this kind of meeting of this select company, the true believers in the church, once a week. They met in a more informal manner, and there they could go over the sermons preached on the previous Sunday, and people would have opportunities for asking questions and discussion. Some gave opportunity for people to relate their experiences, others frowned upon that and did not believe in it at all. In the case of those that appeared in Germany there was a good deal of discussion of doctrine, and indeed at times of philosophy, and they almost became debating societies; whereas in others doctrinal discussions were completely banned and prohibited. So you see there was this considerable variation in the way in which meetings were conducted, but this does not affect the principle.

Another thing that is common to most of these meetings is that they gave opportunities to the laymen. This is where we touch on that question of the universal priesthood of all believers, referred to in an earlier paper. These people felt that the laymen had not been given sufficient opportunity, so in these gatherings the laymen were allowed to speak and put questions. That is an important principle for us to bear in mind. There was a good deal of difference with regard to the place of women. In most of them women were allowed. In the case of Spener, the German to whom I shall be referring, women were allowed to attend these meetings but they had to be behind a screen out of sight, and they were not allowed to speak! Others were very careful to divide even between married men and single men, and married women and single women, and particularly where the question of the giving of experiences was involved.

Another point which is of importance is that they nearly all insisted upon ministerial supervision. Some of them taught that the minister himself should always be in charge of the meetings; others took a freer view and said that the people, if they liked, could choose a pastor of their own. Luther, for instance, took that point of view. But they nearly all agreed about the need of ministerial supervision because there were some instances where people like this met together without such supervision and it ended in a good deal of trouble in the form of excesses. Nevertheless they were all interested in giving the lay people a greater part to play, a greater influence in the life of the church.

## II

Those are some of the general characteristics of these 'little churches within the church.' Let us now turn to some historical examples.

In a sense it can be said that the first example in history of this kind of nucleus within the church in general, strange though it may sound to us, is monasticism. In principle the idea behind monasticism was very much the same; it was a dissatisfaction with the general state of the church and a calling together of men who were concerned about this and anxious to do something about it. They remained within the church; they did not want to go out of it; indeed that was the last thing they thought of. They were in the church, but they were a special body within it. And, of course, as time passed you had the phenomenon of nuclei being formed inside the original nucleus as the original nucleus tended to degenerate. Another pre-Reformation illustration of this idea is found in the case of the United Brethren who certainly started in this way. I think that you can include the Waldensians also under this heading.

I do not want to stay with these because the first really big example which we have of a man seriously considering this whole matter of an 'ecclesiola in the ecclesia' is none other than Martin Luther. This is where we follow on so directly from what we have already been considering. Calvin and Zwingli never considered this idea, and as far as I can discover were really opposed to it. They certainly never tried to put it into practice. Obviously the Anabaptists also never considered it at all. The action that they had taken was the exact opposite of this, and because of the nature of that action they argued that this was unnecessary. What they had done, they said, was right; they had separated, they had gone out. The principle behind Anabaptism is therefore the very antithesis of what we are considering here.

But Luther is a particularly interesting case with regard to this whole matter. I hope to emphasise and point out certain questions which arise in particular out of the fact that Luther of all people not only toyed with and played with, but advocated the formation of these 'ecclesiolae.' He began to think of this as far back as 1522 and 1523; but it was in 1526 that he published something really definite on the subject. It was in his 'Preface to the German Mass' that he put the thing quite plainly and said that something along these lines must be done.

Why did he do so? Here is the interesting thing – he did it because he was profoundly depressed by the state of the church. From 1513 on to 1520 and even 1521 he was on the crest of a wave as it were. There was great excitement and everything seemed to be going well. But then a reaction set in, the reformed impetus seemed to be pausing, nothing much seemed to be happening. A spirit of caution arose, people were hesitant, political considerations came in and Luther became profoundly depressed. But still more important, and still more serious, he was disturbed at the condition of the church to which he himself belonged, the churches which had responded to his teaching. He felt that they were lacking in true spiritual life and vigour, that they were not living the Christian life; so he began to feel the need of discipline. The Protestants had even been defeated in military battle, and baffled, and he felt that that was mainly due to their lack of discipline, that their whole life was lacking in discipline. Therefore a measure of discipline should be introduced into the church. Another thing that greatly aggravated this feeling which developed in him was the phenomenon of Anabaptists. He was upset by them, and he reacted strongly against them. He felt that the true church, which followed him, must be protected against them, and the only way to do that was to impose discipline.

Luther's relationship to the Anabaptists is a most fascinating one; it is a kind of ambivalent relationship. He reacted against them, and yet in a sense he admired them and was a little bit jealous of the wonderful discipline that they were able to exercise in their own churches. He had to admit that there was a quality of life in their churches which was absent in the churches to which he belonged. So he reacts in two ways to them; he has got to discipline his people against them, and yet he wishes to have in his church the kind of thing that was working so well in their churches. The result of all this was that he felt that the only thing to do was to form these nuclei within the churches. He seemed to be failing to reform the whole church; well then, the best he could do was this second best, which was to gather together the people who are truly Christian into a kind of inner church.

Luther went so far as to say that these are the only people who should be allowed to partake of the Lord's Supper. The others are members of the church, remember, but it is only these true Christians whom he would allow to partake of the Lord's Supper; the others are unfit to do so. So he carries this distinction in his mind to the extent that while all are in the church, the general church, the state church, the land church – call it whatever you like – the only people who are fit to come to the communion are those who belong to this inner body.

That was Luther's idea, and he proposed now that this should be put into practice. But he never did so, for two main reasons.

One was that he felt that he could not discover the people who were fit to belong to the nucleus. It was as bad as that; and that is a very serious consideration. But the other was the Imperial Diet of Speier which was issued in 1526. This was a purely political action on the part of the emperor which appeared to be giving liberty to the heads of these states, the Electors, so Luther began to think that perhaps after all he could do the big thing. Here was an opportunity which had not been present hitherto. Everything had seemed to be against him, the Electors were so slow and lethargic and fearful; but at last they seemed to be given freedom to reform by the emperor himself, so Luther felt that he could abandon the second best and go back to the original idea of reform. The result was that, as far as action was concerned, the idea of 'ecclesiola' came to an end there and then. But more than once later on he seems to be looking back wistfully to this idea of the 'ecclesiola.' When he becomes discouraged he goes back to it in his mind; but he never really put it into operation.

Another contemporary proponent of this idea was a man of the name of Franz Lambert. He had been a Franciscan but he had been converted. While travelling, he went to Zurich and met Zwingli and was very impressed by him. Then he went on to Strasbourg and met Martin Bucer (or Butzer, as he preferred to be called). While he was there, Philip of Hesse became anxious to reform the church in his area, and he was advised to consult Franz Lambert who had now developed ideas about a kind of perfect church, a church of true Christian people. So Lambert went to Philip and drew up his scheme. Philip was on the point of accepting it, but he thought that perhaps he had better consult Luther first, and he did so. Luther by this time had changed his mind, and strongly advised Philip not to do this. The result was that Lambert's ideas were never put into practice there. Lambert then took a post as lecturer in the new University of Marburg and died about 1530. The whole thing came to an end at that point.

That incident provokes the following remark about Luther. It does seem to me to be increasingly clear that Luther never really thought out his doctrine of the church truly. He believed, of course, in the church, and in the true church; he was concerned to bring back the church of the New Testament, but I do suggest that he never really thought it through. We have been reminded that Calvin did so in a way that Luther never did. Indeed I think that Luther can be quite honestly and fairly described as an opportunist.

Now in a sense that is not a criticism. We have got to remember the position in which Luther found himself. He had rediscovered the doctrine of justification by faith only and had experienced its liberating power, and what he desired was that that be made known to all people everywhere. His chief idea of the church was that it is a body that does that. But it seems to me that he never worked it out in detail and the result was that he was always improvising. He would often change his mind and his opinion according to changing circumstances. I have already shown that he did so over this one particular matter. He gets influenced by events and he goes back to an idea and rejects it again, and so on. He was a truly great man, and one cannot help but admire him even at this particular point. Yet we do know that what he said and taught tended to be not only adopted but hardened into fixed dogma which has influenced the Lutheran Church ever since. This throws light on the subsequent history of the Christian church; it emphasises the whole danger of regarding any man as an ultimate oracle and that everything he said and did and thought is the only rule.

We come now to another man who is much more important in this connection, and that is Martin Bucer or Butzer, of Strasbourg. He was a man above all others who became concerned about the great need of discipline. You will remember that he influenced John Calvin a good deal because Calvin spent a number of years in Strasbourg with Bucer and found his wife there. He was certainly influenced by Bucer in his whole attitude to the need of discipline. I think it is fair to say that Bucer struggled with this problem, in a sense, more than any one of these men, and what he was concerned about above all else was that discipline in the church should be ecclesiastical and not by the civil power. That was the thing for which he fought and contended, and he had to go on doing so for a number of years.

Bucer published a book in 1546 bearing the title *The Need and Failure of the Churches and how to Improve Them,* and he approached the whole problem in a thoroughly biblical manner. He has been attacked as being a biblicist; well, that is just a compliment to him in that he was concerned to base everything upon the plain teaching of the Scriptures. He drew up a scheme in terms of this which continued for a few years in spite of great opposition, and in the end, owing to a political event, Bucer and a friend had to leave the country and they came to England. In a few years he had died and the whole thing came to nothing. Indeed his ideas were rejected and what he had inaugurated was quite deliberately undone.

Those were the chief attempts at this idea in the sixteenth century. As we move on to the seventeenth century, we come to a most important man, a most important name – Philipp Jacob Spener. He has been called 'the father of Pietism,' and he had a great influence on the religious life of our country through the Moravians, and ultimately the Methodists, in the eighteenth century. He was born a Lutheran and was a very able man. He was early influenced by the book of Arndt called *What is true Christianity?* and also, let us not forget (because there is a two-way traffic in these matters), greatly influenced by a famous book called *The Practice of Piety,* by Lewis Bayly, one time Bishop of Bangor in North Wales.

Under these influences Spener became quite a remarkable teacher and preacher. He got on to this whole idea of the 'ecclesiola' in this way. He was, as I say, a great and influential preacher, influential in the sense that a number of young men, students and others listening to him regularly, were so moved by his preaching that they wanted further instruction from him, and asked if he would be good enough to meet with them. That is how the whole thing started. He began to meet with these men in his own house to start with, then in other houses, and then in public buildings and so on, the whole idea being to give further instruction to these people who were anxious to learn and to live a holy life.

Spener, again, was an orthodox Lutheran. He did not desire to change anything in the realm of doctrine; he did not want to go out of the church; he was not concerned, in a sense, about reforming the church. What he was concerned about was the life and piety of the church; and so he began to meet with these people. He formed what he called Collegia Pietatis, and to help them he published a book called *Pia Desideria,* which has recently been re-published and is available in this country. Translated, this title means, 'Earnest desires for a reform of the true evangelical church,' and it is a most important and valuable book. In it Spener analyzes the position and causes of the spiritual decline, and what, in his view, can be done with respect to it, and so on.

Spener was actively opposed to the idea of separation and he produced a whole series of arguments against it. These were, that the possibility of affecting the others in the church for good is forfeited, and a breach of love is committed; a wound is torn in the side of Christ's body, already sufficiently split and rent; the papists are given an opportunity for derision; it is contrary to the example of divine patience shown by the Saviour and also by the apostles and prophets; the separatists injure themselves; and one separation always leads to another. True Christians must therefore not think of going out and separating; what they must do is to form these 'colleges' within the churches, and then as they grow and their influence increases they will affect the whole lump.

Another, who was contemporary with Spener, though thirty years younger, was again one who has had a great deal of influence on the Christian life of this country. August Hermann Francke. You may have heard of him in connection with the work of George Müller and Müller's Orphan Homes. Francke is famous for the orphanage which he began, and George Müller is not the only one who borrowed his idea. George Whitefield did exactly the same thing in the eighteenth century, and Howell Harris had the idea for his community at Trevecca also from Francke.

It has been rightly said about Francke and Spener that what animated them was the desire to stress the inner spiritual life and experience as over against 'the secularisation of the state church, the ecclesiasticism of orthodoxy, the purely external Christianity that had developed, and the petrification of doctrine.' In the seventeenth-century Lutheranism developed into a kind of scholasticism. The term 'petrification' is quite a fair one. Doctrine had become petrified, it was lifeless, it was useless, it was something purely intellectual. Pietism was a protest, if you like, against formalism.

These two men fought this battle thoroughly and had to suffer a lot. They were both very able theologians and commentators. It is a tragedy that we in this country are so lacking in literature on these two men and in translations of their writings. Wherever they went, and they had to move from one place to another, they started these 'colleges' or 'ecclesiolae,' and they certainly had a potent influence upon the life of Germany.

One man influenced by them – and he is the next I have to mention – is none other than Count Zinzendorf who, of course, belongs mainly to the eighteenth century. Now here again was a man who started as a very orthodox Lutheran and did not want to leave the Lutheran Church. He is an interesting case from the standpoint of this idea of the 'ecclesiolae' because, having started with it, he departed from it. I shall be showing in a moment how that is a tendency that is inherent and incipient, it seems to me, in the whole idea; and in the case of Zinzendorf, as you know, it did eventually lead to a separation and to the formation of the United Brethren, or Moravian Brethren, which became a sectarian body.

## III

There, we have looked very hurriedly at the history of this idea on the continent of Europe. I could mention other countries also. This influence came into Holland as well; in fact there was an attempt at something like this in most countries especially where the works of Spener and Francke became well-known.

But turning to this country, what do we find? Here is a most interesting thing. Were the Puritans believers in the 'ecclesiola in ecclesia'? There is only one answer, and that is that they were not, strange though it may sound at first. Puritanism at its outset was a movement, a spirit, an influence, but not in terms of the idea of an 'ecclesiola.' It was a school of thought, it was not even a society, or a defined group. But the material point for us is that the Puritans were not concerned to form these nuclei within the church. Many of them in practice seemed to be doing that, but I think it can be pointed out that that was not their intention nor their objective. If it did happen it was a kind of accident, because the majority in the church did not respond to what they were anxious to do for them. They never consciously went out to set up these 'little churches within the church'; indeed their primary object was to influence the whole of the Church of England, and to carry on the reform which they felt had stopped instead of going on and completing itself. So they do not come under this particular heading.

Has this idea, then, no advocates in this country? It has. There is a famous example of this in the case of Dr Anthony Horneck. It is he who really first started this idea in this country; and he did so in 1678. He was a German, a very able man, and a very able preacher. He became the preacher at the Savoy Chapel about 1671, and, again, in a most interesting way he was driven, as it were, to form an 'ecclesiola' in exactly the same way as Spener. It was entirely the result of his preaching. He influenced able, thoughtful young men and they came to him with the request that he should meet with them. He began to do so, and out of that the whole idea developed, and from his example the thing spread widely. As in the previous examples they again met every week, and Horneck was very strict in his discipline. He would not allow discussion on controverted points of theology; such discussions were entirely banned. The gatherings were intended to be meetings for devotional purposes. I must go on repeating this, because the primary idea which they all certainly had in all places and at all times was devotional rather than primarily theological.

Others began to follow and to form the same kind of societies. Here I must put in a note. You may have read of 'Societies for the Reformation of Manners.' Now they are not strictly speaking 'ecclesiolae in ecclesia' at all; they had a different object and intention, they had a more purely practical purpose. But the question is, why did Horneck and others ever resort to this expedient of 'the little church within the church'? The answer again is a profound dissatisfaction with the spiritual state and condition of the Church of England. As the result of what had happened in 1662, and the influence of the Restoration period headed by King Charles II and his company, the state of the church, spiritually speaking, had sunk to such a low level that these men felt that it was the only thing to do.

Another great name in this connection is that of Josiah Woodward who preached in Poplar [East London]. I cannot stay with him. He wrote an account of these societies, and the result of the publication of his book, which passed very quickly through several editions, was that the whole idea became extremely popular and these 'Religious Societies' as they were called (they were nothing but these 'ecclesiolae') spread all over the country. Thus when you come to the time of George Whitefield you will find that, when he began to be used of God in that phenomenal manner, he told his converts to go to these societies at Bristol, London, and in other places. He recognised their value, although by this time they had lost most of their spirituality, and it was his hope that they might help his converts and that they, in turn, might be helped by the converts.

Thus we come on to the eighteenth century. Another man who introduced and practised this idea in his church was William Grimshaw, of Haworth. Another was Samuel Walker, of Truro. His case is interesting and very important, especially because of his correspondence, not to say controversy, with John Wesley. Samuel Walker really formed an 'ecclesiola' in his church. Henry Venn did the same thing in Huddersfield, and Charles Simeon did it in Cambridge.

What of Methodism? Here again is a most interesting case. Methodism is, and is not, an illustration of this at one and the same time, very much in the same way as happened in the case of Zinzendorf. The Wesleys, and Whitefield for that matter, and, of course, the Countess of Huntingdon in particular, are a difficult case for this reason, that they were not content to stop at an 'ecclesiola in ecclesia,' but went beyond that. They, of course, were first and foremost concerned about the care of their converts; that was their controlling idea. They could see that their converts could not fit in to the churches as they then were, and they felt that they must make some provision for them. So in that respect, even at the very beginning, there is a difference between them and the idea behind the 'ecclesiolae.' With the Methodists it was not so much a calling out of the most Christian people and forming them into a society, but the needs of the new converts of the revival, and what could be done for them. Others, of course, were allowed to join. In the case of John Wesley he would admit to his societies people who were not members of the Church of England, so there he definitely departs from this whole idea of the 'ecclesiola.' And not only that! Because of his organising genius, it seems to me that from the very beginning there was a powerful and prominent sectarian tendency in the Methodist societies, and the moment the Conference was organised and arranged I feel he had already crossed the line. It is all very well to say Wesley died a member of the Church of England. You can recognise many things on paper, but what really matters is what you do in practice. He really was a sectarian from the time of starting of the annual Conference, although he tried to argue that it was not so. But from the beginning it was surely quite inevitable that Methodism should become a distinct and separate body.

The case of Brethrenism (Plymouth) by definition does not call for consideration because it is essentially separatist.

There is our historical review except for one further case. I think that the most perfect illustration of this idea of the 'ecclesiola in ecclesia' that can be found is in the case of Norway. There was a great revival in that country in the early part of the last century, the main leader of which was a farmer of the name of Hauge. He held very strongly that his converts must not leave the moribund Lutheran Church of Norway, so what he did was to organise them within the church and he called it the 'inner mission.' It is still there today. The famous Professor Hallesby belonged to this 'inner mission.' They are within the Lutheran Church, but they are a distinct and separate body within it. They have their own seminary, their own foreign mission society, their own schools and so on. That is, perhaps, the most perfect example of an 'ecclesiola in ecclesia' that has ever been known.

## IV

What happened to these efforts, these experiments in forming little churches within the churches? The answer is that with the notable exception of Norway they all ended in failure. Luther, as we have seen, himself came to the conclusion that the idea was impracticable because he could not find the people, could not find a sufficient number of good Christian people to form such an 'ecclesia.' There were also the other factors to which I have referred. In the case of Bucer, as I have told you, it ended in ultimate failure. I know that political factors came in, and that circumstances made a very big difference particularly in his case, but the point is that it came to nothing.

But I want to go further and to suggest that this whole idea is bound to come to nothing for various reasons. Here are some of them.

Is it not inevitable that the larger portion of the church, which you may call if you like the nominal church, will always resent this? If you divide up your church and say, 'I am going to call out the true Christians and I am going to have special meetings for them,' what effect is that going to have upon the others? It is bound to arouse resentment and opposition; and it has invariably done so. So that far from helping these other people you create within them a spirit of antagonism.

Secondly, is there not implicit in it, as I have suggested, a sectarian element in its very essence? You are causing a division.

Then another factor which has always militated against this idea is that it has always produced tension over the question of churchmanship and over the relationship of the minister to this. Imagine a minister, a non-evangelical minister, a 'dead' minister, as it were, in a church where such an 'ecclesiola' is formed and in which the people are entitled to choose their own leader. It is inevitable that tensions are bound to arise.

Another cause of trouble – and they all had this, including Spener and Francke – was in connection with excesses. Some people are always ready to go too far and to abuse the privileges. Discussion tended to become wrangling, and the relating of intimate personal experiences and feelings is always likely to lead to trouble, and so the authorities have to intervene.

Another inherent defect in this idea, and again it is practically inevitable, is spiritual pride – spiritual pride in these people whom you call out, and who are ready to be called out because they regard themselves as being better than the others. And there is nothing more dangerous to the soul than spiritual pride.

A further difficulty arose in this way. This idea is all right as long as you have an evangelical minister. But what happens when he leaves and is replaced by a non-evangelical minister? This happened in the case of Samuel Walker. He opposed Wesley. He told the latter that he must not organise his societies as he was doing, that the right method, the only safe method, was a group within the church guided by the minister himself. Samuel Walker scarcely allowed anybody to speak at all, but did all the speaking himself, even in the 'ecclesiola.' He was so concerned that none of the sectarian tendency should come in. However, what actually happened was that when Samuel Walker died the members of his 'ecclesiola' left the church, St Mary's, Truro, and the majority of them joined the two Countess of Huntingdon's churches in Cornwall. Thus the whole experiment came to an end. Exactly the same thing happened when Henry Venn left Huddersfield and went to the little village of Yelling. The 'ecclesiola' disappeared in Huddersfield. Venn got into trouble over this because, having gone from Huddersfield to Yelling, his successor did not carry on in the same way, and the members of the 'ecclesiola' wrote to Venn for advice and instruction. He gave it to them, and thereby, of course, broke the rules. He should not have done that. A minister who interferes in his former church in that way is asking for trouble. Venn regretted afterwards that he had ever done this.

The point is that for these various reasons the experiments of 'the little church within the church' failed. All this is a sheer matter of history; one of two things happened to them all. They either failed in the way I have been describing, or, secondly, they ended definitely in separation and the formation of a new church. That happened, as I have shown, in the case of Methodism in England. It happened in exactly the same way with Calvinistic Methodism in Wales, which became a separate denomination in Wales in 1811.

## V

That leads to the next vital question – can these 'ecclesiolae in ecclesia' be justified on any grounds? First, can they be justified on scriptural grounds? How do you justify this procedure? Many of us, I know, have been tempted to do this very thing in our churches. You have had the idea of calling together your truly Christian people to pray for revival or something like that. Well, is there any justification for this on scriptural grounds? These men were scriptural men as I have been emphasising and they did quote the Scriptures in defence of their procedure. What were they?

These are the only Scriptures they could find to justify this procedure of the 'ecclesiola in ecclesia': 'Where two or three are gathered together in my name, there am I in the midst' (Matt. 18:20); 'And I myself also am persuaded of you, my brethren, that ye also are full of goodness, filled with all knowledge, able also to admonish one another' (Rom. 15:14); 'Speaking to yourselves in psalms, hymns, and spiritual songs, singing and making melody in your heart to the Lord' (Eph. 5:19); 'Wherefore comfort one another with these words' (1 Thess. 4:18); 'Now we exhort you, brethren, warn them that are unruly, comfort the feebleminded, support the weak, be patient toward all men' (1 Thess. 5:19); 'For every one that useth milk is unskilful in the word of righteousness: for he is a babe' (Heb. 5:13). That does indicate that there are different kinds of people in the church; does it do any more? 'Let us consider one another to provoke unto love and to good works: not forsaking the assembling of ourselves together as the manner of some is, but exhorting one another: and so much the more as ye see the day approaching' (Heb. 10:24, 25). Those were the Scriptures that they produced, and the question we have to ask is whether any one of them is really applicable to this point? Does any one of them justify the formation of an 'ecclesiola in ecclesia'?

The New Testament clearly recognises that there are different kinds of people in the church. There are some who are strong, and some who are weak. There are some who are called 'ye that are spiritual,' implying that there are those who are less spiritual. There are all these kinds of divisions and differences and distinctions recognised in the members of the church. We are always exhorted to bear one another's burdens, and the strong must help the weak, and so on. But surely none of these justify this kind of drawing out of some from amongst the others? Not one of these texts does so in any shape or form. I would go as far as to say that this procedure is one which is directly contrary to the New Testament teaching. If you do regard the church as a gathering of true believers, and if you insist upon the three marks of a true church, where is there even a vestige of scriptural substantiation for this kind of practice? The New Testament is always concerned about the whole church. It does not recognise any separation and special treatment for a nucleus. Its teaching always is that the members of the church are sharing and are participating together in these things and are enjoying them together. Surely the New Testament does not cater for anything but that?

The advocates of this idea did not mention, any of them, as far as I can make out, the Parable of the Tares; and rightly so of course, because that does not deal with this kind of issue at all. It is concerned about the question of judgment, but in no way does it justify the minister or anyone else, performing an act of separation and calling out certain people for special treatment and for special instruction. So it seems to me that we are left without any scriptural warrant at all for this procedure. This will, of course, finally determine our whole attitude towards the question.

There is one special question which I should like to raise before I come to a few final questions which this whole story seems to me to pose for us. Some may feel, perhaps, that this is the idea that we ought to adopt as evangelical people at this present time. If there is going to be a great world church does not this teaching and this idea indicate to us that we as evangelicals should be the nucleus, the 'ecclesiola' in the great world 'ecclesia'? Many believe that we should 'stay in' in order to infiltrate and influence in an evangelical direction – 'In it to win it,' as someone has put it.

What is the answer to that? It seems to me that that can be negatived quite easily in this way. As I emphasised in the definition, none of these people were concerned primarily about doctrine. There was no difficulty about that; they were all concerned about practice and about spirituality. Can anyone suggest that any of the men I have mentioned would allow or even tolerate within the church men who deny most of the cardinal doctrines of the Christian faith? We know perfectly well that they would not. They had separated from Rome and they denounced Rome and her teaching. Not only that, we know what they did with people whom they regarded as heretics. They expelled them, and some of them advocated that they should even be put to death. So there is no case for the argument that we can borrow from this idea of the 'ecclesiola in ecclesia' support for the idea that we can remain in the same general 'world church' with men who are not only heretics but who are notorious opponents of the truth of God as it is in Christ Jesus our Lord as we see it.

## VI

Let me therefore put to you what I regard as the urgent questions that this story of the 'ecclesiola in ecclesia' idea raises for us.

Can a view of the church which leads to the necessity of forming an 'ecclesiola in ecclesia' possibly be right? The great Reformation, the great divide had just taken place, yet Luther by 1522 was already having to think of this idea. Was not there something essentially wrong with his whole idea of the church? If you have to resort to this expedient does it not *ipso facto* suggest that there is something incomplete in the Reformation because there is something wrong in your whole view of the church? That question arises, and it is a most important one.

The second question, obviously must be: what is a Christian? Luther said that the majority of the members of the church were not fit to come to the Communion table. Lambert definitely described them as heathen. And yet they were members of the church! He said they were heathens who needed to be evangelised. Well, we have heard of people today who say that they regard the church as 'a good place to fish in.' Is that a New Testament conception? Can people whom you regard as heathens be Christians and church members? You say, 'But how and who are we to decide, how can you define these matters?' But if you call them 'heathen' you are defining. A man cannot be a heathen and a Christian at the same time. So if you call them heathens you are saying that they are not Christians.

Then, thirdly, what is the Christian church? We are really facing this fundamental question. This issue brings it up. It was there immediately after the Reformation; it is with us as acutely today.

Fourthly, who should be admitted to church membership?

Fifthly, are not we today still tending to do what the Reformers did in this whole matter? Are we not failing to learn the lesson of the centuries and failing to go back to the New Testament? I think we have got to face that question. We have been reminded several times already in this conference, that the Reformers did what they did at certain points because that was the position that they found and inherited. We see clearly in the case of Luther that it was accepting what he 'found' that drove him to such depression that he had even to resort to the idea of an 'ecclesiola in ecclesia.' Should he not have seen that? But above all, should not we learn the lesson that these men teach us? We can look on objectively at what they did, and what they failed to do; but are we not tending to repeat the selfsame error?

I would put as my sixth point the familiar argument which says that if you reject this idea, if instead you call for separation, you will have to do exactly the same thing again in a hundred years or so. That is an argument that is often produced in favour of the 'ecclesiola' idea. Spener used it. He said that you would find that, if you start separating, you will have to go on separating.

That, of course, was the famous Roman Catholic charge against Protestantism. It is most interesting to note how many Protestants, even evangelicals, still use it against other Protestants. It is really a Roman Catholic argument, and they are the only people who are really entitled to use it. But in any case it is a foolish argument. Who ever claimed that we are in a position to legislate for the church in perpetuity? We are only responsible for the church in our own day and generation. Of course you may have to go on doing this. We pray that you do not have to; but in any case the question for us is, what are we doing, how are we facing our position, and the challenge of our present position? What our grandchildren may do is not our responsibility; but we are responsible for what is happening now.

Then I go on to the seventh question. Take the argument that Spener used, and it is still being used, that if instead of forming the 'ecclesiola' you go out, you will lose your opportunity of influencing those people and that therefore you must stay in with them in order that you may influence them and make Christians of them. There is only one thing to say about this – it seems to me to be based entirely on a lack of faith in the power of the Holy Spirit. It is true to say today that the religious bodies and denominations that are growing most rapidly in the United States of America are the ones that are most rigorous and which have the highest standard. In any case we have evidence before our very eyes that our staying amongst such people does not seem to be converting them to our view but rather to a lowering of the spiritual temperature of those who are staying amongst them and an increasing tendency to doctrinal accommodation and compromise. But in any case it seems to me to be sheer lack of faith in the power of the Holy Spirit. We are forgetting the 'doctrine of the remnant.' We are trusting to expediency and expedients and not saying that, if we are faithful, the Holy Spirit has promised to honour us and our testimony, however small our numbers and however despised by 'the wise and prudent.'

So I come to the last question which seems to me to be raised, and I think it is the most acute question of all. God forbid that this last question should ever cause a division amongst us who are evangelical, but it does seem to me that this story of the 'ecclesiola in ecclesia' raises this great question. It was there at the beginning with Luther; it is still here. Should we start with the situation and the position as it is and try to reform it, or should we start with the New Testament and apply it? It comes to that! The Reformers began with the situation as they found it, and as we have been reminded several times in the conference, their policy was to reform it. If their premiss was right I think their procedure can be justified. You must then be patient and diplomatic and so on.

But the great question I am raising is this – were they right in that original question? Where do you start? Do you start with the existing situation and try by adjustment and accommodation and meetings and fellowship and readiness to give and take for the sake of the body that is already there, to get the best modifications you can? Is it that? History seems to show that, if you do start with that, you will soon be having to think of starting an 'ecclesiola in ecclesia' because of the dead wood in the church. That seems to me to be the argument of history. Do you start with that then?

Or do you rather start by asking 'What is the New Testament teaching?' Let us start with that. Our one object and endeavour should be to put that into practice, cost what it may, believing that as we are trying to conform to the New Testament pattern we shall be blessed of God. It is a difficult, it is a perplexing, it is a vexing question. As I have tried to remind you, in all fairness, the Reformers were concerned to bring back the New Testament idea; but they failed. There was this kind of polarity in their thinking and they kept on swinging between two basic ideas. That is why I am raising this as the ultimate and fundamental question.

This is the question that remains with us, and the ecumenical movement, it seems to me, has made it a more urgent question than it has been for several centuries. The leaders of that movement are saying, let us throw everything into the melting-pot. They are not actually doing that because they are committed to the principle of modification and accommodation. But they are saying it. Well, let us say it! Let us say that we are living in a situation where we really must and can face these things in a new and fundamental manner. Let us determine to do so in the light of the New Testament teaching and not in the light of 'the scientific man of the mid-twentieth century' or in the light of 'the results of scholarship and of latest knowledge.' It is a profound, it is a fundamental question, and I believe that every one of us will not only have to face it but also have to decide one way or the other, and that very soon. May God keep us all humble, may he give us great charity, give us great patience, but above all may he give us a single eye to his glory and to his praise.

# 1966

# *Henry Jacob and the First Congregational Church*

## I

LET me explain at once why I have chosen this subject on which I am to address you. Indeed, it would be more accurate to say that it has been chosen for me: because this year happens to be the 350th anniversary of the founding of the first Congregational or Independent Chapel in this country, which has had a continuous existence.

It has been my lot on other occasions and in other places to remind people of certain important historical occasions. I am sure that very few, if any of you, knew that this year is the three hundred and fiftieth anniversary of the founding of that first Congregational Chapel. We are living in days when people no longer remember these things, and are not interested in them. It is a very significant symptom of the spiritual malaise that afflicts us, and I would probably have given this address in any case this evening, because a 350th anniversary is an important one.

But, on top of that, something has happened this year which makes this fact still more interesting and throws into still greater significance this thing which happened three hundred and fifty years ago. Last May the Congregational Union of Independent Churches in Great Britain came to an end with the formation of what is called the Congregational Church of England. Now I have no hesitation in saying that the authorities of the Congregational Union were probably completely ignorant of the fact that they were taking this momentous step of doing away with essential Congregationalism on the three hundred and fiftieth anniversary of the founding of the Congregational Chapel to which I am referring. But that is what they have succeeded in doing; and though it means nothing to them it means a great deal to me. So I felt that it would be wrong, apart from anything else, to allow this important occasion to pass without calling attention to it.

I am, as I say, interested in the mere history of this matter: but that is not my only interest. We are living in days when we cannot afford the luxury of mere antiquarian interests, neither can we indulge any historical bent that we may have as a matter of mere enjoyment. The times are too serious and too urgent for that. I am calling attention to this important anniversary because I think it has a great deal to teach us at the present time. It should help the thinking of every one of us.

We must never forget that the Puritans were not only interested in pastoral problems, or problems which come under the general heading of casuistry. They were, of course, vitally interested, as we have been so rightly reminded, in godliness and the outworking of the teaching of the Bible in daily life. But it would be a very regrettable and a most unfortunate thing for us to forget that they were also tremendously, and indeed even primarily, interested in the doctrine of the nature of the Christian church. And it is with that, of course, that I shall of necessity have to deal as I tell you something about Henry Jacob and the founding of the first Congregational Chapel to have had a continuous existence. All this becomes peculiarly interesting and important for us because of the fluid condition in which we find ourselves as ministers and members of Christian churches at this present time.

The task which I am thus attempting to deal with is not an easy one. Clearly, the first thing that is necessary is to give a definition, if we can, of what is meant by Congregational or Independent. Indeed, this whole matter of what is meant by the very term 'Puritan' is an extremely involved one which has been receiving much attention recently. There is a very fascinating essay on this subject under the title of 'Puritanism: the Problem of Definition,' by Professor Basil Hall, of Cambridge, to be found in *Studies in Church History*, vol. II, edited by G. J. Cunning.

There has been from the beginning great confusion concerning this question of the exact meaning of the term *Puritan*. There were many factors which led to that. Daniel Neal's *History of the Puritans* is one of the factors. He was a bit careless in his use of the term, and others have tended to follow him. Furthermore, as Professor Basil Hall points out quite rightly, the leaders of the Congregational and Baptist churches, priding themselves in the fact that their churches have attained unto respectability in this present century, are very anxious to play down their Separatist origins. That is not surprising, indeed it is inevitable, as is often seen in the case of individuals who have 'risen in the world.' These factors then have conspired together to bring a great deal of confusion into this whole question of the definition of the term *Puritan*. The two volumes by Champlin Burrage, which were issued in 1912, on *The Early English Dissenters*, I believe did more good than anything I have come across to clear up this confusion, and since then the position has somewhat improved. But still it is not too clear even now. This term *Puritan* has been used very loosely, and as Professor Hall says again, its meaning has been greatly inflated.

What kind of definition is possible therefore? Well, the first thing we have to remember is that it is used currently, and has been for some time, in a very loose way to include people who differed not only radically from one another on this issue of the church, but even in a very bitter manner. They have all been lumped together always as Puritans. That is where the difficulty has come in. In a sense, of course, they did hold certain things in common but at this point they very definitely divided and disagreed.

I am going to suggest a rough kind of definition. Roughly up until about 1570 Puritans were people who can be described as restlessly critical and occasionally rebellious members of the Church of England who desired some modification in church government and worship. You can think of examples and illustrations of that. They were members of the Church of England. Their one concern was that the reformation should be carried further. They felt that the Church of England had stopped halfway between Rome and Geneva, and they were anxious that the reformation should be carried out more thoroughly in the matter of ceremonies and discipline and things like that. That was the position more or less up until the time that Thomas Cartwright and others began to put forward the Presbyterian view of church government.

It is very important to remember that Cartwright, like those other Anglicans to whom I have referred, was not a Separatist. He believed, and the Presbyterians with him, that they could reform the Church of England in the direction of, and turn it into, a Presbyterian Church. For that reason they were not Separatists. But fairly soon afterwards people called Separatists came into being. Actually the first Separatist church in this country was probably one that was formed here in London in 1567 by a man called Richard Fitz; but it had a very chequered and short history. It is when you come on to the 1580s to people like Robert Browne and Robert Harrison that the Separatists really come to be fairly clearly defined.

These were the people who felt that the principle that Christ's church should be coterminous with the Tudor or Stuart state was wrong; so they believed in separating from the Established Church which took that view. The fact that Browne subsequently recanted and lived a long life as a vicar in the Church of England does not really make any difference to the matter of principle.

After Browne and Harrison there came three men who were still more remarkable, it seems to me, as Separatists. They were Henry Barrowe, John Greenwood, and John Penry, each of whom was put to death for his principles in 1593. Now these men believed in complete separation from the Established Church. The difference between the two groups was sometimes put like this, that the first group believed in 'Tarrying for the Magistrate,' and the second group said *'Reformation without Tarrying for Any'* – the title of a book by Browne.

That, then, was the position until the turn of the sixteenth/seventeenth century. After that it really becomes most difficult. The trouble has been that everybody seems to have assumed that the Independents were the direct continuation of the Brownists or the Barrowists or the Greenwoodites, whatever you like to call them. But I want to try to show that that was not the case. This is the point at which we have to be most circumspect. Certain men arose, and this man Henry Jacob about whom I am going to speak was one of the more important of them, who really were responsible for the beginning of true Independency or Congregationalism.

What then was the difference between Jacob's position, and that of his followers who have sometimes been called 'Jacob-ites' – not Jacobites – and the Separatists like the Brownists or the Barrowists or even the Anabaptists? Well, it can be put like this; the Independents did not regard the Church of England as being altogether wrong, they did not oppose occasional attendance at the services of the Church of England, and indeed were not really opposed to the notion of a state church as such. Oliver Cromwell, for instance, was a true Independent, but he continued the tithe system when he came to authority and to power and his government took an active part in organising the religious life of this country.

We can, therefore, look at it like this, that until about 1640 you had that kind of original Puritan who was essentially Anglican, and who was non-Separatist, of course; then you had the Presbyterian type of Puritan, also non-Separatist; then right at the other extreme you had the Separatists quite plain and clear and open. But then this new group came into being, it seems to me, about 1605 very definitely as the result of the understanding of this man Henry Jacob.

It is very interesting to notice the relationship between Jacob and John Robinson, known as 'the pastor of the Pilgrim Fathers.' John Robinson was first a Separatist, but became an Independent, and this is where Neal and others have gone astray. I have been quite convinced by the argument of Champlin Burrage with regard to this matter. The old idea used to be that it was John Robinson who turned Henry Jacob into an Independent; but it was actually the other way round. It was Henry Jacob who turned John Robinson from being a Separatist into an Independent. This, I think, is something that Champlin Burrage proves quite clearly by quotations from the works of Robinson before 1610 when he met Jacob, and quotations from works which he wrote afterwards, and the way, indeed, in which he behaved afterwards.

This is a matter of some interest for us today as it shows that these men kept their minds open, that they were not rigid and set, but they were always ready to listen to new evidence, new argument, or fresh demonstrations from the Scripture. This is something that we tend to forget about them. There were some, of course, who were thoroughly rigid and set and would never change under any conditions whatsoever; but, speaking generally of them, I think it is true to say that they were prepared to consider other points of view.

From 1640 onwards, however, the position does seem to become quite different. From that time you get terms used regularly. Instead of a general conglomerate term like Puritan, the terms Presbyterian, Independent, Baptist, or Anabaptist came into use. Of course there were others also, like the Quakers and Fifth Monarchy men, the Diggers and others. But the interesting point is that terms like Independent, Baptist, and Presbyterian, rather than Puritan, were used more and more frequently from 1640 onwards. We must not be pedantic about these things, but if we are to understand the essence of the story of this man Henry Jacob it was essential that I should have said that much.

In confirmation of that I have a statement, a quotation from the famous Robert Baillie who wrote so much about the Westminster Assembly 1643–47 and who was one of the Scottish members of it. Robert Baillie says, 'for the Brownists, their number at London or Amsterdam is but very small.' 'The Independent Puritans of London' he likewise reports, 'as yet do consist of much within one thousand persons; men, women, and all who to this day have put themselves in any known congregation of that way, being reckoned.' Then follows an unsolicited testimonial: 'But setting aside numbers, for other respects they are of so eminent a condition, that not any nor all the rest of the Sects are comparable to them.' He is talking there in particular about the Independents. You observe that they were small in number in 1645, less than a thousand, he thinks, here in London.

There, then, is some attempt at a definition. I trust that it is quite clear that the Independents did not believe in breaking altogether with the Church of England. They were prepared to grant that the Church of England was a true church, at any rate that there were true churches within the Church of England, and true Christians; and they did not cut themselves off entirely. They believed in 'occasional conformity' and they would on certain occasions, as I am going to show you by quotations later, join with the Episcopalians in services. They have been rightly called semi-Separatists.

I have tried to describe the situation in a broad and general way. The thing we need to grasp is that there was great confusion during all these years. If ever the position was fluid and uncertain it was then.

## II

We now come directly to the story of Henry Jacob. He was born in the county of Kent, in 1553, and educated at St Mary's Hall, Oxford, later becoming a precentor at Christ Church in Oxford. He was then appointed vicar of Cheriton in Kent, a living which he held, roughly, until 1591. Then, he seems to have gone to Holland. He had already begun to imbibe Puritan teaching (I use the term again generally), and as the result of that he went to Holland and remained there for some time. He was not an extreme Puritan, as we can prove in this way. In 1599 he wrote a book – by the way, he was a very able and learned man – with this title: *A Defence of the Churches and Ministry of England written in two Treatises against the reasons and objections of Mr Francis Johnson*. Mr Francis Johnson was a Separatist and had been pastor of a Separatist Church in Holland. He had written saying that the Church of England was not a true church, and her ministry therefore not a true ministry. Henry Jacob, you see, came to the defence of the Church of England in this *Defence of the Churches and Ministry of England*.

That is very indicative of his position. He had not, obviously, at that time ceased to have communion with the Church of England;

but he rejected all of what he called 'her corruptions.' He regarded the Church of England as having many corruptions, but in spite of that he would not say, as the Separatists did, that she was no longer a true church.

In Holland, somewhere round about 1600, he became the minister of a 'gathered church' at Middleburg in Zeeland in Holland. It was a church consisting mainly of English exiles. May I take this opportunity of saying that I think we as people in this country ought to register our gratitude to that country for the way in which it sheltered and harboured these exiles at that time. Considerable numbers went over from time to time, and they were always given a very warm welcome and great freedom in Holland. Of course, in other times this country did exactly the same thing.

But to go on with this history. In 1604 Jacob published a book with this title – remember he had defended the Church of England in 1599 – *Reasons taken out of God's word and the best human testimonies proving a necessity of reforming our churches in England.* Here are some of the things he maintained in that book: 1. The absolute perfection of the Holy Scriptures in all matters of faith and discipline without any human traditions; 2. That the ministry and ceremonies of the Church of England stood in need of reformation; 3. That for two hundred years after Christ the churches of Christ were not diocesan churches but congregational; 4. That the New Testament contains a particular form of church government; 5. That this form of church government is not changeable by man and therefore no other form is lawful.

In 1605 – you see how busy these men were – we find him back in this country, and joining in what was called 'A Third Humble Supplication' to King James I. Incidentally, Henry Jacob had been one of the men who had presented the Millenary Petition at Hampton Court to James I, who was already James VI of Scotland, in 1603; and he was one of the men who had been grievously disappointed at the king's refusal. But they went on petitioning the king; and here in this 'Third Humble Supplication' they made an urgent request for toleration.

This is what they asked for: 'Permission to assemble together somewhere publicly to the service and worship of God, and to use and enjoy peaceably among ourselves alone the whole exercise of God's worship and of church government, namely, by a pastor, elder, and deacons in our several assemblies without any tradition of men whatsoever, according only to the specification of God's written word and no otherwise, which hitherto as yet in this our present state we could never enjoy. Provided always, that whosoever will enter into this way shall (1) before a Justice of Peace first take the oath of your Majesty's supremacy and royal authority as the laws of the land at this present time do set forth the same; (2) And shall also afterwards keep brotherly communion with the rest of our English churches as they are now established, according as the French and Dutch churches do; (3) And shall truly pay all payments and duties both ecclesiastical and civil, as at this present they stand bound to pay in any respect whatsoever; (4) And if any trespass be committed by any of them whether ecclesiastically or civilly against good order and Christian obedience; That then the same person shall be dealt withall therein by any of your Majesty's civil magistrates, etc.'

That is a good summary of what these men were standing for at that time, namely, about 1605. They desire in their congregations 'a pastor, elder, and deacons,' and they did not wish to be compelled to follow any human tradition. They were willing to take the oath of supremacy, to remain in brotherly communion with the Church of England and to pay all dues, etc.

About the same time in a paper by Jacob called *Principles and Foundations of Christian Religion* he gave his definition of a true visible church: 'A true visible or ministerial church of Christ is a particular congregation, being a spiritual perfect corporation of believers, and having power in its self immediately from Christ to administer all religious means of faith to the members thereof.'

Then with regard to the question as to how such a church is to be constituted and gathered he says – 'By a free mutual consent of believers joining and covenanting to live as members of a holy society together in all religious and virtuous duties as Christ and his apostles did institute and practise in the gospel. By such a free mutual consent also all civil perfect corporations did first begin.' The officers of a church are to be 'A pastor or bishop, with elders, and deacons.' This is his position; he is advocating the employment of covenants in forming a church in the way that afterwards became so well-known and popular, and what he wants is an 'Independent or Congregational non-Separatist Church.' This is most important. He was not a Separatist and he never became a Separatist. But he did believe 'that each congregation in the Church of England was sufficient to determine its own policy and manage its own affairs without the necessity of assistance from archbishops and bishops, or even from classes, synods, etc.' This was his position about 1605.

In 1610 – I reminded you that he met John Robinson at that time – Jacob published a most important book with the title *The Divine Beginning and Institution of Christ's True, Visible, and Ministerial Church.* As this is a most important point in this history I must quote some passages from this treatise of *The Divine Beginning,* as it was generally known. Jacob writes: 'I acknowledge that in England there are true visible churches and ministers, though *accidentally,* yet, such as I refuse not to communicate with. My meaning is, that as these particular congregations have in them godly and holy Christians associated together, to serve God, so far as they see, agreeable to his word: so they are in right from Christ essentially true churches of God, and as such to be acknowledged by us, and in public not to be absolutely separated from.'

Again we are reminded that he was not a Separatist and that there is a difference between a Separatist and an Independent. But here are some further extracts from this famous book, *The Divine Beginning:*

'Two sorts of men there are, Christian reader, who have chiefly occasioned the publishing of this treatise. The first is those who do hold and maintain that Christ Jesus in the New Testament hath instituted no certain form of a visible church nor church government for us; but hath left the same arbitrary, and free to the discretion of men in authority to erect and to set up, to alter and change again, as they in their opinions shall think most fit for the several states and towns wherein they live; and so withal they hold and confess that Christ, in respect of his church and government as it is visible and outward, is *not* king, or lord, or lawgiver to the same. The second sort is those who so plainly and clearly acknowledge that Christ *is* King, Lord, and Law-giver of his church as it is visible and outward, and that he hath instituted in the New Testament, as in the Old, a certain form of his visible church and government, for us everywhere and for ever, not to be altered or changed by any man or men whatever they be. Thus these most truly and soundly do profess and teach that Christians ought so to believe. Yet I know not how, nor on what reason they live themselves, and are well content that others also do live, continue, and remain in a clear contrary practice; that is, first, not at all to participate in any such form of a visible church and government as they profess is of Christ's institution in the New Testament, and consequently is his visible kingdom on earth; secondly, they submit and stand subject unto a provincial diocesan lord bishop's ecclesiastical government and remain apparent members of a provincial church never instituted, yet is contrary to this said reformation and therefore he is not King and Lord of such a church; neither hath he promised nor can we ordinarily have assurance of any spiritual blessing therein.

'These two sorts of men, beloved of the Lord Jesus, have given the occasion of writing this little treatise, which maketh manifestly and I hope soundly and sufficiently against the former, in a direct course of argumentation; against the latter, by necessary infallible consequence; and verily there is no Christian heart, I suppose, if he will deeply and advisably weigh the matter with an upright and single conscience in God's own presence, but will confess with me that both these sorts of persons (especially their errors) are, justly in these our days, needfully to be reproved. For it is evident in the eyes of all men who look into the case, that by the opinions and profession of the former a wide door is opened, and an easy way for libertines to walk in; and Familists, as they are called in England, who taking for their ground that the outward form of the church, ministry, and ceremonies in respect of God's law are things *indifferent,* do make no matter to present themselves upon occasion, either privately or publicly, to the exercise of any religion, and from thence do quickly gather, by a likely consequence of reason as it seemeth to them, that seeing those things so nearly concerning God's special worship are indifferent, therefore other outward things are indifferent also, and ought not to trouble any man's conscience, nor are to be held either as commanded or forbidden by God: *from whence a world of impieties and most unchristian practices do overflow the land'* – and on he goes with a similar kind of argument.

This particular book was one of the things that helped to turn John Robinson from being a Separatist into an Independent.

In the year 1611 Henry Jacob published another book amplifying what he had said, and setting out his arguments still more clearly. He adduced additional proofs from the Scripture, and the testimonies of the learned and the godly men from the days of apostles, that *'church government ought to be always with the people's consent,'* and that *'A true church under the gospel containeth no more congregations but one*. The members of the church created anew in Christ Jesus, have the right and power to choose pastors called to the work by the grace of God, and not by influence transmitted through the polluted channel of the Papacy.'

Then he goes on to show, as he sees it, that the arguments brought forward to justify the Church of England position really play into the hands of the papists at that point: 'Well, will our adversaries say that the Protestant's ministry is justified sufficiently against the Papists, albeit the people have no consent in their minister's calling? Oh, would God-learned men in England would show this substantially. Then would I, for my part, quickly conform. *But otherwise let them be assured the Church of Rome, do what they can, will get ground of them in England, and this maketh me to lay this to heart as I do*. Every day we are challenged by the Papists to prove the lawfulness of our ministry in England, and our calling to it. What say our learned men hereunto? A direct answer must be made to this, men's consciences will not be satisfied with dilatory and shifting answers, nor if we leave scruples and difficulties in that we speak.

'To justify the calling of our ministry in England and to prove the lawfulness thereof, *we must plainly show that the persons who give this calling with us have good authority to give the same.* This is the very point; let our learned men make this clear, and then let the Papists be stopped, then all men are satisfied. For it is a plain case and granted of all, that every true ministry in the church must be received from some persons who have good and just authority to give it; and this is essential to every true ministry.'

Jacob works that out to the point that ultimately the argument, as he sees it, of the Church of England is this: 'The Pope is he who made Archbishop Cranmer and Ridley such bishops. They had no other ordination since. And from them all the rest of our ministers have had their ordination to this day. And so the effect of all this is, that our whole ministry in England successively and derivatively cometh from the Pope, all that maintain the church state in England will thus answer. But oh, miserable defence, and woeful unto us, which indeed, though it be false, yet it is such as the Papists desire, and do triumph in. It is false in two ways. First, *whatsoever the Church of Rome* did give to Archbishop Cranmer, etc., that wholly they took away again, namely, when he fell from them, for then they both deposed him and excommunicated him. So that they left him no whit of that power and function which they had given him. But, *questionless, if they could give it they could take it away,* wherefore, so soon as he was ours, being thus cut off and excommunicated from the Church of Rome, he could not after that have any power (as derived from them) to make ministers, nor to do any other bishoply act. Secondly, we all know the Church of Rome to be the very Antichrist, chiefly in respect of their clergy and spiritual government, and most chiefly of all in respect of the Pope, from whom all the rest, as from the head, do take their power and authority. Now shall we say that very Antichrist can have power from Christ to make ministers? Or that we have a lawful ministry derived from those who had their power only from him? It cannot be. What communion hath light with darkness? What concord hath Christ with Belial? And so what hath Christ to do with Antichrist? Nothing at all. Thus then our consciences can have no assurance, we cannot have confidence in such estate of that ministry. But, certainly, Christ's true ministers among us in England have a better original than this. *Wherefore the answer of our state Protestants must be false.* Yet in this answer who seeth not how the Papists do rejoice, triumph, and insult? Who seeth not how by this they are encouraged, strengthened, and multiplied among us exceedingly. Truly, it would pity a man's heart to behold how this one point putteth life into thousands to stand up against *Christ's Gospel and liberty of their country also*. For when they hear ourselves openly ascribe to the Church of Rome, and to their means, such a gift of grace, even that which is our glory, even the holy instrument of our faith unto salvation, for so is our ministry, they will say: if the branch be holy, the root is more; if the rivers be sweet, the head spring is delicious. And so how can it be chosen, but that the Papists will be graced, and get advantage among us?'

That book, again, of course, influenced Robinson and a number of other people. All that was in 1611.

## III

After this, events moved rapidly, and it became clearer and clearer to this man that he must come back to England, and that he must establish a church on the lines that he had indicated in those books to which I have referred. Thus it came to pass that in 1616 – three hundred and fifty years ago exactly – he came back to this country with that intent. And he put it into operation. At this point let me quote from the second volume of Champlin Burrage where he gives an account of this as gleaned from the Gould Manuscript which is preserved in Regent's Baptist College and in which a history of all this is written in the so-called Jessey Records. This record tells us that Henry Jacob had much conference about these things both here in this country and after that in the Low Countries. He had conversed and discoursed much with Mr John Robinson, late pastor to the church at Leyden, and with others about these matters, and, returning to England, in London he held several meetings with the most famous men for godliness and learning such as Mr Throgmorton and Mr Travers – that is the famous Walter Travers who was, you remember, a colleague of the famous Richard Hooker in the Temple Church, Hooker in the morning saying one thing, Travers saying the exact opposite in the afternoon. Others consulted were Wing, Richard Maunsell, and John Dodd. He was brought to this position by these consultations, 'that having seriously weighed all things and circumstances, Mr Jacob and some others sought the Lord about them in fasting and prayer together. At last it was concluded by the most of them that it was a very warrantable and commendable way to set up that course here as well as in Holland or elsewhere, whatsoever troubles should ensue. Henry Jacob was willing to adventure himself for the Kingdom of Christ's sake, the rest encouraged him.'

And so we come to the formation of this church in Southwark, here in London, in the year 1616. I have completely failed to find the name of the street, we simply know that it was in Southwark, and this is the account: 'Hereupon the said Henry Jacob with Sabine, Staiesmore, Richard Browne, David Prior, and various other well-informed saints have appointed a day to seek the face of the Lord in fasting and prayer, wherein that particular of their union together as a church was mainly commended to the Lord, in the ending of the day they were united. Thus, those who minded this present union, now so joining together joined both hands each with other brother and stood in a ringwise: their intent being declared, Henry Jacob and each of the rest made some confession or profession of their faith and repentance, some were longer, some were briefer. Then they covenanted together to walk in all God's ways as he had revealed or should make known to them; thus was the beginnings of that church.'

Within a few days they gave notice to the brethren here of the Ancient church – which is a reference to the church of the Separatists. There had been several Separatist churches in the time of Barrowe and Greenwood and Penry, but most of the members had been put to death and the churches had been exterminated; but there were still odd people about meeting together; and so

Jacob and his friends gave notice to them: 'In the same year the said Henry Jacob with the advice and consent of the church, and of some of those Reverend preachers before-said, published to the world "A Confession and Protestation in the name of certain Christians showing therein wherein they consent in doctrine with the Church of England, and wherein they were bound to dissent, with their evidence from the Holy Scriptures for their dissent in about twenty-eight particulars."'

I have here a copy of the first edition of this confession: *'A Confession and Protestation of the faith of certain Christians in England, holding it necessary to observe, and keep all Christ's true substantial ordinances for his church visible and political (that is, endued with power of outward spiritual government) under the gospel; though the same do differ from the common order of the land. Published for the clearing of the said Christians from the slander of schism, and novelty, and also of separation, and undutifulness to the magistrate, which their rash adversaries do falsely cast upon them.'*

After a brief introduction, there follow twenty-eight points. I am not going to go through them in detail but will simply give the outline and essence of each:

1. *Christ's offices*. This summarises what I quoted just now from the work Jacob published in 1610. The point is that Christ is the king of the church in these matters of order and of government as well as in the other matters.

2. *Scripture all-sufficient*. Here again it is said that there are clear instructions in the Scripture as to how a church should be formed in that way – that Christ, in other words, has exercised his lordship in this respect through what we find in the Scriptures.

3. *Church's distinction,* or an alternative heading, *Christ's true visible church generally*. 'We believe that Christ's true church is to be noted and considered four ways' – and then the different forms of the church are described.

4. Now comes a much more interesting point. *Christ's true visible political church in a more special manner*. This says: 'We believe that the nature and essence of Christ's true visible church under the gospel is a free congregation of Christians for the service of

God, or a true spiritual body politic containing no more ordinary congregations but one, and that independent. Wherein chiefly two points are to be noted. First, that a true visible political church under the gospel is but one ordinary congregation: and this is to be seen plainly in these scriptures.' A list follows, starting with Matthew 18:17; 1 Corinthians 5:4, 12, 13; 1 Corinthians 11:18, 20, and so on. Then: 'The second point here to be noted is, That by God's ordinance this one ordinary congregation of Christians is a spiritual body politic; and so it is a free congregation independent. That is, it hath from God the right and power of spiritual administration, and government in itself, and over itself by the common and free consent of the people independently, and immediately under Christ, always in the best order they can. Which these places do prove' – again we have a list of scriptural quotations.

5. *Synods and councils*. This is also interesting. 'Howbeit we acknowledge with all, that there may be, and that on occasion there ought to be on earth a consociation of congregations or churches, namely by way of synods.' Now while they believed in Independence in one sense they were not isolationists, they believed in this 'consociation' of churches 'namely by way of synods.' But they go on, 'But not a subordination or, surely, not a subjection of the congregations under any higher spiritual authority absolute, save only Christ's and the Holy Scriptures. They who deny this, maintaining a diocesan and provincial (and neither we nor they themselves know what universal) visible political church both proper and representative, do herein vary from the rule of the gospel.'

6. *Of a catholic, or universal church politic, that is endued with power of outward spiritual government*. 'It is demanded, do we deny an universal visible church under the gospel? We answer, Yea. Under the gospel Christ never instituted, nor God, any one universal visible church either proper or representative, which ordinarily was to exercise outward spiritual government over all persons through the world professing Christianity. No such church is found in the New Testament.'

7. *Of a provincial church independent*. 'It is marvelled, why we likewise deny, that under the gospel there is any true visible political

church, provincial or diocesan; seeing so we shall deny a true visible political church to be now in England, because the English church (as commonly it is holden) is properly a diocesan and provincial, or a national visible political church. We answer, for our parts we acknowledge there are many true visible, yea political churches in England in some degree, and in some respect, yet indeed we deny also a national, a provincial, and diocesan church under the gospel, to be a true visible political church (whether we mean the whole body, or the representative part of such churches) though the public practice among us doth hold them for true political churches. The reason why we deny these also, is, because neither any such is found anywhere set down in God's word of the New Testament, even like as there is no universal church visible political there set down. But only a free congregation, or ordinary assembly is found in the New Testament, as a little before or showed.'

8. *How true visible politic churches are in England.* Here it is shown that though individual churches may be true churches, owing to the system they are in a state of bondage.

9. *Of lord archbishops and lord bishops diocesan and provincial.* 'We believe that the spiritual office, calling, and power, and administration of lord archbishops, and lord bishops diocesan and provincial, with their inferior hierarchy, is contrary to the ecclesiastical order and ordinance of Christ established in the New Testament, and not to be communicated with. The proofs whereof do stand on the grounds of the Article No. 4 before and on those in Article 10 next following after.'

10. *The making of ministers.* 'We believe that the essence of ministers' calling under the gospel is the congregation's consent' – a great point is made of bringing in that whole argument again about the Pope which we saw in one of the other quotations.

11. *Of our communicating with the parish ministers and parishes in England.* 'First, we believe that to think we do, or can receive a ministry essentially from a former minister or a prelate (in these days) is an error, and the thing received is a nullity in that respect. Secondly, this receipt in a parish minister with us maketh not a nullity of the ministry in him in every respect besides; that is, it

maketh not void all trueness of ministry in him.' That is a part of the argument for saying why they could occasionally go to a service in the parish church. They were drawing this distinction between recognising that a man was a godly man, and preached the truth, and the system to which he belonged. So they could go to a service with him occasionally, but they would do so in a way which made it quite clear that they did not believe in nor accept the system of which he was a part.

12. *Touching plurality pastors and non-residents.* This deals with the question of the plurality of pastors and non-residents. They assert that such are 'directly contrary to the order of God in the gospel; and therefore that now they are simply unlawful; and likewise deputed and substituted pastors by private authority, such as curates are. And mere lecturers are little better.'

13. The question of *discipline and censures* is here dealt with: 'We believe that true administering of the holy censures to be by the congregation's consent also. And therefore not to be lawfully done by an absolute diocesan or provincial authority; that is, if it be without any necessary concurrence or consent of that congregation, which it chiefly concerneth.'

14. *Touching the number of pastors in each church; and of the pastor's ordinary power and authority in managing the church's spiritual affairs and government.* It is said that there should be at least one pastor in each church; there may be more, but there should be at least one; and as we have seen already, they believe also in having elders and deacons.

15. *Touching the profane and scandalous mixtures of people in the congregation.* 'We believe concerning mixtures of the open profane with some manifest godly Christians in a visible church, though at once it doth not destroy essentially, nor make void the holiness of that whole assembly, yet truly it putteth that whole assembly into a most dangerous and desperate estate by such their confusion, and by such extreme peril of further infection, especially if they do long tolerate the same among them.' Because of the danger to their souls the people are expected to leave such churches. That is the argument, you see, for a pure church.

16. *Of traditions human.* These they denounced and would not have for the reasons already given in a previous quotation.

17. *Of traditions apostolic.* 'We believe that every ordinance or institution apostolic (and that must unto us out of the Holy Scripture be proved) is divine, that is to say, of divine authority, instituted of God simply unchangeable by men, and such, that of right it ought to be used perpetually and universally among Christians, unless God himself (by his own work) do let it, or make it void.'

18. *Of prophecy, as the apostle calleth it.* 'We believe that the sober, discreet, orderly, and well-governed exercise of expounding and applying the Scriptures in the congregation, by the apostle called prophesying, and allowed expressly by him to any understanding member of the church (but women) is lawful now, convenient, profitable, yea sometime very necessary also in divers respects.' In other words, a man who shows that he has got a gift is allowed to exercise it that way, but not women.

19. *Of the reading of homilies in the church.* 'We believe that with us the reading of homilies in divine service is not lawful, but very unmeet for the congregation of the faithful: namely, where it is held for competent without the employment of a preaching pastor.' You see, if they did that instead of having a preaching pastor it is wrong. 'Whereas a pastor's diligent, discreet, and judicious preaching, and applying of God's word, is the power of God unto salvation ordinarily. Neither doth every of the allowed homilies in every point contain good doctrine.'

20. *Of Christ's descending into hell.* Jacob had had a controversy over that with a bishop about the year 1600, and in this confession he makes his position clear with respect to that, namely, that it simply means that our Lord was at that point under the power of death.

21. Deals with *prayer.* 'We believe concerning prayer: that though every form of prayer prescribed by men be not absolutely nor simply a sin, neither (as we judge) an idol, nor an invention of man, nor a transgression of the second commandment; yet we constantly avouch and profess a prescribed Liturgy, or a Book of Common Prayer by commandment enforced upon a whole

church rightly constituted, to be used still in the very same words whenever they assemble (in comparison of other praying) is not so profitable but rather hurtful in many users of it, as making holy zeal, true piety, sincere godliness, and other gifts of God's Spirit in many of them to languish. The New Testament toucheth no such matter, neither troubleth itself with endeavouring on uniformity in this point, but leaveth all churches herein to their godly liberty, wisdom, understanding, and diligent consideration of themselves,' etc.

22. *Of holy days so-called.* 'Now we believe that under the gospel there is not any holy day (besides the Lord's day) nor any fasting day, or days constant, ordinary, and on certain seasons or times of the year continually to be observed.' You can see the obvious thrust of that.

23. *Of marriage and burying, and churching, as it is called.* 'Concerning making of marriage and burying the dead, we believe that they are no actions of a church minister (because they are no actions spiritual) but civil. Neither are ministers called to any such business; Neither is there so much as one example of any such practice in the whole Book of God either under the law, or under the gospel, without which warrant we believe it to be unlawful whatsoever any minister doth attempt at any time, or in any place, especially as a part of his ministerial office, and function.' That may come as a surprise, but that is their teaching on such matters.

24. *Of ministers also made magistrates by the state.* This is denounced as unlawful and 'contrary to the text of the New Testament.'

25. *Of the gifts and offerings of the faithful.* It is an encouragement to people to bring free-will offerings. Tithes are not altogether condemned. This subject is also partly dealt with in the next point.

26. *Of tithes, and the pastor's fittest, and due and necessary maintenance.* 'We believe that tithes for the pastor's maintenance under the gospel are not the just and due means thereof. Howbeit yet we do not think these tithes absolutely unlawful if they remain voluntary.' They prefer the voluntary system which has been dealt

with in number 25, and encourage the people, as the Scriptures teach, to put their gifts aside on the first day and to take them and offer them to the minister.

27. *Of the civil magistrate's duty, and charge to oversee and order his churches in spiritual matters.* 'We believe that we and all true visible churches ought to be overseen, and kept in good order, and peace, and ought to be governed (under Christ) both supremely, and also sub-ordinately by the civil magistrate: yea in causes of religion when need is.' Here again is very important point of distinction between these Independents and the Separatists who took a very different view of this matter. Later these Independents came to the same view as the Separatists, who saw this point before the Independents saw it. We must be accurate about these matters; and the Independents only came to it afterwards.

This section continues: 'By which rightful power of his, he ought to cherish and prefer the godly, and religious; and to punish the intractable and unreasonable. Howbeit yet always but civilly. And therefore we from our heart most humbly do desire that our gracious sovereign king would (himself or through a magistrate) in clemency take this special oversight, and government of us, to whose ordering and protection we most humbly commit ourselves acknowledging that because we want the use of this divine ordinance, that therefore most great, and infinite evils both to us, and even to the whole kingdom doth ensue, and also because of the spiritual lords their government over us. And notwithstanding the spiritual lords do think it an injury and wrong to themselves not small if the king should substitute civil magistrates to this business, yet that is God's own ordinance.' You see the distinction they are drawing; they will take discipline from a civil magistrate but not from an ecclesiastical one. 'If the king should substitute civil magistrates to this business, yet that is God's own ordinance; and to do otherwise, namely to commit either spiritual or civil government (namely, diocesan or provincial) to ministers of the word, is evil, and (as we believe) a direct transgression of the text of the gospel above rehearsed in Articles 4, 10, and 24.' I am simply reporting, and not expressing my own opinion.

28. *'Touching the necessity that lieth upon us to obey Christ rather than man in our using of the true, and in refusing the contrary ecclesiastical ordinances above specified.'* In other words, this last article enforces the application of the preceding points.

## IV

That, then, is the story. The church was constituted, Henry Jacob was appointed as the pastor, he published these Articles in order to justify what they were doing and to clear themselves from the charge of schism. So the church began and flourished. Jacob was with them until 1624 when he left and went to Virginia in America where he died the following year. He was followed by a succession of godly men, and this was actually the first Independent or Congregational chapel or church that was formed in this country which had a continuous unbroken history.

After the time of the Commonwealth, and still more after 1662, there was a change in certain vital respects and the Independents became true Separatists or free churchmen.

To me, as I said at the beginning, all this is of real interest because it shows us how these men were feeling their way to what they felt was the teaching of God's word, and Christ's will, in these matters. And it is just there, I feel, that it has a real message for us. It is surely a warning to us, therefore, to read the history again, to be sure of our facts, and not to make sweeping generalisations about 'the Puritans said' this or that. Let us try to be sure that we know what we are saying, and that we are accurate in what we are saying as far as we can be.

Secondly, it is a warning to us against rigidity. Let us try to emulate these men in this at any rate. Let us search the Scriptures, let us keep our minds open, let us listen to what others have got to say, and let us recognise that, though we do not understand this there is obviously a human element in all these matters. Some men seem to be able to leap to the true position in one leap as it were, others have to go through steps and stages. To me one of the great lessons I have learned as the result of reading all this once more is that we must be patient with one another, that we must remember that men who are equally honest may differ. We must ever remember what the apostle Paul presses upon the attention of the church at Corinth, namely, that there are strong and weak brethren in every respect practically, in connection with the Christian life; and that it behoves us all to be patient with one another, to try to help one another, and not at any time to quarrel with one another or have bitter feelings towards those who differ. Recognising that these men, who went into all this so thoroughly, took so much time and had to go wearily through these various stages, let us who are in an age when these matters are all being raised once more in an acute way, and who will be called upon to take various decisions of some sort or another in the immediate future, let us try to learn something from this story of Henry Jacob and the first Congregational Church which will be of help and of encouragement to us. May God bless us to that end.

# 1967

## *'Sandemanianism'*

### I

LET me begin by explaining why I have decided to speak on this subject. It is a matter to which I have frequently referred in passing during the whole of my ministry, because I have had an increasing conviction that it is in many ways the most urgent one for us to consider at the present time. If I understand the condition of the church today – and, indeed, during the last fifty years or so – I would say that its great trouble has been that it has fallen into this particular error. I have never before, however, dealt with it specifically or tried to evaluate it as I am now going to do. But a number of things have happened this year and at the end of last year which have crystallised the general vague idea I have had throughout the years and have led me to do this.

Many of you must have noticed that during 1967 the centenary of the death of that truly great chemist Michael Faraday was celebrated; and you may have noticed that he belonged to this particular branch or division of the Christian church which goes under the name of Robert Sandeman. That arrested me at once and brought the subject to the forefront of my mind. In addition, I read a little book called *J. R. Jones, Ramoth and his Times,* by a man called J. Idwal Jones. This was written because it was the bicentenary of the birth of J. R. Jones who was more responsible than anybody else for propagating and spreading the views of Sandeman in North Wales in particular. Reading this out of historical interest made me feel again that this was an indication that I should deal with this matter.

The other thing that brought me to deal with this was that

the great Christmas Evans, who, some would say, was the greatest preacher that the Baptists have ever had in Great Britain – certainly he and Spurgeon would be the two greatest – was born on Christmas Day 1766. Naturally, therefore, I have been reading a good deal about him during the past year; and, as I am going to show you, the whole question of the Sandemanian heresy played a very prominent part in the life of that great preacher. Those are the things, then, that have crystallised my great interest in this subject.

## II

Perhaps the best way of approach would be to tell you something of how this movement, this aberration if you like, began in the Christian church. Here is a little historical background.

It all began with a Scotsman named John Glas in the 1720s. He was a very able man and a minister of the Church of Scotland at a place called Tealing in the County of Angus, not far from Dundee. Glas began to feel uneasy about two matters in particular at first. One was the custom of getting ministers to subscribe to The Solemn League and Covenant which had been introduced in the previous century. This led him into difficulties in his thinking as to the relationship between the church and the state. Principal John Macleod very rightly says of him, that he became a 'voluntary' a century before voluntaryism. 'Glas,' says Macleod, 'made such a thing as a national church, or a national reformation, or a national religion, or a national religious covenant, a sheer impossibility.' He believed in a complete separation of church and state. In other words he became a Separatist.

The other thing that worried Glas was subscription to documents like the Westminster Confession of Faith. He believed that it was sufficient for a man to say that he believed, and accepted, and was prepared to be governed by, the teaching of the Scriptures. He said he was ready to be governed by the word of God, but he was not ready to submit to the words of men. In addition, he began to put forward his particular views as to the nature of saving faith. These three things got him into trouble and he was deposed from his charge and formed an Independent cause in 1733.

John Glas is undoubtedly the father of Independency as far as Scotland is concerned. He was not only a Calvinist, he was a very high Calvinist, and thoroughly orthodox in that sense. But he was in trouble over these other matters. He himself was not a very aggressive man, but he soon had a son-in-law of the name of Robert Sandeman, who was a born controversialist and one who enjoyed writing. He took up the cudgels on behalf of John Glas, and went further than Glas himself ever went. Sandeman became famous through writing a book with the title – *Letters on Theron and Aspasio*. Some of you will recall that *Dialogues between Theron and Aspasio* had been written by the saintly James Hervey of Weston Flavel, now a part of Northampton. Sandeman wrote his 'Letters' attacking the point of view put forward by James Hervey, and in so doing gave a clear outline of the teaching, especially with regard to faith, which had been first propagated by Glas in his sermons and various books.

Added to all this these two men developed various ideas with regard to church government. The first thing was the sharp division between the church and the state. Their desire was, as they felt, to get back to the New Testament pattern; but in doing this they went to extremes. They re-introduced feet-washing, 'the holy kiss,' and a weekly communion. They taught that the possessions of every member of the church should be at the disposal of the church, and that there should be no paid ministers. Incidentally this last is the reason why Lloyd George became a solicitor, and subsequently Prime Minister, rather than a minister of a church. He was brought up in a Sandeman church in North Wales – known there as the Little Baptists of which his shoemaker uncle was the unpaid pastor. They also believed in having a multiplicity of elders in each church, and they prohibited an elder from marrying a second time. They had a very strict church discipline indeed but they always wanted unanimity, and they did not like voting. They wanted a consensus, a general consensus of opinion and unanimity. Furthermore, they believed in casting lots.

Besides these two men there is a third whom I must mention because he became very prominent later on in the century. This was Archibald Maclean, who was at one time a member of John Glas's church, but began to feel that the discipline was too strict, and formed a church of his own in Edinburgh in 1765. While he retained much of the teaching of Glas and Sandeman, Maclean differed from them, in that he became a Baptist. He is really the father of all the Baptist churches in Scotland.

Maclean was a very able man indeed. He was a particularly great admirer of John Owen – that will tell you about his theology, his Calvinism, and so on. He exercised his main influence in the 1780s and the 1790s, and it was he who influenced the Baptist churches in Wales, particularly in North Wales. I should point out, however, that even before that, Glas, and still more Sandeman, who lived for a while in England, had considerable influence. Churches were formed in various parts of England, and the teaching spread into Wales and influenced a man named Popkins, who started a church based on these ideas in Swansea in South Wales. This caused great trouble and was dealt with, as we have heard, by the famous Daniel Rowland amongst others, and also by William Williams the hymn-writer of Pantycelyn.

But it was, as I say, in the late 1780s and 1790s that this Sandemanian teaching really became a menace both in England and in Wales. It produced a reaction from two notable men. The first was the famous Andrew Fuller, who dealt in particular with this teaching in an Appendix to his book *The Gospel Worthy of all Acceptation,* under the heading 'Whether a holy disposition of heart is necessary in order to believing.' This was written in reply to the teaching of Archibald Maclean, who answered it, and then Fuller really dealt with him in a book bearing the title, *Strictures on Sandemanianism in Twelve Letters to a Friend.* It is generally agreed that Fuller more or less demolished Sandemanianism in those twelve letters.

## III

There, then, is the general historical background of this movement. While it is true, as we have seen, that Sandemanianism was in itself a complete system involving matters of church government and order and things of that kind I want to confine attention to one aspect only. That is, the view of faith which was taught by these men. It is important that I should make this clear because Archibald Maclean was constantly at pains to say that he was not a Sandemanian. What he meant by that was, that he did not agree with their entire system. But he did agree with them on this matter that we are going to discuss, namely, their view of faith. This was, in fact, common to them all, and it is interesting to observe that Dr John Macleod says that the great Dr Thomas Chalmers approximates very closely to this particular view of the nature of saving faith.

As we come to consider this subject I want to make it clear that I am not only going to deal with it as it was explicitly propounded by these men, but also with the modifications of it, which I believe have come down even to our day. I want also to stress the fact that this view of faith can be adopted by Calvinists as well as Arminians.

There is a danger sometimes – and I confess I have tended to drop into it myself – to equate this Sandemanian heresy concerning the nature of faith with what we have called 'Believism,' and which we attribute only to Arminians. The fact is, however, that this particular view of faith is one which can be held by Calvinists as well as Arminians. As I have told you, Glas, Sandeman, and Archibald Maclean were all strong Calvinists, and Maclean's great hero was the celebrated Dr John Owen. So you can be a high Calvinist and still be guilty of this particular error or heresy.

The vital question is, What is the true nature of saving faith? Perhaps the simplest way of putting it before you is to read a short extract from Robert Sandeman's book. The matter on the title-page of this book is, 'One thing is needful,' and all along one leading point is kept in view which the author calls, 'The sole requisite to justification or acceptance with God, in opposition to those who while they openly avow only one meritorious cause of justification do yet lead the guilty to seek after some inward motion, feelings, or desires, as some way requisite in order to acceptance with God.' Among 'those' to whom he refers he ranks Isaac Watts, Philip

Doddridge, Thomas Boston, the Erskines, and amongst the others was John Wesley, whom he vilified and regarded as one of the most dangerous men that had ever appeared in the church. 'By the sole requisite' he understands 'the work finished by Christ in his death, proved by his resurrection to be all-sufficient to justify the guilty.' Now here is the point: he maintains, 'that the whole benefit of this event is conveyed to men only by the apostolic report concerning it, that every one who understands this report to be true, or is persuaded that the event actually happened as testified by the apostles, is justified and finds relief to his guilty conscience. That he is relieved not by finding any favourable symptoms about his own heart, but by finding their report to be true.' That is a very good definition of this position.

But let me, to make it still more plain and clear, give you Principal John Macleod's view of it. He says that the teaching of Glas 'is fitted to put a premium upon what is held to be orthodox doctrine, and to lay less stress than is called for on the reaction of the emotional nature to the truth of the gospel, and on the activity of the will as that goes out in the trust of the heart and its attendant obedience in the life.'

The Westminster Confession, as you know, puts great emphasis upon this 'trust of the heart,' that it is not merely an intellectual acceptance of the facts. Indeed, as Principal Macleod points out so rightly, the Sandemanian teaching was in a way a return to the Roman Catholic teaching, which is, that all you have to do is to believe and accept the teaching of the church. You accept that with your mind, and that is all that is necessary. So he ends by saying that 'it held itself coldly aloof from any display of feelings in the exercises of a religious life.' Now that is the very essence of this matter.

The same thing is put quite clearly by Andrew Fuller. He says, 'It is a bare belief of the bare truth. It excludes from it all pertaining to the will and the affections except as "fruits" produced by it.' Everything that happens in the will and in the affections is only the fruit of this belief and is not a part of it. 'They will not have,' he says, 'even a hearty persuasion, but emphasise only notional belief. It is knowledge with approbation.'

William Williams (Pantycelyn) puts it like this, that 'it sets naked faith' – 'naked' faith – 'as the chief thing, believing without power, making little of conviction and of a broken heart.'

There, you have an idea as to what this particular teaching was. Its proponents were very fond of putting it like this; that we are asked to believe the testimony of God in the Scriptures as we believe any other testimony. They said, you believe the testimony of a man so you must believe this. They said, there is a difference in the object of what you believe, but they taught that as regards the belief itself there is no difference between believing the testimony, the ordinary testimony of a man or a witness in a court or in private, and believing the testimony of God in the Scriptures. So they emphasised 'notional belief.' They went beyond saying that faith and other things are not the ground of justification; and said that it must be just naked belief. They therefore excluded all endeavours, and prayers, and religious exercises, and appeals that come to us, and so on. That is the essence of their position.

You may well ask, how was it that able men like this should ever have made such a point of this? What was their object in doing this; what led them to do this? Their answer was that they were trying to safeguard the doctrine of justification by faith only; and they felt that the others were re-introducing works. They were particularly opposed to those whom they called 'the popular preachers,' like Wesley and Whitefield, and the others whom I have mentioned. The same thing was true of their followers in Wales. They were particularly opposed to the popular Calvinistic Methodist travelling preachers, who preached in a very emotional manner, and who provoked visible results in their congregations in the matter of emotions and so on. This was the thing which they disliked so much. They said that these men were turning faith into a work by introducing other elements.

This was put very plainly and clearly by Maclean himself. He said that to include good dispositions, holy affections, and pious exercises of the heart as demanded by law was to re-introduce works. That was the essence of their difficulty. They said that if you introduced any element of feeling, any kind of holy affections or desires you were introducing works, and that the only way to safeguard 'justification by faith only' was to say that faith was something solely in the intellect. It was 'naked' belief by the intellect.

On what grounds did they say this? These were scripturally-minded men, who accepted the authority of the Scriptures. As I say, they not only accepted them, but they thought that they were doing so more than anybody else. They were criticising the Church of Scotland and the Westminster Confession because, as they felt, the church was putting the definitions of men before the word of God. And yet this was the conclusion to which they came.

On what grounds did they do so? Their great text, of course, was Romans 4:5: 'But to him that worketh not, but believeth on him that justifieth the ungodly.' And they interpreted the word 'ungodly' as meaning 'those who were enemies of God,' who at the very time they believed were enemies of God. They argued that it was the only possible meaning you can give to this word 'ungodly.' Thus you have got to say that when they believed they were ungodly. That was their great text.

The other text they used a good deal was, 'Whosoever believeth that Jesus is the Christ is born of God: and everyone that loveth him that begat loveth him also that is begotten of him' (1 John 5:1). That was their position, that it had to be 'naked faith.' That might well lead perhaps to feelings and to actions by the will later, but you must exclude everything like that entirely from your definition of faith.

The questions, therefore, that are raised for us are these. What is the nature of saving faith, is it naked and notional only; or are feelings and the will included? That is the first question. The second is, does faith precede or follow repentance? And thirdly, does faith precede or follow regeneration?

## IV

Those questions show clearly why I suggest that this is a very contemporary subject. Indeed I would go further and suggest that it is one of the main problems before us at the present time. These were certainly the questions that were raised and debated at that time in the eighteenth century. As I have reminded you, William Williams of Pantycelyn, the great hymn-writer, dealt with these questions very strongly in several works, and made great use of his extraordinary gift of ridicule. He settled the matter as regards the Methodists, at any rate in Wales, in the 1760s. Then, as I have told you, Andrew Fuller dealt with it in his way. In addition Thomas Scott, the commentator, dealt with it in his work, *The Warrant and Nature of Faith in Christ.*

What were the arguments of these men against this teaching propounded by Glas, Sandeman, and Maclean? I shall try to summarise them. The first question, obviously, is this – the exegesis of Romans 4:5. What is meant by 'the ungodly'? As these protagonists, and especially Andrew Fuller, pointed out very clearly, the very cases quoted by Paul in Romans 4 made the Sandemanian interpretation quite impossible. The apostle is actually dealing at that point with the case of Abraham in the first instance. He is showing how this teaching of justification by faith only, which he has been elaborating in the first three chapters of that epistle to the Romans and especially as he summed it up in chapter 3, is not anything new, but that this is what happened in the case of Abraham.

They went on to show quite clearly that as you read what Paul goes on to say about Abraham, you find that all this happened, not when he was in Ur of the Chaldees, but long afterwards when for some time he had been a godly and a God-fearing man. It is, therefore, ridiculous to describe Abraham at the point when this term is used with respect to him, as 'ungodly' in the sense of meaning an enemy of God. In the same way Andrew Fuller pointed out that the case of David, which Paul also quotes in that chapter, is exactly parallel with that of Abraham, and that, if you take the trouble to turn up the Scriptures, you will find that both Abraham and David cannot at any point be described as 'enemies of God.' They were both godly men.

What Paul is concerned to show and to emphasise is that they were not justified by their works. He is not trying to say that they were enemies of God at this point, but he is saying that it is not their works that save them. It is through the faith which has been given to them that they are justified; that is how it comes to them. It is the action of God, and not their action. As Fuller and others pointed out, verse 20 of that chapter really settles the matter. There, the apostle, coming back to the case of Abraham, actually says about him, 'He staggered not at the promise of God through unbelief; he gave God the glory.' 'He gave God the glory'! The argument is that in no sense can this be described as something 'notional,' 'purely intellectual,' or 'naked faith,' but that of necessity it includes these other qualities of heart and will.

Then, of course, you have to deal with a statement like that in Romans 10, verses 9 and 10. This statement inevitably played a great part in the whole contention, 'That if thou shalt confess with thy mouth the Lord Jesus, and shalt believe in thine heart that God hath raised him from the dead, thou shalt be saved. For with the heart man believeth unto righteousness; and with the mouth confession is made unto salvation.' Of course the followers of Glas and Sandeman had to say that the 'heart' there simply means the mind. But it was pointed out to them that this is not the way in which the Scripture uses the term 'heart.' It does not confine it to the affections, but it means the centre of the personality, the centre of man's being including all these various faculties, not exclusively the mind but including the others also. We shall come to the exegesis of 1 John 5:1 later on.

That is the general answer to the Sandemanian view of faith. But we must get a little closer to this and examine more clearly what the Scripture tells us directly about the nature of faith. Here are the answers which these men gave between them. They pointed out, in the first instance, that faith is a duty, and therefore of necessity the will is included.

Secondly, they pointed out that faith is a grace given by the Holy Spirit. Here, they quoted 1 Corinthians 13, 'Now abideth faith, hope, charity …' As it is a grace, it cannot be confined to the head only and to the intellect; it is not merely something notional.

Again, they pointed out how in Romans 4:20, Paul says that faith 'gives glory to God,' and you cannot give glory to God only with your mind. The whole person is involved. So they argued that if you just look at what we are told about faith by way of definition in the New Testament that is what you find.

Then they went on to point out that faith, according to the Scriptural teaching, depends upon choice, or upon the state of the heart with regard to God, or towards God. At this point they quoted a great deal, and rightly, from the Gospel of John, chapter 5 towards the end, where our Lord says things like this: 'Ye have not his word abiding in you; for whom he hath sent ye believe not. Search the Scriptures; for in them ye think ye have eternal life; and they are they which testify of me. And ye will not come unto me, that ye might have life' (verses 38-40). 'I know you, that ye have not the love of God in you' (verse 42). 'How can ye believe, which receive honour one of another, and seek not the honour that cometh from God only?' (verse 44).

There they were able to show clearly that a question of choice is involved, and that that is determined by the state of the heart towards God.

In addition to that, they said that the whole idea of faith is expressed in terms which indicate the exercise of affection. They produced many examples of this. Take the word 'receiving' or 'receiving not' for instance in 2 Thessalonians 2:10, where you find 'receiving the love of the truth that ye may be saved.' The whole term 'receiving' is something that includes the affection; it implies the engagement of the affections. The very term 'receiving' or 'not receiving' carries that implication.

Further, as we have already seen in Romans 10 the apostle puts his emphasis upon 'believing with the heart.' 'Confession is made with the mouth' but you believe in the 'heart.' He deliberately says that, in order, as Fuller and the others argued, to show that it is not merely a matter of giving an intellectual assent, but that you wholeheartedly do this, that this has become now something vital to you and the whole of your personality. You believe with the heart. Then you have in Acts 8:37 the report of the Ethiopian eunuch asking Philip to baptize him. The reply he got was, 'If thou believest with all thine heart, thou mayest.' So again you have this same emphasis upon the heart.

Another most powerful argument, it seems to me, is that want of faith is generally ascribed to moral causes, or to a want of a right disposition. Take again those verses at the end of John 5, and still more striking, the series of statements in John 8 from verse 33 onwards. You remember our Lord had just said, 'If ye continue in my word, then are ye my disciples indeed; and ye shall know the truth, and the truth shall make you free,' and then the Jews answered him, 'We be Abraham's seed, and were never in bondage to any man: how sayest thou, Ye shall be made free?' Here is the conflict, here is the unbelief; and what our Lord says to them is this: 'I know that ye are Abraham's seed, but ye seek to kill me, because my word hath no place in you. I speak that which I have seen with my Father: and ye do that which ye have seen with your father' (verses 37, 38). They objected to this and said, 'Abraham is our father.' And he said, 'If ye were Abraham's children, ye would do the works of Abraham. But now ye seek to kill me, a man that hath told you the truth, which I have heard of God … Ye do the deeds of your father,' and so on. 'Jesus said unto them, if God were your Father, ye would love me; for I proceeded forth and came from God' (verses 39-42). Their whole unbelief is based upon their not loving him, their antagonism to him in fact, and that is something, of course, that we can link up with various other statements also. You have the phrase in Hebrews 3 about 'an evil heart of unbelief.' An evil 'heart' of unbelief!

Moreover, there are those statements which are to be found in Ephesians 4, verse 17, and following: 'This I say therefore, and testify in the Lord, that ye henceforth walk not as other Gentiles walk, in the vanity of their mind, having the understanding darkened, being alienated from the life of God through the ignorance that is in them, because of the blindness of their heart; who being past feeling have given themselves over unto lasciviousness to work all uncleanness with greediness,' and so on.

All these statements show that unbelief is due always to a state of the heart. That is what produces it and governs it. It is not a mere error of the understanding; indeed it is what Paul says in Romans 8:7. 'It is enmity against God; it is not subject to the law of God, neither indeed can be.' The trouble with the unbeliever is not simply in his mind; it is much deeper, it is an 'enmity against God,' it is 'an evil heart of unbelief.' There is the essential trouble.

Those were the main arguments that were brought against the Sandemanians to show the true nature of faith – saving faith – and that it clearly, in the light of all these Scriptures, is not something that you can confine to the mind or to the intellect.

Then what about that second question about the relationship between repentance and faith? Here is something which, you will agree again, is very important at this precise time. Sandeman and the rest taught that faith comes first and is followed by repentance. Others in their replies were concerned to show that it is the other way round, that faith implies repentance, and that therefore if there is no repentance there is no true faith. They quoted large numbers of Scriptures here as we must of necessity do. Fuller puts it in a phrase. 'Faith without repentance is not genuine.'

What were the Scriptures with which they were concerned at this point? There are many Scriptures which demonstrate that repentance always comes first. You find this in the Gospels. John the Baptist precedes our Lord and he preached a baptism of repentance. 'Prepare ye the way of the Lord,' was his message. You will find this summary of the beginning our Lord's own ministry in Mark 1:15, 'Jesus came into Galilee, preaching the gospel of the kingdom of God, and saying, The time is fulfilled, the kingdom of God is at hand: repent ye, and believe the gospel.' That is the order, repentance first and belief of the gospel following.

There are also a number of other passages which we can quote. You remember how at the very end, just before our Lord ascended you have the account in Luke 24 of how he spoke in that upper room with his disciples and said, 'Thus it is written, and thus it behoved Christ to suffer, and to rise from the dead the third day: and that repentance and remission of sins should be preached in his name among all nations, beginning at Jerusalem.'

When you move on to the book of the Acts of the Apostles you have the notable event on the Day of Pentecost reported in Acts 2. As Peter was preaching, they cried out saying, 'Men and brethren, what shall we do?' And the reply was, 'Repent, every one of you, and be baptized in the name of the Lord Jesus Christ for the remission of sins' (Acts 2:37 and 38). But note the order – 'Repent' is the first thing, and then the other follows.

You have exactly the same thing in Acts 3:19 – the same order. You have got it again in Acts 5:31. You have it in that most beautiful and lyrical statement in Acts 20 where Paul is saying farewell to the elders of the church at Ephesus, and makes his appeal to them. He calls them to witness with regard to the character of his own ministry: 'Serving the Lord with all humility of mind, and with many tears and temptations, which befell me by the lying in wait of the Jews: and how I have kept nothing back that was profitable unto you, and have taught you publicly, and from house to house, testifying to the Jews, and also to the Greeks, repentance toward God, and faith toward our Lord Jesus Christ.' The order: repentance first, and faith following it. You get precisely the same thing in Acts 26:18, in the commission given by the risen Lord to Saul of Tarsus. Indeed, as the opponents of the Sandemanians pointed out, the case of the publican in our Lord's parable of the Publican and the Pharisee who went up into the temple to pray indicated precisely the same thing (Luke 18:9-14). The feeling, and the sorrow for sin is what is emphasised.

That is the evidence which goes to show that you cannot have saving faith without repentance. You can have an intellectual assent to propositions, you can have a notional faith, but you cannot have saving faith without repentance. Repentance is involved in it, and it is in a sense because you repent that you believe. It is that which leads you to believe. It is that which shows you the necessity of believing in the Saviour. To say that you can have faith without it, and that faith is something that leads to it, is clearly to be going contrary to the teaching of the Scriptures.

That brings us to the last issue that I suggest was raised by all this; the relationship between faith and regeneration. You will agree that we are living in an age when it has been the custom to say, and to teach, that faith leads to regeneration, and that one of the inducements held out to people for believing is, that if they will believe then they become regenerate and will receive a new nature. This teaching is generally based upon the teaching of 1 John 5:1; and others would try to produce evidence from John 1 verses 12 and 13: 'To them that received him gave he power to become the sons of God.'

This, again, is surely a very important point. How did Fuller and the other opponents of Sandemanianism deal with this matter? Their method was the obvious one, if we are going to be governed in our thinking by the Scriptures. You start, for instance, with what our Lord said to Nicodemus. Here is a man who patently comes with the idea, and the supposition, that there is a new teacher who has got some novel teaching and he wants to know what it is in order that he may evaluate it and add it to his own. At once he is interrupted by our Lord's statement, 'Verily, verily, I say unto thee, Except a man be born again he cannot see the kingdom of God.' There has got to be this radical change. He has got to be 'born of the Spirit.' 'That which is born of the flesh is flesh; that which is born of the Spirit is spirit.' This miraculous, marvellous thing that no one can understand, comparable to the wind, as the eighth verse puts it, must happen to us before we either understand or accept his teaching. This is the whole basis.

Added to that, as I have said, you have Romans 8:7, 'The carnal mind is enmity against God: it is not subject to the law of God, neither indeed can be.' It is impossible. Before a man can believe and accept God's word and God's way of salvation he must have a new mind. It cannot be done with the carnal mind.

But this is put still more plainly and strongly and clearly in the series of statements Paul makes in 1 Corinthians 2. We read there, 'We speak the wisdom of God in a mystery,' but Paul has already said that it is 'not the wisdom of this world, nor of the princes of this world, that come to nought.' That puts out the natural man, who is an enemy against God. That is not the wisdom of which he is speaking. 'We speak the wisdom of God in a mystery, even the hidden wisdom, which God ordained before the world unto our glory: which none of the princes of this world knew: for had they known it, they would not have crucified the Lord of glory' – and so on. Then from verse 10: 'God hath revealed them unto us by his Spirit ... What man knoweth the things of a man, save the spirit of man which is in him? even so the things of God knoweth no man, but the Spirit of God. Now we have received, not the spirit of the world, but the Spirit which is of God; that we might know the things that are freely given to us of God. Which things also we speak, not in the words which man's wisdom teacheth, but which the Holy Ghost teacheth; comparing spiritual things with spiritual. But the natural man receiveth not the things of the Spirit of God: for they are foolishness unto him: neither can he know them, because they are spiritually discerned. He that is spiritual judgeth all things, yet he himself is judged of no man. For who hath known the mind of the Lord, that he may instruct him? But we have the mind of Christ' (verses 10-16).

There, the apostle is surely demonstrating beyond any question that the natural man – man as he is – is incapable of believing and receiving the word of God with regard to salvation or anything else. That surely demonstrates that until a man is born again he cannot believe, he cannot exercise faith. It is an utter impossibility. It is all 'foolishness' to him, and he dismisses it and rejects it as folly.

At this point I must mention what is – I may say it in fairness – a kind of complication in this whole matter. Glas, as I have told you, was a Calvinist, and he took very great pains to say that this man who is still not born again accepts the witness and the testimony of the Scriptures as the result of the operation of the Holy Spirit upon him. He has got to say that as a Calvinist, has he not? And he does say so; yet he still says that faith is something entirely notional. Sandeman accepted the same position. That was an attempt on their part to answer an obvious difficulty. But still it does not face, as it should have faced, the whole question of the relationship of faith and regeneration.

With regard to 1 John 5:1, 'Whosoever believeth that Jesus is the Christ is born of God,' what that says is, not that he shall be, but that he has been, and the fact that he believes that 'Jesus is the Christ' is the proof of the fact that he has been born of God. It is John's odd way of putting things. As you go through his Epistles you will find that John constantly uses that kind of expression. He seems to put the consequence before the cause. It is an arresting way, and the Spirit used him in that way to give us this truth. So he puts it: 'Whosoever believeth that Jesus is the Christ is born of God' – as if to say, show me a man who says Jesus is the Christ. I tell you that man is born of God. For as Paul puts it, 'No man can say that Jesus is the Lord but by the Holy Ghost.' It is just John's way of putting it.

That is how the answers were given to these three main questions that were raised by this Sandemanian teaching.

## V

What conclusions do we draw from all this? Have I been wasting your time in considering all this? I suggest that I have not, for this reason, that the consequences of this teaching are most serious. And we must examine ourselves in the light of this.

What are the consequences? Clearly it immediately affects evangelism. These men were much opposed to Boston and the Erskines and Flavel in the previous century, and all who preached the law and called to repentance. They said that they were trying to create feelings in their listeners, and that you must not do that. You must just give them the evidence that God has sent his Son into the world to save them. You must not preach the law, and you must not call men to repentance.

There is a good deal of that kind of teaching in our age. A lady came to me in distress in my vestry not long ago, saying that she belonged to a certain group of Christian people in Ireland who taught that it is wrong for a preacher to call people to repentance. They teach that that was only for the Jews at the time of our Lord, but that it is no longer the case: and what we must do is to introduce people to Jesus. They say that that is evangelism – not preaching the law, not trying to create any feelings or holy desires or aspirations or any sense of grieving for sin, or any of the weeping and wailing that we have heard took place under the preaching of Daniel Rowland. All that they would dismiss as entirely wrong, saying that you are introducing works, and that you must not do that; you just call upon people to believe that 'God so loved the world, that he gave his only begotten Son …' and that you accept him as your Saviour.

In the same way, of course, on this teaching you call for an immediate decision, and you do everything you can to produce one. A man has just got to receive the evidence. You put it like that to him. You have received the evidence in a lawcourt, you have received the evidence of something that a man tells you in secular affairs, why do you not receive this evidence? And you are just asked to believe that evidence without any feelings, without any awareness of any change in yourself at all, without any holy desires – these are dangerous because they are 'works,' and they must not be allowed. So you emphasise this 'naked faith' which accepts the testimony, the evidence given, and it is obviously something that you should do at once. If you are going to wait and delay and query and question, it is obvious that you are dropping back under works once more.

So this teaching makes a very big difference to evangelism – it did so immediately at that time. Christmas Evans pointed out how these people were always bitterly opposed to what was called 'warm preaching.' They did not like that. You see, you simply had to present the evidence, and you did it more or less like a barrister. You get Finney in the next century doing precisely this. He was a man of such an ardent constitution that he introduced a good deal of energy and of power, and perhaps almost a passion into his preaching; but he did not believe in doing that theoretically. He was still the barrister presenting the case, and all people had to do was to accept the case, and there it was. Those holding Sandemanian views are always opposed to warm, emotional preaching, and any preaching which would have the effect of bringing people to a feeling, and a sensible knowledge, of the fact that they were sinners, and the terrors of the law, and that they were to face a holy

God, and that they would have to be holy before they could face him. So it has this great influence at once upon evangelism and preaching.

But it also has a great effect, obviously, upon the type of Christian that it produces, and this was the thing that so concerned William Williams. He said, 'It chills one's feelings until they despise heaven's pure breezes.' They were against emotion as such, and in particular at the point of believing. This is something that concerns us. I shall never forget how a few years ago a very well-known evangelical leader came to me and asked if I had been yet to a series of meetings that were being held here in London. I said, 'No, I have not had the opportunity so far.' He said, 'It's marvellous, it's wonderful. The people are streaming forward. No emotion! It's marvellous. It's wonderful – no emotion.' He was glorying in the fact that the people who were going forward to register their decision were not showing any emotion at all; this was something to be gloried in. It is just here that this teaching becomes so serious. Can you have saving faith without any emotion? Can you be a Christian without emotion? 'It produces,' says William Williams, 'a coldness, it chills men's feelings.'

But let me quote what Christmas Evans says about it. Now Christmas Evans, that great Baptist preacher, was influenced by this teaching for a number of years; he fell to it, and this is what he tells us was the effect of doing so upon him: 'The Sandemanian heresy affected me so far as to quench the spirit of prayer for the conversion of sinners, and it induced in my mind a greater regard for the smaller things of the kingdom of heaven than for the greater. I lost the strength which clothed my mind with zeal, confidence, and earnestness in the pulpit for the conversion of souls to Christ. My heart retrograded in a manner, and I could not realise the testimony of a good conscience. Sabbath nights, after having been in the day exposing and vilifying with all bitterness the errors that prevailed, my conscience felt as if displeased, and reproached me that I had lost nearness to and walking with God. It would intimate that something exceedingly precious was now wanting in me. I would reply that I was acting in obedience to the word, but it continued to accuse me of the want of some precious article. I had been robbed to a great degree of the spirit of prayer and of the spirit of preaching.'

This is the point at which we examine ourselves and especially those of us who are preachers. The question is not so much, are we still praying, are we still preaching – but have we got the spirit of prayer, have we got the spirit of preaching? You can preach mechanically, you can preach coldly; you can pray mechanically, you can pray coldly. The effect of this teaching upon Christmas Evans was to rob him of the warmth and the feeling and the urgency which he had known, and to introduce this terrible coldness into him. William Williams says, 'Love is the greatest thing in religion, and if that is forgotten nothing can take its place.'

Sandemanianism leads to coldness of spirit, to lack of prayer; it affects very profoundly also one's assurance of salvation, and especially the highest form of that assurance. These people taught – and many have taught it since, often following them quite unconsciously – that you must not talk of your feelings in the matter of assurance, that assurance is something that you obtain only from the Scriptures. They say that the way to get assurance is to go to the Scriptures, where you read, 'Whosoever believeth in him shall not perish.' They then ask, 'You believe the Scriptures, do you not?' 'Yes.' 'Well, then, you are not going to perish.' They say that our assurance is established in an objective manner, and that it is a mistake to introduce the element of feelings even into full assurance of faith. The teaching that countered this (and which I would most certainly advocate and can support with quotations from the Puritans, John Owen included) was that the highest form of assurance is the immediate assurance that is given by the Spirit himself. There is a mediate assurance that one can get from the Scriptures. I am not disputing that. But that is the lowest form of assurance, that is the first form – you believe the word of the Scriptures.

But you can go to a second form of assurance which is better, and that is the application of the tests suggested in the First Epistle of John: Do you love the brethren? Do you delight in his commandments and no longer find them grievous? and so on. Test yourself by those.

But there is yet another and a higher form of assurance: 'The Spirit beareth witness with our spirits that we are the children of God.' The first two I have mentioned refer to our spirits; but the Spirit himself also beareth witness 'with' our spirits that we are the children of God. This is the highest and the most glorious assurance of all and it is 'given' to us and is not the result of our deductions from the Scriptures. Goodwin, and Owen, and Bolton, John Preston, John Howe, and many others of the Puritans, as well as Jonathan Edwards and indeed John Wesley have eloquent teaching concerning this. Here is something in the realm of 'feeling': immediate and direct, and not indirect. Sandemanian teaching does away with that.

It also does away with the spirit of brokenness, and a spirit of humility. Is not this the most serious thing about us as modern Christians? When did you last see someone weeping because of sinfulness? Is there evidence of brokenness of spirit amongst us, and humility? We are all so healthy, we are so glib. Why this essential difference between the type of piety that you see so clearly in the seventeenth and eighteenth centuries and what we have today? Can what we have today be truly called piety? Can it be called 'godliness'? It appears rather to be an intellectual acceptance of certain propositions, accompanied by hardness, an absence of feeling, a distrust of feeling, a dislike of feeling. As if the whole man were not involved, not only in faith, but in salvation!

The result is that you get a mechanical performance of duties; and people are taught to evangelise and to do 'personal work' almost by numbers, and are drilled to pray. Everything is organised and arranged, you pass examinations in them, and so all these duties are done in an external mechanical manner instead of rising out of the heart.

What a contrast this is with what we are told in Acts 8 about the people who were 'scattered abroad from Jerusalem because of the persecution' – the ordinary Christians, remember, the apostles being left in Jerusalem. What are we told about these ordinary Christians?

'They went everywhere preaching the word' (verse 4). That does not mean proclaiming it from pulpits; it just means 'speaking' it. And then we are told in the next verse that Philip 'heralded' it. He was an evangelist and a preacher. But they all spread the gospel. Not because they were trained to do so, or because they were told, This is what you have to do now that you have been saved. There is no sign of the mechanical stages we are supposed to go through. You take your decision, then you are given some work to do. You are taken from step to step; and it is all organised and arranged. And it is all done in this mechanical manner.

We expect that kind of thing from the cults, and that is always their great characteristic, but it is not the New Testament way. But if you start with a definition of faith which makes it something notional, and naked, and intellectual, and deliberately exclude the feelings and the emotions, that is the inevitable result. So you get a hardness, a coldness, a mechanical type of Christianity. What makes this so serious is that it is so discouraging to a true visitation of the Spirit of God. You cannot read the accounts of the revivals of the past without observing that the emotional element was always prominent. But, today, so many are terrified of emotion and have almost a phobia concerning excesses. Indeed I fear that it can be said of many that they seem to be so afraid of what they call excesses that they are 'quenching the Spirit.' When have you known a congregation to be really moved? When have you heard a congregation crying out? Are you explaining away the great phenomena accompanying the revivals of the past in terms of the twentieth century, and saying that the people at Llangeitho listening to Daniel Rowland were a sort of primitive people lacking education, and just emotionalists? The apostle Paul reminds the elders of the church at Ephesus of how he preached 'with tears.' And Whitefield used to preach with tears. When have you and I last preached with tears? What do we know, to use the phrase of Whitefield, about preaching a 'felt Christ'? Is not this the cause of the trouble today?

How can we get out of this cold and arid and mechanical type of worship and Christian living? What can we do to relieve the situation? Let me read a glorious statement from the Life of Christmas Evans. He tells us how he came out of it. There he was, under that blighting teaching of Sandemanianism for about five years. He says, 'I was weary, weary of a cold heart towards Christ and his sacrifice and the work of his Spirit.' (Are you weary of that? Do you feel anything at the Communion table? Do you 'feel' anything?) 'I was weary of a cold heart towards Christ and his sacrifice and the work of his Spirit, of a cold heart in the pulpit, in secret prayer and in the study. For fifteen years previously I had felt my heart burning within, as if going to Emmaus with Jesus. On a day ever to be remembered by me as I was going from Dolgelley to Machynlleth and climbing up towards Cader Idris I considered it to be incumbent upon me to pray, however hard I felt in my heart and however worldly the frame of my spirit was. Having begun in the name of Jesus I soon felt as it were the fetters loosening and the old hardness of heart softening, and, as I thought, mountains of frost and snow dissolving and melting within me. This engendered confidence in my soul in the promise of the Holy Ghost. I felt my whole mind relieved from some great bondage, tears flowed copiously, and I was constrained to cry out for the gracious visits of God, by restoring to my soul the joys of his salvation, and that he would visit the churches in Anglesey that were under my care. I embraced in my supplications all the churches of the saints, and nearly all the ministers in the principality by their names. This struggle lasted for three hours; it rose again and again like one wave after another, or a high flowing tide driven by strong wind, until my nature became faint by weeping and crying. Thus I resigned myself to Christ body and soul, gifts and labours, all my life, every day and every hour that remained for me; and all my cares I committed to Christ. The road was mountainous and lonely and I was wholly alone and suffered no interruption in my wrestling with God.

'From this time I was made to expect the goodness of God to the churches and to myself. Thus the Lord delivered me, and the people of Anglesey, from being carried away by the flood of Sandemanianism. In the first religious meetings after this I felt as if I had been removed from the cold and sterile regions of spiritual frost into the verdant fields of divine promises. The former striving with God in prayer, and the longing anxiety for the conversion of sinners which I had experienced at Lleyn were now restored. I had a hold of the promises of God. The result was, when I returned home the first thing that arrested my attention was that the Spirit was working also in the brethren in Anglesey, inducing in them a spirit of prayer, especially in two of the deacons who were particularly importunate with God, that God would visit us in mercy and render the word of his grace effectual amongst us for the conversion of sinners.'

That is our only hope: 'All coldness from my heart remove.' What do we know about warmth of spirit, warmth of heart, warmth in prayer, warmth in preaching, to be moved to the depth of our being and feel the love of God flowing into us and flowing back out of us to him? Is Sandemanianism merely a matter of antiquarian or historical interest, or is it our major problem today – Calvinists as well as Arminians?

# 1968

# *William Williams and Welsh Calvinistic Methodism*

## I

LET me start by giving some kind of explanation as to why I am dealing with this subject; it is quite a simple one. Last year I should have been doing what I am going to do tonight, because it was the two hundred and fiftieth anniversary of the birth of William Williams. He was actually born at the end of 1717. But I felt constrained to deal with the question of Sandemanianism first. It came in a kind of logical sequence in my own mind with regard to the addresses that I have been delivering at the close of this conference, and I suddenly realised that it would make quite a good introduction to this subject tonight, because the greatest proponent against Sandemanianism in Wales was none other than William Williams. So it has seemed to me to be right to give this address this year. It does also serve, I trust, as an interesting link with what has been before us almost throughout this conference because I shall be dealing with Calvinism and Methodism and what I shall say will, in a sense, perhaps, help to sum up the various matters that we have discussed together.

I am not going to say very much about William Williams himself. One could not attempt to deal with him without taking a whole evening, because he was such a many-sided man, who stands out as one of the three, or perhaps four, great leaders of Methodism in Wales in the eighteenth century. Daniel Rowland was the outstanding preacher, as we heard last year. Howell Harris was the great exhorter and the great organiser. But William Williams was a many-sided man.

We think of him instinctively first and foremost as a great writer of hymns, and he was, I would say, supreme in this matter. Certain literary authorities in Wales, who are not Christian themselves, are ready to grant that he is, in their judgment, the greatest of all Welsh poets. This is something of very real significance, because here you have such an outstanding, natural poet, now, under the influence of the Spirit, writing these incomparable hymns. An indication of his place as a writer of hymns, and indeed a writer of prose in addition, is the fact that the University of Wales Press are in process of republishing Williams' *Complete Works*. Two volumes have already appeared. So we are dealing with a very remarkable man, a man of very unusual ability.

In addition to being an outstanding poet and writer of hymns he was also, we can say, the theologian of Welsh Calvinistic Methodism. He showed that in his attack upon Sandemanianism, but he showed it in many other ways positively. He was the theologian of this group of three or four men, and he showed great ability there. He would give his theology sometimes in verse and sometimes in prose. But in many ways I would say that the greatest of all his gifts was the gift which he had of instructing the little societies or companies of Methodists that used to meet together. He was acknowledged by everybody to be supreme in this matter. He wrote a book which he called *Drwo y Society Profiad* or *The Door to the Experience Society,* or *The Door to the Society in which experiences are dealt with*. It is quite a classic. I had intended at one time to devote my whole paper to that, because it might be very useful and instructive for us in this phase through which we are passing at the present time, when we have little groups of Christians meeting together for fellowship in different parts of the country. The early Methodists had to face that problem. They had new converts whom they formed into societies. The question, then, was, how could they be instructed? They needed leaders; they might be good men but still they would not know how to handle people. Well, Williams wrote the book in order to instruct them and to guide them as to how to do this all-important work.

There, then, are the outstanding characteristics of this man. He was born, as I have said, in 1717, and was converted while quite young under the ministry of the great Howell Harris. Williams intended to be a doctor, and he was preparing to become a medical student. As he was going home one day, quite heedlessly and thoughtlessly, he saw a crowd of people listening to a man. He joined them; it was Howell Harris preaching. There and then he was converted and immediately, almost, felt a call to the ministry. Eventually he was ordained as a deacon in the Church of England, and as such he was one of the men present at the first great Association held by the Calvinistic Methodists in Wales in 1743 with Whitefield presiding.

## II

These are the main facts about Williams. You can see how easily one could spend the whole time with him, but I propose to look at him as one of the leaders of the Calvinistic Methodists, and particularly in Wales. Our theme, then, is going to be 'Calvinistic Methodism.'

I have often found during the years that people, both Arminians and Calvinists, have regarded this term as a contradiction in terms. 'Calvinistic Methodism?' they say; 'this is impossible, it is a contradiction.' I remember speaking at an anniversary in a church not so far from here about twenty-five years ago. I said I was glad to be present as a Methodist and as the representative of Whitefield and Calvinistic Methodism. And the then minister of that church said that he regarded this as a contradiction in terms. Well, that was because he was seriously defective in his understanding of the term Methodism. But there are others, on the other side, who have been astounded at this. The term 'Methodism' on the continent in particular is a dirty word, and there are Calvinists who dislike any association between Calvinism and Methodism. Again this is due to a serious defective understanding, as I hope to show, of both Calvinism and Methodism. So it is clear that this is a subject that has a good deal to tell us at the present time.

The best way of approaching it, I think, is for me, first of all, briefly to outline how Calvinistic Methodism ever came into being. We have to start, of course, with the rise of Methodism. Consider first the condition of England at that time, when Methodism really began in the 1730s. The Church of England was generally Arminian. You remember the famous dictum of the great Lord Chatham with respect to the condition of the Church of England. He said that she had a Calvinistic creed, a Popish liturgy, and an Arminian clergy. And that was an accurate description. She was not only Arminian but also spiritually asleep.

What about the other churches? Presbyterianism had ceased to be. There had been a Presbyterianism in England, but it had become Arian in its doctrine. The Westminster Confession of Faith does not guarantee that you cannot go wrong doctrinally. It was the Presbyterians who went most astray and became guilty of Arianism, and Presbyterianism literally died. The Presbyterian Church of England which we have today is something quite new which only started in the last century. As regards Congregationalism, these Arian tendencies for a while even affected people like Isaac Watts and Philip Doddridge. The Congregationalists had also been affected by the Hyper-Calvinism, to which reference has been made, and we have been reminded also that among the Baptists there was this Hyper-Calvinistic teaching.

That was the condition in England in general. In Wales it was very similar. The Church of England was in the same condition in Wales as in England. In the nonconformist bodies there was an occasional good man here and there; we must not depreciate them. The Methodists in their enthusiasm, and perhaps William Williams himself, tended to do so. In his 'Elegy' on the death of Rowland and of Harris he tends to give the impression that there was no light at all. There were good men, but unfortunately these good men were given to argumentation and disputation among themselves. So that from the standpoint of a live spirituality they did not count very much.

It was into that kind of condition in England and in Wales that Methodism came. How did it come? I cannot, obviously, go into detail. As regards England the real origin and genesis is to be found in the Holy Club that was founded in Oxford, mainly at the instigation of Charles Wesley. The story is well-known. However, the Holy Club in and of itself would never have led to Methodism. The real beginning of Methodism is found in the mighty experience through which Whitefield passed in 1736, and through which the Wesley brothers passed in May 1738. In Wales Methodism was quite independent and spontaneous. Welsh Methodism owes nothing to English Methodism. It started before that in England, in 1735, with the conversion of both Howell Harris and Daniel Rowland, and again, quite independently. They had never heard of each other and knew nothing at all about one another. But the Spirit of God dealt with these two men in a most amazing way, and it was only in 1737 that they met and came together.

That is how Methodism began. At first they were all one – in England and in Wales when they eventually met and came together. There was one Methodism, including all these men to whom I have referred. But then, as we have already been reminded, a division came in and Methodism divided into two groups, Calvinistic and Arminian. In Wales they were all Calvinists. In England they were not all Calvinists. On the Calvinistic side you have the great names, Whitefield, Berridge, Toplady, Romaine, and the two Hill brothers, Rowland Hill and Sir Richard Hill, and also the Countess of Huntingdon. On the Arminian side there were the Wesleys, John Fletcher, Thomas Olivers, and various others.

These are historical points which are of considerable interest. The Methodism in Wales was entirely Calvinistic. The Wesleys visited there but they did not have any churches there until the beginning of the nineteenth century. But again I would emphasise this fact – that we have a Methodism that is common to both. This is a basic point. Actually the term 'Calvinistic Methodist' in Welsh emphasises this very strongly, for it is not Calvinistic Methodism, but Methodism-Calvinistic. And so you have Methodism-Wesleyan. The Methodism comes first, and the other is an adjective describing the particular type. At first they all worked together, but, owing to the division, it was Whitefield who became most intimately associated with the men in Wales, and he was actually the Moderator of their first Association in 1743.

## III

We must now face this question – What then is Methodism? Let me first answer negatively. It is not primarily a theological position or even a theological attitude. Methodism was not a movement designed to reform theology. It was not that at all. Actually in Welsh Calvinistic Methodism they did not have a catechism or a confession of faith until the next century – emphasising this point, that it was not primarily a theological movement. We must not think of it in terms of theological reform.

What was it then? Well, Methodism is essentially experimental or experiential religion and a way of life. I think that is an adequate definition of it. What produced this? How did this ever come into being? The answer is that it was born of a number of things. The first was the realisation that religion is primarily and essentially something personal. This was the thing that came to all of them. They all became aware of their own personal sinfulness; they underwent conviction of sin, and it was an agonising process. But they all experienced this terrible need of forgiveness. This became a burden to them – both parties. Then there was also a great desire for a knowledge of God – a direct knowledge of God: not to believe things about God – they had already got that – but the desire to know God. 'This is life eternal, that they might know thee the only true God, and Jesus Christ, whom thou hast sent' (John 17:3). All this led on then to a desire for assurance of sins forgiven.

Many have probably read the account of the first meeting between Whitefield and Harris in Cardiff in 1739. The first question that George Whitefield put to Howell Harris was this: 'Mr Harris, do you know that your sins are forgiven?' He did not ask him, 'Do you believe that sins can be forgiven?' or 'Do you believe that your sins are forgiven?' for various reasons, but, 'Do you *know* that your sins are forgiven?' And Harris was able to say that he had rejoiced in this knowledge for several years. This again was a point that was common to all of them – assurance of salvation, assurance of sins forgiven.

The next thing that was common to all types of Methodism was the desire for 'new life.' So you had that great emphasis on the doctrine of regeneration and re-birth. You know how they were all influenced by the book of Henry Scougal, *The Life of God in the Soul of Man*. This was their longing and desire. Whitefield preached constantly on regeneration, and so did the others. You remember that he even had to be corrected on this point, actually by the Wesleys, though he had gone before them. They felt that he was not making enough of justification by faith. There was this tremendous emphasis on the need of a new birth, a new beginning.

The next thing I have to stress is the emphasis which they all placed on 'feeling.' They were very concerned about what Whitefield once called a 'felt' Christ. They were not content with orthodoxy, correct belief; they wanted to 'feel' him. They laid tremendous emphasis upon the place of feelings in our Christian experience. This I could illustrate at great length. Unfortunately there are only two of Williams' hymns in the Congregational Hymnary, and they are translations, of course. You get there no true idea of his greatness as a hymn-writer and as a poet. He cannot be translated. In his hymns you have an incomparable blend of truly great poetry and perfect theology. We have, 'Guide me, O thou great Jehovah,' and 'O'er the gloomy hills of darkness,' but one of the greatest of all his hymns has been translated like this, and it is so typical of Williams:

*Speak, I pray Thee, gentle Jesus!*
*O, how passing sweet Thy words,*
*Breathing o'er my troubled spirit*
*Peace which never earth affords!*
*All the world's distracting voices,*
*All the enticing tones of ill,*
*At Thy accents mild, melodious,*
*Are subdued, and all is still.*

And he goes on:

*Tell me Thou art mine, O, Saviour,*
*Grant me an assurance clear,*
*Banish all my dark misgivings,*
*Still my doubting, calm my fear.*
*O, my soul within me yearneth*
*Now to hear Thy voice divine;*
*So shall grief be gone for ever,*
*And despair no more be mine.*

Now that is so typical of him. There are endless hymns by him on that theme in the Welsh hymn-book. He wanted to 'feel' these things. He believed, but he was not satisfied with that; he wanted to know.

Of course you get the same note in the English Methodist hymn writers in exactly the same way. Let me give one example out of the writings of Toplady:

*Object of my first desire,*
*Jesus crucified for me;*
*All to happiness aspire*
*Only to be found in Thee:*
*Thee to please, and Thee to know,*
*Constitute my bliss below;*
*Thee to see, and Thee to love,*
*Constitute my bliss above.*

*Lord, it is not life to live*
*If Thy presence Thou deny;*
*Lord, if Thou Thy presence give,*
*'Tis no longer death to die:*
*Source and Giver of repose,*
*Only from Thy smile it flows;*
*Peace and happiness are Thine;*
*Mine they are, if Thou art mine.*

*Whilst I feel Thy love to me,*
*Every object teems with joy;*

*May I ever walk with Thee,*
*For 'tis bliss without alloy:*
*Let me but Thyself possess,*
*Total sum of happiness:*
*Perfect peace I then shall prove,*
*Heaven below and heaven above.*

And as you read Toplady's Diaries you find this kind of thing emphasised repeatedly.

That brings me to say just a little more about this whole question of assurance, because in many ways it was the distinguishing mark of Methodism and the same thing that was common to Methodism. They divided over holiness teaching, as we have already been reminded, and over other matters, but here there was this great unity, this teaching concerning assurance. What was it? It was this, that our assurance of salvation is not only, and not merely, something that is to be deduced from the Scriptures. They agreed that that was part of it. I would say that the bulk of evangelical people today, in this and other countries, stop at that. That is their only assurance, that which you deduce from the Scriptures. 'Whosoever believeth in him is not condemned.' So they say, 'Do you believe in him?' 'Yes.' 'Very well, you are not condemned, and there is your assurance. Do not worry about your feelings,' etc., etc.

New Methodism taught the exact opposite. That is the point at which you start, and you can go on and test yourself in terms of the teaching of the first Epistle of John. As you do so you will get a better assurance, an assurance which will save you from a kind of 'believism,' or an intellectualism that just says that it believes and accepts all this, and which emphasises the importance of evidences of new life. But these men were concerned to go on to a further source of assurance, which to them was the one that they desired and coveted above everything else. That was the direct witness of the Spirit himself to the fact that they were the children of God. So they made much, of course, of Romans 8:15 and 16; and also of Galatians 2:20: 'The Son of God, who loved me, and gave himself for me,' etc.

This, I repeat, was common to all of them. We are all familiar with the experience of John Wesley in Aldersgate Street on May 24,

1738. 'My heart was strangely warm, and I did know that my sins, even mine, had been forgiven.' William Williams made a great deal of this. Let me give two quotations to establish this point. I am translating out of his book, *The Door* (or 'Entry' if you like) *to the Experience Meeting – the Experience Society*. He was giving instructions to the men in charge of the societies as to how they should question and catechise and cross-examine the people who were anxious to be admitted to the societies, and, indeed, how they should examine the experiences of those who belonged to the societies. He drew a distinction between the way in which you questioned and catechised young members, new members, and the way in which you catechised older members. He says: 'You must not expect as much of the light of faith, and certainly amongst those whom you are receiving for the first time, as you must expect amongst those who have been in for some time' – although he goes on to say that 'sometimes you will get a shock and you will find that people's early experiences are very much better than their later experiences.' However, that is his main point of distinction – that you do not expect as much light and clarity and certainty from the young convert as you do from the older one.

How, then, do you question and examine the young convert? This is one of his ways of putting it – that the examiner is to say to the young convert, 'Though you have not yet received the testimony of the Spirit (to your salvation), nevertheless, are you seeking God with your whole heart, and with this as the main rule of your life? Not by fits and starts or occasional touches of conviction – Is this the main thing in your life?' But notice how he starts: 'Though you have not yet received the testimony of the Spirit.' Then when he comes to the way in which they should question the older men he says, 'You must examine them concerning the clarity or the clearness of their testimony, how they first received their testimony, whether they have lost any of it or not.' Then he tells them to ask: 'Has this testimony which you have in your own spirit been doubled by the Holy Spirit?' That is the term he used – 'doubled.' In other words, that was Williams' view of 'the Spirit himself also beareth witness with our spirits that we are the children of God' (Rom. 8:16). Our spirit tells us this, 'the Spirit of adoption, whereby we cry, Abba, Father.' But the Spirit, as it were, doubles it, seals it, guarantees it, gives an extra, an overplus on top of it, confirms it. That is the term which he uses with regard to these older converts.

That was their teaching, and, of course, it was their own experience. This comes out very clearly in the case of Daniel Rowland, who having come to see the doctrine of justification by faith as he had heard it preached by Griffith Jones at Llanddewi Brefi, still did not have certainty about it. But one day when he was reading the litany at the communion service in his own church in the village of Llangeitho, suddenly the Spirit came and did this 'doubling'; and he knew. And it was from then on that he began to preach in that amazing way and with that amazing power, of which Ryle writes in his famous book, *Christian Leaders of the Eighteenth Century*.[1] The same thing is very clear in the case of Howell Harris. Howell Harris, being convicted of sin on the Sunday before Good Friday 1735, got an assurance at Whitsun. But it was only three weeks later that he had this 'doubling' by the Spirit, and that was the thing that made him an evangelist. They taught this, and they taught people to expect this, not to be satisfied with anything less, as my quotation from Williams' book has already shown you.

I go on from this to add another vital point about them all – Methodism in England and in Wales and in all parties. They met together in little groups or classes; whatever you may like to call them. What did they do there? Well, the main thing they did was to state their experiences to one another, and to examine one another's experiences, and to discuss them together. They told of the Lord's dealings with them, what had happened to them since they last met, of anything remarkable that had occurred to them, and so on. This was the main element in these societies; that is the thing that Williams treats of in that book to which I have referred – this great emphasis on experience, and on assurance, on this 'felt' element. They were primarily 'experience' meetings. Indeed I think we are justified in using this term, that the thing that characterised

[1] Reprinted Banner of Truth Trust, 1978.

Methodism was this pneumatic element. Over and above what they believed there was this desire to feel and to experience the power of the Spirit in their lives.

All this was expressed in their lives, about which they were so careful and so meticulous. They were taught to be so, and were examined in order to make sure that they were so. That is the picture of their life in their societies. These people, under the preaching, had undergone an experience, and they had made application to join the Society, and they had been received; and that is how they went on.

One other great thing we have got to emphasise is their evangelistic zeal; and again it was common to all of them. Who can decide as to which had the greater evangelistic zeal, John Wesley or George Whitefield? You cannot answer the question. They both had it. And it seems to me that both these branches or divisions of Methodism showed exactly the same zeal and enthusiasm in this desire to bring their fellow men and women to a knowledge of God's salvation in Christ Jesus, and that they were equal also in the success which they attained.

All this was common to all Methodism. Then there came the division. When I say that they had these things in common, 'and then,' it sounds as if I were saying that from there on they did not have them in common. But they did. After the division all that went on, all that remained common; but they became divided into those two groups, the Arminian and the Calvinistic.

The question has often been asked as to why this ever happened. I remember it being asked in a final meeting at this conference a number of years ago. The answer is very difficult. I suppose in a sense it cannot be answered. Dare I make one suggestion? (We might very well have this as a topic for discussion some time.) Is there even a national element in this? I mean by that, that it may have something to do with national characteristics. I am not going to go into this, I am simply asking a question. What is the place of nationality in these matters? Can you allow it any place at all?

Let me just say this before I leave the matter. I have always felt that John Wesley was about the most typical Englishman of whom

I have ever read. I could substantiate what I am saying. However, we do know this, and we have been reminded of it already, the Church of England at that time was thoroughly Arminian. The Wesley family, the father and mother, had become Arminians, and were proud of it. Not only that, there is very interesting evidence brought forth by Professor Geoffrey Nuttall to show that Arminianism had had a particular vogue in the village of Epworth, where the Wesleys lived. So they had been brought up and nurtured in a thoroughly Arminian atmosphere. No doubt that has a great deal to do with it. But in Wales, as I have reminded you, the whole thing was entirely different, and they were all Calvinistic.

It is interesting to notice that they only became Calvinistic after a while. They all started as Methodists, but in Wales they became Calvinistic. Howell Harris tells us this quite plainly, in his own Diary, and as to how he became a Calvinist. The same thing is true of Whitefield. Whitefield 'became' a Calvinist. I am not going into the details as to when, but the fact is that he became Calvinist. I believe that in the case of Rowland and Harris in particular, and probably also in the case of Whitefield, it was their study of the Thirty-Nine Articles and of the Puritans, that brought them to this position. However, the fact is that they became Calvinistic, and in Wales they remained purely Calvinistic until the end of the century.

## IV

We come now to look at the characteristics of Welsh Calvinistic Methodism. These are quite clear. First and foremost there was the great preaching. That was the outstanding characteristic. I am one of those who believes that Calvinism should always lead to great preaching; and when it does not I query the genuineness of the Calvinism. You cannot have great preaching without a great theme; and they had that great theme, and so you had great preaching all over the country. And the great characteristic of the preaching, as of the life, was warmth, and enthusiasm, and rejoicing. Some of them went through an early phase in which they tended to be a bit legalistic; but it did not last long and the other element came through.

Welsh Calvinistic Methodism was also characterised by singing. Williams produced most of the hymns, and the people would sing them to old tunes and ballads. Moreover, there was often great shouting during the preaching. They would interrupt the preacher, they would cry out their 'Amens' and 'Hallelujahs,' and sometimes the excitement was quite marked. This joy and rejoicing and singing and assurance was the great characteristic of Welsh Calvinistic Methodism.

The other thing that one must mention, because it is of such vital importance, is that they had a succession of revivals. I trust it is not necessary for me to define and describe the word 'revival.' I know that in some countries the word 'revival' has now come to mean the holding of an evangelistic campaign. This is not revival! In a sense I cannot think of anything that is further removed from revival than just that – a man-made, man-organised series of meetings. That is not it! Revival is 'a visitation from on high,' an outpouring of the Holy Spirit. They had a whole succession of them. One of the great revivals in that eighteenth century broke out as the result of the publishing of a new hymn-book by this man William Williams in 1763. The very publication of the hymns and the fact that the people began to sing them led to one of these new outbursts. There had been a period of dryness and of aridity, because, unfortunately, there was a quarrel even amongst the Welsh Calvinistic Methodists. It is a blot on their story. It was almost entirely a personal matter: not entirely so. But it seems to me, the more I have read about it, that it was a clash of personalities, as so often happens, alas, in the church, between Rowland and Harris. Harris undoubtedly had also been going astray somewhat in his doctrine, and this had happened about 1751–53. Following that there had been this period of dryness, but then William Williams' new hymn-book came out and as the people began to sing these great expressions of theology a revival broke out.

The hymns of William Williams are packed with theology and experience. That is why I once, in giving a lecture on Isaac Watts, ventured to say that William Williams was the greatest hymn-writer of them all. You get greatness, and bigness, and largeness in Isaac Watts; you get the experimental side wonderfully in Charles Wesley. But in William Williams you get both at the same time, and that is why I put him in a category entirely on his own. He taught the people theology in his hymns; as they sang the hymns they were becoming familiar with the great expressions of the New Testament doctrines of salvation and the glory of God. But this element of 'revival' is something I want to emphasise, because it was a peculiar feature of 'Calvinistic' Methodism. You also had activity amongst others, and occasions when there was a movement of the Spirit; but they were much less frequent and they were not so clearly 'special' visitations as was the case amongst the Calvinistic Methodists.

Those, then, were the great characteristics of Calvinistic Methodism. It seems to me that it might be of some help if we now considered this question: Was this an entirely new phenomenon? Is the Calvinistic Methodism of the eighteenth century something without antecedents? I suggest that it is not and that there were precursors of it. Again I think we are dealing here with a most interesting point – the relationship of this Calvinistic Methodism to what had gone before. Where do we get hints or adumbrations of this previously? Well, I have always felt that you get a good deal of it in the saintly Hooper, Bishop of Gloucester, martyred in the time of Queen Mary I. The same is true also of John Bradford. You get there the same stress upon feeling and the same warmth. Let us not forget that these two were really the first two Puritans, though the name was not then used. We are in grave danger of forgetting the Puritans of the sixteenth century in our concentration on those of the seventeenth century, yet let us never forget that but for them the seventeenth-century Puritans would probably never have come into being. I find in these first Puritans something more akin to Calvinistic Methodism than one finds even in those who are sometimes described as the 'Pietistic' Puritans, such as William Perkins and others like Lewis Bayly, and so on. These were men who put their emphasis on practical and pastoral theology. They were interested in the application of the law of God in the life of the believer. They put this great emphasis upon 'practising' it. So you get their 'casuistry' and their dealing with 'cases of conscience.' That does lead to a kind of piety, but it is not the same thing as you have in Calvinistic Methodism. There, the emphasis was on the teaching of the law and its application in the daily life of the Christian. Of course I am not excluding the other element altogether, I am talking about the main emphasis; whereas in Calvinistic Methodism the great emphasis and stress was upon 'experience.'

When you come to the next century you get something that is similar to, though not identical with Calvinistic Methodism, in people like Walter Craddock and Morgan Llwyd (Lloyd, as he is called in English). But they were more mystical. It is wrong to say of these Calvinistic Methodists that they were mystics. There is a mystical element in them; you cannot exclude it; but you cannot classify them with the mystics. They were suspicious of and opposed to mysticism, as was shown in their opposition to the quietism that became such a characteristic of the Moravians. And yet, surely, there is a true Christ-mysticism which we must not exclude, and which I maintain you get in the apostle Paul himself, as well as in many others throughout the centuries.

There is much about people like Walter Craddock and Morgan Lloyd that seems to suggest what blossomed so fully in the eighteenth century. They were entirely different from the Quakers. They did not just believe in an 'inner light' and tend to depreciate the Scriptures. No, they had this great theological content as well. I have often felt that you get something of the same thing appearing here and there in John Flavel and Thomas Brooks – touches of it. But it seems to come in as 'touches'; it is not given the centrality that it is given in the Calvinistic Methodists. Personally, I would not hesitate to describe the Jansenists, including the great Blaise Pascal, as Calvinistic Methodists before their time. And certainly I would say that there is more of an affinity with some of the men in Scotland, such as William Guthrie and even before him, Robert Bruce and John Livingstone, than there is with the bulk of English Puritans.

This is a most interesting point. We know that these Calvinistic Methodists read the Puritans a great deal. They fed on them. Puritan writings were their food next to the Bible, and they learned a great deal from them. Yet I am suggesting that Calvinistic Methodism was not a mere continuation of Puritanism. A new element has come in – this emphasis upon the feeling aspect, the revival aspect, and this whole matter of assurance, all the things I have been describing as the essence of Calvinistic Methodism. I venture again to suggest that Jonathan Edwards must be called a Calvinistic Methodist. You have the same combination in Edwards. I know the brilliant intellect tended to obscure this at times, but I would say that essentially Jonathan Edwards as a type was a Calvinistic Methodist, though actually a Congregationalist.

When you come to the Continental Pietists, again we are in a slight difficulty. There were affinities, clearly in the case of Spener, Francke, and people like that, and the Moravians. We know the association between the Moravians and the Methodists, especially at first. They did separate and go apart for certain reasons, but from the beginning they were aware of something in common, and, what was in common was again this very thing which I have been trying to emphasise as being the main characteristic of Calvinistic Methodism.

## V

Let us now attempt some kind of assessment, or attempt to draw out some lessons from all this. We have been dealing with the history of this Methodism that split in two directions, and yet in a sense kept together right through and in spite of the divisions. What are the lessons?

The first, it seems to me, is the grave danger of hardening our terms. We are ever in danger of so 'hardening' the terms that in the end they come to stand for something which is no longer true of the original. It is assumed today that if you use the word Methodist you are speaking of Arminians. That is the general assumption, that you are speaking of John Wesley and his followers. It is to me ridiculous that a religious denomination in this country should call themselves 'The Methodists.' They have no right to do this. It is not true historically. But this is the sort of thing that happens and terms become hardened.

It also shows us the danger of party spirit. Labels generally lead to a spirit, and we must avoid this as Christian people. We must avoid this hardening and rigidity which leads to a wrong spirit and lands us eventually in a position in which we are tempted to ask, as people have asked before us: 'Can any good come out of Nazareth?' God save us and preserve us from ever becoming victims of that terrible spirit!

But there is another lesson that may be of great value to us at this present time through which we are passing. We are in an age of change, and there is no doubt that in a few years the religious situation in this country is going to be very different from what we have known, and there will be new groupings of Christian people. The many will doubtless be in one 'Territorial Church' together, or even in a 'World Church.' There will be others who will not. And the problem will arise for those who do not belong to a 'Territorial Church' as to what they are going to call themselves, the problem of 'denominations.' We are familiar with all these terms – Congregationalism, Presbyterianism, Baptists, and so on – and the multiplicity of divisions and names that our friends in America know so much better than we do. But I am raising this question now: Is it not time that we put an end to all this, and that we cease to use and to bandy about these names of men? I know the difficulty. The argument is: 'Well, you have got to call the church something, you have got to show how one differs from another.' But I am raising the question as to whether you should do that; whether we should not merely as the result of all we have been considering in this conference, and all we know about the history of these matters, decide that in future all we put on the notice-boards of our buildings is – 'Christian church.'

If a man should come and say to me, 'But what do they teach in there?' I would reply, 'Go in and listen.' Why should we put up a notice that is going to exclude people? Let it be known that the gospel is going to be preached here. That is what a church is for. Let them go in, let them listen; they will soon find out what is being preached and they can then decide for themselves whether they are going there again or whether they are not. Why is it necessary that we should harden the things about which we disagree, and on which we differ, and harden them to the extent of 'placarding' the thing? It has caused great confusion to the world outside always. And we know that it is doing so at this present time. Is not this one of the greatest hindrances of all in evangelism? In other words, are we not guilty of the sin of schism in this very respect? And we are adding to it by putting up these labels. All we need to announce is that this is a Christian church, a place where the gospel is preached. Can we not leave it at that?

But having said that, let me come to more particular statements with regard to my assessment of Calvinistic Methodism. First of all I would say that Calvinistic Methodism is true Methodism, and the only 'true' Methodism. Why do I say that? I say so because I assert that Arminian Methodism is inconsistent with itself in the following ways. It starts by emphasising 'grace.' The Arminian Methodists claimed and still claim that they were preaching 'grace.'

> *His only righteousness I show,*
> *His saving grace proclaim,*

says Charles Wesley in a well-known stanza. They laid great claim to this. But then it has become equally clear, has it not, that they introduce works again with their whole notion of free will, and the part that the man himself plays. I have never found an Arminian who can satisfactorily interpret 1 Corinthians 2:14: 'The natural man receiveth not the things of the Spirit of God: for they are foolishness unto him: neither can he know them, for they are spiritually discerned.' Their difficulty is this. They say, 'Quite right: all men by nature are sinners.' They believe in depravity. But then they go on to say that God in his grace has given this power to believe and accept the gospel to 'all men.' That, therefore, means this, that all men now are spiritual, whereas Paul says quite plainly that all are not spiritual, that you have 'carnal' and 'spiritual' men.

So if you say that grace is given to 'all,' it must follow that all are spiritual, because it is the only grounds on which they can possibly believe and accept this gospel and not regard it as 'foolishness.' So while they start with grace they go on to deny it.

Secondly, though they emphasise – I am dealing still with Arminian or Wesleyan Methodism – the re-birth and regeneration, they then go on to deny it by saying that we can lose it. Re-birth is the action of God, and yet they say that we can undo this and we can lose it. From this it follows – and you get it in its extreme form, of course, in the Salvation Army, which came out of Arminian Methodism – that you can be regenerate today and unregenerate tomorrow, and regenerate again, and back and forth. This whole notion of 'falling from grace,' and coming in and out of salvation, is surely a fundamental denial of the doctrine of regeneration.

The same thing applies to their teaching concerning assurance. What is the value of an assurance that you can lose? I mean by that, what is the value of an assurance of salvation if you can lose your salvation? If your persistence in grace and in salvation is dependent upon you, where is your assurance? Can you rely upon yourself? Would any man be eventually saved if it were left to us to persevere in grace? It is not a doctrine of assurance. It leaves it all back with me, and I am in all the uncertainty that I was in before. Of course, that is why so many turn to the Church of Rome, where you hand it over and the church looks after it for you. It is because you cannot possibly do it yourself. The Church of Rome does not offer you assurance of salvation. What she says is, 'You cannot get it, but leave it to us and we will put it right for you.' And then you get all the paraphernalia that characterises that church, by which they tell you they are going to do this. So the whole emphasis of the Arminian Methodist upon assurance is nullified.

I would sum up this section like this. One of the greatest proofs of the truth of the doctrines emphasised by Calvin, what is known as 'Calvinism' – though I have already said I do not like these terms – is John Wesley. He was a man who was saved in spite of his muddled and erroneous thinking. The grace of God saved him in spite of himself. That is Calvinism! If you say, as a Calvinist, that a man is saved by his understanding of doctrine you are denying Calvinism. He is not. We are all saved in spite of what we are in every respect. Thus it comes to pass that men who can be so muddled, because they bring in their own human reason, as John Wesley and others did, are saved men and Christians, as all of us are, because it is 'all of the grace of God' and in spite of us.

Calvinistic Methodism is the true Methodism for those reasons. But in addition to that, Calvinistic Methodism saves Methodism from degenerating into mysticism. There is always this danger. Put your emphasis on feeling, upon the 'felt' aspect, and you are already in danger of degenerating into mysticism, or into a false asceticism, or into a kind of 'illuminism.' And all these, of course, have made their appearance in history. But Calvinistic Methodism saves us from that because of its great emphasis upon the doctrines. Here, you have got the doctrines, but in addition you have got this other element, the 'felt' element; it is a perfect combination of both. Not only does it guarantee our doctrinal correctness, it also saves us in the realm of experience itself from many aberrations, which have often ended in what seems to me to be nothing but a kind of Spiritism. Calvinistic Methodism saves us from that. So I argue that Calvinistic Methodism is true Methodism.

Secondly, I argue that Calvinistic Methodism is also true Calvinism. I want to show that a Calvinism that is not Methodist as well is one which we need to examine carefully. Calvinism without Methodism has certain dangerous tendencies, which we must recognise. If we do not we are in a very dangerous position.

Calvinism without Methodism tends to lead to intellectualism and scholasticism – that is its peculiar temptation. The result is that men talk more about 'the truth we hold,' rather than about 'the truth that holds us.'

Another danger which Calvinism without Methodism is prone to is that confessions of faith, instead of being subordinate standards, tend to be the primary and supreme standard, replacing the Bible in that position. I am only talking about tendencies, and not saying that this happens to all Calvinists. Officially we say that these confessions are the 'subordinate standard'; the Bible comes first, then these. But there is always a danger that the Calvinist may reverse the order.

A question arises here – it has already been suggested in one of our discussions. It is the whole question of the rightness of preaching from and through the [Shorter] Catechism rather than preaching through and from the Bible itself. I am simply putting it up as a question which we need to examine. The Calvinistic Methodists did not preach through the catechism. Their whole tendency was to say – as was the tendency of Charles Haddon Spurgeon – that you should not even preach a series of sermons, but that each sermon should be 'given' to you, that you look to God for your sermons. I mean by that, that you look to God for your text and the message you are to deliver. That was the emphasis of Calvinistic Methodism. So I put it in this general way by saying that there is at any rate a danger that we may change the position of the Confession, and it ceases to be the 'subordinate' standard.

A third danger always, as a tendency in Calvinism unless it is corrected by Methodism, is to discourage prayer. This is a very serious matter. The Calvinistic Methodists were great men of prayer, and their churches were characterised by prayer-meetings – warm, moving prayer-meetings, which would sometimes last for hours and where great experiences would come to people. I am suggesting – and I could produce facts – that Calvinism without Methodism tends to discourage prayer. I have known Calvinistic churches in which they have no prayer-meeting at all, and in which prayer is really discouraged.

Lastly, Calvinism without Methodism tends to produce a joyless, hard, not to say a harsh and cold type of religion. I am saying that this is a tendency. All this results from intellectualism of course; and the more the intellect dominates the less joy there will be, and a hardness, and a coldness, and a harshness, and a bigotry tend to come in. I had almost said that Calvinism without Methodism tends to produce 'dead Calvinism.' But I am not saying that. Why not? Because I regard the term 'dead Calvinism' as a contradiction in terms. I say that a dead Calvinism is impossible, and that if your Calvinism appears to be dead it is not Calvinism, it is a philosophy. It is a philosophy using Calvinistic terms, it is an intellectualism, and it is not real Calvinism.

Why not? Because true Calvinism not only does justice to the objective side of our faith and our whole position, it does equal justice to the subjective; and people who cannot see this subjective element in Calvinism seem to me never to have understood Calvinism. Calvinism of necessity leads to an emphasis upon the action and the activity of God the Holy Spirit. The whole emphasis is upon what God does to us: not what man does, but what God does to us; not our hold of him, but 'his strong grasp of us.' So Calvinism of necessity leads to experiences, and to great emphasis upon experience; and these men, and all these older Calvinists were constantly talking about 'visitations,' how the Lord had appeared to them, how the Lord had spoken to them – the kind of thing that we have seen Toplady expressing in the hymn already quoted and in his Diaries. They also talked about 'withdrawings.' Why have those terms disappeared from amongst us modern Calvinists? When have you last spoken about a 'visitation' from the Spirit of God? When did Christ last make himself 'real' to you? What do you know about 'withdrawings' of the Spirit, and the feeling that your Bridegroom has left you and that he has not visited you recently? This is of the essence of true Calvinism; and a Calvinism that knows nothing about visitations and withdrawings is a caricature of Calvinism. I object to its using the term with respect to itself.

But more, Calvinism leads to assurance, and assurance of necessity leads to joy. You cannot be assured quietly and unmoved by the fact that your sins are forgiven, and that you are a child of God, and that you are going to heaven: it is impossible. Assurance must lead to joy. Not only that; knowing this leads to prayer. God is my Father. I am adopted. I know him. I have an entrance, and I want to go there. I want to speak to him and I want to know him. This is true Calvinism. And that, of course, leads to a love of his word. You meet him in the word. The word instructs you as to how to find him; it helps you to understand the visitations and the withdrawings. You live on the word. Nothing so drives a man to the word of God as true Calvinism.

Then, in turn, as I have been trying to say, true Calvinism is bound to emphasise the element of revival, the 'givenness' of the activity of God, the visitations of God. It is only since the decline of Calvinism that revivals have become less and less frequent. The more powerful Calvinism is the more likely you are to have a spiritual revival and re-awakening. It follows of necessity from the doctrine. You cannot work up a revival. You know that you are entirely dependent upon God. That is why you pray to him and you plead with him and you argue, and you reason with him. These Fathers used to do this. How different is our approach to the condition of the church today from that which was true of these Fathers and their successors for several generations. Today we look at the situation and we say – 'Well, things are very bad, everything is going down – what shall we do? We had better have an evangelistic campaign.' So we call a committee together and we begin to organise, and to talk about what is going to happen in a year's time or so.

Calvinistic Methodists did not look at the problem like that. This is how they looked at it. They said, 'Why are things like this? What is the matter? We have offended God, he is grieved with us, he has turned his back on us. What can we do about this? We must get down on our knees and ask him to come back, we must plead with him.' And so they would use the kind of arguments you find Moses using in praying to God in Exodus 33, or such as you get in Isaiah 63. They would reason and argue with God, and say, 'After all, we are your people, not those others. Why do you not come back to us? We belong to you, your name is involved in all this.' They would plead the 'promises' with God, they would agonise in prayer until God heard them and visited them again.

This is Calvinism. Nothing so promotes prayer as Calvinism. Calvinists who do not pray, I say, are not Calvinists. These things follow the one the other as the night follows the day. The true Calvinist is concerned about revival. Why? Because he is concerned about the glory of God. This is the first thing with him. Not so much that the world is as it is, but that the world is behaving like this, and that God is there. It is God's world, and they are under

God. The glory of God! This is the great thing which dominates all the thinking of the Calvinist. So he is waiting, and longing, and pleading with God to 'show' this glory, to show this power, to arise and to scatter his enemies, and to make them like the dust, and to show the might of his almighty arm. This is Calvinism. They want this. They are zealous, and they are jealous, for his name.

At the same time, having an understanding, through their doctrine, of the condition and the state of the unregenerate, they become burdened about them also, and they are anxious to do everything they can to bring them to a knowledge of salvation in Christ Jesus. And when this happens it ends in – what? Well, in great praise and thanksgiving.

My argument is, that cold, sad, mournful, depressing Calvinism is not Calvinism at all. It is a caricature; something has gone wrong somewhere. It is mere intellectualism and philosophy. Calvinism leads to feeling, to passion, to warmth, to praise, to thanksgiving. Look at Paul, the greatest of them all. We should not talk about 'Calvinism'; it is Paul's teaching. He tells us that he wept. He preached with tears. Do you? When did we last weep over these matters? When did we last shed tears? When have we shown the feeling and the passion that he shows? Paul could not control himself, he got carried away. Look at his mighty climaxes; look at the way in which he rises to the heavens and is 'lost in wonder, love, and praise.' Of course, the pedantic scholars criticise him for his *anacolutha*. He starts a sentence and never finishes it. He starts saying a thing and then gets carried off, and forgets to come back to it. Thank God! It is the truth which he saw that led to these grand climaxes of his; and it is bound to do so. If we understand the things we claim to believe we are bound to end in the same way. 'Who shall separate us from the love of God?' And the answer is, 'I am persuaded' – and in the language of the Welsh Calvinistic Methodists it is much better and stronger – 'I am certain.' It is sure, it is certain, 'that neither death, nor life, nor angels, nor principalities, nor powers, nor things present, nor things to come, nor height, nor depth, nor any other creature, shall be able to separate us from the love of God, which is in Christ

Jesus our Lord.' Or listen to him again at the end of Romans 11, 'O the depth of the riches both of the wisdom and knowledge of God.' How often have you had that 'O' in your preaching – you Calvinists? Calvinism leads to this 'O'! – this feeling, this passion. You are moved to the depths of your being, and you are filled with joy, and wonder, and amazement. 'O the depth of the riches both of the wisdom and of the knowledge of God! how unsearchable are his judgments, and his ways past finding out!' – and so on. Or take the same thing at the end of Ephesians 3. These are men dominated by a sense of the glory of God, and who are concerned about his praise.

In other words I am arguing that the first Christians were the most typical Calvinistic Methodists of all! I am just describing them to you. Not only the great apostles – Paul and others – but the people, the ordinary people – joy and rejoicing, praising God and thanking him always 'from house to house' as they ate their bread together. Peter can say of them: 'Whom having not seen, ye love; in whom, though now ye see him not, yet believing, ye rejoice with joy unspeakable and full of glory.' That is first century Christianity! It is also the very essence of Calvinistic Methodism. It leads to praise and thanksgiving and rejoicing. It always leads to something like this:

*We praise, we worship Thee, O God,*
*Thy sovereign power we sound abroad:*
*All nations bow before Thy throne,*
*And Thee the Eternal Father own.*

*Loud alleluias to Thy Name*
*Angels and seraphim proclaim:*
*The heavens and all the powers on high*
*With rapture constantly do cry –*

*'O holy, holy, holy, Lord!*
*Thou God of hosts, by all adored;*
*Earth and the heavens are full of Thee,*
*Thy light, Thy power, Thy majesty.'*

*Apostles join the glorious throng*
*And swell the loud immortal song;*
*Prophets enraptured hear the sound*
*And spread the alleluia round.*

*Victorious martyrs join their lays*
*And shout the omnipotence of grace,*
*While all Thy church through all the earth*
*Acknowledge and extol Thy worth.*

*Glory to Thee, O God Most High!*
*Father, we praise Thy majesty,*
*The Son, the Spirit, we adore,*
*One Godhead, blest for evermore.*[1]

* * *

*Glory be to God the Father,*
*Glory be to God the Son,*
*Glory be to God the Spirit,*
*Great Jehovah Three in One,*
*Glory, glory* – [that was the great shout of the Calvinistic Methodists]
*While eternal ages run.*

[1] Quoted from Philip Gell's Collection, 1815.

# 1969

# *Can We Learn from History?*

## I

There is nothing, perhaps, that has so detracted from the glory of God as the history of his people in the church. That is why I am going to deal with this subject of learning from history. Hegel's famous dictum reminds us that 'We learn from history that we learn nothing from history.'

Now as far as the secular world is concerned, that is undoubtedly perfectly true. The history of the human race shows this quite clearly. Mankind in its folly and stupidity goes on repeating the same old mistakes. It does not learn, it refuses to learn. But I will not accept this as being true of the Christian. My contention is that the Christian should learn from history, that because he is a Christian it is his duty to do so, and he must rouse himself to do so.

My basis for saying this is the teaching of the Bible itself. How often do we find, for instance, in the book of Psalms that the Psalmist, in order to enforce his lesson and to make his appeal to the nation, recapitulates their history in order to show that the error into which people were falling again is precisely what their forefathers had done. And you remember how in the New Testament, in the book of the Acts of the Apostles, Stephen's famous defence of himself before the Council was really just a recapitulation of history in order to bring out his point. There is also an account of Paul doing the same in Acts chapter 13.

All this surely indicates that the Christian should learn from history. The real trouble with the world is that it cannot think straightly. But the Christian should, and it is therefore his duty to learn in this way. My argument is that it is always essential for us to supplement our reading of theology with the reading of church history. Or if you prefer it, that we should at any rate take our theology in an historical manner. If we do not, we shall be in danger of becoming abstract, theoretical, and academic in our view of truth; and, failing to relate it to the practicalities of life and daily living, we shall soon be in trouble. How many of us who are in the ministry went into a church with theoretical ideas, not aware at all of the practical problems and difficulties? But we soon had to learn that what seemed so plain and clear in theory could not be done in practice because of the state and condition of the people. Now it seems to me that if we are careful to learn the lessons of history, and to supplement our reading of theology by that, we shall already be prepared, and we shall avoid many of the pitfalls and the dangers into which we shall inevitably fall if we do not do this.

This is my introduction to what I am going to do. I am going to take a general view of the history of the church, particularly in the sixteenth and seventeenth centuries. I want to emphasise that I am going to take a 'general' view. In this conference we spend a good deal of our time, and rightly so, in dealing with particular problems and particular questions; but there is a danger that if we do not from time to time take a more general view we may well 'miss the wood because of the trees.' In any case it is sometimes more comfortable to be dealing with particulars than to look at the general situation. But I believe that we are living in an age in which it is very important that we should take this general view.

It is obvious, is it not, from the history of the church that at different times and in different epochs certain particular questions have had unusual prominence. We are all familiar with the facts that in the early ages, for instance, it was the questions of the person of our Lord and the doctrine of the Trinity that were uppermost, and had to be fought out. At other times there have been other subjects that have stood out more prominently. But at the Reformation the first great and immediate question was the doctrine of justification by faith, as we have already heard in this conference several times. But it is interesting to notice that you cannot isolate these things; they are all inter-related. So almost immediately that problem led to another, the problem of the church and the nature of the church. All these different doctrines belong to a whole, and whichever you may start with, sooner or later you will arrive at the others. Thus the problem of the church was a very prominent one in the sixteenth and the seventeenth centuries.

By today there is no question at all but that this is the biggest problem and the most urgent of all. The Ecumenical Movement is compelling us to consider it constantly. In addition to that, we are undoubtedly living at one of the great turning-points of history. I sometimes have a fear that we who are evangelical, of all people are most guilty of failing to realise this. We are so immersed in our local situations, or in our particular fields of study and of interest, that we are not alive to the fact that we are at one of these great climactic points of history. Indeed I have said before, and I say again, that it seems to me that the church has not been in the position that she is in today since the great era of the Protestant Reformation and the century that followed it. Therefore we can do nothing better than to take a general view of the history of those two centuries and learn certain vital lessons from that history.

## II

I need not take any time in painting the background or in explaining why the sixteenth and seventeenth centuries were such a great climactic age. Up until then, speaking generally, the church in the West, at any rate, had been one and united. Then came the Protestant Reformation. Going further back, before Constantine brought the Roman Empire into the church in the early fourth century, the unity of the church had been expressed in terms of faith and worship and a kind of spirit, or 'inner spirit.' But with the coming in of Constantine, and what followed, the institutional element became much more prominent, and the church from there on became an institution and was governed as such by its hierarchy. So that you had a very rigid kind of church government, exercising discipline and control, excommunicating, punishing by death, and so on. But with the Protestant Reformation came the great division in the church in the West into the Roman Catholic and the new Protestant church. The Protestant Reformation seemed to shatter the idea of the unity of the church as being something vitally important, and therefore, immediately, the Protestants were charged with schism.

But – and this is the thing that I want to deal with in particular – the really important thing from our standpoint is what happened after that. That original division led to a whole succession of divisions, with the result that the Roman Catholics have always said that there is something inherently wrong in Protestantism, and that it is fissiparous in its very nature and being, that its history has proved this. This has been the charge that they have brought against Protestantism constantly, and there are many Protestants today who are concerned about the success of the Ecumenical Movement and who repeat the charge.

Very well, let us look at the facts. I think we have to admit immediately that the facts seem to be on the side of that charge. You start with Luther and the movement connected with him over against Roman Catholicism. But history shows that very soon there were divisions even amongst the Lutherans, and right up till about 1580 and the Formula of Concord there were constant wrangles and difficulties and groupings within Lutheranism itself. In addition to that you had the Reformed Church coming into being in Switzerland, and looking particularly of course to Calvin and Geneva; and added to this, the various divisions and subdivisions of the Anabaptists. That was the general picture on the continent.

Coming to our own country, you had the formation of the Church of England. But very soon other divisions began to appear. I do not want to take too much time on this, but eventually a position was reached in which you had those who were Church of England practically in the full sense of the term, and in addition, Puritans, Presbyterians, Brownists, Separatists, Barrowists, Anabaptists, and later, Quakers, Levellers, Diggers, and many other sects which arose during the time of the Commonwealth. In fact, endless divisions came into being.

The history of the Church of Scotland shows this perhaps still more clearly, and it takes a real expert to be able to follow the various divisions and sub-divisions and ramifications. There are books which have charts showing this. When we come to modern times and look at the United States of America, a few years ago I know there were at least two hundred and sixty-one different Protestant denominations. (I do not know what the latest figure is.)

Those then are the sheer facts of history. What do we say about this? How did this happen? What is the explanation of this? A very general explanation, I think, is that this was due to the fact that the Protestant Reformation liberated men and taught them to think for themselves. When you have been under the bondage and tyranny of a rigid system and you are suddenly given freedom, it is almost inevitable that you should get certain excesses. But that is only a very general explanation, and I want to address myself to this problem: can we justify what has happened in Protestantism? Are the Roman Catholics right in what they say about us?

The first answer to that is, of course, that the Roman Catholic Church herself is in no position to bring this charge against Protestantism. Before the Reformation ever came about there had been schisms and divisions and even separations in the history of that very church. Even before Constantine came in there were divisions that occurred. They were regarded as heresies and some of them lasted many centuries; the Novatianists, the Donatists, and many others; and there was always a running quarrel between what became the Church of the East and the Church of the West. The idea that Rome had always been recognised as supreme, and that there were no problems and no divisions, is simply not true to history.

The same continued even after the fourth century and right up to the Protestant Reformation. But Rome, of course, had such tremendous power that she could in a sense contain these divisions. I always feel that the analogy which is helpful at this point is the analogy of the political situation in this country. The great characteristic of the Conservative Party is that she can contain her divisions and subdivisions. The Liberals and the Labour people bring them out into the open and expose them to the public. The Conservative Party do these things amongst themselves and nobody knows what is happening; but when you get behind the scenes you find that there are as many divisions as anywhere else. That, then, is the answer to the Roman Catholics, and we need not be troubled about that. What is of concern to us is, can we justify what has happened in any way?

I will now give you my thesis. The division between Roman Catholic and Protestant I am prepared to defend to the death; but the other divisions, I am prepared to assert, were sinful. They were manifestations of schism and all involved in them were guilty, and we are guilty, in the sight of God.

Let us proceed to substantiate this contention. The extraordinary thing about all that happened in Protestantism, and happened so quickly, is that, apart from the Anabaptists and the various sects, they were all really concerned about comprehension. This is the enigmatic factor which seems to me to come out so strikingly as one reads this history and keeps on re-reading it from different angles – they were all seeking for comprehension. Take Luther for instance: this was his great concern. Luther was afraid that these divisions would lead to the loss of the whole of the Protestant Reformation, that the princes and the powers seeing this happening would be annoyed, and everything that he had fought for, and had suffered for, and had contended for, would be completely lost. So he was very concerned about comprehension, and particularly within his own group.

In the same way, as I am going to show, Calvin was very concerned about Protestant unity from his angle; and when you come to this country, Anglicanism and Queen Elizabeth I were of course dominated in their thinking by the idea of comprehension. Hence their Acts of Uniformity and so on. And as we have been reminded in this conference the Presbyterians held exactly the same view. All these people wanted one national church. That is even true of the Congregationalists at the time of the Commonwealth. It was only later that they ceased to believe in this. Up until the end of the Commonwealth and the Restoration this was the great idea, the idea of comprehension. Here, you see, is this extraordinary fact that while all of them were claiming to aim at the idea of comprehension they nevertheless divided in this extraordinary manner.

The question we have to ask, then, is this: What was it that caused these divisions? What were the factors that operated to nullify this great idea of comprehension? I have tried to tabulate them, trusting as we look at them that we can receive guidance for our day, and situation, from this particular history.

The first cause of trouble as I see it, the first thing that hindered Protestant union, was the idea of national churches. Now it is not at all surprising that they should have thought of it in that way, because reform tended to take place independently in the different nations and countries. Not only that, in all these countries there was the time-honoured connection and relationship between the church and the state. So when they broke with Rome it was almost instinctive for them to think in terms of their own national position. They did not want to divide up, but they desired to separate from Rome; and they all viewed it within the sphere of their own knowledge. So they all tended to do it in a national way. You find the city-states in Switzerland doing exactly the same thing. They were concerned about themselves primarily, and because of this old and traditional relationship between the church and the state, the church tended to take the form of a national or state church. That happened not only on the continent but also here in England, and in Scotland, and in various other places. In the case of England the kings and queens became the head of the church as well as the head of the state. This is a most important factor; and one cannot understand this particular history without seeing that very clearly.

In the second place certain national characteristics operated very powerfully. Here, of course, is something that one could take up and deal with at length. I am not going to do so now because of lack of time. Should this factor operate at all? What is the place of national characteristics in the Christian life, and especially in connection with the church?

Well, the fact is that this has been a very important factor in the case of England. There was a natural independence of spirit and a national consciousness before the Reformation. England had several times objected to the power and the influence of the Pope over her church. There had been many movements in this direction and many protests. A national spirit was arising in most European countries and nations at that time, and therefore when the church separated from Rome it was quite natural for them to do so in their own particular way.

But, in addition to this, I believe that national characteristics operated in many ways. This is a subject which needs to be discussed in greater detail, but it is surely difficult to evade the conclusion that the ecclesiastical differences in different countries have been the result of these differing national characteristics. Let us take as an illustration the difference between England and Scotland. The typical Englishman has a dislike of definitions; the glory of the British Empire to him was that it had not got a written constitution. It had just happened, and with the principle of empiricism enthroned, her chief glory was that she had 'muddled through.' I do not want to make too much of this, but there is this innate dislike of over-precision and too much definition. I am speaking about the average Englishman; there are exceptions, but they are very much exceptions. It is surely very clear that at the time of the Reformation and in the Elizabethan period this national characteristic operated in England. The *via media* appeals to the Englishman, he likes the idea of compromise, he dislikes extremes and excesses and over-precise definitions.

I am not criticising, I am describing; and I am asserting that we have to bear all this in mind, and that if we fail to do so we shall not be learning the lessons of history. I am suggesting that with regard to the danger today of basing too much of our discussion upon confessions drawn up at that time we tend to neglect this particular factor; and we do so of course to our own confusion.

The Scots, on the other hand, are very different in this respect. They like definitions, and precision and exactness. They demand them, and insist upon them. The whole outlook, the mentality, is a different one. This is something that I could work out in terms of other nations like the Dutch, etc., in exactly the same way. One must not go too far with regard to all this. I know that there is the danger of trying to explain everything in terms of psychology and so on. I remember once reading a book by a man who said he could explain everything in terms of geography. He did not hesitate to explain John Calvin in terms of the cold climate of Geneva. You know the theory that the further south you go the more likely the people are to be Catholic, the more north the more likely they are to be Protestant! At that point, of course, it becomes ridiculous; all I am asserting is that you cannot exclude this particular factor of these general characteristics of people.

This is not only true of nations, this factor is very important also with regard to individual persons. Temperament comes into these matters, and I defy you to exclude it. I am quite sure that a great deal of the trouble in the sixteenth century was due to the personality of Martin Luther. He was a giant of a man, he was a kind of volcano, and so different from John Calvin. Luther was not systematic in the way that Calvin was; he was not governed by reason to the same extent. There was something explosive about the man, and as I am going to show, in certain details this really is a most vital part of the explanation of what I would regard as a tragedy. But I must be fair to Luther. His own history influenced him, perhaps unconsciously. If you read the history of the Lutheran Church from, say, 1518 or 1520 right on to 1580 you will find that Luther was in great trouble over the question of condemning people and excluding them from the fellowship of the church. I have no doubt but that this was largely due to the way he himself had suffered at the hands of the Roman Catholic Church. He had a horror of doing to others what had been done to him. He at any rate was intelligent enough to see this, that if you fought for freedom against a rigid system you must at all costs avoid becoming a dictator yourself. He was aware of this, and, I believe that at certain times it made him hesitate to condemn where perhaps we might think he should have condemned.

But then, in addition to that, his views on the 'hiddenness' of the church, and the 'hiddenness' of the word of God, and the markedly spiritual element in his whole outlook and teaching, militated against his defining things as clearly as Calvin, and putting his ideas into practice in the matter of discipline. I leave it at just that, taking the one example of Luther. There are many other men who appear in the history of that time, and many since, whom one could use in exactly the same way. I am asking this basic question, let me remind you, as to whether things of this nature should influence the Christian position. My contention is that they should not; but I am asserting that they have done so.

But let us look at a third factor – politics! Here, of course, was a most potent factor in the sixteenth and seventeenth centuries. What was really the explanation of Luther's violent antagonism to the Anabaptists? Surely there is no question at all about this. It was his fear, especially after the Peasants' Revolt, that the views and activities of these people whom at first he had rather liked, would jeopardise the whole of the Reformation. He knew the reaction of the princes and governments, so he did everything he could to prevent this. But that was a political motive.

In the same way, it seems to me, the case can be made out very clearly that Melanchthon – a very different kind of man – in drawing up the Augsburg Confession was very largely governed by a political motive. The Roman Catholics were saying that Protestantism was heretical, that Protestants were departing from the Christian faith, and that the emperor and the various princes should therefore oppose it. So Melanchthon's primary concern in drawing up that confession, was to prove that Protestantism was not heretical, that really it was teaching very much the same thing as the Roman Catholic Church had been teaching except for certain things. This was his emphasis. So if we forget this and stand too rigidly behind that confession, as the Lutherans did afterwards, and ignore this particular factor in history, namely, political considerations, we shall be taking a false view of the Augsburg Confession. The same thing, of course, is equally evident, and more so, in connection with the Huguenots.

But when you come to this country this factor is still plainer and clearer. The person who really determined the character and the nature of the Church of England was none other than Queen Elizabeth. I do not think there is any question about this. A recent book, *Queen Elizabeth and the Reformation in England*, by Haugaard, is most illuminating in this respect. It deals particularly with the crucial Convocation of 1563, and the history leading up to it. In many other books one can read about the influence of Walsingham, and of Burleigh himself, and of the Earl of Leicester and others who were more or less favourable in general to the Puritans. But the point is that the dominating factor was the political one. Elizabeth was in an extremely difficult position. She was especially afraid of France, so she had to keep on the right side of Philip of Spain. On the other hand the Roman Catholics said that she was illegitimate, that she was a bastard. She naturally disliked that, and so at that point she was against the Roman Catholics. The result of all this was that Elizabeth was always engaged in a balancing exercise. She felt that if the Puritans were given their head, and the church was allowed to go in that direction, then the Roman Catholics would of necessity be alienated and everything might be lost. But she did not want to go too far on that side either, because she knew that if she gave the impression that she was too favourable to the Roman Catholics she would be annoying the great body of her people.

The principle that emerges so clearly is that she was governed by these political motives and ideas. I believe that it can be stated further that in her own nature and temperament she was a true daughter of her father, and that her sympathies were very largely on the Catholic side. There is much evidence that can be produced and adduced to demonstrate that. But above all else she was concerned about her throne, and about her whole position and that of the country. We should give her very great praise as a statesman; but we are concerned about the nature of the church.

But when you come on to James I and Charles I all this is much more obvious. They held the view 'No bishop, no king,' and that determined all their thinking and behaviour. The political factor came in so powerfully on that side; but we have to admit that it came in on the side of the Puritans also. People like Hampden and Pym and others, on constitutional grounds, and on political grounds, were opposed to these sovereigns, and there developed a mixture of motives. The religious and the political became bound up together, and the issues became confused; and having at the back of it all this idea of comprehension, and of a national church, the real spiritual element was generally over-ridden, it seems to me, by the political one. It is agreed by many historians that the real reason why the Solemn League and Covenant was signed by England in 1643 was political expediency. The English did not want to do this, but the Parliamentary army was doing very badly and they needed help; so they had to turn to Scotland. The Scots saw their opportunity, and they laid down this condition: they bargained, and they won the bargain.

Somebody was asking in one of our discussions – if I may digress for a moment – why it was that there was a failure to impose Presbyterianism in the seventeenth century whereas Protestantism had been imposed in the sixteenth century? I think the answer to that is quite simple. In the sixteenth century you had a tyrant like Henry VIII in control; and the power of the Crown and of the Throne was so tremendous that they could enforce anything. But when Presbyterianism became official and the attempt was made really to make it permanent, there had been a rebellion, a revolution; the king was being fought, and the army was becoming more powerful. The king was eventually beheaded and the army gained control; and the army, with Cromwell, was mainly Independent. It was they, very largely, who would not endure this imposition of Presbyterianism. And, later, in 1660 we must not forget the conservatism of the English mentality, and its liking of ceremonial, its liking of titles and names. This is one of the few great countries left in the world that has a monarch. That is not an accident, it is typically English. A fondness for kings and queens, a liking for titles and names, is a part of the whole outlook. The Welsh, for instance, are a peasant people and they have never had the veneration for titles that is found so commonly in England. You cannot exclude this kind of thing, and it did turn out to be a very powerful factor. The English did not like these upstarts who were getting into positions of authority. They preferred, and had always had, a king in control, and while they had more or less endured Oliver Cromwell, when his two sons did not turn out to be too successful they turned with great relief even to such a man as Charles II. They were encouraged, unfortunately, in doing that, as we know, by the Scots who, deceived by the duplicity of Charles, thought there was a real opportunity of establishing Presbyterianism, or at the very least modifying episcopacy very considerably in that direction.

Added to this there is the whole question of tradition. I have already been referring to it – a dislike of change. This manifested itself particularly over the question of episcopacy. It was partly also responsible for the desire to hold on to certain ceremonies which had been taken over from the Roman church, modified I know, but still essentially Romish ceremonies. But episcopacy stands out. You cannot read the history of 1560 to 1640, or even to 1660, without seeing that the one great stumbling-block to every attempt at comprehension was ultimately episcopacy. This was the rock on which they all struck and at which they all foundered, in a sense.

Take, for instance, those attempts that were made to get a modified episcopacy. This was all very good. But Archbishop Ussher's attempt and all others failed. And then after the Restoration when Clarendon got into control, and the exiled bishops came back, episcopacy was flying high and it ruled and governed. Everything was in its hands, and so you had the Great Ejection of 1662 and all the other persecutions with which we are familiar.

Then we come to the fifth great cause of these tragic divisions; and that was the trouble over the definition of fundamentals. To put it in other language, it was the trouble concerning the line of division between essentials and non-essentials in connection with the Christian faith. Or, to put it in yet a different way, it was a desire for uniformity in too much detail. This, to me, is one of the great and most important lessons of that hundred years.

Let me give an example or two. Take Luther, for instance, and in particular Luther's view of the sacrament of the Lord's Supper. This is surely one of the great tragedies in the history of the church, this division between the Lutheran and the Reformed churches. It was almost entirely due to a division on this one thing. There were other differences, but I am satisfied by the evidence produced by those historians who say that the cause of the collapse at the Colloquy of Marburg in 1529 was really this one thing. Luther himself drew up fifteen points or articles, and Zwingli and Oecolampadius, who was there with him on the other side, accepted fourteen of the points in their entirety, and had even accepted part of the fifteenth. But Luther took up his bit of chalk, you remember, and wrote on the table, 'This is my body' – not that it 'represents' it, it *is* it – and so wrecked the conference on his notion of consubstantiation.

Luther wrecked the whole prospect of comprehension or of Protestant unity on this one thing, on this one particular. As somebody has put it so well, 'The sacrament of communion became the apple of discord.' It is a terrible thing, but it is true. And Luther as the result of this attacked Zwingli and his followers violently, and Calvin also. He said the most outrageous things about them. I am not at all sure but that at that point one can almost invoke medical illness in the case of Luther. There seems to be some evidence for that. However, that is doubtless another dangerous thing to say; but you cannot even exclude that. These are the historical factors that come in and determine men's decisions and their attitudes. However, the whole prospect of union was wrecked, and the whole situation became hardened over this one thing.

There is a very tragic footnote to this. Luther just before his death in 1546 read a little book by John Calvin which bore the title *A Little Treatise on the Holy Supper of our Lord,* and having read it this is what he said to Melanchthon: 'In this matter of the sacrament we have gone much too far, I will commend the thing to the Lord. Do something after my death.' Pathetic, is it not? But it was too late, the damage had been done; and though he had now come to see that they had gone much too far the position had become hardened. Later it became even worse and the whole prospect of unity vanished because, after the Formula of Concord of 1580, this became part of the exclusive and irreformable system of the Lutherans. That led to the hardened orthodoxy against which there arose the movement associated with the name of the Pietists.

One of the Puritans of the seventeenth century made a very acute remark on all this. He said: 'Witness the bickering between some Lutherans and Calvinists, as they are by some nicknamed, which have given religion since the last Reformation thereof a greater blow than all the thunderbolts of Rome together.' That was his view of the division between the Lutherans and the Reformed, that it had done greater harm to true religion than all the thunderbolts of Rome together.

That is but one illustration out of many that could be adduced from the history of England and Scotland, and what became the United States, of this tendency to insist upon particulars which I am suggesting are non-essentials. It was part of this whole problem of deciding what is essential and what is non-essential, what is fundamental and what is not fundamental. It was the failure to arrive at this decision, this conclusion, in a charitable manner that so often wrecked every attempt at true evangelical and Protestant unity.

Yet, and in spite of all I have been saying, the astonishing thing is that the ideal of Protestant union was fought for during this whole period in a most remarkable manner. William Farel, the man who persuaded John Calvin to stay in Geneva, was most concerned about this and he fought for this. Bucer, or Butzer, again was outstanding in his concern and his striving for Protestant union. And as you know, Bucer had a great influence upon John Calvin and in many ways influenced him in this same direction. With regard to the dispute and difference of opinion on the sacrament of the Lord's Supper, what Bucer said about this was that the dispute was 'only a matter of words' – and surely he was right. Calvin, on the same topic, said that the difference 'was not very grave.'

But, most interesting and important, let me remind you of some of the manifestations of this desire for Protestant unity on the part of John Calvin. In spite of the vituperative and unkind things that Luther said of Calvin, Calvin's references to Luther were always not only gentle but generous and full of expressions of admiration. But listen to Calvin writing to Melanchthon: 'Let us mourn together the misfortunes of the church, yet rejoice that we cannot be utterly overwhelmed.' Listen to him writing to Bullinger on the sacrament: 'If we could only talk together for half a day we would agree without difficulty.' That is John Calvin. He is a much maligned man.

Calvin wrote to Matthew Parker, Queen Elizabeth I's archbishop, in 1560 urging him to induce the queen to convoke a general assembly of Protestant ministers to frame a plan of worship and government, not only for the Church of England but for all the Reformed and evangelical churches. He urged her to do this; and you remember his famous statement, that he was prepared to cross oceans, and so on, to do anything he could to help in this respect. The reply he got to that was that the Church of England would retain its Episcopate, which Matthew Parker argued derived not from Rome but from Joseph of Arimathaea! That is how that ended.

Then you are aware, I trust, of Calvin's advice to the Puritans in this country who wrote to him. They asked his advice as to whether they should stand out on the question of episcopacy and of ceremonies in England; and though it may surprise you, Calvin told them not to stand out on that. He did not believe in episcopacy, but he was so concerned about Protestant unity that he could just see that perhaps in the peculiar circumstances of England – perhaps he was a bit of a psychologist and knew something about these national characteristics – they should not stand out on these particular things. They did not accept his advice, but that was the advice that he actually did give to them. Let it be said to the honour of Cranmer that he tried to call a conference in the days of Edward VI to deal with his matter, again encouraged by Bucer, who was by then professor of theology in Cambridge.

Here, you see, during all these times of divisions and ramifications and sub-divisions there was this great effort after Protestant unity. It is very interesting to notice that the last two great results of this seeking for Protestant unity were, first the Authorised Version or Translation of the Bible, and the other was, of course, the Westminster Confession of Faith. That was the last expression of this concern about unity – Protestant evangelical unity – in this country. But alas, it all came to nothing, and Milton could complain that 'new presbyter' was very similar to 'old priest.'

## III

There, then, is a very hurried review of the history. Let me try to draw some lessons and conclusions from all this. My whole contention is that our situation today provides us with an opportunity such as the church has not had since the Protestant Reformation. I want to go further. I suggest that in the light of this history we are in an altogether better and more advantageous position than our forefathers were in the sixteenth and seventeenth centuries. On what grounds do I make this assertion? I do so on the grounds of the tremendous differences between our position and theirs. One is that politics is no longer the dominating factor that it was then. It really did dominate then. It had been the tradition throughout the centuries – church and state – and almost inevitably they were driven to do what they did, as I have tried to show. That is no longer the case.

Not only that, there is an increasing manifestation of a desire to separate church and state, not only in other countries but even in this country. But more than that, we are living in an age where nationalism of the type that you had in the sixteenth and seventeenth centuries is no longer present. We are living in an international age. Even the proposal and the desire to have the European Economic Community is a manifestation of this. There is a readiness now to surrender certain elements of national sovereignty which as far as I know has never existed before. All this is a part of the climate in which we are living, so that our position is very different. Then in the religious realm there is all this talk and activity with respect to ecumenicity.

I argue, therefore, that we have a new freedom of manoeuvre which our Protestant Reformers did not have. We have possibilities that they never had. They were bound by what they had inherited in a way that we are not. Say what you like about this age, there is a freedom of manoeuvre possible today which I am not aware of as having existed at any other time. And so the question that I would address to you is this – and I am concerned at the moment merely to ask questions – have we got the same burning desire for Protestant evangelical unity as Calvin and the others whom I have mentioned had? It is our duty to have it. Division in the church is a scandal. Schism is a deadly sin. The ideal for the church has been put by our Lord himself in John chapter 17; and we have other similar passages in the New Testament. If we have not a burning desire and longing for this unity of true believers I say we are false to the New Testament. So we must examine ourselves. If they in their extraordinarily difficult situations and circumstances had this desire, how much more so should we have this desire?

What then are we to do? Once more I am only going to put forward some matters for your consideration and deliberation. Each one of these matters, of course, would take a long time in and of itself, so I am only going to give some headings. The first thing I suggest is this, that we really must say farewell once and for ever to the idea of a national church. There has been no national church in this country since the Restoration; that finished at the Great Ejection. Every Act of Toleration has been a denial of the national church idea – the recognition of nonconformists and ultimately Roman Catholics in the 1820s. This has put an end to it in actual fact, though of course, it is a characteristic of this country to say 'Yes' and 'No' at the same time. You have it and you do not have it.

Now that may be allowable in politics, but I am asking in the name of God whether it is right in the realm of the Christian church. That is the question that I am putting. I suggest that there is all the difference in the world between the idea of a national church and the recognition of the churches in a particular country. 'The churches' in a particular country is inevitable, that is right. You have to have a minimum of organisation and naturally churches in a country will work together and operate together; but that is totally different from the idea of a national church. So I suggest that is the first move, to get rid of that notion.

Then the second step will be this – we shall have to face squarely this question of the definition of fundamentals and essentials. Here

I start with two negatives. We do not take the position, I assume, as Evangelicals, that was taken by Dr Samuel Johnson. He said: 'For my part, Sir, I think that all Christians, whether Papists or Protestants, agree in the essential Articles and that their differences are trivial and rather political than religious.' The great Lexicographer could sometimes talk nonsense! That is, of course, something we do not even waste time in considering.

But we also have to reject, it seems to me, the position of Richard Baxter. He said that all who accept the Apostles' Creed as a summary of belief, the Lord's Prayer as a summary of devotion, and the Decalogue as a summary of duty are truly Christians and members of the catholic and universal church of Christ. That, as was pointed out to him when he said it in a conference to which I shall refer in a moment, would have included Papists and Socinians into the fellowship of the church, and so it was turned down.

What we have to do is this: we have to discover a position between – the border-line, if you like – between 'a binding condemnation spoken in the name of the whole church, and an arbitrary hereticising in the name of a scholastic pedantry.' Let me put that in other language. We have got to avoid the extremes of 'an unrestrained or unrestricted laxity and an egotistical rigour.' Those are the extremes between which we have to work – an unrestrained laxity and an egotistical rigour. As I have tried to show, it was the failure to draw the line that led to so much of the trouble during the century which we have been considering.

What is the next step? Well, it seems to me that there is this broad division still, as there was at the time of the Protestant Reformation, between the notion of a general comprehension with Rome, modified but Rome nevertheless, included on the one hand, and an evangelical attitude towards the church on the other hand. This is the big broad distinction. You had it at the time of the Reformation, but unfortunately, as I have tried to show from the history, they divided up and Protestantism became fragmented. I am suggesting that we now have another opportunity of restoring the true position. There is this big, broad division – the Catholic view, the Comprehensive view, the all-inclusive view on the one hand, and the evangelical view which is more restricted and particular on the other hand.

Then, having laid down that broad distinction, I am suggesting that the next step is that we must avoid the danger of being bound by tradition, that we must even avoid the danger of being legalistically bound by the confessions of faith that were drawn up in the sixteenth and the seventeenth centuries. We must remember that the confessions are only subordinate standards. They are not of equal authority with the Scriptures, and we must be careful lest we allow ourselves to be jockeyed into positions in which we are just defending the confessions of those two centuries at all costs and not facing the realities and the practicalities of the situation in which we find ourselves in this present age and generation.

The American Presbyterians seem to me to provide us with a most instructive and excellent example at this point. The American Presbyterians in the eighteenth century did not hesitate to modify the Westminster Confession. They modified it over the question of the relationship between the church and the state. They wanted a wholly free church, a church that was entirely free, so they modified Chapter xx, Section iv, Chapter xxiii, Section iii, Chapter xxx, Section i, of the Westminster Confession.

Now that, to me, is spiritual and biblical thinking. The Westminster Confession was not divinely inspired, and we must be free. We must use these confessions of faith as guides and not allow them to be tyrants. They are not to be rigid codes which we must never vary or change in any respect. Let us use them, let us thank God for them, but let us claim that as Christian people we are born again, that we have the Spirit, and are equally capable of determining the teaching of the Scriptures and the true doctrine with regard to the church. We must remember that in all these confessions – I trust I have brought this out – there was that historical element; there was the factor of the historical condition at that time because of their peculiar circumstances, and therefore I argue that it would be wrong for us to insist upon adhering to them always in all points and details. We have got to recognise the historical element, and so must examine the confessions in the light of Scripture. The church must go on being reformed and she must continue to put herself under the Scriptures.

There is surely a great misuse of the confessions today. Some are dishonestly paying lip-service to them, and then just throwing them into the museum. And there are others, it seems to me, who are fighting a rear-guard action by hiding behind them. It is a matter of ecclesiastical policy sometimes rather than truth. I suggest that these are two very bad uses of the confessions and that the honest thing to do is to examine them in the light of Scripture, and to realise that God calls upon us to do this in our day and generation, even as he called upon the Protestant Reformers to do so and the Fathers in the seventeenth century.

I am urging this for this reason, that if we do not avoid the mistake into which they fell we shall also fail; and we have to avoid, in particular, this tragic mistake of going to extremes, and insisting upon particulars which are non-essential, in a rigorous manner. Take what we have been hearing in this conference this year. Are we not all agreed that the story is a tragic one – the Christian church divided up, all the troubles and the persecutions and the misunderstandings and the alienations? We are 'the body of Christ,' the custodians and the guardians of the faith, and people are dying and going to hell round and about us. It is a tragic story, and we ought to be ashamed of it. I say that the call to us is to learn these lessons and to avoid the mistakes into which they fell. There are many distinctions which we must bear in mind, and which I can merely mention. But we must learn to distinguish between error and heresy, between false teaching and a mistaken belief.

Let me quote Melanchthon at this point: 'It is possible that we should tolerate as brothers Christians who err but who do not defend the error; yet those cannot be regarded as brothers who promote and defend teachings that have no scriptural foundation.' In other words, you see, there is to be a fundamental division, and I am suggesting that it is still the fundamental one, the division of Catholic and Protestant, or a comprehension that includes the Roman Catholics on the one hand and the evangelical, truly Protestant, position on the other. There is this dividing line – 'we cannot regard as brothers those who promote and defend teachings that have no scriptural warrant.' I believe we are back very much in the position of the Reformers of the sixteenth century, except that we have this additional factor of modernism and liberalism, and so on, which they did not have to contend with, and which really should not constitute a problem to us at all, for it is not a gospel in any sense. Where then do we draw the line?

Let me quote some of the Puritans. Take Robert Harris. 'I will not undertake to define what is so merely fundamental and absolutely necessary to salvation as that without it there is no hope. This much I am sure: First, the fundamentals are fewer than many of both sides make them. Secondly, that every lean-to and superstructure doth not raze the foundation.' They talked about 'lean-to's' you see in the seventeenth century! Robert Harris was a member of the Westminster Assembly. He says there that he is quite convinced of this 'that every lean-to and superstructure doth not raze the foundation.' That is the thing to watch, that you do not raze the foundation: then you can be more tolerant about these lean-to's. He says, 'Men of humble and of sincere hearts, though differing in opinion can and do walk together, pray together, and love one another.' Surely that is something to which our hearts must respond.

Charles Herle: 'But for those differences that are among us, whatever they be, let us rather strive to pray them less than argue them more.' Are we ready to say 'Amen' to that? Here is another member of the Westminster Assembly – 'Let us rather strive to pray them less than to argue them more.' Again he goes on: 'However, for the difference between us and our brethren that are for Independency, 'tis nothing so great as you seem to conceive it. We do but with Abraham and Lot take several ways. We are, as Abraham speaks, "brethren" still, and as they were ready to rescue each other on all occasions against the common enemy, our difference 'tis such as doth at most but ruffle a little the fringe and not in any way rend the garment of Christ.' And, surely, this is the position. These differences are about 'fringes.' I am talking about true Evangelicals – nobody else! The differences are about 'fringes' and they 'do not rend the garment of Christ.'

Is there any kind of practical proposal therefore that I can put before you? There is, and with this I close. In 1654 Oliver Cromwell – with his idea of toleration – and the Parliament called upon the divines to define what should be tolerated or indulged among those who profess the fundamentals of Christianity. In effect they said, we have all these divisions and sects and groups; what are the fundamentals of Christianity on which we can have fellowship together? So a committee was set up and the members of the committee were these: Mr Richard Baxter, Dr John Owen, Dr Thomas Goodwin, Dr Cheynel, Mr Marshall, Mr Reyner, Mr Nye, Mr Sydrach Simpson, Mr Vines, Mr Manton, Mr Jacomb. As I said earlier, Baxter tried to short-circuit the whole proposal at the beginning by saying that nothing was necessary but the Apostles' Creed, the Lord's Prayer, and the Ten Commandments. But that was rejected. Then they proceeded to work, and they produced sixteen articles which they felt stated the fundamentals on which, and on which alone, true fellowship is possible between Protestant evangelical people. Here they are –

1. That the Holy Scripture is that rule of knowing God and living unto him which whoso does not believe cannot be saved.

2. That there is a God who is the Creator, Governor, and Judge of the world, which is to be received by faith, and every other way of the knowledge of him is insufficient.

3. That this God who is the Creator is eternally distinct from all creatures in his being and blessedness.

4. That this God is one in three persons or subsistences.

5. That Jesus Christ is the only mediator between God and man without the knowledge of whom there is no salvation.

6. That this Jesus Christ is the true God.

7. That this Jesus Christ is also true man.

8. That this Jesus Christ is God and man in one person.

9. That this Jesus Christ is our Redeemer, who by paying a ransom and bearing our sins has made satisfaction for them.

10. That this same Lord Jesus Christ is he that was crucified at Jerusalem, and rose again and ascended into heaven.

11. That this same Jesus Christ being the only God and man in

one person remains for ever a distinct person from all saints and angels notwithstanding their union and communion with him.

12. That all men by nature were dead in sins and trespasses, and no man can be saved unless he be born again, repent, and believe.

13. That we are justified and saved by grace and faith in Jesus Christ and not by works.

14. That to continue in any known sin upon what pretence or principle soever is damnable.

15. That God is to be worshipped according to his own will, and whosoever shall forsake and despise all the duties of his worship cannot be saved.

16. That the dead shall rise, and that there is a day of judgment wherein all shall appear, some to go into everlasting life and some into everlasting condemnation.

They were the sixteen points. We have the authority of Richard Baxter for saying that it was Dr John Owen who worded those articles, that Dr Goodwin and Mr Nye and Mr Simpson were his assistants, that Dr Reynolds was the scribe, and that Mr Marshall, a sober, worthy man did something, but the rest were little better than passive.

Now these articles were designed and intended to exclude not only Deists, Socinians, and Papists, but also Arians, Antinomians, Quakers, and others. What I am asking is this: Cannot we accept those as the fundamentals? Are those not sufficient? We remember, of course, that bishops, deans, etc., etc., had been abolished at that time, and therefore did not need to be mentioned; and also that they did not have to contend with a 'higher critical' attitude to the Scriptures. They were agreed also in their attitude towards 'tradition.' Their object was to define the irreducible minimum on which evangelical people could work together. We, today, need to elaborate some of these statements in view of our peculiar circumstances; but, still, I suggest, we should seek the minimum definition and not the maximum. Then, united on that basis, we can as brethren work together, and meet together for discussion of the matters on which we differ, and for our mutual edification.

# 1971

# *Puritanism and Its Origins*

I CALL attention to this subject for the reason that I believe that periodically we need to remind ourselves as to what Puritanism is. I have attempted to do this on two previous occasions. In an address I gave at the Evangelical Library in 1962 on the Ejectment of 1662, I dealt with it hurriedly in order to provide the background to what happened in 1662.[1] Then in 1965 in a paper on 'Henry Jacob and the first Congregational Church in London,' I again summarised it briefly. However, I feel that it is necessary to return to it once more, and chiefly because of an element of confusion that has arisen with regard to the definition of Puritanism.

I do this not in any academic sense. My interest in this subject is not academic, and never has been. Puritanism can become a snare and a real danger. There are these voluminous tomes, and very easily one can play a most exciting intellectual game picking out subjects and having most interesting theoretical discussions. That has never been my approach to Puritanism.

My interest in it arose in this way – if you will forgive me a word of personal confession and reminiscence. Brought up as I was in what is called the Welsh Calvinistic Methodist Church, and having become interested in their history, I observed that the leaders of that movement – Daniel Rowland and others – were obviously diligent readers of people called Puritans. They would quote from them, and indeed at times were charged with having preached some of their sermons. That had aroused my general interest. But my real interest arose in 1925 when, in a way that I need not explain now, I happened to read a new biography of

[1] See Appendix p. 471.

Richard Baxter which had just appeared. I had read a review of it in the then *British Weekly*, and was so attracted that I bought it. From that time a true and living interest in the Puritans and their works has gripped me, and I am free to confess that my whole ministry has been governed by this. A later element which encouraged this yet more was my discovery of Jonathan Edwards. One cannot read him without being driven back again to the same sources. I am interested in Puritanism because it seems to me to be one of the most useful things any preacher can do. Nothing so encourages a true ministry of the word because these men were such great exemplars in that respect.

This is why I am so concerned about a true definition of Puritanism. This has become increasingly difficult because of the plethora of books which are being published on this subject. It is very difficult to keep up with them. Some of the best are *Tudor Puritanism* by Knappen, *The Rise of Puritanism* by Haller, *The Elizabethan Movement* by Patrick Collinson – a more recent and very important book. Then there are *Reformation and Reaction in Tudor Cambridge* by Porter – again a very important book, and *Anglican and Puritan* by New, and many others which deal with particular aspects. This makes the problem difficult because the whole question of the definition of a Puritan has been raised acutely by all these books.

However, the most important reason for considering this particular subject now is our situation today. We are back in a position very similar to that of the sixteenth century. That was a time of great change as we have been reminded in several of the papers in this conference. It was a time of new beginnings; and we are in an era of new beginnings. That is why it is so important for us to consider this particular history.

The problem has arisen with regard to the definition of the term Puritan, and there has been much writing concerning this in books and journals. When did the term Puritan appear? When was it first used? The historians have become interested, and they are more interested in the history, or perhaps in the historiography rather than in the spirit and in the teaching. It is just there that they become a danger. They have the scholarly, not to say pedantic, precision which is peculiar to them, and that is where the confusion comes in. There were also differences among the Puritans themselves, and there were those who changed from one position to another as the years passed.

All this has made the question of definition somewhat difficult and complicated. An essay by Professor Basil Hall of Cambridge in one of the volumes of church history is now being regarded by many as having more or less settled the semantics of this question: and he claims to have arrived at a true definition of what is meant by a Puritan. He says that the only true Puritans – in the true sense of the meaning – were these Anglicans who did not leave the Church of England but who held to Puritan doctrine. He excludes Presbyterians, Separatists, and others.

It is easy to see how he arrived at that conclusion. From the standpoint of neatness of definition, and mechanical classification, there is a lot to be said for what he argues; but I shall attempt to show that it is an almost ridiculously inadequate definition of what Puritanism really means.

There is what can be called the Anglican view of, and definition of, Puritanism which virtually says and assumes, that Puritanism began with Richard Greenham and Richard Rogers in the late 1570s and early 1580s and was then continued and elaborated by the great William Perkins who lived on into just the beginning of the next century. According to this definition Puritanism is essentially pastoral theology – an interest in pastoral theology and cases of conscience, etc. That was the interest of those men, of course. Greenham was the first. He began to teach young men who went to stay and to live with him and thus quite a school of teaching arose. They were, of course, interested in all the great doctrines, but their peculiar emphasis was on this pastoral aspect. They dealt with 'cases of conscience,' namely, the difficulties that arise in the living of the Christian life.

Now I am concerned to show that that is not only an inadequate definition of Puritanism, but that if we accept it we are excluding what I am hoping to show is the main essential characteristic of Puritanism. Others make light of what separated the Puritans from other Anglicans; they minimise it, and say that it is merely a matter of temporal and economic and administrative differences, and nothing else. They maintain that it has nothing to do with doctrine, but only with matters indifferent, and that the trouble with the Puritans was that they would keep on turning molehills into mountains. They were quite unimportant differences.

But then, J. F. H. New, to whom I have referred, in his book *Anglican and Puritan,* goes so far as to say that there was always a fundamental difference between the Puritan and the Anglican in matters of fundamental doctrine, such as the doctrine of man, the doctrine of the church, the doctrine of the sacraments, and doctrine in respect of eschatology. This is a really important book, but I find that most writers are hesitant about his point of view. They do not deal with him truly; they just say that he has gone too far. But he has certainly caused many to think again. His contention is that over and above the 'matters of indifference' to which I am going to refer there was always from the beginning a fundamental difference, a difference with regard to those key doctrines of the Christian faith. Having read New several times I am almost persuaded that he is entirely right. He may go a little too far, but I am convinced that on the whole he is essentially right. The only qualification I would add is that what he says is plainly true when the Anglican position had truly crystallised as a result of the work of Richard Hooker, and you have true Anglicanism, but that it was not as true in the earlier period. The great difficulty always in handling this matter is that one is almost driven to use terms in a proleptic manner. It is very helpful from the standpoint of clarity of thought to talk about Puritanism and Anglicanism, but, to be strictly accurate, Anglicanism as such only really emerged with Richard Hooker; yet it was implicit before that and was only made explicit by Hooker. In a sense, therefore, we are justified in talking about Anglicanism from the beginning and to talk about Puritanism from the beginning of the Reformation in England. I suggest, therefore, that the best way to get out of this morass is first of all to approach our subject in a purely historical manner.

The first question to ask is, When did Puritanism begin? Those who follow Professor Basil Hall will point out that the term Puritan was not used until 1567, and that therefore Puritanism began then. That is doubtless true as a mere statement of fact, but it completely misses the spirit of Puritanism. Puritanism, I am prepared to assert with Knappen in his *Tudor Puritanism,* really first began to manifest itself in William Tyndale, and as far back as 1524. Why does one say that? For the reason that Puritanism, as I am hoping to demonstrate, is a type of mind. It is an attitude, it is a spirit, and it is clear that two of the great characteristics of Puritanism began to show themselves in Tyndale. He had a burning desire that the common people should be able to read the Scriptures. But there were great obstacles in his way; and it is the way in which he met and overcame the obstacles that show that Tyndale was a Puritan. He issued a translation of the Bible without the endorsement and sanction of the bishops. That was the first shot fired by Puritanism. It was unthinkable that such a thing should be done without the consent and endorsement of the bishops. But Tyndale did so. Another action on his part which was again most characteristic of the Puritans was that he left this country without the royal assent. That again was a most unusual act and highly reprehensible in the eyes of the authorities. But in his anxiety to translate and print the Scriptures, Tyndale left the country without the king's assent, and went to Germany, and there, helped by Luther and others, he completed his great work. Those two actions were typical of what continued to be the Puritan attitude towards authority. It means the putting of truth before questions of tradition and authority, and an insistence upon liberty to serve God in the way which you believe is the true way.

From the time of Tyndale this spirit, this attitude, this mentality continued to manifest itself. Henry VIII, as is well known, was concerned really about one thing only and that was to be able to secure a divorce from his wife and to marry again. That led to the desire to get rid of the Pope and his authority in order that he himself might become the head of the Church of England. Doctrinally he died a thorough Roman Catholic. This mixture of motives and muddled thinking and divided counsels meant that he was in difficulties constantly and kept on changing his policy. For instance, in 1532 he authorised Ten Articles in which, while he still retained all the various ceremonies which were characteristic of the Roman Catholic Church, he modified the view of purgatory somewhat, and the worshipping of the saints, and the cult of relic worship, and images and pilgrimages and things of that kind. But that was only temporary, because in 1538 he changed his whole position again and more or less reverted back to where he had started. Having encouraged the translation of the Bible he now tended to go back on that. In 1539 he authorised Six Articles under which if you denied transubstantiation you were regarded as a heretic, and such heresy was to be punished by death. You were not allowed to have the two elements in the Mass; auricular confession to the priest was compulsory once more. In other words he was attempting now to retain all the doctrines and ceremonies of the Roman Catholic Church. All he was concerned about was that he should be the Supreme Head of the church. So he would not allow the clergy to marry, services had to be in Latin, images were brought back, and the Roman Catholic costumes were to be worn.

This action on the part of Henry VIII brought out the typical Puritan attitude once more. It caused a division amongst people who had been persuaded of the truth of the Protestant faith. On the one hand there were those like Cranmer and others who said, 'Well, we must put up with this. The king is capricious, you never know what he will do next. This is what he says now, but let us hope that in a year's time he will have changed his mind, and the position will be easier again.' So they decided to stay in England and submitted to all this. I am not querying their motives, and I am not out to condemn anyone; I am simply concerned about clarity of understanding concerning the origins of Puritanism. That was the position of Cranmer and others. But there was another school of thought consisting of those who said that this was intolerable and who therefore fled the country and went on to the continent. Who are they? Among them were people like Miles Coverdale – another famous name in connection with the translation of the

Bible – the great John Hooper, eventually Bishop of Gloucester, Hills, and others. These went to the continent, and while there they came under the influence of Bullinger, and still more the teaching of Zwingli who had been teaching at Zurich before Bullinger, and John Calvin at Geneva, and others. Now Zwingli was a very radical reformer. He had made a clean sweep in the matter of ceremonies and the dress of the clergy. These Englishmen were greatly influenced by this, with the result that quite soon they were not content merely with being opposed to Roman Catholic doctrine. Until this point that had more or less been the position. They had had their eyes opened to the errors of Roman Catholic teaching and were objecting to it and denouncing it. But now under this continental influence they went a step further and began to object to religious ceremonialism.

They now began to feel that the Reformation was incomplete, and that it was not enough merely to change the doctrine and get rid of false Roman Catholic teaching. The Reformation had got to be carried through and worked out in terms of practice also. The notion of an incomplete Reformation came in. That, surely, is the essential and most characteristic note of Puritanism – the feeling that the Reformation had not gone far enough.

They were not unanimous about this. Tyndale was prepared to tolerate these ceremonies and dresses and so on as long as they were explained to the people. But there were others who said that this was intolerable. These things were relics of Catholicism and they must be got rid of. They argued that the steps which had already been taken, and acknowledged as being a necessity, must be completed. Very often at this point many of them used our Lord's statement at the end of the ninth chapter of Luke's Gospel, about how a man who has once put his hand to the plough must never look back. This was their obvious illustration in urging that the work must be carried through to completion. Thus, as early as that, this division was already taking place among those who had become Protestants, those who felt that reformation was incomplete and that the ceremonies must be got rid of, and those who did not.

The former, I suggest, are the true Puritans. I do not call them the precursors of the Puritans; I call them Puritans, because that was typical Puritan thinking and Puritan action. We can perhaps summarise the position by putting it like this. These men came back after a while and influenced thinking in this country. There was a great deal of persecution under Henry VIII right to the end of his reign and there was much coming and going back and forth to the continent.

But we can jump now to the Edwardian period when the influence of these men and their teaching came more into the open. A crisis arose when a bishopric was offered to John Hooper. He was prepared to accept it, but he was not prepared to be put into office in the way that was being dictated to him by Cranmer, Ridley, and others. He was told that he had to wear the customary vestments, but Hooper, who had been on the continent way back in 1539 would not consent to this and withstood them. Eventually he was put into prison for a while. Hooper was perhaps the first who clearly stated this argument about the vestments.

His essential argument was as follows. He put his argument in the form of the following syllogism:

*Major Premise* – All things to be required in the Christian church are either ordained in the Bible or are things indifferent.

*Minor Premise* – Vestments are neither ordained in the Bible for use in the Christian church nor are they things indifferent.

*Conclusion* – Therefore they are not to be required in the Christian church.

He amplified this a little. To the major premise he attached a definition of a thing indifferent. This is the important term here. The thing indifferent, he said, was when the use be not profitable or the non-use be not harmful. Then to his minor premise he attached these four notes: (1) Things indifferent are to be grounded on Scripture; (2) Or if not in Scripture they are things to be left free to be done or not done as each individual's conscience may direct, provided they are not in conflict with the Christian faith; (3) They must have a manifest and open utility known in the church; (4) Things indifferent would be instituted in the church with lenity and without tyranny. Things indifferent degenerated or abused are no more indifferent. That is Hooper's essential argument.

These matters became the centre of disputation, and here, already, in the time of Edward VI you have clear indications of the division between Puritanism and Anglicanism. Hooper on the one side, Cranmer and Ridley on the other side. The difference about these things that were described as indifferent! There were two main views. The Anglican view was that these things are unimportant; it is the gospel alone that matters. Also we should be supremely concerned about the preservation of the church. That was the typical Anglican attitude. These indifferent matters are unimportant, and as long as the gospel is being preached, and the church is being preserved, all should be satisfied. We have had this deliverance from Roman Catholicism, they said, and we must not go back to that under any consideration; and as long as we have liberty to preach the gospel these other things are unimportant and can be ignored.

To which the Puritans replied, 'If they are indifferent then why do you enforce them?' That is the essence of the Puritan argument. 'If you say that they are indifferent, why do you compel us to submit to them? Why must we conform to these things?' Thus at the time of Edward's reign you see beginning to emerge two basically different views of ecclesiasticism. The Anglican's is a progressive view, a developing view, the typically 'Catholic' view; whereas the Puritan's is a static view which says that these things are determined by the New Testament, and that, once for all.

That is a broad statement of the difference. Anglicanism has always taught this progressive idea, this developing idea which emphasises that the church in her experience and wisdom continues to make discoveries and gains new insights into the teaching of Scripture. This leads to certain developments and additions in the church in the matter of government and ceremonies and so on. The Puritans on the other hand said 'No, the teaching is fixed in the New Testament, and we must abide by that.' The clash of opinion on this matter led inevitably to a difference in their view of bishops in particular. What is a bishop? Is a bishop to be described as a lord? Has he the right to dictate in the way that he has hitherto done? The Puritan began to query this, and preferred the continental pattern of government that many of them had seen at first hand, and of which they were hearing constantly in their correspondence with some of the great continental teachers.

I wish I had time to develop this, but it seems very clear to me, and increasingly so as I read about these matters, that what seemed to be almost a determining factor at this stage – and we are in the Edwardian period still, remember – was whether or not a man had been on the continent. I have already referred to this in connection with what happened back in 1539. What explains much of the trouble was the fact that Cranmer by the time of Edward had not been out of England for fifteen years. Ridley had never been abroad at all. Latimer, the great preacher, was really primarily concerned about morality and not with these matters. The men who had been on the continent, and had seen the way things were being done in Geneva and other places, were so influenced by that that it changed their thinking, while Ridley and Cranmer who had not come under this influence saw things in a different way, in a more insular way. It is interesting to notice that Ridley, just before his death, had come to agree with John Hooper, according to John Foxe in his great *Book of Martyrs,* and denounced the wearing of the surplice, and the wearing of clerical dress outside the church, and various other vestments in connection with the service of the church. Ridley said just before his death that these things were 'foolish and abominable, yea too fond for a vice in a play.' I maintain, therefore, that you have true Puritanism already in the Edwardian period.

When you come to the period of Queen Mary I this becomes still clearer. She reigned from 1553–58, and what is most important in her reign is not so much what happened in England as what happened on the continent. Once more a number of true Protestants escaped to the continent. Some remained in England, such as Latimer, Ridley, and Cranmer, who were put to death; but many escaped to the continent. There, some went to Geneva, some to

Strasbourg, others to Zurich, and so on. But the really interesting people were those who went to Frankfurt-am-Main, and it is what happened there that is of great importance. A great dispute took place there which had far-reaching consequences. I can but briefly summarise what happened in order to show how what had been not only incipient, but had already been showing itself, now began to show itself still more plainly. The great William Whittingham, the man who was undoubtedly mainly responsible for the translating of the 'Geneva Bible,' was at Frankfurt. He drew up an order of service for the English church there in which he departed entirely from the Edwardian Prayer Book of 1552. He left out the Litany, the surplice was not to be used at all, and he introduced a system of discipline which demanded a declaration of faith on the part of the people before they could join the church. He appointed a pastor or superintendent, preachers, elders, and deacons. This was the model for the English church – the church of the exiles as it was known – that was meeting in Frankfurt. Most of the worshippers accepted this. Edmund Grindal, a truly great man – to me one of the most fascinating of all these people – was at the time at Strasbourg, and did not agree with all this. But the man who really caused the trouble was Richard Cox, and the trouble at Frankfurt eventually centred round the personalities of two men, Richard Cox and John Knox. Whittingham had drawn up this scheme, and eventually John Knox was appointed as pastor of this church; but, almost immediately, Richard Cox – he was an Anglican who had escaped from England – came there. He was a strong man, a powerful character, and he was able to influence many. He objected to all this and said that 'they would do as they had done in England, and they would have the face of an English church.' Now that was a typically Anglican statement – 'They would do as they had done in England, and they would have the face of an English church.' To this John Knox replied, 'The Lord grant it to have the face of Christ's church.' English church – Christ's church. There you have the essential division between Anglican and Puritan. Eventually John Knox was forced to leave Frankfurt and he went to Geneva where Calvin received and accepted him. There he learned a great deal which later found expression in the Church of Scotland. That dispute at Frankfurt crystallises in a very clear manner the difference between the Anglican and the Puritan.

But, and this is an astounding fact, even after he had had this victory over John Knox, Richard Cox was able to make certain concessions. He did away with private baptism, confirmation of children, the observation of saints' days, kneeling at the Communion table to receive the communion, the wearing of linen surplices, and various other matters such as the use of crosses.

Even in such an hour of victory Richard Cox had been so influenced by the teaching of the Continental Reformers that, though so concerned about 'the face of an English church' he was prepared to say that those things must go. That is a very important bit of history. It happened during the Marian exile.

In the meantime, back in England, some remarkable things had been happening. Certain people, generally outside the ranks of the clergy, began to form little churches here in London. There is no record of anything much outside London. It is astonishing to notice the great part London played in all this great history. London was a very great city in the sixteenth and the seventeenth centuries in particular, and she gave a lead frequently to the whole of the country, and in that same Marian period independent churches arose. I mention that fact mainly for this reason, that these churches were often referred to afterwards by William Bradshaw, one of the Pilgrim Fathers. William Brewster and Bradshaw referred to these churches, pointing out that what they were doing in New England was really but a continuation of what had actually happened in the time of Queen Mary back in England. But the big thing was that which happened in Frankfurt-am-Main. There the real difference and cleavage became manifest. These men were all Protestants, they were all anti-Roman Catholic, but there was this difference. And this is the difference between Puritanism and Anglicanism.

We come now to the accession of Queen Elizabeth I in 1558, an event which aroused in all true Protestants a spirit of hopefulness. The new queen was a true Protestant, unlike her half-sister Mary, so they had great hopes that what was left off incomplete at the end of the reign of Edward VI would now be continued. However, they were soon cast down almost to the depths of despair. Elizabeth soon began to assert herself and to claim that she was the supreme governor of the Church of England and that the appointment of bishops was in her hands. She would not relinquish this to anybody else, and insisted upon doing it herself. Not only so, but she insisted upon retaining the ceremonies against which protests had been made in the earlier years. John Jewell, famous for his *Apology for the Church of England* later opposed these vestments quite definitely. Edmund Grindal again, writing to Bullinger and others later on in life, said that he had contested long and earnestly for the doing away with the Prayer Book and the vestments and the other ceremonies. Grindal became first the Bishop of London and then Archbishop of Canterbury, but that is what he wrote later. These men came back from the continent where they had had a taste of Reformed worship, and they wanted to apply this now in England. Grindal said that he had contended 'long and earnestly' for the doing away of those things. But it was not to be! Elizabeth stood solidly against these men for several reasons. Undoubtedly one of the chief reasons was political. She was in a very difficult position. I could put up a fairly good apologia for Queen Elizabeth! She was a very able and subtle politician. But the tragedy is that anyone should ever have been allowed to have such control over the destiny of the church. That was the fundamental fallacy.

Her attitude brought out the same division again, the same old division which we have already seen, even back in the days of Henry VIII. What were these men to do with this situation? They were all Protestants, and numbers of them had been together on the continent; but now they were face-to-face with a real dilemma. What were they to do? The old cleavage reappears. Some said, 'We must not desert our churches for the sake of a few ceremonies, and these not unlawful in themselves, especially since the pure doctrine of the gospel remains in all its integrity and freedom.' That is the statement of Edmund Grindal. We must not desert our churches because of these few ceremonies. We have liberty to preach the gospel. We have the pure doctrine; surely we are not to leave the church. What then did they do? They protested. All honour to them. They protested to the queen and to Burleigh and afterwards to Leicester and others. They protested, but having protested they accepted official positions in the church, bishoprics and others. Their argument was that if they refused these offices Elizabeth would put in Roman Catholics instead of them. That was their argument. Let us try to be fair to these men. Put yourselves back in imagination into their position. How easy it is to look back and to condemn them; but that is what they felt. They had liberty to preach the gospel, the doctrine was right, so they felt that if on the grounds of their attitude towards these ceremonies – and really none of them believed in them – if they refused to take up offices in the church they would just be abandoning the field either to crypto-Catholics or plain Catholics, and the whole church would be lost to true Protestantism. That was the attitude taken by Archbishop Parker, by Richard Cox, Edmund Grindal, John Jewell, and others. That was the typical Anglican reaction.

What was the Puritan view? It was very different. This was represented by men like Thomas Sampson in Oxford, Miles Coverdale, John Foxe, Laurence Humphrey at Oxford, Lever, and others. What did they do? They just defied the queen. They felt that it was not enough merely to adopt the attitude of the others and say 'Well, we will go on and hope for better times, and trust that we shall be able to change the situation.' They did not adopt the policy of 'In it to win it' as it is now put, and indulge in passive resistance. They felt that that was wrong, and that these ceremonies and other matters were too important for that. So they continued to fight.

We come now to an important bit of history. Sometimes the course of history depends entirely upon one incident; and there was such an incident on the 10th October 1562. Queen Elizabeth went down with a bad attack of smallpox, and she appeared to be dying. The hopes of the Puritans began to rise. They felt sure that if Elizabeth died, they would be able to manipulate a more thorough-going Protestant into the position and all would be well. But, unfortunately, Queen Elizabeth, unlike Queen Anne later, did not oblige! You recall the rejoicing of the nonconformists at the death of Queen Anne. Unfortunately for the Puritans, Queen Elizabeth recovered and things were never the same again. There followed the famous and crucial Convocation of 1563. The Puritans put up what was to be in many ways their last fight in that Convocation. Their contention was that in the services of the church the Geneva gown should be used, not the surplice. The surplice played a big part in this controversy. To the Puritans it was a relic of Roman Catholicism, so they opposed it. Ministers should wear the Geneva gown. They suggested also the abolition of kneeling at the Communion, and that all 'saints days' should be banished, and that the sign of the cross in baptism should be prohibited. In the Lower House of Convocation they were only beaten by one vote, fifty-nine were against them and they were fifty-eight. But that was enough for the 'Anglican' party. Elizabeth and the bishops made use of this 'victory,' and in a sense the Puritans were so defeated in that Convocation in 1563 as never to recover again.

But they went on fighting what had now become a kind of rearguard action. They went on fighting about these vestments, and you have from 1563 to 1567 what is called the Vestment or Vestiarian Controversy. It was at this time that the name Puritan actually began to be used in any generally accepted sense. They were called Precisians and other names prior to that. The Puritans admitted that, in a sense, the vestments – the copes and all the other vestments, and the surplice especially – were in substance indifferent; but they said that there was a difference between saying a thing is indifferent in theory and the practice of this. What that means is this; that though you may say that the wearing of a surplice is nothing in and of itself, their argument was that because of its use by Roman Catholics it was popish. The surplice was not important of itself, there was nothing wrong in a surplice as such; but as the Roman Catholics had made so much of it, it had become important. That is the explanation of one of those points made by Hooper as we have seen. The surplice, they said, was popish and idolatrous because of its associations. They also argued that decency and reverence at the sacraments cannot be secured by the wearing of copes and other vestments, and that these in any case had become a hindrance because they had been used by the Roman Catholics, and had the effect of defacing that rite.

But above all, the Puritans objected to the enforcing of these things. Elizabeth commanded her bishops to do this. She was clever enough not to do it herself. She did not want to lose her popularity, so she always handed over the task to these poor bishops. One cannot read about Parker, Grindal, and others without feeling heartily sorry for them. Their whole sympathy was really on the other side, but now that they had taken up these positions in the church they had to carry out the queen's instructions, and so the fight continued.

As this went on a further point arose. These Puritans began to ask, 'Is it right that the secular power should have this authority in these matters and in this realm?' That was clearly the next logical step in the argument. They started with the things themselves, but as the enforcement of these things was pressed upon them they began to ask questions about the secular power. Who is to settle the affairs of the church? That began to emerge as a great principle and bone of contention. What is the limit of the public authority in the sphere of 'things indifferent'? This question became increasingly prominent from 1563 until about 1570. It is very important for us to remember that while there was this division among these men, who were all Protestants, over these matters, outside the Court circles none of them regarded the 'Anglican' compromise as anything but a temporary expedient. They all felt that this was only something for the time being, that given time they would be able to educate the people, and that perhaps the queen might change her mind, and political considerations might work in the opposite direction. It is essential that we should understand this. The position of these men whom I am describing as Anglicans was that they were holding a temporary position by means of a temporary expedient. There is no evidence that they ever intended it to be permanent. In extremely difficult circumstances they were living from day to day, and having to accommodate themselves to the frequent changes in the mind of the monarch.

Patrick Collinson, in a very interesting phrase, says that Anglicanism is a kind of 'Reformed Catholicity characterised by centrality and moderation.' They were holding on to the best possible; they were trying to moderate; they were holding a central position. That was certainly not true of the Puritans, and at the same time there are indications of certain influences coming in from the Anabaptists on the continent which were driving some of the Puritans to great extremes.

The position began to harden on all sides. This is the real tragedy, it seems to me, of that Elizabethan period. Think again of all these men coming back from the continent at the beginning of the reign of Elizabeth. They were really in fundamental agreement even about these matters that are called 'indifferent'; but then there was that cleavage. Some of them took office, others refused to do so, and those who refused began to agitate and to fight in various ways. The queen commanded the bishops to keep these others in order, and gradually you can see what began to happen to these men. The office began to influence their views. The holding of office is always dangerous. The carrying out of one's duties tends to be uppermost in one's mind. You have taken your vows so you have to carry them out. In addition, their memories of what they had known on the continent were beginning to fade. There was no longer persecution such as they had endured under Mary, and they began to settle down. Some of them became very wealthy men. Bishops were wealthy in those days, and all these things began to influence them. They forgot about their wonderful agreement when they were fugitives together on the continent; and the idea of discipline became paramount. You must have discipline, you must have order. The result was that eventually bitterness arose between these men who had been such friends and coadjutors in the difficult days of Mary and the persecution. A hardening and a separation took place.

Then a dramatic event took place in 1570 in connection with Thomas Cartwright in Cambridge. He had been appointed Lady Margaret's Professor of Divinity, and he began to lecture on the early chapters of the book of Acts. Incidentally, it is interesting to note that many Anglicans today object to the drawing of any doctrine from the book of Acts. That attitude began way back in 1570. Cartwright raised the whole question of the nature of the church and in so doing started the story of Presbyterianism in England.

Here was an entirely new factor. Some of these Puritans had seen that the monarch should not have this power over the affairs of the church, and that the bishops also should not have this authority. Indeed, the question was raised as to whether there should be bishops at all. They decided that there should be no such office in the church. They had seen the Presbyterian model in Geneva, and it had commended itself to them, so they began to introduce the idea of Presbyterianism into the Church of England.

What of the other Puritans whom we have been describing as 'Anglicans'? They decided that the best expedient was to appoint lecturers. These men were unhappy and troubled. Fundamentally, in their doctrine, they were concerned about thorough reform, but for the reasons I have given, they felt that they had to conform, and many of them did so on the grounds of conscience. They argued that as they had taken an oath they had to honour it, and that they would be breaking their vows if they became Presbyterians. So they continued. But they were unhappy. The expedient they adopted was to appoint people whom they called lecturers. What were these? It is important to remember that they were not incumbents. They were simply preachers and did not have the responsibility of the parish and the pastoral side of the work. Their work was to preach the true doctrine as they understood it. These lecturers soon became popular and especially in the market towns.

Another idea introduced was what were called 'prophesyings.' This meant gatherings of people within the church, sometimes ministers only, at other times laymen also, to consider the Scriptures. One was appointed to expound a passage and then the others gave their criticisms of the expositions, and they discussed it together. These 'prophesyings' also became very popular and were held regularly, again in the market towns.

The essential difference between the Puritan and the Anglican seems to be crystallised and put before us graphically in two men

– Walter Travers and Richard Hooker. These two men used to preach regularly in the Temple Church here in London, Richard Hooker in the morning, and Walter Travers in the afternoon. Richard Hooker was the typical Anglican. As I said at the beginning, it was in Hooker, and with Hooker, and by Hooker that Anglicanism received clear definition. His *Laws of Ecclesiastical Polity* created the ultimate pattern for Anglicanism. On the other hand, Walter Travers espoused the Presbyterian standpoint. The position was now becoming much more clearly defined. The temporary positions were becoming hardened; and Anglicanism as defined by Richard Hooker is something very different indeed from the standpoint of Parker and Grindal and those men who came back from the Marian exile on the continent. A real change had taken place, and as I see it, an inevitable change. The temporary accommodations and compromises of 1558–63 ultimately must lead to the Hooker position.

On the other hand, the position taken by the others, the true Puritans, led in different directions. One was to Presbyterianism. It had already taken that course in Scotland under John Knox. But it also began to take another line here in England. People called Separatists began to appear. These were men who said that there must be a complete break away from the state church idea altogether. They talked and wrote about 'Reformation without tarrying for any,' meaning the Crown and the magistrates. So you have the great story of the Separatists. I am not concerned to trace it out, but simply to state that the more radical or true Puritanism divided up into Presbyterianism and Separatism. The former still believed that the Church of England could be reformed into a Presbyterian church, the latter abandoned her.

What of the Anglican Puritans at this point? This is interesting and most important. It had become fairly clear by now that as the result of the attitude of the queen and the bishops and certain powerful courtiers, there was virtually no hope of reforming the Church of England in a truly Puritan direction. At the beginning of Elizabeth's reign they were all determined to do that. Then came the cleavage, as we have seen. The Puritans believed that it could still be done. The others temporised and hoped that by a long-term policy it could be achieved. They were all concerned to do this at first, but when you come to the end of the 1570s and the 1580s it was clear that it could not be done in that way. It became still clearer in the 1590s. In 1593 John Penry and Henry Barrowe and others were put to death because of their Separatist teaching and practice.

How did the Anglican Puritans – that is my term for them – react to this? It was at this stage that they turned to moral and pastoral teaching – 'cases of conscience,' and pastoral theology. The attempt to turn the whole of the Church of England into a Presbyterian church (the classical movement as it is called) had failed. They therefore began to concentrate on pastoral teaching and pastoral theology while not neglecting general Protestant theology. This is what Prof. Basil Hall identifies as Puritanism. That alone to him is Puritanism. But I trust that I have shown that this was but a late development on which they were driven back. The big thing, the original idea, seemed impossible, so they turned in this direction, hoping that ultimately times might change and true reform of the church might be possible. This pastoral, yea pietistic element, had been there always, but, hitherto, subsidiary to the desire for true reform of the church. Indeed, the underlying argument is that it is only a truly reformed church that guarantees the possibility of that full flowering of the truly religious type of life.

Queen Elizabeth died eventually in 1603, and James VI of Scotland became James I of England. At this point many thought, 'What a wonderful opportunity. This man, having been brought up in Scotland under the influence of John Knox and his successors, is interested in theology and is a Calvinist. This is the man who is going to put everything right.' So they took a great petition to him which was considered at Hampton Court, known as the Millenary Petition; only to be completely rejected. He was even worse than Elizabeth. How did the poor Puritans react? Large numbers emigrated – some to Holland, becoming eventually the Pilgrim Fathers who, in 1620, went to America. What of those who stayed on in England, and in the church? They went on with their spiritual and moral teaching and preaching such as is found in the works of Richard Sibbes, John Preston, and many others. But then a new element came in. Charles I, in his folly, introduced the political element, so that, in addition to the purely spiritual fight and endeavour, a political element came in and the Puritans began to feel that there was hope once more. The fight went on until you come to 1640 and the outbreak of open warfare between the king and the Puritans. This led to the Commonwealth and the Cromwellian period when Anglicanism was abolished and for a while Presbyterianism was set up officially; and when that ceased Congregationalism held sway. But there was much confusion.

Then you come to 1662 and the Great Ejection, and what was really the end of Anglican Puritanism. We call it the Ejectment, and of course that is a correct term. But there is a sense in which it was not an Ejectment. These men held to a position that compelled the authorities to eject them. It was because they would not continue any longer to accept and to submit and conform to things which they regarded as compromises and worse. It had become clear to Thomas Goodwin way back in the 1640s that they would never win the Church of England to a truly Reformed position, that she was committed to the 'via media' and that she would never be anything else. So he had espoused Independency. John Owen having been convinced of Independency in the 1640s, had left a year before the Ejectment, in 1661. But in 1662 up to 2,000 men saw it so clearly that they stood at all costs and were ejected from their livings. Thus you have the beginning of what is called nonconformity. There had been a kind of nonconformity before, but it was now official nonconformity. Puritanism as such ceased to exist in the Church of England, though there were people like William Gurnall of Lavenham and others who remained. They were negligible in number and ceased to have any influence. The attempt to contain Puritanism in the Church of England had completely failed at last; but the issue was really decided in 1563.

In the meantime the Pilgrim Fathers had gone to what is now the United States, and you had 'The New England Way.' Most of the men who followed the Pilgrim Fathers were Anglicans, men like John Cotton, Richard Mather, and Thomas Hooker; but when they settled there they had no bishops. They formed Congregational churches. They did not say that the Church of England was not a true church, however; they all agreed in establishing this New England Way which is the Congregational way. My contention is that true Puritanism – which is not merely theoretical or academic – can never rest content with being a mere wing or emphasis in a comprehensive Episcopal church, but must always end in Presbyterianism or Independency.

Let me now endeavour to sum up. What are the marks of the Puritan? What are the differences between the Anglican and the Puritan? Let us never forget this, that they were all Protestants, and that until towards the end of the sixteenth century they were virtually all Calvinists. The position of Whitgift, who became Archbishop of Canterbury, is perhaps a bit doubtful, but let us grant that Whitgift and the others were Calvinists. They were all Protestant, all Calvinist, and all believed in a state church. All these things were common to both parties. What then was the difference? I accept the remark of someone who has put it like this – that the real difference was, that though they were all Protestants, the Anglicans always had 'a Catholic undertone,' and that is the essential point of difference. They all believed in a comprehensive church and in the state connection, etc.

What then is the difference between the Puritan and the Anglican? My reply is, as I hope I have shown, that it is not simply a matter of emphasis and a greater concern about the pastoral side of the work. What then? I hope I have demonstrated that it is a concern about the nature of the church. It is a desire for full and complete reformation. It is something that started with objection to ceremonies and vestments but developed into a full doctrine of the church. Is it not interesting to notice how here in England the same steps were retraced as had happened in the case of Martin Luther? You remember that at first Luther was only concerned about the question of Indulgences. But the moment you begin to question any one of these great systems at any point, if you are consistent and if you are logical, you will soon be querying the whole doctrine of the church – the government of the church and all these other matters. Luther had gone through those steps. You remember how he nailed up his famous Theses in 1517, but he did not denounce the Roman Catholic Church fully until the following year and afterwards there was the same kind of development here in England. It started with ceremonies and vestments, and eventually led to a querying of the whole condition of the Church of England, and a desire to carry out the Reformation thoroughly. The Puritan could no longer be satisfied with a partially reformed church but desired a fully Reformed church.

A second difference between the Puritan and the Anglican is the difference, if you like, between an international and a national outlook. I mean by that what I quoted earlier about the difference between Knox and Cox. John Knox had an international outlook, and all the Puritans had an international outlook. They had seen church life on the Continent, and they said, 'We are all Christians: we all belong to the same great church.' They had an international outlook. The others, the 'Anglicans' had a national outlook, and with Richard Cox were concerned primarily about 'The face of the English church.' I am speaking very broadly. I know that at times there were influences from the continent on Cranmer which led him to favour certain ideas of some kind of ecumenical Protestantism. But it all came to nothing. I believe it is fair to say that Anglicanism is, and always has been essentially national in its outlook, essentially English. It was an exception to what happened in the other Protestant churches. The Church of England was the exception: she was different from the Protestant churches on the continent. I believe this was determined very largely by this national, as over against the international, outlook.

Another way in which the same point can be put is this. The Puritan always wants to go back to the New Testament only, the Anglican is also concerned about tradition and custom and continuity. Anglicanism has always put an emphasis on continuity; that is why, today, she is regarded by many as 'the bridge church.' She has always claimed to be Catholic as well as Reformed. Continuity and tradition!

Another way of putting it is that the Puritan bases all on the teaching of the Scripture only, whereas the Anglican brings in reason. That particular emphasis began to come in with John Jewell, but it became still more evident in the teaching of Richard Hooker. The place Hooker gives to reason has been a controlling factor in the Anglican outlook.

Yet another way of putting the difference is to say that the Puritan says that the evangelical view is the only view, whereas the other says that Evangelicalism is one view, one emphasis, one attitude, and that we should be content with being a wing of a comprehensive church as long as we are given liberty to proclaim our emphasis. This is a fundamental point. The Puritans would not have that, but the Anglicans have always contended for that.

When you come to practice, I can summarise the difference like this. The Puritan emphasises the spirituality of worship; the Anglican emphasises the formal aspect of worship, and is more interested in the mechanics of worship. The Puritan is interested in fellowship, the Anglican is more individualistic. The gathered church is at the heart of the Puritan idea – the fellowship; the Anglican is more individualistic. Puritans believed also in the ferreting out of sin and in a rigid church discipline; the Anglican tends to be content with an outward conformity.

Those it seems to me are the main differences. I can well understand the attitude of many of these great men, particularly at the beginning of the reign of Queen Elizabeth. They submitted to many things they disliked, from the standpoint of expediency, and as a temporary measure. Calvin, you remember, advised them to do so and to accept episcopacy though he did not believe in bishops. He said that for the time being it was right to do so in England. That is expediency. Bullinger and others also gave them the same advice. I can understand the attitude of many of those men, and I can understand in many ways those who continued to maintain it right through the reign of Elizabeth, and in the reign of James I and Charles I. While disagreeing I can fully understand them, because there was always the hope that things might change. It was not much of a hope – many said there was no hope – but there was still hope that eventually the Church of England might be fully Reformed. I can understand it even until 1662. But I cannot see any place for it after 1662, and the history of the subsequent three hundred years has demonstrated the rightness of those men who preferred to be ejected rather than to submit to what they regarded as relics of Catholicism. Puritanism, in other words, is ultimately a mentality, a spirit. True Puritanism, I argue, is ultimately found in Presbyterianism. It is found in John Knox; it is found in Thomas Cartwright. It is found also in Separation. It is found in the New England churches. It is found in nonconformity, in Independency and the Baptists. You see it in Thomas Goodwin, you see it in John Owen. This surely is essential Puritanism because it has kept the church, and the doctrine of the church, in the central position. You get essential Puritanism in the same way in Spurgeon. He is a perfect example of Puritan thinking. By today there is a great deal of Anglican thinking among the members of the Baptist Union, the so-called Congregational Church of England, and in Methodism and other branches of churches which had their origin in Puritanism. They think as Anglicans not as Puritans; and they are denying their own origins.

The Puritan is primarily concerned about a pure church, a truly Reformed church. Men may like aspects of the Puritan teaching – their great emphasis on the doctrine of grace, and their emphasis on pastoral theology; but however much a man may admire those aspects of Puritanism, if his first concern is not for a pure church, a gathering of saints, he surely has no right to call himself a Puritan.

Puritanism began with this concern about a thorough Reformation, and that led on to the whole doctrine of the church; and while we thank God for other aspects of Puritanism, for those things that became a part of their great corpus of teaching, if we fail to put the doctrine of the church in a central position we are departing from the true Puritan attitude, the Puritan outlook, the Puritan spirit, and the Puritan understanding.

# 1972

# *John Knox – The Founder of Puritanism*

Most people think of John Knox solely in terms of Scotland, and feel therefore that it is for the Scots people only to commemorate him and his work. The answer to that can be put in this way. All who have visited Geneva, and have seen the famous plaque or memorial to the great Reformers will have noticed that John Knox is included among them. He is in that august company with Calvin and Farel; and that should be sufficient to make us realise not only that John Knox did great and marvellous things in Scotland, but also the international character of his work.

I propose to consider this great man with you in terms of a statement made by Thomas Carlyle – a fellow Scot, of course, but nevertheless a historian of repute who did not say things lightly. He refers to John Knox in his book *Heroes and Hero Worshippers* in these terms. He says, 'He was the chief priest and founder of the faith that became Scotland's, New England's, and Oliver Cromwell's – that is of Puritanism.' Carlyle does not actually include England – he should have done – but he includes New England and Oliver Cromwell. He claims for John Knox that he was the father and founder of a movement that led to remarkable events, not only in the British Isles, but far beyond, events which influenced the whole course of history. Is that statement of Carlyle justifiable? Can we substantiate his claim? I propose to demonstrate that Carlyle was in no sense guilty of exaggeration.

## I

Before we come to think of Knox in particular as the founder of Puritanism let me give a brief sketch of his life. He was brought up in Roman Catholicism and became a priest. At one time he was known as Sir John Knox. He was brought up in poverty in a poor family, with no aristocratic antecedents, and no one to recommend him. He became the great man he was solely as the result of his own remarkable natural gifts, and still more as the result of his conversion. He was converted in a remarkable manner through the instrumentality of certain of the great first lights of the Reformation in Scotland – George Wishart and others. He underwent a very thorough change, and turned his back, of course, upon Roman Catholicism. He found himself eventually in St Andrews where he began to participate in affairs. At first he did not preach, but later he was forced to do so. As a result of this, when the French captured St Andrews and took a number of prisoners, John Knox found himself working as a slave in a French galley for nearly two years. This was a most exhausting experience in which he suffered, not only the rigours of such a life, but intense cruelty also. This undoubtedly left its mark on the whole of his life, because it undermined his health; and he had a constant struggle against ill health.

Eventually he was able to get out of that situation, and came back to England and Scotland. The situation became too difficult for him in Scotland, so he settled in England. He was appointed as minister and preacher in Berwick-upon-Tweed, and he remained there and in Newcastle upon Tyne from 1549–51. (There is much dispute as to whether he was born in 1503 or 1504 or about 1513 or 1515. That does not matter. The important point is that he was a man of age when he was converted somewhere in the 1540s, and became a preacher in Berwick and Newcastle.) After that he came down to London; and by this time Edward VI was on the throne. Knox became one of the Court chaplains and Court preachers. He was thus right in the centre of affairs in England, and preached on many occasions before Edward VI and the Court. Edward VI died at the age of sixteen, and Mary, 'Bloody Mary,' came to the throne of England. Knox and a number of others had to escape for their lives. Eventually he went to the continent and began to study under John Calvin at Geneva; but while there he was called to become joint pastor of the English refugees who had formed a church at Frankfurt-am-Main. So, very reluctantly, and mainly as the result of the persuasion of Calvin, he went there and ministered to the church. After much trouble and disputation he was turned out from Frankfurt and went to Geneva with a number of other refugees, and there again became the pastor of the English church from 1556–59. Then in April 1559, after the death of Mary, and when Elizabeth had come to the throne in 1558, he was able to return not only to the British Isles, but to Scotland. He began his great work, his life's work in one sense, in Scotland, in April 1559 and continued there until he died on November 24th, 1572.

There, we have a mere skeleton of an outline of the story of this man. There are many excellent biographies of him. I would commend one of the latest by Jasper Ridley. It well repays careful study and consideration. It is one of the best that has ever been written on him, altogether superior to one that came out some thirty years ago by Lord Eustace Percy.

## II

Let us now look at the man himself. No man has ever been more maligned than John Knox. This happened to Calvin also; but it is much more true of Knox. There were elements, perhaps, in his character which called this forth even more than in the case of Calvin; but it is all based upon ignorance and, of course, the malice of Roman Catholics and every other type of Catholic. Inevitably in these days of ecumenicity a man like John Knox becomes the target of vitriolic attacks. The chief interest today is in Mary, Mary Queen of Scots, who is painted up, and idealised, even more than she painted herself!

However, I am not concerned to defend John Knox. He does not need me, or anyone else, to defend him. Let us look at this amazing man. He was of short stature – a fact not without significance! Someone once said that the greatest things in this world had been done by small men and small nations! He was not a handsome man, or in any way distinguished in appearance as judged by modern standards. He was a strong man, a rugged man, and from the physical standpoint there was nothing to recommend him except for the fact that there was something that came into his eyes now and again that literally put the fear of God into people. The most striking thing about him was his ability. He was not able in the sense that Calvin was able, nor was he a scholar in the sense that Calvin was; but a man can be able without being a scholar. So when I talk about his ability I am thinking in particular of his sense of discrimination, of his ability to 'differentiate between things that differ.' This seems to have been one of his most outstanding characteristics, as we shall see.

Another thing about him was his astounding energy. Here again is a characteristic of all the great men whom God has used throughout the centuries. How he accomplished all he did can only be explained in terms of the grace of God, but there was something even in the very constitution of the man that accounted for this. I was reading recently that the same thing was true of Daniel Rowland, the great Welsh preacher of the eighteenth century; and I noticed that his contemporaries always commented on his extraordinary energy. This quality is not only characteristic of great statesmen, and great military leaders and others, it is generally a characteristic of great preachers also. We are reminded of Demosthenes' definition of oratory: it was 'action, action, action.'

Another characteristic of Knox was his shrewdness. If ever a man needed shrewdness it was John Knox in the situation in which he found himself. We have been reminded in this conference of the alliance, or relationship at any rate, between the State and the church, between politics and religion. This was inevitable in those days, and it meant that John Knox had to co-operate with certain politicians in Scotland. One is struck by his extraordinary insight into, and understanding of, the thinking of these men and their duplicity. Several times he saved the Reformation simply because of this shrewdness. Jasper Ridley refers to him as 'a consummate politician'; and so he was, and had to be! These men would have sold the pass many times because they could not see what was really happening. They could not see what the enemy was doing; but John Knox could see it, and with that extraordinary shrewdness of his he was able to save the situation. In many instances he was able to see through the subtleties of the mind and behaviour of Mary, Queen of Scots, and her efforts to nullify his endeavours.

Then I come to his wisdom. I am emphasising these points for this reason, that this man is generally regarded as a bigot, a harsh man, a man who was driven by tremendous conceit and ambition, a man who would brook no disagreement or any kind of opposition. But you cannot read any objective account of him without being amazed at his extraordinary wisdom. He seemed to know exactly how far he could go at every stage, and he never tried to go beyond that point. Some would be urging him onwards, and others would be restraining him: but he always seemed to follow the path of wisdom. For instance, when he was in Berwick he did not openly attack the Book of Common Prayer which was officially to be used; he just did not use it. You see the distinction. I emphasise this because I have often had to suggest to some of my younger brethren that this is an important point. You need not always announce, and talk about what you are doing; and to act is more important than to talk. Knox did not attack, and call attention to it, and put up a placard and say that he was not going to use the Prayer Book; he just did not use it. That indicates moderation and great wisdom.

Knox has sometimes been charged with cowardice because he several times escaped from Scotland – both to England and to the continent – in times of persecution and great danger. But to me he was being governed by this principle of great wisdom and of shrewdness. He realised that if he stayed in Scotland he would undoubtedly be put to death, as were George Wishart, Patrick Hamilton, and others before him. He knew that that would not further the cause; so he escaped. I would justify him in doing so. Sometimes it takes greater courage to escape than to stay and become a martyr.

Then consider his moderation. To many people it sounds utterly ridiculous to talk of moderation in the case of John Knox – 'that fanatic, bigot, and extremist.' But the moderation of the man is almost incredible. Take, for instance, the advice he once gave to the people at Berwick. He was down in London just as Edward VI was coming to the end of his reign, and just before Mary became queen. He knew that these members of his old church at Berwick would soon be in great difficulties. The Prayer Book, though officially introduced, had not been enforced in the diocese of Durham because the then Bishop of Durham, Tunstall, was more Catholic than Protestant, and did not like this Protestant Prayer Book; so its use had never been enforced. This had helped Knox, of course, to pay no attention to it; but now he could see that there would be a change, and discipline would be enforced; so he writes to these friends in Berwick and Newcastle and urges moderation upon them.

On what matters should they stand? The great question that was raised at first was, as I shall point out later, the kneeling at the reception of the Communion. Knox's advice to them was, that for the sake of the bigger principles and the greater truths, they should conform on this, and he would excuse their doing so. Now that is the principle of moderation in practice. Take some further examples. When he went to Frankfurt as one of two ministers he found that they had already decided to introduce Calvin's Order of Service. They were agreed about this, and they thought that he would agree immediately, because he was such a great admirer of Calvin. But John Knox was not willing to agree and for this reason. He said that they must not do that without consulting all the other English refugees in Strasbourg, Basel, and other places. That is moderation. He would only act in unison with the other brethren. Later he and others drew up an Order of Service of their own, and there was opposition to it. He was more ready than anyone else to accept modifications and various additions to it. Further, as I pointed out in my address last year on the Origins of Puritanism, when you contrast him with Richard Cox, the Anglican who came to Frankfurt and insisted that the church, as he put it, should have 'an English face,' and that they must go on using the Prayer Book as they had used it in England, Knox did everything conceivable, everything a man could possibly do to accommodate the opposition and to find agreement. But the intransigence of Richard Cox, and those who followed him, was such as to make agreement totally impossible. This man who is so often traduced as being intolerant and full of bigotry, stands out in shining contrast as a model of moderation over against those Anglicans who not only opposed him but hounded him out of Frankfurt and made him escape to Geneva.

Let us turn now to his originality, which again I want to emphasise. John Knox is sometimes thought of as if he were but a 'gramophone record' of Calvin. That is a complete mistake. Some are perhaps guilty of that charge; but John Knox was an original thinker. He thought for himself, and when his understanding of the Scriptures demanded it, he did not hesitate to disagree with, and to oppose, and to speak against, the views that had been advanced by people such as Tyndale and Calvin himself. He disagreed with Calvin and Tyndale, for instance, about the duty of Christian people with regard to their princes and rulers. He advocated opposition to rulers in certain circumstances, and even revolution, before they came anywhere near – and Calvin in particular – to accepting that teaching. That was a mark of his original thinking. He was not governed by Calvin in this matter, or indeed in anything else, unless he agreed. He thought things out for himself. I am emphasising this because it is a very important matter. We must not swallow automatically everything we read in books, even from the greatest men. We must examine everything; and Knox did so and, as I say, when he disagreed he was very ready to say so. The same was true of his attitude towards the various ceremonies in the Church of England services. He was ahead of others, as I am going to show, in this matter also, and when he wrote his book concerning *The Monstrous Regiment of Women* he was again quite original.

That brings us to his courage. It was said of him when he died that he 'never feared the face of man'; and that is true of him.

In addition I might add that he never feared the face of women either! And he had to face two women. One was a very strong woman; and the other, Mary Queen of Scots, was strong because of her weakness. Weak women can make use of their good looks and their femininity in a way that gives them a kind of strength. Elizabeth I of England lacked the good looks, but she had real strength of character. John Knox had to deal with both of them, and he was not afraid of either. Their great power made no difference to him. His courage is almost incredible. He, in the same way, opposed Cranmer, Ridley, and Peter Martyr. He was never afraid to be alone, and to stand alone. His was the same heroic character that you see in Martin Luther standing in 'the Diet of Worms' and elsewhere.

But consider him as a preacher. His great characteristic as a preacher was vehemency. Great preachers are generally vehement; and we should all be vehement. This is not the result of nature only; it arises from the feeling of the power of the gospel. Vehemence is, of course, characterised by power; and John Knox was a most powerful preacher, with the result that he was a most influential preacher. The effect of his preaching upon Edward VI, to which I shall refer later, was quite remarkable; and that was not only true of Edward VI but of many others also. It is traditional to refer to the effect of his preaching on Mary Queen of Scots. He could make her weep; not under conviction but in anger. She was afraid of him; she said she was more afraid of his prayers and his preaching than of many regiments of English soldiers. Randolph, a courtier and an ambassador, said this about him and his preaching: 'The voice of one man is able in one hour to put more life into us than 500 trumpets continually blasting in our ears.' The voice of one man! Many times did one sermon delivered by Knox change the whole situation. When the Lords and others were alarmed, and frightened, and all ready to give in, Knox would go up into a pulpit and preach a sermon; and the entire situation was transformed. One man 'more influential than the blustering of five hundred trumpets in our ears!'

That is what preaching can do, and often has done. This was constantly the case with Knox. Perhaps one of the greatest tributes paid to him in this respect was that done unconsciously by an English ecclesiastic. After Mary had come to the throne of England a certain Hugh Weston was appointed to be chairman of a discussion on the Communion Service and other matters which took place in Oxford between Cranmer, Ridley, and others on the one side, and the Roman Catholics on the other side. During the discussion Weston said, 'a runagate Scot' – which meant a refugee Scot – 'did take away the adoration and worshipping of Christ in the Sacrament; by whose procurement that heresy was put into the last Common Book, the Prayer Book of 1552. So much prevailed that one man's authority at that time.' Weston was not referring to what had happened in Scotland, but in England. There you have a striking testimony to the power of the preaching of Knox, from the enemy. According to these Roman Catholics John Knox was more responsible for the abolition of the idolatry of 'worshipping the host' in the Communion Service than anyone else. That illustrates the power of his preaching.

## III

We come now to consider John Knox as 'the founder of Puritanism.' Is Carlyle right? Is it true to speak of John Knox as 'high priest and founder of Puritanism'? I touched on this subject last year when dealing with the Origins of Puritanism. I referred to it in passing, and also said that in many ways we could trace back the origins of Puritanism to William Tyndale. I still maintain that; but I also contend that, from the standpoint of an organised body of thought and organisation, what Carlyle claims is justifiable. William Tyndale emphasised certain principles both by his spirit and his action, but they became explicit, I would say, in the case of John Knox. I agree with a writer of the last century, of the name of Lorimer, when he says that the only other candidate for the title of 'founder of Puritanism' was John Hooper, Bishop of Gloucester. I further agree with Lorimer when he says that undoubtedly we have to put Knox before Hooper. They agreed on many things, but there were certain differences between them which will emerge as we proceed.

In what sense, then, is it right to say that Knox was 'the founder of Puritanism'? The first answer is provided by his originality of thought, his independence. The Puritan, by definition, is a man of independence, of independent thought. The Puritan is never an establishment man. I mean that not only in terms of 'the establishment of religion,' but in terms of any aspect of establishment. This is, to me, a most important point. There are some people who seem to be born 'establishment men.' Whatever sphere of life they are in, they are always on the side of the authorities, and of what has always been done, and conditions as they are. Their great concern is to preserve the past. They are found in the free churches as commonly as in the Anglican communion and other forms of Christianity. They are establishment men; and they always start from that position. Now I maintain that the Puritan, by his very nature and spirit, is never an 'establishment man' because of his independence and originality, his reading of the Scriptures for himself, and his desire to know the truth irrespective of what others may have said or thought.

Secondly, Knox is 'the founder of Puritanism' because he brings out so clearly the guiding principles of Puritanism. That is, first and foremost, the supreme authority of the Scriptures as the word of God. I need not go into this. Roman Catholicism puts the church, its tradition and its interpretation of Scripture first; and all imperfectly reformed churches have always continued to do the same. But the peculiar characteristic of the Puritan is that he asserts the supreme authority of the word of God. This was Knox's guiding principle. If a thing could not be justified from the Scriptures he would not have it, and he would not allow it to be introduced.

The second guiding principle was that he believed in a 'root and branch' reformation. That is not my term; it is his term, and it became the term of others. In other words, the Puritans were not content with a reformation in doctrine only. This is where Knox, and they, disagreed with the leaders in England. All were agreed about the changes in doctrine. They were all Calvinists and so on, but the differentia of Puritanism is that it does not stop at a reformation of doctrine only, but insists that the reformation must be carried through also into the realm of practice. This involves the whole view of the nature of the church. To the Puritan, reformation not only means a modification or a slight improvement; it means a 'new formation' of the church – not a mere modification of what has already been – governed by the New Testament and its teaching. That was his second guiding principle.

He desired to get back to the New Testament idea of the church. In conformity with that he said that the church had to be reformed in the matter of her ceremonies, in other words, in her conduct of worship and in the administration of the sacraments. He put it in this way. 'In the worship of God, and especially the administration of the sacraments, the rule prescribed in Holy Scripture is to be observed without addition or diminution,' and 'the church had no right to devise religious ceremonies and impose significations upon them.' It was because of this that charges were brought against him. It was said that he contended 'that man may neither make nor devise a religion that is acceptable to God, but man is bound to observe and to keep the religion that from God is received without chopping or changing thereof.' He also taught that 'the sacraments of the New Testament ought to be administered as they were instituted by Jesus Christ, and practised by the apostles. Nothing is to be added to them and nothing to be diminished from them.' Again, 'the Mass is abominable idolatry, blasphemous to the death of Christ, and a profanation of the Lord's Supper.' He was charged with teaching such principles; and he was guilty of the charge. This was his position.

Such were his guiding principles. But, and this is most vital in this matter, he applied his principles. There is no such thing, it seems to me, as a theoretical or academic Puritan. There are people who are interested in Puritanism as an idea; but they are traitors to Puritanism unless they apply its teachings; for application is always the characteristic of the true Puritan. It is all very well to extol the 'Puritan conscience,' but if you do not obey your conscience you are denying Puritanism. Hooper agreed with Knox in so many things, but Hooper had a tendency to go back on what he believed. When Hooper was to be ordained as bishop he said that he would not wear the vestments that were customary, and was sent to gaol; but then, afterwards, he gave in and wore the vestments. The point I am establishing is that the true Puritan not only sees these things, and holds these views, he applies them, he acts on them. This is where Knox is so notable, and superior to John Hooper. He stands out in his conscientious application of what he believed to be the New Testament pattern regarding the nature of the church, and the ordinances and the ceremonies, and the exercise of discipline.

## IV

Let us now watch him putting these principles into operation. First in Berwick-upon-Tweed and Newcastle-upon-Tyne. As we have seen he did not carry out the Edward VI Order of Common Prayer of 1548, neither did he follow the instructions of the Book of Common Prayer of 1549. He was helped in this respect by Tunstall. Most other preachers were conforming to it; but not John Knox. He was not governed in his administration of the sacraments by the decrees of the official body in England under which he was now preaching, nor by the Prayer Book.

Secondly – and this is one of the vital points – it was customary to receive the sacrament in a kneeling posture. This is Anglican practice. John Knox was the first to teach people – and not only to teach them, but to put it into practice – to take the Communion in a sitting position. This is Puritanism in practice. Quite on his own, and by his understanding of the Scriptures, he came to the conclusion that it is wrong to kneel in the reception of the sacraments. There is very good evidence, I think, for saying that he had already put this view into practice in St Andrews, before he had become a slave in the French galleys; but whether so or not he certainly introduced this practice in Berwick; and it was a great innovation. For centuries under Roman Catholicism the sacrament had been received in the kneeling position, and this was the custom and the practice in the Reformed Anglican church. Another innovation, in which he was the leader, was that he substituted bread for the wafer. He no longer used the wafer as had been the custom for centuries in the Roman church, and as was still the custom in the Anglican church up to this time. They soon changed this; but Knox was the first to do so; and he did so when he was minister at Berwick-upon-Tweed.

With regard to baptism he refused to baptize the children of people who had been excommunicated. Other ministers did so. He refused private baptism, and he refused to make the sign of the cross in connection with baptism. Those who are familiar with the subsequent history of Puritanism will know that these are all vital matters which became crucial in the Puritan position throughout the years. Knox had introduced these Puritan ideas, in practice, in his ministry both at Berwick and Newcastle.

Knox was taken to London by the Duke of Northumberland and became Court Chaplain, and a popular preacher. We are concerned with his story there only as the founder of Puritanism. A great crisis arose in 1552. A reformed Prayer Book had been introduced in 1549, but almost everyone came to agree that it was inadequate, and that there were still too many relics and remnants of Roman Catholicism in it. So it was decided that they must have a new Prayer Book, and also new 'Articles of Religion.' They began to prepare them, and by September 1552 a new Prayer Book was produced, largely by Thomas Cranmer. They had already also drawn up Forty-Five Articles of Religion – which became the basis of what ultimately became known as the Thirty-Nine Articles. Here is the crucial point. This new Prayer Book had actually been sent to the printers, and was due to come into operation on November 1st, 1552. Copies of this book had been sent to John Knox and the other chaplains and preachers, as a matter of courtesy, assuming, of course, that they would all be in agreement. But, immediately, John Knox saw that it contained something with which he could not agree. He was also unhappy about some of the Forty-Five Articles. Article 38 stated, 'that the Second Book of Common Prayer was holy, godly, and provable by God's Scriptures, and every rite and ceremony, and at no point repugnant thereto, both as regards the common prayers and the administration of the sacraments as well as the ordinal.'

This immediately made Knox feel that the position was intolerable. Why? For this extraordinary reason, that in this new Prayer Book there was a rubric which commanded the recipient of the Communion to receive it in a kneeling position. Now that had not been stated in the Prayer Book of 1549. Why not? For the reason that that had always been the custom and the practice. That had been done under Roman Catholicism, and it had been continued in the Church of England; so it was not mentioned in 1549. Hooper and others had been querying this practice, as well as Knox, and his practice at Berwick and Newcastle had become known. So Cranmer, Ridley, and Peter Martyr and others felt that an instruction should be put into the new Prayer Book telling people that they had to receive the sacrament in the kneeling position. Immediately Knox was in trouble. How could he agree to Articles which stated that everything in this new Prayer Book was 'holy, godly, and provable by God's Scriptures'? That was not true; it was a lie. So what did he do? Fortunately he had an opportunity of expressing himself. The king (Edward VI) and his Court were at Windsor, and it fell to the lot of John Knox to be the preacher. With his customary courage he preached on this very matter, and did so with such power and effect that he shook the king to his foundations on this matter, and many others with the king. Knox maintained that kneeling was sinful and idolatrous. Remember that he had against him, Cranmer, Ridley, and Peter Martyr, and also that the book was already in the hands of the printers, and that in six weeks' time, or less, it was due to be introduced officially on November 1st. Well, this one sermon of Knox caused consternation and led to much activity. Knox, with one or two others, drew up a memorandum stating their case against kneeling, and pleading that the king and the authorities should not insist upon this kneeling because it was sinful and idolatrous. They presented this memorandum to the king and council. After much conferring and arguing the authorities eventually arrived at a compromise. Knox did not get his wish that this rubric should not be put into the new Prayer Book; but he did obtain a vital improvement. He had so convinced the king that the king signed a Declaration which was to be added to the Prayer Book. This was a rubric which was to be inserted in order to safeguard against the dangers that arose from kneeling at the reception of the Communion, and especially the possibility of idolatry.

There is little doubt but that this rubric was drawn up by Cranmer. It has the marks of his peculiar genius for compromise. The new Prayer Book was already printed but still in the hands of the printers. What could the authorities do? They printed this new rubric, this new declaration on this subject, on a separate sheet of paper, and the king issued a decree that this sheet was to be stuck into the new Prayer Book. The few copies of the original printing of that Prayer Book that remain still have it.

This is the rubric that John Knox, through the king, had forced Cranmer to produce. It says, 'Although no order can be so perfectly devised, that it may be of some, either for their ignorance and infirmity, or else of malice and obstinacy, misconstrued, depraved, and interpreted in a wrong part: and yet, because brotherly charity willeth that, so much as conveniently may be, offences should be taken away: therefore we, willing to do the same; whereas it is ordained in the Book of Common Prayer, in the administration of the Lord's Supper, that the communicants kneeling should receive the Holy Communion, which thing being well meant for a signification of the humble and grateful acknowledging of the benefits of Christ given unto the worthy receiver, and to avoid the profanation and disorder which about the Holy Communion might else ensue; lest yet the same kneeling might be thought or taken otherwise, we do declare that it is not meant thereby that any adoration is done, or ought to be done, either unto the sacramental bread and wine there bodily received, or to any real and essential presence there being of Christ's natural flesh and blood. For as concerning the sacramental bread and wine, they remain still in their very natural substances, and therefore may not be adored, for that were idolatry to be abhorred of all faithful Christians; and as concerning the natural body and blood of our Saviour Christ, they are in heaven, and not here; for it is against the truth of Christ's true natural body to be in more places than in one at one time.'

This rubric became known as 'the Black Rubric.' My point is that Knox was the man who was chiefly responsible for its introduction. It was added to the Prayer Book as a safeguard against the terrible danger of idolatry. Now that was a purely Puritan action. Queen Elizabeth, when she came to the throne, excluded that Black Rubric from the Prayer Book, and it was only restored with slight modification in 1662.

Here is proof positive that this man was the leader of the Puritan party in this explicit manner. He fought about many other things also, but failed. He tried to change the doctrine in Article 26 on the nature of the sacraments. Knox taught 'that God confers grace independently of the sacraments, though sacraments are a sign of grace.' Cranmer on the other hand said, and printed that 'grace was conferred through the two sacraments which were not merely a sign or a channel of grace.' There, again, Knox was contending for the Puritan attitude to the sacraments over against that of Cranmer, Ridley, Peter Martyr, and the other typical Anglicans.

Further evidence of Knox's 'puritanism' during this period in London is this. As a result of the trouble over the Prayer Book, Knox had become such a prominent man and leader that he was offered the bishopric of Rochester. But he refused it. Hooper accepted the bishopric of Gloucester, but Knox would not accept; and the only explanation of this refusal was his Puritan principles. He never really believed in bishops at all.

## V

Going on to his time in Frankfurt, here, again, a very interesting thing happened. As we have seen, Knox was asked to go from Geneva, where he was studying under Calvin, to be one of the two pastors of the church of the English refugees meeting in Frankfurt. This is surely extraordinary. Here is an English church, a church founded by some great Englishmen who had had to flee for their lives; and they ask this Scotsman to be their minister. Why? Thomas Fuller, a typical Englishman, and not a Puritan, writing in the next century put it thus, 'You may account it incongruous that among so many and able English divines that were then abroad that a Scotsman should be pastor of the English church at Frankfurt, the most visible and conspicuous beyond the seas; and it was seeing Mr Knox's reputed merit did naturalize him though a foreigner.' That puts it well.

While he was at Frankfurt Knox did something which is typically and characteristically Puritan. He and Whittingham, the main translator of the famous Geneva Bible, drew up an Order of Service to replace that of the Common Prayer Book which they disliked. Modified mainly because of Knox's moderation, this Order had been accepted by the church until Richard Cox and his party arrived. I emphasise the point that John Knox, by drawing up this Order of Service, repudiated the Book of Common Prayer. He did not say this openly, once more, until confronted by the militant and ungentlemanly opposition of Richard Cox whose behaviour can only be described as quite abominable, intransigent, and rude – not the last time Puritans have had to suffer in that way at the hands of Anglicans. Cox having adopted this attitude, John Knox was no longer prepared to remain silent. He was prepared not to shout about these things as long as there was a hope of carrying people with him, but when Cox behaved in that scandalous manner, John Knox preached the next day and now stated plainly and clearly his views of the Book of Common Prayer. 'At the time appointed for the sermon,' he says in his subsequent history of these matters, 'I began to declare what opinion I had … (and how) I was driven away from my first opinion.' Here is evidence of a big man: he changes his opinion. It is the small man who never changes his opinion. He went on to explain why he had changed, and to say that he believed that the troubles in England under Mary were the punishment of God upon them for not carrying out reformation more thoroughly, and especially with regard to this matter of the Prayer Book.

There he states plainly and openly his attitude towards the Prayer Book. This resulted in his being driven out from Frankfurt; so he went to Geneva. The first attempt at a Puritan church amongst English people was that in Frankfurt. It was a failure because Cox and his friends resorted to the despicable resort of charging John Knox falsely with high treason against the emperor, the political judge. This charge was based on certain things he had said, and had printed, in a sermon once preached in Amersham.

The first attempt to form a Puritan church having thus failed in Frankfurt, Knox and his supporters then went to Geneva; and what had failed at Frankfurt became a success in Geneva. Here Knox introduced the Order of Service which had been tried and rejected in Frankfurt. This became the Order of Service in Geneva. It is known as the Geneva Book. This Order in the Geneva Book was not Calvin's Order. Calvin also had his Order; but this was John Knox's primarily, and this was the Order of Service which he subsequently introduced when he returned to Scotland, and which has been used in the Church of Scotland ever since as their official Book of Order.

In Geneva, therefore, we have the first truly Puritan church amongst English people. This provides one of the strongest arguments for asserting with Carlyle that John Knox is the founder of English Puritanism. It was also while at Geneva that he formulated his view with regard to princes, and the attitude of the Christian towards 'the powers that be.' Here he was ahead of Calvin, and this is again a sign of his true Puritanism. I maintain that one cannot truly understand the revolution that took place here in England in the next century except in the light of this teaching. Here was the first opening of the door that led to that later development.

Also while at Geneva he published his famous treatise *The First Blast of the Trumpet Against the Monstrous Regiment of Women,* the monstrous 'government' by women. John Knox believed that it was contrary to Scripture to have a queen ruling over the people, and he produced specific statements from the Scriptures to justify his attitude. As the result of this, Knox mortally offended Queen Elizabeth I. She never forgave him; but he nevertheless prepared a second *Blast* which he did not actually publish.

This, again, is not only indicative of his courage and his independence of thought, but, I maintain, it is also a part of his essential Puritanism coming to the surface. I should add, perhaps, to make my story complete, that Knox at times could indulge in a little casuistry. He put forward an explanation of how, in spite of the clear scriptural teaching on this question of a woman monarch, in the peculiar circumstances then prevailing it was allowable for Elizabeth in England and Mary in Scotland to act for the time being as monarchs. That was a bit of casuistry. However, his main position was the one stated in the first *Blast*.

One further fact must be mentioned here. Queen Mary Tudor died and Elizabeth came to the throne in 1558. Knox saw at once new possibilities arising, so he wrote *A Brief Exhortation to England for the Speedy Embracing of Christ's Gospel Heretofore by the Tyranny of Mary Suppressed and Banished*. He sent this from Geneva in 1559; and Elizabeth strongly objected to this Scotsman who was writing to the English to tell them how to conduct their affairs. He wrote in a very strong manner. He was naturally very much concerned about the state of the English church. He had been pastor amongst English refugees in Frankfurt and Geneva, as well as previously in Berwick-upon-Tweed and Newcastle. So he addressed this great appeal to them. He reminds them of what had taken place in Mary's time, and again presses upon them the idea that it was God's judgment upon them. He called them to repentance and conversion, and then went on to make an extreme statement which I cannot defend. He was intolerant at this point. He said that 'none ought to be freed from the yoke of the church discipline, nor permitted to decline from the religion of God.' Further, prince, king, or emperor who should try to destroy God's true religion and introduce idolatry should 'be adjudged to death according to God's commandment.' Let me say this in mitigation. Knox never was the means or the cause of anyone being put to death. He stated that in principle, but he never carried it out himself in practice. That was one of those extreme statements which it is difficult to defend.

In this exhortation to England, this programme of ecclesiastical and educational reform, he advocated the setting up of schools where people could be taught and instructed in the Scriptures. This was a programme for ecclesiastical and educational reform and, I would claim, is the first printed outline of reform ever published by the Puritan party of the national church. This is a weighty document. It is the first printed statement of Puritan principles with regard to the church and her management. In it Knox shows his dislike of bishops and suggests as a practical reform that every bishopric be divided into ten parts, that where there had been one lord bishop there should be ten preaching men, that these men should be preaching regularly, and that these great dioceses, and these princes of the church should be abolished. Big dioceses should be reduced to ten manageable bodies, and godly, learned men should be instructed to preach and to give instruction to the people in every city and town. In addition he advocated the setting up of schools.

## VI

Then he returned to Scotland and remained there for the rest of his life. But this did not bring to an end his connection with English Puritanism. He began to hear that the people who had followed him, in other words the true Puritans, were being persecuted by the bishops, some of whom were men who had been members of the congregation in Frankfurt or in Geneva. So he wrote a letter from Scotland to the bishops in England remonstrating with them, and pleading with them not to persecute the Puritans. He writes as a true Puritan to those other Puritans who were beginning to compromise in England, and shows clearly his attitude to vestments, surplice, etc., which he describes as 'Romish rags.' There speaks the true Puritan.

He also wrote a letter to the sufferers in England in 1567. This letter causes perplexity to some because he seems to discourage them. Some of these suffering Puritans wrote to him and pleaded with him to come out plainly on their side. He had already done so, in a sense, in his letter to the bishops; but he wrote back to these people and exhorted them not to break, or to trouble the common order 'thought meet to be kept for unity and peace for a time.' In other words, he told them not to secede, not to be separatists. He was opposed to separation; but let me emphasise the fact that he introduced the term 'for a time.' Knox is often misunderstood at this point. People argue that he did not believe in separation, and that he was really on the side of the 'conforming Puritans.' That was not the case. This letter is but another example and illustration of his extraordinary spirit of discrimination. Knox always seemed to understand that the position of England was a peculiar one; and he was surely right. This Scotsman had the sense and the understanding and the ability to see that the Englishman is *sui generis*. The Englishman – and you cannot ignore these things – has a genius for compromise. He has a hatred of definitions and precise statements. He still boasts of the fact that when he had an empire it did not have a written constitution! He glories in the fact that he has always 'muddled through.' Knox always recognised this, so when he was in London he was prepared to do things which he had not done in Berwick and Newcastle, and which he most certainly did not, and would not do, in Frankfurt and Geneva, and when he went back to Scotland. But when he writes to these people in England he knows the position is different; and so, appearing to contradict himself, he advises them to tolerate certain things, and to conform. He argues that, while the authorities are still preaching the truth in general, they should not break with them over this particular matter.

Note that he emphasises 'for a time.' He felt that there was still hope that the force of truth would soon prevail, and that all would come to see that they should get rid of the 'Romish rags' and all the other relics of Romanism. Of course, that did not come to pass; and Knox himself died in 1572. So what appears to be inconsistency is, rather, a mark of wisdom and understanding.

His influence upon Puritanism in England did not end there. It went on even after his death. Knox wrote a *History of the Reformation in Scotland*, and it is very interesting to notice that that *History* was first published, not in Scotland, but in England by the English Puritans in 1587. Not only so, John Field, a leading Puritan who printed another treatise by John Knox, in introducing that treatise paid him a most glowing tribute, referring to him as 'so worthy and notable an instrument of God' and describing the treatise as 'a seal of his godly and wonderful labours, carrying in the forehead thereof of what an heroical and bold spirit he was.'

## VII

Knox's influence even continued into the next century. John Milton, in writing a treatise justifying the putting to death of Charles I leaned heavily upon John Knox. That is why I put such emphasis upon his perspicacity, and his understanding of the Scriptures, in this matter of not only opposing rulers at times, but even, if necessary, of putting them to death. The fact that John Milton recognised this is surely a powerful proof of the fact that Knox is the founder of Puritanism. In 1683, when Charles II was beginning to show openly that he was a Roman Catholic, at the command of the authorities the works of John Knox were burned in public in Oxford, and a prohibition was issued that his works should not be read. 1683, and Knox died in 1572! His influence continued and was feared. He is indeed the founder of English Puritanism as well as of that of Scotland.

Consider the case of the Pilgrim Fathers. Knox is behind their whole attitude towards the state and the rulers; and so he is, as Thomas Carlyle claims, the founder of American Puritanism in exactly the same way. Indeed, I would argue that he is in many ways the father of the American War of Independence which came to a triumphant conclusion from the standpoint of the colonists in 1776. He was the one who opened the door to all this.

What do we make of this man? He was a man for his age; a man for his times. Special men are needed for special times; and God always produces such men. A mild man would have been useless in the Scotland of the sixteenth century, and in many other parts of this country. A strong man was needed, a stern man, a courageous man; and such a man was John Knox. Martin Luther was of the same mould. God uses different types of men, and gives them different personalities. Different men are needed at different times. In those times an heroic, rugged character was needed; and God produced the man.

Lest any should continue thinking that he was a hard man, I close by referring to his extraordinary humility. 'Humility in John Knox?' says someone. He was a most humble man. The fact that a man stands boldly for the truth, and does not yield, does not mean that he is not humble. He is not standing for himself, he is standing for the truth. I can prove that John Knox was a very much humbler man than many in the ministry today. He was in St Andrews after his conversion, and was invited to preach; but he refused. He would not preach, alleging, and these are his words, 'that he would not run where God had not called him,' meaning that he would do nothing without a sense of lawful vocation. Knox would not preach without being absolutely certain of his call. A chaplain called John Rough turned to Knox on a certain day, and called on him to preach and not to refuse the burden. He asked the congregation to show that they had instructed him to call upon Knox, and the congregation called out that this was so. Here was a whole congregation calling upon Knox to preach. What was his response? 'At this Knox burst into tears and withdrew to his room.' He remained in a state of deep depression and anxiety until the day of his first sermon came. 'Everyone could see how gloomy he was, for he never smiled, avoided company as much as possible, and spent all his time by himself.'

What a contrast to men who are always ready to run up pulpit steps to preach! This is true humility, and also the Puritan spirit. It is 'the fear of the Lord,' the dread of standing between God and man, and proclaiming 'the unsearchable riches of Christ.' The Puritan never believes that every man who is converted is thereby called to preach, or that he can run whenever he likes at his own calling. He wants to know for certain that he is called, because he is so deeply conscious of the sacredness of the task. Like Paul the apostle he does this 'in weakness, and in fear, and in much trembling.'

Knox is generally regarded as being an arrogant man, and one who was rude in the presence of Mary, Queen of Scots. But that is all based on the fallacy of what makes a man a 'ladies' man.' It is based also on a misunderstanding of true womanhood, and what a true woman really likes. The general idea of a 'ladies' man' is one of a 'society fop.' But that is not a 'ladies' man,' and a woman worthy of the name has no regard for a fop. A true woman likes a strong man; and as you read the life of this man you find that many of his correspondents were women. This stern reformer, this man who battled with lords and princes, and who would stand up to all authorities, spent much of his time in going into the details of what Charles Lamb once described as 'the mumps and measles of the soul.' These women had their personal problems and difficulties, their 'cases of conscience'; and he always had time to write to them. He often wrote at great length, with great tenderness. When he was in Geneva two women took a dangerous journey over land and sea in order to be near him and to partake of his ministry. His correspondence with his mother-in-law, Mrs Bowes, and also Mrs Ann Locke, over many years is proof positive that this man had a most tender spirit when you really got to know him, and when he knew he was dealing with a true and honest and genuine soul. That is another sign of his humility. A further sign was this. When he went back to Scotland he appointed superintendents in the church – not bishops. He did that because it was essential at the time. It was only a temporary expedient, and it was dropped later; but the interesting point is that he never became a superintendent himself. He was only a preacher to the end. He did not appoint himself as a superintendent, still less as an arch-superintendent. All these things are signs not only of his humility, but also of his essential Puritan spirit.

So let us take farewell of this noble, rugged, and yet tender, and even lovable spirit, as he came to leave this world, and to receive his eternal reward. This is the account given by his daughter. 'At about mid-day, he asked his wife to read aloud the 15th chapter of the 1st Epistle to the Corinthians, and said that he commended his soul, spirit, and body to God, ticking off his soul, spirit, and body on three of his fingers. At about 5 p.m. he said, "Go and read where I cast my first anchor," and his wife read to him the 17th chapter of John's Gospel. When evening prayers were read about 10 p.m. his physician asked him if he heard the prayers. Knox replied, "I would to God that ye and all men heard them as I have heard them; and I praise God of that heavenly sound."' 'Now it is come' he shortly added. Those were his last words, and there can be no doubt that as he crossed, the heavenly trumpets sounded on the other side as this great warrior of God entered in, and received his eternal 'crown of glory.'

# 1973

## *Howell Harris and Revival*

SOME may wonder why we devote a meeting in this conference held in London to a Welshman of the name of Howell Harris. The first answer is that this year happens to be the bi-centenary of his death. He died on July 21, 1773. It has been our custom from the beginning of this conference to call attention to great men of God the anniversary of whose birth or death falls in any particular year; and that is the main reason why I call attention to Howell Harris. But quite apart from that, Harris is one of the great heroic figures in the Christian church, and his story is truly an astonishing one. It is very necessary that we should call attention to him because the ignorance of people concerning this man is almost indescribable. For instance, there was a review of a book by J. Pollock on 'George Whitefield' in the *Western Mail* of Cardiff on June 2nd this year – the very year in which the bi-centenary of the death of Howell Harris is being celebrated – and the reviewer, who was a schoolmaster, actually wrote these words, 'The story of Whitefield deserves to be better known especially in Wales where Calvinistic Methodism may be claimed to be a legacy from him (*i.e.* Whitefield) through the Countess of Huntingdon.' I have only one comment to make on that; it is an example of 'invincible ignorance'! But lest anyone should think that this feeling that Howell Harris has been sadly neglected is due to nationalistic prejudice on my part, let me quote some words by Dr Geoffrey Nuttall, a well known contemporary historian, of New College, Hampstead, who wrote a little book on Howell Harris and gave it the title *Howell Harris: The Last Enthusiast*. Dr Nuttall, an Englishman, writes 'I have sought to rescue Harris from his neglect by English writers, and to restore him to his original place in the Evangelical Revival as a whole'; and again

'This is one reason why I have chosen to speak of him, in the hope of introducing him to the ignorant Englishman.'

But why should people in England, in London, be interested in him? The answer is that he paid no less than thirty-nine visits to London during his hectic life. He deputised for George Whitefield in preaching in the Tabernacle at Moorfields more frequently than anyone else, and he was for some three years the head of the Calvinistic Methodists both in England and in Wales. So Nuttall is quite right in saying that Harris played a very prominent part in the Evangelical Awakening and Revival of two hundred years ago. He was a particularly close friend of Whitefield, and, because of his Calvinistic views, was more friendly with Whitefield than with the Wesleys. Nevertheless, he was also a great friend of both John and Charles Wesley. He attended their Annual Conference on many occasions, and he was always concerned about reconciling Whitefield and Wesley and bringing them together. I shall refer to that later on. At the same time he was a great friend of the Countess of Huntingdon. However, my main reason for calling attention to him, over and above everything else, is that I believe a consideration of this man's story will help us come to an understanding of the true nature of revival.

Fortunately there is an abundance of material concerning him. He wrote endless diaries. He was always writing. After a heavy day's preaching he would write in his diary, and spend hours at it; and fortunately they are still available. The first diaries were in Latin, then others were in English. Because he wrote in such a minute hand, and in addition, wrote across what he had written previously, they are very difficult to decipher; but a number of men have been engaged in this work for years, and copious extracts from these diaries have been published in several volumes by the Welsh Calvinistic Methodist Book Room. The special value of the diaries is that in them Harris gives us such an intimate insight into what was happening in that great period of revival, and especially the relationship between the various great men of God who were so mightily used.

## I

Let me hurriedly deal with some of *the salient facts*. The condition of Wales at the beginning of the eighteenth century was, from the spiritual standpoint, very low indeed. The same was true also, of course, in England: but in certain respects it was worse in Wales than in England. Wales as a whole was about a hundred years behind England even in shedding Roman Catholicism, and whilst there had been great Puritans in Wales, such as Morgan Llwyd, Walter Craddock, and Vavasor Powell and others, spiritually speaking things were at a very low ebb indeed. There were one or two evangelical men in the Church of England, and there were nonconformists – Independents and a few Baptists – but they were small in number. That was the state of the church.

The state of the people was one of spiritual ignorance, indeed death, with the consequent and inevitable immoral condition. I do not want to over-paint this picture, as has sometimes happened, according to the modern historians. Writers of the eighteenth century and of last century may have been guilty of over-painting the blackness and darkness of the picture. However, we can be quite certain that the position was very sad and deplorable. But then suddenly there came this great awakening, this great revival, in which one of the chief instruments – many would say the chief instrument, though I cannot quite agree – was born in January, 1714 – this man Howell Harris.

He was born in a little hamlet called Trevecca; it is not even a village. He had but little education, yet he became a schoolmaster. The schoolmaster of today is not the same as in those days. The vital event in his life took place in 1735; but for this we should never have heard of him at all. It was his conversion. How did it happen? In this connection I cannot but refer to a most amazing incident. The Calvinistic Methodist Church of Wales has paid just a little attention to the bi-centenary of Harris' death this year. In their General Assembly held last June in a place called Lampeter in Cardiganshire, they asked a professor of church history at Westminster College, Cambridge, Dr R. Buick Knox, to deliver an address on Howell Harris. It is, to me, almost incredible, but this is what Dr Knox said, 'The decisive moment in his life was at the solemn sacrament in Talgarth Church on Easter Day 1735.' That is astonishing, and for the simple reason that it is not true! What amazes me is that a professor in church history should be capable of such a statement, and that the official Journal of the Historical Society of the Presbyterian Church of Wales should publish it.

What then actually did happen? On Palm Sunday, March 30th, 1735, Harris attended the parish church at Talgarth, which is a short distance from the hamlet of Trevecca where he was born and where he lived. During the service the vicar, announcing that there would be a Communion service the following Sunday, said that he knew there were many people who did not come to the Communion service because they felt they were not fit to partake of it. He went on to say, 'If you are not fit to take Communion you are not fit to pray, and if you are not fit to pray you are not fit to live, and if you are not fit to live you are not fit to die.' These words hit this thoughtless schoolmaster with great force. He had never been a riotous person but he had lived a loose life; so these extraordinary words of the vicar announcing a Communion service began a process of conviction of sin which from then on led to an agony of repentance.

I emphasise this incident because it reminds us of one of the amazing things about being a servant of God. You can bring people to conviction of sin even through an announcement! You never know what God is going to use; your asides are sometimes more important than your prepared statements. Well, Howell Harris went to the Communion service, and it but increased his conviction of sin. He continued in an agony of repentance – trying to find peace and unable to find it – until Whit Sunday, which was May 25th, when he went again to a Communion service in the same church. He describes how during a part of the service he had a tremendous fight with the devil. He had found a certain amount of peace in a neighbouring church called Llangasty where he had given himself to God as best he could in his ignorance. That gave him a measure of peace, but the devil came and attacked him in this Communion service on Whit Sunday, violently trying to shake his faith in everything. However, before the service was over he had found peace. Here are his own words describing this: 'At the table, Christ bleeding on the cross was kept before my eyes constantly; and strength was given to me to believe that I was receiving pardon on account of that blood. I lost my burden; I went home leaping for joy, and I said to my neighbour who was sad, Why are you sad? I know my sins have been forgiven, though I had not heard that such a thing was to be found except in this book [*The Practice of Piety*]. Oh blessed day! Would that I might remember it gratefully ever more!'

Howell Harris was now converted, he knows that his sins are forgiven; and he has lost his burden. But still more important is what happened to him over three weeks later, on June 18th, when he had a further experience. He was reading the Scripture, and praying in the tower of the Llangasty church, where he had given himself to God, when he received a further experience which eclipsed all previous experiences. It is from that moment that this man began to be the flaming evangelist of whom we speak, and whose memory we commemorate this evening. As a result of this experience he felt a compassion for souls and a sorrow for all people who were in sin. It was this experience which led to his evangelistic activity.

At first he just began to visit people who were sick, and to read to them out of certain books, *The Practice of Piety* and other books which had helped him. But he read with such power that people were profoundly affected. After a while, whenever it was heard that he was going to read out of a book in any sick room or anywhere else, people crowded together to listen to him; and this went on in a cumulative manner until eventually the crowds became so great that he began to preach to them in the open air. Great crowds began to gather, and large numbers of people were brought under conviction, and many were brought to conversion. It was as a result of this that he began to establish the Society meetings, the Experience meetings of which we have already heard in this Conference.

I am just selecting some of the outstanding facts in his life. It was in 1737, two years after his conversion, that he first met the great Daniel Rowland of Llangeitho, situated in another part of Wales in the West. He met George Whitefield for the first time in Cardiff in 1739, and eventually these various contacts led to the formation of an Association of all these Societies so that they might regularize and control their conduct and development. The first Association was held in 1742, but a more famous one was held near Caerphilly in 1743. The man who was appointed Moderator on that occasion was the great George Whitefield. Harris and the others went on preaching, and enduring terrible persecutions and hardships. Harris was brought very near to death on several occasions. The antagonism in the Church of England, and among the vicars, was indescribable, and the hostility of the masses at times was violent. But this man went on, with his life in his hands, and was indefatigable. I have scarcely ever read of any man who has worked as hard as Howell Harris did. He would preach many times during the day, and after that would hold private societies with the converts, and after that would write his diaries. Very often he had no sleep at all, and would go back to his school the next day; or he would have a couple of hours' sleep and then travel and preach somewhere else. On and on he went, working in an almost superhuman manner. His voice became permanently husky quite early on in his preaching career, but he still continued.

This went on until 1750 when a dispute arose, for various reasons, between him and Daniel Rowland and the other leaders, which led to a disruption and separation, and he retired to his home in Trevecca. This led eventually to a most interesting enterprise. He had read about the community that August Hermann Francke, the German pietist, had established in Halle. It was a kind of orphanage and religious community. Harris had been greatly impressed by this, as many others were, and he decided to start such a 'family' in Trevecca. There he gathered together quite a number of people, up to one hundred. One would be a blacksmith, another a carpenter, another working on the farm, another a miller, and so on. They were a religious community, and he taught and instructed them in the faith. Later, he did another extraordinary thing. There was a war at this time with the French, so Harris became a soldier, a captain in the militia. As captain in the militia he came to England, to Great Yarmouth, and then went down to Devon and Cornwall and other places. He preached in his uniform and there are extraordinary stories of what happened sometimes.

However, he turned to the Methodist Societies in Wales in 1763 and continued to work with his old friends and colleagues. Another interesting thing about him was that in 1768 the Countess of Huntingdon and he and others established a college for the training of preachers. It was established at Trevecca and a great building was put up in 1768. The founding of the college in 1768 was a great occasion, as were the anniversaries which were held every year. Whitefield preached at the opening, and in 1769 Whitefield, John Wesley, Rowland, and others preached. All this went on until, quite exhausted, weary, and tired, Harris died on July 21, 1773.

Out of all this came first the Calvinistic Methodist Society, and eventually a 'Connexion.' Harris and the others died as churchmen. Their followers departed from the Anglican church and held their own first ordination of ministers in 1811. Were there nothing else but the coming into being of the great Welsh Calvinistic Methodist Church, which played such a prominent part in the life of Wales in the nineteenth century, it would have been a wonderful story; but we know that in addition to that, Harris' ministry greatly added to the numbers of the Congregationalists and the Baptists. They benefited greatly from his ministry, and they are very ready to acknowledge that. Likewise his efforts here in London were a great means of encouragement to the saints. He recorded all these things in his diaries, and in them you get glimpses of men like John Cennick and many other of the subsidiary personalities in the great Evangelical Awakening, in addition to the Wesleys and Whitefield.

## II

Those are the main facts in connection with this man. I want now to refer to what I call *matters for special comment.* I am going to select certain matters out of the life story of this man which, as I see things, are most relevant to our condition today. We do not have a merely antiquarian interest in these things; we are not academic historians; we are spiritual people – many of us are preachers, pastors, and others are leaders in Sunday School work and in other spheres. So we turn to history to derive some benefit, some help, and some encouragement. We need it badly at a time such as this, for the state of affairs in Wales and in England today is almost identical with what it was before this great religious revival of the eighteenth century. We are back in very much the same kind of situation. There are differences. I must not digress to mention them. I would say the main one is that they did not have to contend with the liberalism and modernism that we have known. It was rather a deadness. What was needed then was an awakening ministry. We are called upon to do something in addition to that.

What are these matters that deserve special comment? First, and foremost, the sovereignty of God! Professor Buick Knox, in his address in the General Assembly this year, uses the following phrase: referring to Harris he talks about the 'movement which he began.' What can one say about such a statement? It indicates a sheer lack of spiritual perception and understanding, and savours of twentieth-century thinking and the starting of various movements. Howell Harris never started a movement. His story, as I have reminded you already, is one that can only be explained in terms of the sovereignty of God. Here is this man going to a church rather reluctantly, and here is this strange announcement of a Communion service; and he is immediately apprehended, arrested, and convicted. That is what started the whole of this great story. Howell Harris did not start it. We must not think of him in terms of a man who starts a crusade or a movement. That is really to deny the essential message of this wonderful story. No, no! It is the sovereignty of God; and we see this not only in the story of Howell Harris, but also in the fact that at almost exactly the same time as God did this to Howell Harris, he was doing the same to Daniel Rowland. They had never heard of each other – long distance separated them from one another – but it happened at the same time; and we know that things were happening to George

Whitefield at the same time. We know also that much the same was happening to Jonathan Edwards in America and others at the same time. What is this? The sovereignty of God! The sovereignty of God as regards time, place, persons!

If you have visited Trevecca you will know that it is still a hamlet; and if you had been asked to say where a great movement of revival is likely to start you might have been tempted to say St Paul's Cathedral, or somewhere else in London. But that is not what happens when God acts. It is often in a hamlet like Trevecca, some unknown place of which no one has ever heard; but that is the kind of place God chooses and the time and the persons – this poor schoolmaster and others of a similar type. Read the history of revivals and you will find that God has constantly repeated this kind of action – 'not many wise men after the flesh, not many mighty, not many noble, are called.'

Another aspect of the sovereignty of God which I would emphasise is the way in which revival comes. The story of Howell Harris is one illustration of the fact that revival does not always come after a preliminary reformation. Revival sometimes follows reformation, but revival sometimes precedes reformation; and for us to lay it down that reformation must precede revival, and that doctrinal orthodoxy is essential to revival is simply to fly directly into the face of facts.

Secondly, what is revival? Revival is an outpouring of the Spirit of God. It is a kind of repetition of Pentecost. It is the Spirit descending upon people. This needs to be emphasised in this present age. For we have been told so much recently by some that every man at regeneration receives the baptism of the Spirit, and all he has to do after that is to surrender to what he has already. But revival does not come as a result of a man surrendering to what he already has; it is the Spirit being poured out upon him, descending upon him, as happened on the Day of Pentecost.

That brings us to a third point, which is seen particularly clearly in the case of Howell Harris. We come, in other words, to that crucial experience, to which I have referred, which took place on June 18th 1735, when he was in the tower of the church at

Llangasty. To me, this is the key to the understanding of Howell Harris, as it is the key to the understanding of revival. I am amazed that both Dr Geoffrey Nuttall and Professor Buick Knox make no reference to this at all. Others deal with it in a very cursory manner too – they just slip it in as one of the facts and one of the events – but as I have always understood this man's story, and as I still understand it more and more, you cannot explain him or understand him, or what happened through him, except in the light of this crucial experience of June 18th. Here let me recommend the little book published by the Banner of Truth a number of years back. It is called *The Early Life of Howell Harris* by Richard Bennett – in the original Welsh it is *The Dawn of Welsh Calvinistic Methodism*. Bennett gives an excellent account of this crucial experience. What was it? To me, there is only one expression to use. It was the expression used by these men themselves and by their successors. It was a baptism 'of fire' or a 'baptism of power.' What I would emphasise particularly is that Harris was already converted, had already received forgiveness of sins, and he knew that he had it, and had been dancing in joy. But it was now just over three weeks later that he received this crucial experience which turned him into a flaming evangelist. What was it? This is how he describes what happened as he was there sitting in the tower and reading and praying: 'Suddenly I felt my heart melting within me like wax before a fire, and love to God for my Saviour. I felt also not only love and peace, bur a longing to die and to be with Christ. Then there came a cry into my soul within that I had never known before – Abba, Father! I could do nothing but call God my Father. I knew that I was his child, and he loved me and was listening to me. My mind was satisfied and I cried out, "Now I am satisfied! Give me strength and I will follow thee through water and fire."'

As Richard Bennett says, 'Doubtless the experience of forgiveness in Talgarth church was sweet. Yet it left a feeling of further need in his soul which he could not define. But when he was at secret prayer in Llangasty church, God now gave himself to him. He was there cleansed from all his idols, and the love of God was shed abroad in his heart. Christ had come in previously, but now he began to sup with him; now he received the Spirit of adoption, teaching him to cry "Abba, Father," and with it a desire to depart and be with Christ. All his fears vanished for months and pure love took their place.'

That is the account of this crucial experience; and I emphasise that it was *the* crucial experience. I do so by showing how Harris keeps on referring to it. He never forgot it. It was the biggest and most momentous event in his life. If you read his diaries or extracts from them, you will find that when he comes to June 18th he generally refers to what happened to him in Llangasty church. It is to this he points back rather than to what happened on Whit Sunday in the month of May. For instance, in 1739 he writes in his diary on this date, 'The love of God was shed in my heart four years ago to give myself to God.' Again in 1746, 'A day to me memorable. This day eleven years ago I was sealed to the day of redemption.' Again, 'Had a seal through reading Revelation 21:7. Oh! Sweet day. I had this before in Llangasty church of old, but through yielding to sin and carelessness and being curbed by almost-Christians, and because it was not given through a scriptural promise I fell again into doubts.' On June 29th, 1763 he seems a bit confused with his dates, but he writes, 'This day twenty-eight years ago I was (when I did not seek it as I had never heard of it) sealed by the Spirit of adoption and feeling that I loved God with all my heart, that I was in God and he in me. I longed to be dissolved and to be with my own dear Father.'

Another very interesting reference in his diaries – not to his own experience but to an experience of a little maid – must be quoted in this connection. 'The Lord revealed himself to her in an amazing manner for some hours, so that she was lost in his love that she knew not where she was. Sinking to nothing in the discovery of his majesty and glory in Jesus Christ her eternal portion, and by the uncommon earnestness the Spirit gave her to pray for the church, she thought an uncommon work on the earth. Many such instances of the outpouring of the Spirit have we among us.' If you read extracts from his diaries you will find that this is his constant emphasis, this to him was the turning-point, the crucial event that made him an evangelist. It is essential to an understanding of revival. We can further demonstrate this by showing that he had several repetitions of this experience. He not only refers to it, and reminds himself of it, or the date brings it back to him, he also had similar experiences. Richard Bennett referring to events in 1736 says, 'He speaks again and again of a spiritual feast which he enjoyed about this time on Grwyne Fechan mountain while returning home from Cwm Iau, for he seemed to see God so smiling upon him that his heart was near to bursting under the powerful influences of divine love. The place became a holy mountain for him ever afterwards.' Although his body was weak and aching, and though he could eat nothing, the realities of the spiritual world appeared so naked to his mind throughout the time, that his weak body was clothed with unparalleled power, so that his very appearance dispelled all opposition.

Another extract from his diary says, 'In private society till two in the morning like a drunken man. Could say nothing but glory, glory for a long time. Who can write all the Lord did here?' In 1747, 'God came down as he used in Wales and our hearts did burn within us.' This was in London. He has a reference then to Lady Huntingdon, 'Hearing her declaring her sentiments of the new birth, and all she insists on from the bishops is the necessity of knowing forgiveness of sins and receiving the Holy Ghost.' May 1749, 'The Lord came, overpowering me with love like a mighty torrent that I could not withstand or reason against or doubt.' There is always this distinction between receiving forgiveness of sins and receiving the Holy Ghost; in other words, the difference between what happened to him on Whit Sunday 1735 and what happened to him on June 18th in the same year.

This is the only explanation of this man. This is what created within him a compassion for the lost. This is what urged him to go out and to tell the people about their condition and do something about them. His concern for the lost and the perishing was the consuming passion of his soul. I would make this comment at this point. Is not that always the crucial test which we must apply to those who claim to have received the baptism of the Spirit?

The crucial test is the concern for souls, compassion for the lost. That was the great characteristic of our Lord. He saw the people as 'sheep without a shepherd.' He 'had compassion upon them'; and the man who is filled with the Spirit in this way is like his Lord. His outstanding characteristic is his *compassion for the lost;* his concern for them is the test of 'the baptism of the Spirit.' It does not lead to an inward-looking, self-indulgent church movement that turns in on itself and spends its time reciting and even boasting at times of experiences. It always leads to this concern for others. There have been movements in the church claiming great things for themselves, as there are certain similar movements at this present time, but they have had to admit that the evangelistic concern has not been prominent among them. The baptism of or with the Spirit, however, shows itself primarily by giving its recipients a great evangelistic concern. That is not to deny the great value of experiences; but I would suggest in the light of this history that this deep concern for the lost is the most prominent and chief characteristic of such an experience.

Another matter that must be emphasised under this heading is that Harris always stressed the importance of *new* experiences, *fresh* experiences. He reprobated the kind of person who was always talking about an experience he had had many years before, but who never seemed to have had it again. Even in his 'dying testimony,' as it is called, he says 'that we are not to speak of what we have had from the Lord, but what we have now afresh from him.' This was of great concern to him. This great vital experience could be repeated, and if it was not being repeated, and people had to live on the memory of a first experience, he thought they were in a sad state, and he would reprimand them for that.

Under this same heading one cannot but refer to *his spirituality*. Howell Harris lived in the realm of the Spirit. He believed in direct leadings. He often would not act at all without such a direct leading. Some would criticise him on those grounds, and it may be that at times he did become what Nuttall describes as 'an enthusiast.' Indeed he was perhaps in danger, at times, of crossing the border into fanaticism; but the point is that he lived in close association with God, and was sensitive to the Holy Spirit's influences. If you read in his diaries his accounts of meetings when he had been preaching, and when others had been preaching, the expressions you keep on finding are these – 'The great gale came down when I shewed of our Saviour's infinite death.' 'The Lord came down in power'; 'I had great freedom and a strong gale came down when I shewed the greatness of salvation.' That was what he always sought and longed for. 'The Lord came down in power.' Another favourite term of his was 'the authority.' If he was not conscious of 'the authority' when he preached he was troubled, but when 'the authority' came all was well. This was what he longed for, and craved for, and what he believed was absolutely essential in connection with the preaching of the gospel.

## III

I turn now to certain other *interesting features in his ministry,* which are perhaps primarily of interest to preachers. First, *his method of preaching.* He referred to himself always as an exhorter. He was very sensitive on that point. He had intended originally to be a parson, a clergyman. But he was never ordained; the bishop of the diocese in which he lived would not ordain him; and he was very careful not to trespass upon the prerogatives and the privileges of ordained men. At the same time he was never slow to point out to them that he was 'in the field' before all the ordained men, and he did not hesitate to reprimand them when the occasion arose. He did so quite frequently. He reprimanded Daniel Rowland, he reprimanded George Whitefield, he reprimanded the Countess of Huntingdon, though he was not an ordained minister but only an exhorter. He felt that he had authority from God to deal with these people, and to tell them how they should conduct and comport themselves.

His method of preaching was most unusual. He described how he began to preach. We have seen that he at first began by going to visit the sick, and reading out of a book. Having done that for some time he began to add to what was in the book. He was really exhorting, preaching to them, but still kept looking at the book. This is how he describes the situation: 'All the people began by now to assemble by vast numbers so that the houses wherein we met could not contain them. The word was attended with much power that many on the spot cried out to God for pardon of their sins. I took no particular texts but discoursed freely as the Lord gave me utterance. As to the subject of my discourse it was all given unto me in an extraordinary manner without the least premeditation, it was not the fruit of my memory, it was the effect of the immediate strong impulse felt in my soul. 'Tis the presence of the Spirit only that is my call to preach.' And again, 'In all my discourses, before the power comes I open the contexts.' He felt he was capable of himself of opening the context, and that is what he did until 'the power' came; but when 'the power' came he just allowed these words that were given to him to pour out. Here are some other statements which he makes in this connection. He says on one occasion, 'I attempted to speak without the divine commission and I was humbled.' Do we know anything about that? He writes again, 'Learning not to speak when not called; if I do, I shall do no good.' Then he says on another occasion: 'Because I still read, and no one took any notice of my gift of speech which I now exercised, they thought that everything was in the book, and that I prayed from the book, because I kept it before my eyes, seeing no harm in this at the time.' 'No preparation. Leaning wholly on God. Receiving such ability and blessing that I wondered where the words came from, so clear, so prolific, so appropriate. There for nearly nine hours till broad daylight. No weariness. How sweet everything is while he works with me. I feared that pride might rise in my heart, so extraordinary was the gift.' In other words he took these books with him, and read out of the books; but when he reached this point when the Spirit came, he began to speak to them directly. He was no longer reading, but he still looked at the book. Eventually he gave up the reading altogether and just spoke directly to the people. Richard Bennett says that, 'In 1737 his ministry became more scriptural than it was before. He preached more and more in the following months on Zaccheus, Revelation

3:20, and portions of the last chapter of St Luke.' He still came to the people without any preparation, his head throbbing with pain, his voice hoarse, and he would pour out that which was given him at the time. It is true that he now divided the matter under headings, but he did not allow himself to be fettered by headings or anything else.

I ask a question at this point. Was not this what the New Testament calls prophesying? Was this not the prophesying that we read of in 1 Corinthians 11 and 14? I would venture the opinion that it is. This is a man delivering what is given to him. It is immediate inspiration and it pours out through him. It is not revelation, but inspiration.

I turn now to another interesting aspect of this man's life, namely his doctrinal development, or, if you prefer it, *his development in the knowledge of doctrine*. This is most important for many of us gathered in this conference. Here are quotations from his diaries:

'For a time I endeavoured to convert myself and the people by reasoning, without looking upon it as the work of the Spirit. I fell into the error of exalting the power of man, arguing that all men could repent and turn. I knew but little concerning Christ, although I spoke much of him, and was deeply conscious of him in my heart. My inner teachings compelled me to confess that I could not do anything of myself; however, I spoke in this inconsistent manner for a long time. Although the gospel was within me I was led by the principle of the law, because I simply did not follow my inner teachings, but sermons, books, and my own carnal reason. For a short while Christ left me too, even as he did the apostles of old. I hesitated when I understood that the carnally minded clergymen were pleased that I was calling election the doctrine of the devil. When I denounced election many who formerly hated me began to love me; but yet I continued to proclaim that man could turn himself, as otherwise my preaching was in vain.'

In other words there was a conflict between his head and his heart. To continue:

'Although experience always taught me that I could do nothing except it be given to me, yet I was a strong Arminian, and at Wernos I debated with great zeal against those who held pre-destination. I withstood that doctrine for a long time, and all the people, and all the reasons in the world, could not bring my proud stubborn heart to embrace it. I was taught the doctrine of election slowly, in stages. The seed of belief in it was sown when, quite early on, I became certain of the immutability of God. But the doctrine did not develop for some time after that, and I, because of the darkness of my understanding, denied it and opposed it, till it pleased God to instruct me further. Little by little my eyes were opened to know the mystery of the gospel. The Lord kept me from reading the mere letter of Scripture, from increasing merely in head knowledge. But as I grew inwardly I gradually came to see and to understand this verse and that. I received the gospel not from man, nor from a book, but from God. That which I experienced, proved, and felt and saw and heard of the word of life, that also I proclaim.'

He goes on to say that this change in his doctrine and in his understanding took place towards the end of 1736. Remember that the great experience had taken place in June 1735. He writes, 'About Christmas 1736 I began to think of Christ. Before, I had placed the emphasis on man's work. At Merthyr (Cynog) in 1737 I was first enlightened to see the doctrine of free grace, although my experience had shown me from the beginning that I could do nothing in my own power.' Then he adds, paying tribute to his great contemporary, 'Rowland was the means whereby I was brought to the knowledge of the truth about Christ. It was in that same year also, I think, that I came across a book called *The Sincere Convert* by Thomas Shepard which was used to turn me from duties and frames to depend only upon Christ.' Again he says, 'At Merthyr church heard the doctrine of free grace being pressed home warmly, clearly, and powerfully – so I had been under a cloud until this hour. I cried out, O Lord, let me hear this wholesome doctrine in every pulpit. Never before had I been so stripped of self. How thankful we should be for a good ministry.'

That is a brief account of his doctrinal development. At this point I would make a comment, and put it in the form of a question. Is there not a real danger of our becoming guilty of a very subtle form of Arminianism if we maintain that correct doctrine and understanding are essential to our being used by the Spirit of God? It is sheer Arminianism to insist upon a true and correct understanding as being essential. The case of the young Harris disproves this. For eighteen months he was used in this mighty manner while still not merely confused, but actually wrong in his doctrine. The same, of course, is true in the case of John Wesley. I remember speaking once in the Anniversary at the Central Hall, Westminster. I said that I felt I was there to represent George Whitefield, and in discoursing a little on the difference between the theological standpoints of Whitefield and Wesley I made a remark which I repeat on this occasion. I said that John Wesley was to me the greatest proof of Calvinism. Why? Because in spite of his faulty thinking he was greatly used of God to preach the gospel and to convert souls! That is the ultimate proof of Calvinism – predestination and election. It certainly comes out quite clearly in the case of the young Howell Harris.

The next matter to which I would refer is in connection with the Societies which Harris and others formed, and as we were reminded so well by Dr Eifion Evans, these were primarily 'experience meetings.' Harris says that they were meant for people 'to read and to talk together about the state of their souls, to show the result of what they had learned by self-examination, and to ground the ignorant in the principles of religion.' Let me emphasise and underline that in the innermost Societies there were full members who gave proof of 'having the witness of the Spirit in their hearts.' There were Christians who had not received that, but this was the first demand for admission to this innermost circle, that they had proof of the witness of the Spirit in their hearts. This was a point that was frequently emphasised by all these men.

I pass on next to his irenic spirit. I do not like to refer to it as an 'ecumenical' spirit. That word has such overtones at the present time that I doubt whether we should use it at all in connection with Harris. But as to his irenic spirit there is no question whatsoever. You cannot read his diaries, or the diaries of Whitefield and of

Wesley concerning him, without being struck by this powerfully. This man, of all these men, was the one most concerned about unity amongst true Christian people; but to suggest, as Professor Buick Knox seems to do, that Howell Harris was the great precursor of the modern ecumenical movement is simply ridiculous. It is not difficult to imagine what he would have thought and said of so-called Christians who deny the deity of Christ, his atoning blood, and the person of the Holy Spirit. But he was grieved at the divisions among those who held the true faith and shared a common experience of 'life in the Spirit.' Thus we find him in 1742 in London saying, 'We should not espouse the names put on us to our shame – Presbyterians, Quakers, Church of England, Anabaptists, Methodists, etc. and espouse only the name given to us in the Scripture – Christians; for I am sure, infallibly sure, that it is God's will that all his followers should be as one as the Father and the Son are one.' I could adduce many similar quotations to demonstrate this point. Here is another most interesting quotation, 'I will not look on small things lest they should obstruct me in great things, as they do with so many.' That was his constant rule. He was constantly troubled by the question of whether he should stay in the Church of England, or whether he should leave that church and join the nonconformists. He went through agonies concerning this matter and especially in the early years. In his diaries there are constant references to this.

But he did remain in the Church of England. Why did he do so? It seems to me that there are a number of reasons. One was certainly his great humility. He was a curious man in whom there was a combination of a strange humility – almost of morbid introspection at times – and a timorousness and a self-abnegation, but, on the other hand, he could roar like a lion, rebuke great people, and be afraid of no one. But he was essentially a humble man. His upbringing had been in the Anglican church. His great experiences had been in connection with such churches; and this always influenced him. Then there was the influence of that great man Griffith Jones of Llanddowror, who started the circulating schools, and who was a kind of 'morning-star' of the great revival.

Harris trembled to go against the advice of such a man. He was also greatly influenced – and I would say this was the overriding consideration – by the evangelistic need and opportunity among the Anglicans. The national church was then the church of the people, and everyone was supposed to be a member of it. If people ever went anywhere they went there, particularly on special occasions such as christenings, weddings, and burials. Harris saw in that a great evangelistic need and opportunity. He felt that the nonconformists had the truth, but here were these masses of people in utter ignorance; and he trembled to do anything which might militate against this evangelistic opportunity. He felt that if he left the Church of England those people would no longer listen to him. They would say that he had become a Dissenter. Thus he would be shutting the door of evangelism in his own face. It seems quite clear to me that this was the overriding consideration. It led to many difficulties, but I would put that as the chief argument that constantly prevailed with him.

Again, he could see very clearly that neither the Church of England nor the nonconformists, the Dissenters, could nurture the converted that had come into being as a result of his great evangelistic ministry. So, as neither could deal with these people, why not stay in the Anglican church and form the societies and go on in that way? But let us not forget that the state of the nonconformists at that time was not a very spiritual one. The story of the nonconformists in the early part of the eighteenth century in Wales, as indeed in England, was one of doctrinal disputations. They were learned men, they were able men, and they were well versed in doctrine; but they spent most of their time in arguments and disputations with one another. Furthermore, many of them were hyper-Calvinists. There is no doubt at all in my mind that Harris was held back from accepting the doctrines of election and predestination very largely by the hyper-Calvinism of some of the Dissenters. That has often hindered people from accepting the doctrines of grace. As a result of these various considerations Howell Harris remained in the Church of England for the whole of his life.

## IV

I close with certain remarks concerning his end, in June and July 1773 – two hundred years ago. During those last days he wrote a great deal. Let me give a few quotations which show how this man faced the end of his earthly journey. He writes;

'My spirit is like one at the door waiting to be called in. I could have no access to ask for anything but that I may go home, and that he would make haste and make no long tarry. Oh, thou who didst bleed to death, and who art alive, come and take me home; and as for the passage, I have committed that to thee to take care of me. I am thine here and for ever. I am one of thy redeemed, the fruit of thy blood and sweat, and thy will is my heaven. I feel my spirit continually, as it were, from home, and that I am one of the Lamb's company and belong to him and cannot be long from him. My spirit cries, Lord, thou canst not be God and not pity and love me, because thou hast given me what thou hast promised in pity to a poor, broken, penitent, and humble spirit, and also faith to lay hold of thy righteousness and blood. Oh Lord, thou canst not leave me long here, thou must pity and call me home, for I am a stranger here. I love the glorified spirits and long to be among them because they behold his glory and because they have no guile, nor deceit, nor sin, nor strange gods, nor any other corruption; no wisdom, no righteousness but only in the Lamb.'

He writes again; 'My dear Saviour did shine upon me so sweetly this afternoon. Oh let me eat no more the bread that perisheth, but be thou to me from henceforth bread and food for ever.' 'I feel my Spirit' he writes again, 'leaving all places and men here below and going to my Father and to my native country, home, yea my own home, and though I am here below in his kingdom yet whilst I wait to be called home my longings and cries are insatiable indeed, and when the Lord of glory answers me that I shall soon go to him my spirit does so burn with love to that dear Saviour that I flee to him and can take no denial. I cannot stay here, and though I am but a bit of dust and nothing before thee, yet, O Father, may I without offending ask thee one special favour. Oh Saviour, give me leave, though a worm, to ask without offending that my time be shortened. Oh my dear Lord, I must love thee and weep at thy feet and wrestle with thee till thou appearest unto me. This is thy lower house and thou art gone before me and therefore I must come. Thou canst not leave me long. Thou art both here and there, also my Heaven. I must have the Saviour indeed, for he is my All. All that others have in the world and in religion, and in themselves I have in thee – pleasures, riches, safety, honour, life, righteousness, holiness, wisdom, bliss, joy, gaiety, and happiness, and by the same rule that each of these is dear to others. He must be dear to me, and if a child longs for his father, a traveller for the end of his journey, a workman to finish his work, a prisoner for liberty, an heir for the full possession of his estate, so in all these respects I cannot help longing to go home.'

Very often, according to his first biographers, he joyfully repeated these words, 'Glory be to God. Death hath no sting.' And again he broke out as one full of faith and assurance, 'it is more clear to me that God is my everlasting Father and that I shall go to him soon.' He over and over again expressed how exceeding dear and precious the Saviour was to him. 'This is following Jesus; we are come to Mount Zion. I saw a great glory before in that God-man Jesus, but nothing to what I now behold in him.' That is how he triumphantly and gloriously faced the end.

I cannot refrain from quoting the brief account of his funeral written by the Countess of Huntingdon. 'On the day Mr Harris was interred we had some special seasons of divine influence both upon converted and unconverted. It was a day never to be forgotten, but I think ought to be remembered with holy wonder and gratitude by all who were present. No fewer than 20,000 people were the assembly on this solemn occasion … We had three stages erected and nine sermons addressed to the vast multitudes, hundreds of whom were dissolved in tears … Though we had enjoyed much of the gracious presence of God in our assemblies before, yet I think I never saw so much at any time as on that day; especially when the Lord's Supper was administered, God poured out his Spirit in a wonderful manner. Many old Christians told me they had never seen so much of the glory of the Lord and the riches of his grace, nor felt so much of the gospel before.'

That is what happens, you see, even in the funeral of such a man. In the same way, on the day that Daniel Rowland died in Llangeitho a revival broke out. The news of the death of these men could lead to revival. Here are the last words in the Countess' account: 'When the long and mournful procession arrived at the parish church at Talgarth, the service was to have been conducted according to the rites of the Church of England. But amidst the sorrow and tears of the audience that thronged the building an interruption took place. The officiating clergyman, being unable to proceed on account of his emotion, handed the Prayer Book to another – that does not often happen – but the second clergyman also lost self-control and passed the book to a third, when he again by reason of the same cause was unable to go on; and thus in silence were the remains of the great man laid to rest in the chancel in the parish church at Talgarth, and in the same grave in which his wife had been buried a few years before.'

## V

I close by asking a series of questions in the light of all this. How many churches do you know of today in which experience meetings of the type held by Howell Harris and others could be conducted? Secondly, are we aware of the rich possibilities in this life for the Christian believer, especially in the matter of direct dealings with God? Does our doctrine of the Holy Spirit, and his work, leave any room for revival either in the individual or in the church; or is it a doctrine which says that we have all received everything we can have of the Spirit at regeneration, and all we need is to surrender to what we have already? Does our doctrine allow for an outpouring of the Spirit – 'the gale' of the Spirit coming upon us individually and collectively? Do we recognise and acknowledge that in the sovereignty of God an Arminian may be 'filled with the Spirit' and greatly used by God in the salvation of souls, and the edification of the church? It is an inevitable question.

Is not the greatest sin among evangelical people today that of 'quenching the Spirit'? Do we regard the exhortation of the apostle in 1 Thessalonians 5:19, as being applicable only to the church in the time of the apostles? Do we recognise that this is our greatest sin, or do we satisfy ourselves, and pacify our hearts and consciences, by saying that that only applied to the early church and the apostolic era? Is not our greatest need today an outpouring of the Spirit of God individually, as well as upon the churches in a more collective sense? We are again in a condition of darkness and of deadness so similar to that of the early years of the eighteenth century. What produced the change then? The outpouring of the Spirit of God! Is this not our greatest need? We are not simply to exhort people to surrender to what they have already, but rather to pray that God would shed forth his Spirit again as he did on the Day of Pentecost, as he has done repeatedly in the great revivals in the history of the church, and as he did, not least, on Howell Harris on June 18th 1735.

# 1974

## 'Living the Christian Life'[1] – New Developments in the Eighteenth- and Nineteenth-Century Teaching

THIS conference has concentrated attention on the theme of living the Christian life. So far we have been brought to the end of the seventeenth century. We have been following the chronological order. We started with Luther and Calvin; then we came on to the early English Reformers, after that we were brought to William Perkins, at the end of the sixteenth century, and some of the men he influenced, especially in the earlier part of the seventeenth century. Then in considering the problem of antinomianism we were brought right to the end of the seventeenth century. I take up the story from that point and propose to deal with the departures from what we have been hearing. The fact is that something happened in the 18th century which brought a new element into this discussion. To put it generally, it is the idea of 'Christian perfection,' or the possibility of perfection in Christian life and living, in this present world of time.

I am attempting an impossible task, for I have to review two hundred and fifty years of history. All I can claim to do is to call attention to the salient features. A volume of mine on Romans 8 verses 5-17, recently published, deals in detail with what I am now going to review very hurriedly.[2] This perfectionist teaching can be considered under three main headings. The first I would describe as Evangelical, the second as Ethical, and the third as Psychological.

[1] The general title for the 1974 conference.

[2] *Romans, The Sons of God,* 1974.

The first, the Evangelical Perfectionist teaching brings us directly to the teaching of John Wesley. Whatever we may think of him, and his teaching, John Wesley was a phenomenon; and his teaching, and the Denomination which resulted from this, is a phenomenon which we have to recognise in the history of this country. You are familiar with the statement of Halévy that it is probably this which saved England from a revolution such as they had in France in 1789. What he originated accounts in large measure for the history of the nineteenth century; and apart from anything else, the political impact of this teaching upon the life of this country was quite remarkable. So it cannot be regarded lightly.

## I

I must emphasise that what I am going to say applies almost entirely to England. John Wesley was really a failure in Scotland and in Wales. The reason for that is fairly obvious. It is not national but doctrinal. Those two countries were Calvinistic in their outlook. In Wales Methodism took the form of Calvinistic Methodism – the leaders there sided with Whitefield rather than John Wesley; and though he paid a number of visits to Wales the followers of John Wesley had no churches there until about 1800 and thereafter. So this teaching scarcely influenced Wales as such at all. There were certain people who went to live in Wales from England who tended to bring his teaching with them; but it was not a phenomenon in Wales. Exactly the same is true of Scotland. Wesley's visits made practically no impact at all there, whereas Whitefield's made a very profound impression. So we are dealing with teaching that became prominent in the religious life of England, and which has continued to be so ever since in various forms. What was this teaching? The main difficulty that confronts anyone who attempts to deal with this subject is that there is such a plethora of material that it is almost impossible to know what to select. Moreover John Wesley stated his teaching so frequently and in so many ways, and modified his statements so many times, that it tends to become confusing. But fortunately in 1765 he wrote what he called *A Plain Account of Christian Perfection*. It was published in 1766, and re-published in 1777 when it was described as *A Plain Account of Christian Perfection as taught by John Wesley from 1725–1777*. He gave several other summaries of his teaching and preached many sermons on this subject.

Let us start with the actual history. John Wesley underwent his crucial experience in Aldersgate Street in London on May 24th, 1738. It was then he knew that his sins were forgiven; and it was a turning-point in his life. He began to evangelise and to be a prominent preacher. The same had just previously happened to his brother Charles, and still earlier to Whitefield; and so they began to co-operate and preach together in London, Bristol, and other parts of the country. That happened in 1738, but by about 1740 John Wesley had already begun to preach this notion of what he called 'Christian perfection' or 'perfect love.' It came in as early as that. He published what he called *The Character of a Methodist* in 1742 and in that his teaching on 'Christian perfection' or 'perfect love' is very prominent. Indeed, even before that, this teaching had appeared in a hymn-book which he had published, and in many of his sermons. There was a famous sermon on 'Christian perfection' which he preached in 1740, and which, as a result of his conversation with Dr Gibson, Bishop of London at the time, he published. It was a sermon on Philippians 3:12. That was as early as 1740. He then stated the doctrine very plainly in the preface to his second volume of hymns published in 1741. In another volume of hymns in 1742 he published it again. And so he went on. He called the first Conference of his preachers and helpers in 1744, and on the second morning of that Conference he expounded in detail his teaching concerning perfection. He continued to do so in his various annual Conferences. Then he reviewed the whole teaching in *A Plain Account of Christian Perfection* which he published in 1766.

All this led to great controversy with the men with whom he had worked. This was true of the Moravians who had greatly helped and influenced him when he was travelling on the boat to America, and later after his return to this country. He paid a visit to their 'colony' in Herrnhut in Germany in August of 1738.

These men had a profound effect upon him, and he and they had worked together in meetings in Fetter Lane here in London. The same was true of Whitefield and others. As he continued to preach this doctrine he provoked controversy and caused much confusion; and this became one of the main causes of the separation between George Whitefield and John Wesley and the division in Methodism. The question of election and predestination was also involved, but the preaching of 'Christian perfection' was the real cause of the trouble. John Wesley said many times that he felt that the Methodist people had been raised up by God to bear witness to this truth and doctrine concerning 'Christian perfection,' so he nailed his colours to the mast. This was the peculiar treasure of Methodism, the thing that Methodism had been called to propagate. The teaching was based upon certain favourite texts, such as the 6th chapter of Romans, 1 Peter 4:1, 2; 1 John 3:8; and 1 John 5:18. It is interesting to note that he never seems to have used – as some of this followers have done, and particularly in this century – Acts 15:9 and 26:18 where the term 'sanctified by faith' is used.

What then was this teaching? Perhaps the most helpful thing I can do is to read out a summary of his teaching as it is found in the first volume of *The Study of Methodism* published in 1966, and edited by two leading Methodist scholars, Professor Rupert Davies and Professor Gordon Rupp. Professor Rupert Davies has an excellent summary of the teaching, but as it is rather long I am going to read a summary of Rupert Davies' summary by Jack Ford who was until recently the principal of the College of the Church of the Nazarenes in Manchester. This is found in Ford's *In the Steps of John Wesley: The Church of the Nazarene in Britain,* and as it is briefer I quote it:

(1.) 'Justification and Sanctification are two distinct things and must not be confused; but the latter invariably follows the former.'

(2.) Entire Sanctification is 'an instantaneous change which eradicates all sin.'

(3.) 'Sanctification, of course, is the gift of God; it is received, like justification, by faith alone.'

(4.) 'The one (justification) implies what God does for us through his Son; the other what he works in us by his Spirit; and when God has done the one thing, his Spirit is at once at work to do the other.'

(5.) 'It is accompanied by the witness of the Spirit to itself. "But how do you know that you are sanctified, saved from inbred corruption? … We know it by the witness and the fruit of the Spirit." '

(6.) 'Of the perfect Christian Wesley says: … he is "pure in heart." "Love has purified his heart from envy, malice, wrath, and every unkind temper … " '

(7.) 'The fruit of the Spirit is the necessary mark of sanctification.'

(8.) 'Christian perfection is, above all, loving God with all our heart and mind and soul and strength, and our neighbour as ourselves … The best possible description of it, therefore, is perfect love.'

(9.) 'In one view (perfection) is purity of intention, dedicating all the life to God. It is giving God all the heart: it is one design, ruling our tempers. It is devoting, not a part, but all, our soul, body, and substance to God.'

(10.) '… It is clear that Wesley here and always teaches a "relative" perfection. The perfect, he says, grow in grace to all eternity.'

(11.) 'The "perfect" man is not free from errors … He is not exempt from infirmities … Nor is he free from temptation.'

(12.) 'They who are sanctified, yet may fall and perish.'

That is the essential teaching of John Wesley. You may well ask, How did he come to propagate or even to hold such teaching? That is a very interesting question. John Wesley is one of the most complicated characters in English religious history. He was a combination of opposites, and a very difficult man to assess for that reason – especially from the stand-point of psychological understanding. He did and said things that were contradictory. The answer as to how he came to hold such teaching is fairly clear. You will notice that he described the *Plain Account* he published in 1777 as being his teaching from 1725–1777, and he always emphasised the point that this was what he had always taught and preached from 1725 onwards. He was not converted until 1738, but he says that he began his teaching on perfection in 1725. This is undoubtedly true, and it provides us with the solution to the problem of his teaching.

How did he come to teach it? His father and mother, though they had had Puritan forbears, had drifted away from that outlook, and had become non-jurors. They had both been interested in mystical theology and had read a great deal of it. I mean by that Roman Catholic mystical teaching. Before the Reformation there were in the Roman Catholic Church those who were very interested in holiness and godliness and in coming to a knowledge of God. These were called mystics, and some of them were very 'evangelical' mystics. There was, for instance, John Tauler in Germany who used to preach in a church where great crowds gathered, and there were many conversions. If you read his sermons you come to the conclusion that this man was almost an evangelical. Then there was the famous book *Theologia Germanica* which helped Luther so much in his early days. John Wesley had read these books, and also *The Imitation of Christ* by Thomas à Kempis. But beyond that he had read authors belonging to the seventeenth century, and two in particular. One was the famous Madame Guyon, a most remarkable woman, who published various works, and who was a great friend of the Roman Catholic Archbishop Fénélon. Two of the latter's books can still be found in second-hand bookshops – *Letters to Men,* and *Letters to Women*. These mystics were concerned about knowing God – 'the beatific vision.' 'Blessed are the pure in heart for they shall see God,' expresses what they were striving after. In addition to these, and I believe his favourite author, was a layman in France called Marquis or Baron de Renty. This was a remarkable man, an aristocrat who was so intent on getting to know God, and to live a godly life, that he followed the 'mystical way' and lived a very rigorous, disciplined life in order to attain to that. John Wesley published a life of him more than once, and exhorted his people to read it. This had a very profound influence upon him. Later he came across the famous book by Henry Scougal – *The Life of God in the Soul of Man*. That is not a work on mystical theology, but it has the same general idea of a true and living knowledge of God. Wesley started with this and pressed it to an extreme. Scougal's book influenced not only Wesley but also Whitefield and all the members of the Holy Club. Then, to cap them all, there were the writings of William Law, who again was a mystic, but a Protestant mystic. He wrote a book on perfection as well as his famous book *The Serious Call.* That again influenced Wesley and Whitefield and others.

These are the influences that came to bear on Wesley even before his conversion, and it was these influences that led Charles Wesley, brother of John Wesley, to start the Holy Club in Oxford. These facts are important for this reason. We should always be interested in any man who is concerned about holiness; and these men were. They were not content to know God. So they formed their Holy Club and they practised fasting, visiting prisoners, and so on. This was the way to know God – good works. They tithed – in fact they went beyond that – they gave their money until they were almost penniless, and were so vigorous in their fasting that they even affected their health in their attempt to achieve this holiness. That is the background to Wesley's teaching.

Then came the great experience in May 1738, and after that his visit to the Moravian settlement in Germany. There he was profoundly impressed by the testimonies of two men, one called Arvid Gradin and another called Christian David. These men both testified to being entirely delivered from sin, and to being filled with God's perfect love. While this deeply affected him it also raised a problem in his mind as to how to reconcile it with his evangelical experience and his understanding of the doctrine of justification by faith which had brought him to conversion. The teaching of the Moravians, and especially Peter Bohler, had brought him to see and believe the doctrine of justification by faith. He saw that he had been trying to justify himself by works. This grasping of the teaching of justification by faith, and seeing that it was a denial of what he had previously believed, caused a conflict in him which lasted just under two years. For two years he was able to fight the old mystical tendencies, but by 1740 he had reverted to the old position. Indeed it is clear that this conflict continued in him throughout his life. Having started in favour of mysticism he turned against it at his conversion. When justification by faith was dominant, down went mysticism; but when he became somewhat confused, as he did several times, concerning justification by faith, mysticism came up again. So we find that at different periods in his life he held different attitudes towards mysticism. It is important therefore that we should bear this in mind. In 1740 he made statements about justification by faith – which he had only come to believe two years before – which were really denials of that doctrine; and Whitefield and Count Zinzendorf and the Moravians here in London protested.

He did the same again in 1770. In his Conference in 1770 he made a statement in which he virtually went back to 'justification by works' quite openly, and it was printed in the minutes of the Conference. It led to a great quarrel, and particularly between him and Augustus Toplady. The contradiction between this and his former teaching was pointed out to him; whereupon he again did a most extraordinary thing. He virtually withdrew what he had said, and confessed that he had been too extreme; but one of his assistants, John Fletcher of Madeley – a very saintly, godly man – defended what Wesley had said in the 1770 Conference. But though Wesley himself had now virtually withdrawn his statement he did not restrain John Fletcher from publishing his defence of it. That was what led to the acrimonious controversy. I remind you of this in order to show that there was a curious kind of instability in his temperament, and particularly in his thinking. It seems to me that the only way to understand John Wesley is to see that there was a perpetual conflict in him between the mystical notions leading to 'perfect love' and the doctrine of justification by faith, and that he oscillated between the two. And of course, as controversy arose, he was inclined more and more to make extreme statements.

How do we evaluate this teaching? In a sense we have already had the answer in this conference. Wesley's teaching is a reversal of the teaching of Luther and Calvin, the early English Reformers, and William Perkins and the Puritans. How did he arrive at this?

It seems to me that we are driven to conclude that it was due to over-intellectualism. John Wesley was a typical intellectualist. He called himself 'a man of one book,' but he was a prolific reader; moreover it is clear that his own thinking dominated and coloured his reading even of the Scriptures. The trouble with John Wesley was that he was too logical. Intellectualist and logical as he was, instead of being guided by the Scriptures, and being controlled therefore by the balance of the Scriptures, he took certain statements and pressed them to their logical conclusions irrespective of other statements in the same Scriptures. For instance he would take words such as 1 John 3:8, 'He that is born of God sinneth not,' and say, 'That is true.' It says, 'If a man is born of God he does not sin, therefore it must be true of the Christian. Therefore any man who has been reborn or regenerated does not sin and cannot sin!' That was the kind of argument he employed; and the result of this is that there are constant contradictions in his teaching. How could he make such a statement when he knew that Christians sinned? That led him to give a definition of sin; and this perhaps is the 'Achilles heel' of his whole teaching. He had a defective doctrine of sin. His definition of sin was that it is 'the voluntary transgression of a known law.' He seems to have ignored the doctrine concerning the pollution caused by sin. He regarded sin only in terms of this voluntary transgression of a known law.

That led to various other defects. He completely ignored the exhortations of the Scripture. He takes positive statements such as 1 John 3:8, etc., and so presses them to their logical conclusion that he lands himself in difficulties. The exhortations, the appeals to us to apply the teaching of holiness and to do various things ourselves, are ignored. His main error was to confuse assurance of salvation with perfection. Ultimately he is confused, I believe, over the doctrine of the baptism of the Spirit. Sometimes he gives the impression that it is this baptism that completely sanctifies a man, then at other times he says that it is this which testifies to the fact that a man has been cleansed from sin. However, the point is that he did teach that one could be entirely delivered from sin, that sin could be eradicated out of our natures.

However, there were certain qualifications which he added, and which I must mention in order to be fair to his teaching. He would never use the term 'sinless perfection' for the following reason. He said that a person filled with the love of God is still liable to 'involuntary transgressions,' so he would not talk about 'sinless perfection.' Another matter, which constantly troubled him, was this. People used to say to him, as the Bishop of London did: If you teach this possibility of being perfect, or having 'perfect love,' in this life, where are the examples and illustrations of this? He was in great trouble over this. He examined a number of his followers, and at one time he felt he could produce thirty such people; but only one of the thirty seemed to persist – the others fell away. Another interesting fact concerning him is that he never claimed this experience for himself. He was a very honest man. He taught this perfectionism but he would never say that it was true of himself. He said it was true of John Fletcher of Madeley, but not of himself. For many years he had great difficulty in producing any examples of it, but in 1762 there was a period of great blessing in his Societies in the London area, and many people came forward at that time to testify to this blessing. He gives an account of their experiences in his book. But he was really always in trouble over this factual aspect of his teaching.

Again, he was in trouble as to when this happens. He said that he had never known a single case where this perfection was attained at the time of regeneration. He said the rule was that a man was born again, and that that in a sense already made him perfect in the matter of not committing any voluntary transgressions, but he still had to grow, the old nature was still struggling, and he had to fight it. He went on and on struggling until he was delivered entirely from sin. He taught that this must be sought diligently, and generally had to be sought for a long time; yet it could happen at any moment because it is a gift. As you have your justification by faith, so you have your sanctification by faith; and it is a complete and an entire sanctification although there is this relative element in it. It does not mean perfection of knowledge and wisdom and understanding. It is perfect only in the sense of not being guilty of any known or voluntary sin. Another aspect of the teaching which perplexed him was: Should he exhort his people to confess this blessing and bear testimony to it in public? On the whole he was against doing so because he was wise enough to see the dangers. If someone professed this and then fell into sin – because he taught that you could fall into sin, indeed he even taught that one could fall away from grace altogether – it would do more harm than good. So on the whole his tendency was to discourage people from publicly confessing this experience or laying claim to it. That is, I fear, but a hurried review of his teaching.

What is the subsequent history of this teaching? It dominated the life of the Methodist Societies right to the end of the eighteenth century. They became a separate denomination almost as soon as John Wesley died. There again he was inconsistent. He would not leave the Church of England himself, but he drew up plans for his followers to do so after his death. These are the odd characteristics of this man. I suppose that ultimately it was the result of a kind of honesty. He saw both sides of a problem and was drawn both ways; so he did nothing. He would not leave the Church of England, but he turned himself into a kind of bishop and ordained men whom he sent to America in order that they might ordain others there. He broke many of the rules of the Church of England. He had his own Societies, his own Conference, his own chapels, and yet, as the Anglicans are never tired of reminding us, he died as an Anglican. They should not boast of that because it is merely an expression of his inconsistency and of one of his greatest weaknesses!

His teaching continued into the nineteenth century, but the Methodism that came directly from him began to lose its fervour and there was a revolt against it. In particular two extraordinary men arose in the early years of the nineteenth century, both of whom were workmen. One was Hugh Bourne and the other William Clowes. These men passed through a great experience which they interpreted as being 'a baptism of the Spirit.' They called it a 'spirit of burning,' a burning away of the dross. They formed what afterwards became known as the Primitive Methodist Church or Connexion. They called it Primitive Methodist because they claimed that it went back to the original Wesleyan teaching from which the others had departed. This became a very powerful movement. A man came over from America called Lorenzo Dow and he brought with him the idea of 'tarrying meetings.' The rationale of these meetings was this: If this cleansing of the heart, this eradication of sin out of one's nature is something that is received from God, then should we not wait until we receive it? So they held great preaching and tarrying services in America. The people would go in their wagons and carts and would listen to the preaching for days on end. Gradually they developed this idea of 'tarrying' for the blessing, waiting until you receive it and saying 'I will not go home until I receive this. If it can be received in a moment, I want it and I am going to get it; and I am going to wait until I get it.' Lorenzo Dow introduced this idea to Hugh Bourne and William Clowes, and they held a series of extraordinary meetings at a place called Mow Cop. There they would meet for preaching and praying; and there is no doubt but that amazing things happened. That became a mighty movement in the 1810s and onwards to 1830 and beyond that. It is an extraordinary story, and I commend the reading of the biographies of these two men and, indeed, any of the better histories of the Primitive Methodists. I believe these men confused in their thinking a baptism of power with sanctification. There is no doubt about their power – the historical records prove this – but they clearly got confused in their doctrine as between power to witness and to preach and sanctification. However they exercised a great ministry and had a profound influence over masses of people.

The next big movement that came out of Methodism was the Salvation Army. William Booth was originally a member of the Methodist Church, and a Methodist preacher; and so the Salvation Army taught the typical full-orbed Wesleyan teaching concerning 'Christian perfection' or 'perfect love.' I believe that it still continues to do so. But in the beginning, and until the death of the original General, this was an essential part of the teaching. At the same time Methodism developed in America, and became the largest denomination in that country. The Methodists took greater advantage of the Great Trek towards the West in America than any other religious body. Their circuit riders were aggressive men who spread the gospel widely. The result was that their teaching became widespread in the life of America. After a while it began to wane, but that led to various holiness movements based on this same teaching, and then holiness churches. Among many such churches the most notable is the one to which I have already referred, namely, the Church of the Nazarenes which started somewhere in the 1890s. A man of the name of Bresee was greatly used in its formation, and the Church of the Nazarenes became a strong church which is now to be found in this country also. At the same time certain holiness churches arose in this country – the Calvary Holiness Church started by Maynard James and Jack Ford and others. There was also a man called David Thomas in Battersea who led a similar movement. All these came together and eventually all became part of the Church of the Nazarenes. There is one other movement I must mention. It started in Scotland towards the end of the last century and is known as The Faith Mission. It was started by a man called J. G. Govan, and it is to it that the late Duncan Campbell belonged. The Faith Mission of Scotland also perpetuates the teaching of the Wesleys with regard to sanctification.

## II

There, hurriedly and inadequately, we have looked at what I have ventured to call 'Evangelical Perfectionism.' We turn now to the second division which I have described as 'Ethical Perfectionism.' This is really the teaching of Charles G. Finney. We think of him primarily as an evangelist, but actually Finney was only an evangelist for some ten years. After that he became professor in a college in a place called Oberlin, and there he began to teach and to propagate his teaching concerning perfection. It is known as the Oberlin School of Perfectionism. Why do I differentiate between this and the previous teaching? It is because it is essentially different. Here again was a strange man. Finney was trained as a lawyer; and he never ceased to be a lawyer! In many ways that accounts for his teaching. He was so much the lawyer who followed his own logical reasoning in such a rationalistic manner that he did violence to the teaching of Scripture and seemed to be entirely oblivious of the great teaching of the preceding centuries. He was influenced by Wesley's teaching, and that of the Methodists, but he elaborated a system of his own which contradicts that of Wesley in certain vital respects. This was partly the result of his being influenced by the teaching of a man named N. W. Taylor who was a professor at Yale University in New England. N. W. Taylor was really one of the originators of what became known as the New England theology. Finney swallowed this teaching and carried it to an even greater extreme than Taylor himself. The teaching can be summarised simply thus. John Wesley was an Arminian, but he believed in original sin and also that a man could do nothing about his salvation apart from grace. But he also believed that this grace was available to all, and that it was left to man himself to decide whether to take advantage of it or not. Finney was not an Arminian; he was a Pelagian. He did not believe in original sin, and he believed that the natural man, by a process of reason, was able to grasp the truth and to put it into operation. The result was, as is clear in his autobiography, or his system of theology, or any of his sermons, that he always preached like a barrister. He said that he had a case to present, and as a barrister, he tried to influence the mind and the thinking of his hearers in order to produce a verdict. So he taught that you could have a 'revival' whenever you liked. That is his teaching concerning revivals which has been copied and adopted by so many. You have only to do certain things and you will have a revival. That is Pelagianism, pure and simple. No original sin, no original depravity! Man, he taught, is morally capable. Wesley had never taught that. Finney taught, further, that obligation is limited by ability, that a man is never expected to do anything beyond what he is capable of doing, beyond his ability. So he introduced a sliding scale of perfection. When you are but a 'babe in Christ' you can be perfect at that level. Of course, compared with a more advanced man you are not perfect, but you are perfect at that level. That is your ability at that stage. You cannot do more at that stage. So he introduced a sliding scale of perfection; and at the same time he taught that nothing is sinful but a voluntary action. Righteousness is adjusted to the fluctuating ability of man. Even the claims of the law, he said, are graduated to the sinner's ability.

He taught that the law applies to everyone. It applies as much to the Christian as to the non-Christian. Christians, said Finney – somewhat reminiscent of certain others we have been hearing about – are still under the law, and under the same demands of the law as everyone else. So 'Christian perfection' is perfect obedience to the law of God. Furthermore, Finney denied very strongly what he called Wesley's idea of 'physical' sanctification. Wesley taught a kind of physical sanctification in the sense that something happened to us; our natures were rid of sin. Finney denounced that and denied it. He said that we remain exactly what we are from beginning to end, and though you may live to be a hundred years old you are still essentially the same in your nature as you were at the beginning. Our Lord said, 'Make the tree good and the fruit will be good.' Finney denied that and said that the tree cannot be made good.

A good summary of his teaching can be stated thus. Christ reveals himself to us, and reveals ourselves to us, and we, induced by the revelation, receive him and put him on. Christ gives us the revelation; we do the rest. We get this revelation of the truth about ourselves and the truth concerning Christ, and then, having seen this truth, we can accept it or not. If we accept it we then proceed to put it into practice. At the same time he talked about a baptism of the Spirit; but it is very difficult to discover what exactly he meant. He shifted in his statements and in his definitions. Scripture was twisted and forced to fit into his rationalistic system. He completely ignored all previous teaching and exposition of Scripture, and thus he got into this position of denying any possibility of growth in grace. John Wesley taught growth in grace and in knowledge, and that you can mature in the Christian life though you are perfect in the sense described by him right through this process. But development was possible. In the case of Finney no development is possible.

## III

We turn now to the third and last group, which I am designating 'Psychological Perfectionism.' First a brief historical survey. About 1859 a man called W. E. Boardman began teaching a kind of perfectionism in America. He started conventions for holiness. He was mainly influenced by the teaching of Wesley, and in a sense he held a modified Wesleyan teaching. There was another man called Asa Mahan, somewhat difficult to categorize, who was the president of the Oberlin College where Finney was professor of theology. He did not stay very long at Oberlin because he came to disagree with the teaching of Finney. Personally I would put Mahan into the category of Wesley. At that point I disagree somewhat with Warfield, but that is a mere technical point. However, Asa Mahan and Boardman began this new kind of holiness teaching which was a modification of the Wesleyan teaching.

This teaching, however, was made popular in America, and especially in this country, by Mr and Mrs R. Pearsall Smith. Both Mr and Mrs Pearsall Smith had been born and brought up as Quakers – a most significant fact. They had always held the Quaker teaching concerning the inner light and passivity, etc. But they began to be influenced by Methodist teaching, and particularly in 1867 when a young Baptist became a tutor in their home. Pearsall Smith was quite a wealthy businessman, and was able therefore to keep a tutor for his children in the home. This young man told them that he had had a great experience as a result of which he 'simply trusted' and 'Jesus delivered.' This was the teaching: he had been fighting the battle against sin within and without, and was failing, but he now had come to see that all he had to do was to trust in Jesus. He had done so, and had been delivered. He laid the care of his life, he said, moment by moment, on the Lord, and the Lord took it, and made his life, moment by moment, what he would have it to be. The Pearsall Smiths accepted and adopted this teaching in 1867. In 1871 Pearsall Smith claimed that he had received the baptism of the Spirit, and as the result of this he began to teach, preach, and propagate this new teaching. In 1873 they paid their first visit to this country and held meetings in London.

It is of interest to note that D. L. Moody also paid his first visit to Britain in 1873. Pearsall Smith and his wife came and held meetings in London in the Spring of 1873. In July 1874 they held the famous Broadlands Conference which was described as a 'mighty meeting.' Most of the teaching was done by Pearsall Smith. In September 1874 he conducted similar meetings, helped by Asa Mahan, in Oxford, which became known as the Oxford Meetings.

But then we come to 1875, and especially from May 29th to June 7th, when a great convention to propagate this kind of teaching was held in Brighton. It is known as the Brighton Convention, and the speaker here again was Pearsall Smith. Then a most extraordinary thing happened. It was the collapse of Mr Pearsall Smith. He was more or less dismissed from the movement because of erroneous teaching and faulty conduct. He passed under a cloud because of some kind of moral failure; and he disappears off the scene. We hear no more about Mr Pearsall Smith. After that, in the same year, the same kind of convention for the deepening of the spiritual life, or for holiness, or sanctification, was held in Keswick at the request of a vicar in Keswick. So the Keswick Convention meetings began, and have continued to be held annually ever since; and that is why the centenary of this convention is to be celebrated in July 1975. It is interesting to note that 1975 has been chosen rather than 1973, which I would have thought was the real centenary year. It may have something to do with the disappearance of Mr Pearsall Smith? I am simply stating the facts.

While Mr Pearsall Smith disappeared from the scene Mrs Pearsall Smith did not; and in some ways she was the better teacher of the two. She wrote a book which has had a very widespread influence. She called it *The Christian's Secret of a Happy Life*. J. B. Figgis writing an official book called *Keswick from Within* about 1913–14 says, 'Mrs Pearsall Smith's book had a greater effect than any other, apart from Frances Ridley Havergal. In fact it did more than any other publication ever written to extend the knowledge of the truth of sanctification.' This became the most famous book connected with this teaching. There were later teachers, one of whom called Evan H. Hopkins has been described as 'the theologian of the Keswick

Movement.' His most famous book on this theme is called *The Law of Liberty in the Spiritual Life*. It was re-published in 1975 by Marshall, Morgan & Scott.

The Keswick Movement has been mainly an Anglican movement, with an occasional free churchman such as F. B. Meyer and Graham Scroggie taking a prominent part. It is interesting to notice that though it was mainly an Anglican movement Bishop Ryle never spoke at the Keswick Convention, though he was Bishop of Liverpool. I suggested in my Preface to the reprint of his book on *Holiness* that it was because Bishop Ryle did not agree with the Keswick message that he had been so neglected in evangelical circles during the first half of this century. His book, *Holiness,* was really written to controvert the 'Keswick teaching.' A well-known evangelical reviewing the reprint of Ryle's book in *The Life of Faith* found himself in difficulties. He had to agree, of course, that Bishop Ryle had never spoken at the Keswick Convention; but he pointed out that Ryle had once sat on the platform there! C. H. Spurgeon likewise never spoke at Keswick, and for the good reason that he did not agree with the teaching. Bishop Ryle and Spurgeon were so deeply indebted to the Puritans, and so governed by their teaching, that it would be impossible for them to have accepted this teaching which departed so seriously from that earlier teaching.

What, then, was the 'Keswick message' as it was called? The big point I am anxious to establish is that this is not the Wesleyan teaching. There has been some confusion concerning this, and it has been increased in recent years by the appearance of certain speakers on the Keswick platform. Up until a certain point the distinction was observed, and the Keswick Council did not invite people of the Methodist school to speak at the convention. That was right because they did not hold the Wesleyan teaching. Indeed the Keswick teaching always strongly opposed the teaching concerning perfection. It rejected all forms of perfectionism.

The Pearsall Smiths not only came to this country but also went to Germany where they were even more successful than in this country. One of their chief followers in Germany, a man called

Theodor Jellinghaus used to refer to the 'perilous' Wesleyan teaching of a complete deliverance from sin. The old leaders of Keswick likewise denounced the Wesleyan teaching of deliverance from sin, or eradication of sin, as dangerous, perilous teaching. They taught what is called 'sanctification by faith.' This is the essential Keswick message. It asserts that justification and sanctification are separated – not only is a distinction to be drawn between them, they are actually separated. Both are 'taken by faith,' but you can have the one without the other. You can be justified only without being sanctified, where the Puritan teaching, the old evangelical teaching coming down from the Reformers, is that the moment you are justified you are regenerated, and sanctification begins. In the Keswick message they were really separated; both are to be taken by faith; and you can have full salvation through full trust. There was a man who used to teach this in a popular way by putting it in this manner. He used to put a sixpence on his right hand and say 'Take that,' and you took the sixpence. There, he said, you are taking your justification. Then he put a sixpence on his left hand and said, 'Take that also; that's your sanctification!' As you took the first sixpence so you can take the second sixpence. You 'take' sanctification by faith, and thereby you can be immediately delivered from conscious sin.

It was often stated in the following manner. The Christian believer comes to a crisis when he is tired of the struggle against sin. He then meets the teaching which tells him that he can be delivered, and that he must take this deliverance by faith. So he comes to a crisis of decision and decides that he will abandon everything, himself included, and give himself to the Lord. He hands himself and everything over to him in a great act of surrender. This is a critical experience. It is followed by an experience and by growth. But this depends on what was emphasised by the tutor in the household of the Pearsall Smiths in 1867, namely on our 'moment by moment' abiding in Christ.

That is the essence of the teaching. It is 'the rest of faith.' You 'let go and let God.' You can never fight the world, the flesh, and the devil successfully. You must abandon yourself and give up the struggle. There should be no struggle, there need be no struggle, to struggle is wrong; 'hand it over to the Lord, and he will do it for you.' A speaker in Keswick some years back used an illustration that has often been used there. 'Here you are in a room,' he said, 'it is dark, but the sun is shining outside. Why is your room dark? It is because the blinds are drawn. How can you get that light of the sun into your room? All you have to do is let up the blinds! Quite simple,' he said, 'quite simple.' 'Let up the blinds, and the light will come streaming in; and that is all you have to do. Nothing more. This is your surrender.'

Or take the famous illustrations that were used so much by Evan H. Hopkins. He had a great illustration which emphasised that the important thing is to 'abide in Christ.' As long as you abide in Christ, and leave it to him, you will be delivered from all sin. Sin still remains in the nature, sin has not been eradicated, but you can be delivered from all conscious sin as long as you abide in Christ. And here is the illustration: 'Take a poker,' said Evan Hopkins. 'It is cold, it is black, it is rigid. But now, put it in a fire and keep it there. What happens to it? It becomes hot, it becomes red, it becomes malleable. Yes, but only as long as it is in the fire. Take it out of the fire and it becomes cold, black, and rigid again.' Another illustration was that when people who cannot swim put on some kind of wings they can keep afloat; but only as long as they use the wings. If they wriggle out of the wings they will sink to the bottom. These were the analogies that were used to illustrate this teaching of 'Let go and let God' or 'Take it by faith.'

Another matter which they particularly emphasised was that you must not be at all concerned about your feelings. To do so is a great error, they said. Pearsall Smith had said that 'true religion resides in the will alone'; so you must not worry about your feelings. Many of them, in giving an account of their critical experience, went out of their way to emphasise, 'I felt nothing at all, nothing at all.' Perhaps two or three days later they had been deeply moved, but at the time, 'nothing at all.' This was right, they argued, because in your justification you felt nothing; indeed you realised the danger of trusting to your feelings; you took it by naked faith. You must do exactly the same, they said, with regard to sanctification. So the slogan was, 'Do not bother about your feelings.'

Let me try briefly to evaluate this teaching or 'message.' Surely one significant word in the title of Mrs Pearsall Smith's book gives us the key to the essential weakness. *The Christian's Secret to a Happy Life*. Happy! Happiness is put first; that is why I put this teaching under the heading of Psychological. These people were primarily concerned about happiness. Of course happiness is a product of holiness; but their primary concern was with happiness. As a result they become guilty of faulty exposition of Scripture. They started with a theory. They suddenly 'saw' this; it came to them; and now this became the controlling factor in their exposition of the Scripture. There is to be seen in the history of this movement, not infrequently, a contradiction between the Bible Readings which were given in the mornings and the convention addresses in the evenings. Certain men were called upon to give Bible Readings who were not called upon to give a convention address. My predecessor, Dr Campbell Morgan, once referred to this fact jocularly when he and I were having a meal with the then Keswick chairman, and went on to say, 'I am not complaining, you know. As long as you leave me with the Bible I am quite happy!' But he was asked to give the Bible Readings. As a result of their being controlled by the theory, they used to divide up their messages and allocate particular themes for the different nights. On Monday you had a message which chiefly emphasised repentance, then you gradually graded the message until it led to the 'critical experience.'

Another general criticism I would offer is that instead of expounding the great New Testament texts, they so often started with their theory and illustrated it by means of Old Testament characters and stories. You will find that so often their texts were Old Testament texts. Indeed their method of teaching was based on the use of illustrations rather than on exposition of Scripture. An inevitable result was that they virtually ignored everything that had been taught on the subject of sanctification during the previous eighteen centuries. That is not merely my statement. Many of them boasted of this. They said that this great truth had been missed through all those long centuries. It had only been discovered by them in the mid-nineteenth century. Surely any teaching that makes such a claim is suspect? The Keswick message asserted that the Reformed teaching produced miserable Christians, people who were still living in Romans 7. But they had found a message which could enable you to 'pass over Romans 7 to Romans 8'! Thus you could find the happiness and the victory that had eluded you, and the weary struggle would cease. The very terms and expressions that were used suggest that the approach was not so much biblical as psychological; the teaching was designed ultimately to make us happy, to produce a happy and joyous Christian life. Now the Christian is meant to experience joy, but it must never be placed in the first position. 'Blessed are they which do hunger and thirst after righteousness: for they shall be filled' (Matt. 5:6). The blessedness results from righteousness; you do not start with it. It is always an error to start with happiness or joy.

A further criticism that can be levelled against this teaching is that it is always wrong to found a movement on one particular doctrine. Doctrines must never be treated in isolation; but this convention was designed to preach this one doctrine. This always leads to a loss of the balance so characteristic of scriptural teaching.

Another serious criticism is that the 'Message' was not presented in a church context. It was an inter-denominational movement which did not face the problem of the church, or think of the life of the Christian in terms of the church. We are reaping the result of this at the present time. Evangelical people soothed their consciences and found peace and happiness by adopting this teaching, and through meeting with other Evangelicals on an inter-denominational basis while still belonging to their various churches or denominations, many of which had become apostate. Christian living was taken right out of the context of the life of the church; and any teaching in holiness which is divorced from the life of the church is already in error.

But still more serious, this teaching is guilty of 'dividing' Christ. It was taught explicitly that you can 'take Christ' as your justifier alone, without 'taking him' as your sanctifier. Thus you are dividing

Christ. In the same way it divides salvation. There is a distinction between sanctification and justification, but no division. I once used an illustration to show the difference between distinction and division in a booklet called *Sanctification by Faith*. I put it this way. The Alps consist of one range of mountains; but there are particular peaks. They are not separate mountains standing out in a plain: they all belong to the same range, but each one stands out distinctly. In that sense we must not divide doctrines from each other, but at the same time we can draw distinctions.

My ultimate criticism of this teaching, however, has always been that it ignores completely the great 'therefores' of the Epistles. The New Testament teaching on sanctification can surely be stated in this way. In the Epistles, particularly those of the apostle Paul, the first chapters are doctrinal – he reminds them of the doctrines they have believed. For instance, in the Epistle to the Romans the first eleven chapters are devoted to doctrinal teaching; then in chapter 12 the apostle begins to apply the doctrine to the living of the Christian life and says, 'I beseech you, therefore, brethren, by the mercies of God.' In other words, in the light of all he has been saying, he appeals to them to apply it to the practicalities of Christian living. We find precisely the same at the beginning of chapter 4 of the Epistle to the Ephesians. You have the doctrine in the first three chapters, and then in chapter 4 verse 1 ff., 'therefore.' But the 'Keswick message' ignores that completely. In other words, the New Testament does not teach sanctification as a theory, as something isolated from the other great doctrines. It is something which is deduced from them. It is always the working out of the doctrines, and so it is always couched in terms of appeals and exhortations. Take for example Romans 8:13. Paul says in Romans 8:12 that 'we are debtors, not to the flesh to live after the flesh' and then goes on in verse 13 to say, 'but if ye through the Spirit do mortify the deeds of the body ye shall live.' This is something we have to do; we are not to 'let go' and 'let God' do it. We are not told to abandon ourselves to him, or to 'hand it over to the Lord' to do it for us; but we, through the help and the aid given to us by the Spirit, are to mortify the deeds of the body. Or take 2 Corinthians

7:1 where the apostle exhorts us saying, 'Having therefore these promises, dearly beloved, let us cleanse ourselves from all filthiness of the flesh and spirit, perfecting holiness in the fear of God.' We have to do this. In the same way, Philippians 2:12 and 13, 'Work out your own salvation.' We have to do this. While 'it is God that worketh in you, both to will and to do,' we have actually to do this. But the Keswick message ignores completely this 'therefore' which is the key to the understanding of the New Testament teaching on the doctrine of sanctification.

I could show how, in the same way, this message completely misunderstands the teaching of Romans 6 and 7 as well – and it is interesting to notice the number of times those two chapters were dealt with in the convention. I suggest that it is psychological in the sense that it ignores these exhortations and statements such as we find in Romans 6:12, 'Let not sin therefore reign in your mortal body.' That is an exhortation to you – in the light of your position in Christ, and the fact that you are no longer under law, but under grace – to do certain things and not to do others. Ignoring all that, the 'message' is a kind of Couéism. The treatment of Romans 6:11, 'Reckon ye yourselves therefore' often comes to this, that though you know that it is not true of you, you must say to yourself that it is; and as you keep on saying to yourself that it is true, that it must be true, you will feel happier. I cannot see any difference in principle between that teaching and the teaching of Couéism which exhorts you to say to yourself when you are ill, 'Every day and in every way I am getting better and better' and that, doing so, you get better.

Finally, it is a self-contradictory teaching because, although on the one hand it tells you that you are not to strive, that you have but to 'hand it over to the Lord,' it nevertheless tells you that if you do not 'abide' in him he cannot do it for you. So ultimately all depends on your abiding. You are only delivered while you abide in Christ – 'while you keep the poker in the fire.' If you pull the poker out you are back to where you were. So ultimately it leaves the problem with you. You are not fighting sin directly but you are still striving against everything that is discouraging you from abiding in Christ.

Let me conclude by describing the position today. As regards the Wesleyan teaching, apart from the Church of the Nazarenes, and a few small groups and sects, I would say that it has virtually disappeared. A convention held every year at Southport still teaches it. Let me say this: they are godly men, and honest men who have a genuine concern about holy living and the state of the church. Methodism, speaking generally, has departed from it. The Free Methodist Church in America has not; I am speaking generally and particularly of this country. The Faith Mission in Scotland, as I say, still teaches it also.

With regard to the Keswick Message, or teaching, the position is this. There are but few men today who teach and preach the Keswick message, even in the Keswick Convention. Most of the Keswick speakers in the last ten years no longer believe what was called the 'Keswick message.' Read their addresses, and particularly the Bible Readings given in the morning, and you will find that they teach the traditional Reformed view of Romans 6 and 7. I can only think of some three men who are exceptions to this. The Keswick message has virtually disappeared, and we are back to the older evangelical teaching concerning the way in which we are to live the Christian life. That is why I said at the beginning that we are at an interesting historical point. The teaching which, starting with Wesley, has taken several different forms since then, has in many ways virtually come to an end, and there is a welcome return to a teaching which is more biblical, expository, and exegetical. Today we are confronted not so much by the kind of teaching which considers the work of the Holy Spirit with regard to holiness, as by an emphasis upon the gifts of the Spirit. This teaching which emphasises the gifts of the Holy Spirit seems to me to have given the final blow to that older teaching which paid greater attention to the doctrine of holiness. So the Higher Life or Victorious Life teaching is not a live issue for us today; but I felt it was good that we should be acquainted with the history, that we should be able to draw these distinctions, and know exactly what confronts us.

We are left with the challenge of how to teach our people to live the Christian life. I have criticised these various teachings; but once more I would pay tribute to the men who taught them. They were men who were concerned about holiness. Are we equally concerned about holiness? Our danger is, perhaps, to be so concerned about correctness of doctrine as not to be sufficiently concerned about correctness of life. I regard what I have been criticising as erroneous teaching by men of God. I am a humble follower in this matter of George Whitefield who gave instructions that John Wesley should preach his funeral sermon in spite of their disagreement and difference on these matters. The things about which they agreed were more important, and they had much fellowship together during the last years of Whitefield's life. We must follow these men. There are these differences, and we must be clear about them. But let us examine ourselves. It is easy to denounce false holiness teaching; but what is your holiness teaching? Have you the same desire for holiness? These men suffered, and sacrificed much in order to be holy men. They may have been confused about doctrines at times, they may have confused 'things that differ,' but they were zealously concerned to be holy men of God, and many of them were concerned to have a holy and a pure church. There, we surely are with them, and agree with them; and if we criticise what they taught, let us make sure that we have, and can preach and practise, 'a more excellent way.'

# 1975

# *'The Christian and the State in Revolutionary Times':*[1] *The French Revolution and After*

OUR object in studying this subject of the Christian and the State in Revolutionary Times has a very practical intent. We have not considered this matter in a theoretical manner for the simple reason that we are in the midst of such a situation ourselves. I have thought several times during the conference of a friend who was many times in this very room in recent years, Josef Ton, a Baptist pastor in Romania, who is in the midst of the fiery furnace, if one may use such an expression, at the present time, and also a colleague of his, Prof. Valish Talosh, who is professor of history in the Baptist Seminary in Bucharest. These men are already in this very situation.

The former periods of which we have been hearing were revolutionary times like ours, but as we have been seeing, each period tends to have its own special features. So if we want to consider this subject in a practical manner we have to bring it up to date; and it has fallen to my lot to do that very thing. We cannot stop even at the American War of Independence and the Declaration of Independence. We must go on beyond that; and so my title is 'The French Revolution and After.'

My whole thesis is to show that something entirely new emerged, and came into being, with the French Revolution. It is one of those great turning-points in history comparable to the Reformation – not in the same way, of course, but quite as definitely a

[1] The title for the Conference of 1975.

turning-point as was the Protestant Reformation. I start by saying that it was something which was essentially different both from the rebellion and revolution in England in the seventeenth century and also from what happened in America in 1775–76.

This new thing that came to expression in the French Revolution can be traced to a number of influences, particularly in France. It was the age of the so-called Enlightenment. The man who played a very prominent part in that was Diderot. He edited what was called an Encyclopaedia in thirty-five volumes, between 1751 and 1780, which was meant to cover the whole of knowledge, a complete conspectus of life. He was aided in this by many men but in particular by two men. The first was Jean Jacques Rousseau. Rousseau is vital to any consideration of the French Revolution. He was a voluminous writer and an undoubted genius. He published a number of books that had a profound effect on the thinking of the French people. In a book on education in 1762 he said that education was to be based entirely on natural instincts, and was to be entirely free from every competing influence of society, and especially the church. He introduced a rational view of everything. He discounted revelation and all revealed religion. He believed in a kind of natural religion based upon feeling and an experience of God; and he denounced any belief in a supernatural revelation. Then came his famous book called *The Social Contract*. In this book his argument is that the laws of the state are not of divine appointment and are not based upon divine law but upon 'the will of the people.' We know about the view of John Locke and others but there is something that is quite new here. Those men, after all, were deists. But we now reach a point when that is no longer the case in these matters. These Frenchmen held a very optimistic view of human nature, and they refused to take the Christian revelation, and especially as regards salvation, seriously. The basis of society, they said, is to be that the members of the society are to agree to a social pact, not under God, but among men themselves. There had been an acknowledgment of God so far, but now that had ended. Men are to combine for freedom and for just government in the interests of the majority. That was essentially the teaching of *The Social Contract*. Then came Voltaire, who was much more violent that Rousseau, and very violently anti-Catholic and 'anti' all Christian dogma.

These two men had a tremendous effect upon the whole outlook of the French people. They were living under the government of their dissolute kings – it was a tyranny and all that resulted from that. These new ideas came in, and at the same time Jean Astruc – the father of Higher Criticism, and, I regret to say, a physician – introduced his teaching. That introduced a yet more direct attack upon the authority of the Bible. Men had more or less, in a general way, accepted the Bible and its teaching, but now all this began to be queried. All these tendencies worked together. In other words man became the centre, not God. Not only in matters connected with the state but also in matters of religion. Reason is supreme, not revelation. The idea of the 'sovereign people' came in, and all this led in 1789 to the Revolution and the great slogan of 'liberty, equality, and fraternity.' This referred not only to political but also social matters and the whole of life; and so you get the beginning of the French Revolution. There were other elements, other strands. The teaching of Kant worked in this same direction. And in this country there was Thomas Paine who wrote his famous book *The Rights of Man*.

All this led to the French Revolution. It was a phenomenon that in a sense shook the world. At first most intelligent people welcomed it. In this country, for instance, it was eagerly welcomed by people like Coleridge and Wordsworth. One cannot really understand Wordsworth's poetry apart from the French Revolution, especially such expressions as 'Bliss was it in that dawn to be alive.' *The Prelude* gives the history, and frequent references to the Revolution are found in other poems. These men, Wordsworth, Coleridge, and others, really believed that this was the dawn of a new era – not the millennium in the biblical sense, but in their sense a kind of millennium. Men were going to be set free from all restraints and shackles, and a great new world was going to develop. However, it did not last very long. These men soon became disillusioned. The 'reign of terror' followed in France, and that in turn led to the dictatorship under Napoleon. That disillusioned Coleridge and Wordsworth and others and caused them to revert to their former views. John Wesley denounced the Revolution from the very beginning, and prophesied that this was going to be the introduction of 'the time of the end.' William Wilberforce, the leader in the cause for the abolition of slavery, regarded it with absolute horror. So there was a reaction against it in this country.

Coming to the nineteenth century we find the popular teaching of the German philosopher, Hegel, with its new view of history. It rejected the view that God guides history and taught that there is a dialectical process which governs history – thesis and antithesis producing a new synthesis. This changed people's view of history altogether; and they believed that this dialectical process produced inevitable progress. This obviously meant that there was an entirely new attitude towards the church, the State, man, everything; indeed there was a complete new view of life. Hegel, in turn, was followed by a man whom he had influenced, Karl Marx, whose teaching is essential to an understanding of our own century. Whatever we may think of his views, Karl Marx was an extremely able man who thought about these problems very deeply, both political and social. In a sense his central thesis was the inevitability of revolution, and that the course of human history had followed a certain dialectical pattern which would lead on inevitably to the 'dictatorship of the proletariat.' This was inevitable. So this stimulated men to think about revolution. There were, of course, many variations among his followers as to the details of the teaching. Some tended to say that as this process was inevitable then there was no need for us to do anything. Others taught that we can hasten the process, we can help it along. The result of all this was that the nineteenth century in many ways was the century of revolution. We came very near to revolution several times in this country. There was unrest in the Manchester area, the 'Peterloo Massacre' of 1819 being long remembered. There were revolutions on the Continent in 1830, and very nearly a revolution in this country. Many like Macaulay held the view that if the Reform Bill which was passed in 1832 had not been passed, undoubtedly there would have been a revolution in this country. But *the* year of revolution was 1848 when there were revolutions in many countries on the continent.

All this was the result of this entirely new thinking that had gained currency. It was an attack on all established institutions, including the church and the state. It meant the rejection of all authority and the setting up of 'the sovereign people,' and their reason and understanding, as the arbiters in these matters.

## I

We must now look at the way in which people reacted to all this. We have already seen that in this country, at first, people reacted against it. There is the oft-quoted statement of Halévy that the Methodist Awakening of the eighteenth century undoubtedly saved this country from a revolution such as that experienced in France. This country was cautious, and I believe there is much in what Halévy said. I would add to that that there was also the influence of the history of what had happened in the seventeenth century. After all, we had had a revolution in the seventeenth century; and you will remember that there was a reaction against that. The restoration of Charles II cannot be understood except in terms of a disillusionment with the Commonwealth period, and a feeling that government was impossible without some kind of a head, preferably a king. That introduced a note of caution and carefulness into the thinking of this country. The 'Glorious Revolution' of 1688 and the passing of the Bill of Rights in 1689 establishing a constitutional monarchy produced a settled order. So the tendency in this country right through the nineteenth century was to turn to political reform. The controlling belief was that you must have progress with order.

While that was true of the main church bodies and leaders it was not true of many of the followers. While most of the leaders of Methodism were really rank Tories, many of the Methodist people turned to Chartism, the teaching of Robert Owen and others, and became actively interested in Trade Unions. They believed and felt that the people had a right to liberate themselves from the tyranny and oppression under which not only industrial workers but also farm labourers suffered. So they entered into these movements of reform. Sometimes there was violence such as was seen in the Luddite activities, and the story of the Tolpuddle Martyrs; but on the whole the prevailing view was that which trusted to liberalism and reform. In brief I think that that is a fairly accurate picture of what happened in this country.

I turn now to something extremely interesting; to me, the most interesting reaction of all to the French Revolution. It was what took place in Holland. Here I call attention to a fascinating and most important man whose name was Groen Van Prinsterer. He was on all counts a most remarkable man. Born in very comfortable circumstances, he was trained in law and philosophy and history. He became secretary to the king, and eventually secretary to the cabinet. He had been brought up in a nominal religious atmosphere – the religion of his parents – and he was quite satisfied with it. He was sent on one occasion to do business for the king and the government to Brussels, and there he met and came under the influence of Merle d'Aubigné, the great historian of the Protestant Reformation. Under this influence – and that of the whole movement known as the *Reveil* which had started in Switzerland under Robert Haldane who had gone to live out there, and who influenced some students – Groen Van Prinsterer's life was entirely changed. D'Aubigné was one of the people who was converted under that movement, and he happened to be in Brussels when Groen went there, and as a result of that meeting he was truly converted in 1828. This, of course, profoundly affected his whole view of politics and of everything else, and as he continued to think deeply he became increasingly a first-class historian. But he could not be content with being an academic historian. He felt that he must become involved also in politics. And the more he thought the more he saw the dangerous character of the French Revolution and all that it had introduced. The result of this was that he published a great book in 1847 with the title *Unbelief and Revolution*. It is a book of fifteen chapters, only one of which has so far been translated into English, namely, chapter eleven. I am glad to be informed by friends who are in this conference that two further chapters are on the verge of being published in English, and I do hope that some of our publishers will take this up and see that eventually the whole of this great book is published in English. Notice that it was published in 1847, the year before the many revolutions which took place in 1848.

In order to indicate Groen Van Prinsterer's viewpoint let me quote his own words as they are translated into English. Writing about the French Revolution he says, 'As respects theoretical origin and course, the Revolution cannot be compared with any occurrences of former times. Change of rulers, re-allocation of authority, change of forms of government, *political* controversy, many a difference of religious conviction – all these have, in principle, nothing in common with a *social* revolution whose nature is directed against every government, against every religion; with a social, or rather yet an *anti-social* revolution which undermines and destroys morality and society; with an *anti-Christian* revolution whose chief idea develops itself in systematic rebellion against the God of revelation. So Stahl: "I take the Revolution in its world-historical idea. It did not exist in its complete form before 1789. But since then it became a world power and the battle for or against it fills history." "The Revolution is a unique event. It is a revolution of beliefs; it is the emergence of a new sect, of a new religion; of a religion which is nothing but irreligion itself, atheism, the hatred of Christianity raised into a system."

'The revolution of the United Netherlands has been compared with it; also the revolution in North America. As respects the Netherlands I appeal to what I have often said, that "liberty of Christian exercise of religion was its chief object as oppression of the gospel was the chief cause of the war." As respects America, I appeal to the remarkable work of Baird, who said: "In separating themselves from Great Britain and in reorganising their respective governments, the United States modified their institutions much less than one would be able to expect there. King, parliament, and Britannic justice were replaced for president, congress, and the supreme court; but it was at bottom the same political system plus independence." Still less may I recognise in the English revolutions a likeness of the French. If you find agreement between the revolutions of 1688 and 1789, read Burke on the similarity in outward appearance, the contrast in essence and principle. He says: "The present Revolution in France seems to me to be quite of another character and description and to bear little resemblance or analogy to any of those which have been brought about in Europe upon principles merely political. It is a revolution of doctrine and theoretic dogma." Even with 1640, with the democratic tendency and with the tyranny of Cromwell, no comparison can be allowed in its chief conception. Says Tocqueville: "Nothing could be more dissimilar ... In my opinion the two events are absolutely not to be compared." And Stahl remarks: "The liberty of England and of America is permeated with the breath of the Puritans, the liberty of France is permeated with the breath of the Encyclopaedists and the Jacobins."'

There we see Van Prinsterer's essential point of view and his teaching. He did his best to propagate these views but he was very much a voice crying in the wilderness. But he was able to form, in a very embryonic manner, what became known as the Anti-Revolutionary Party. But fortunately another man arose, the great Abraham Kuyper, and Van Prinsterer soon recognised that Kuyper had public gifts which he himself lacked. Kuyper was a born orator, and a born statesman and eventually he became the Prime Minister of Holland. Groen Van Prinsterer brought Kuyper into the movement and soon handed it over to him; and so we know of, and tend to think of, Kuyper as the leader of the Anti-Revolutionary Party, the Christian Party, and the many battles he fought in the political arena. Kuyper gave up being a minister of the church and eventually his professorship in the Free University which he himself had founded, in order to give himself to this political activity where he could introduce his Christian ideas and especially with regard to education. I wish I had time to go into all this thoroughly; but time only allows me merely to mention this most extraordinary and striking opposition to the whole principle of the French Revolution which took place in Holland. It did not take place in England; it did not take place in the United States of America; but in that little country it did. And there it stands as a great monument to the only real opposition to the whole notion behind the French Revolution.

Coming to this present century we find several striking events. Many of us, because these things were taking place in our own lifetime, do not realise what has been happening; but the Revolution in Russia in 1917 is a great landmark. The leaders of that Revolution, Lenin and Trotsky, claimed that they were putting into operation the theories and the teaching of Karl Marx. They have not done so; and it has been proved clearly that nothing could be further removed in a sense from the teaching of Marx, which advocates ultimately a class-less society and the end of all government, than the tyranny which we know exists in Russia and has done so for nearly sixty years. On the other hand, and at the other extreme, we have seen Mussolini and Fascism, and Hitler and Nazism. All these are essentially religious, as Van Prinsterer saw that the French Revolution was in reality a new religion, and not merely a political theory. There is an element of worship in them, and also an apocalyptic element. They are not merely political programmes, there is something much deeper and almost demonic. This is true of Fascism as well as of Communism.

These movements have had an effect and an influence in this country. Movements have arisen on what is termed the extreme Left and also the extreme Right; but until comparatively recently all this has taken a mainly political form. But when we come to the 1960s we are confronted by a new phenomenon. I refer to the appearance of what is known as 'the theology of revolution' or the 'theology of liberation.' This is an amazing phenomenon because it has mainly affected South America which is a Roman Catholic-dominated subcontinent. The movement has been led by various Catholics, the most prominent of whom was a Roman Catholic priest, Camilo Torres. He was actually killed in a gun battle as a guerilla fighter. Among his sayings was that 'every Catholic who is not a revolutionary and is not on the side of revolutionaries, lives in mortal sin.' An Archbishop of Brazil calls for the complete revolution of present structures on a socialist basis and without the shedding of blood. It is very interesting to observe that there have been these divisions in every century between revolutionaries who have believed in fighting and those who have said that you must not fight. Under the teaching of these men, and there are many others, conversion becomes 'one's commitment to the liberation of man from all sorts of oppression.' The love of Jesus Christ becomes love for your neighbour. We are told that we meet God in an encounter with man, and so the division between the church and the world is reduced. We have seen elements of this in the notorious book *Honest to God* by John Robinson and others. Mission – this is their great word – becomes denunciation of, and a confronting of the present state of social injustice. In other words they teach that real Christianity means to liberate people from poverty, from political oppression and so on, and that the Christian church should be leading in this revolution.

What is particularly interesting is that this movement has mainly risen in the ranks of Roman Catholics. It is perhaps linked up with Pope John XXIII and his talk of liberation and various other ideas. This 'theology of liberation' has had considerable influence upon many of the leaders of the World Council of Churches. They have been discussing it recently at Nairobi. There are of course the two views again, but it is such an insistent emphasis that the leaders cannot ignore it; and there are many in this country and other countries who are interpreting the whole of the Bible in this way. But this teaching does violence to the whole notion of Christian salvation in a personal sense. According to it Christ came to set people free politically, socially, and then in other respects. They use the story of the liberation of the children of Israel from Egypt and their going to Canaan as the great illustration of this. This is what God wants and this is the great purpose of Christianity – to give people political and social liberty.

To sum up, we find that that which began in 1789 in France has spread world-wide and has been manifesting itself in these various ways. So by now we find ourselves in a world, and in a situation in society, in which men are asserting that they are the supreme authority. This expresses itself in this country in the attitude which says that, though Parliament may pass Acts, if we do not agree with them we need not observe them. The resulting lawlessness leads many people to ask the question: Is this country any longer governable? Can life and government continue when men cease to recognise any authority except what they think and what they believe? This is the state in which we find the world at the present time.

## II

The question that arises therefore is, What are we to do in this situation? We have made this great review of history in this conference – what conclusions do we draw from it all? I start by making certain general statements which must of necessity take a very dogmatic form because of the limitation of time. The Christian is not only to be concerned about personal salvation. It is his duty to have a complete view of life as taught in the Scriptures. That is common to all the views that have been considered, apart from those which are non-religious, to which I have been referring. As far as the Christian is concerned – and that is what we are interested in now – we are not to be concerned only about personal salvation; we must have a world view. All of us who have ever read Kuyper, and others, have been teaching this for many long years. I must add, immediately, that it is equally clear, surely, from the study we have been making, that we all tend to be creatures of our times and much of our thinking is conditioned by the age in which we live. It is surely clear that this was true of the Reformers. It was true also of the Puritans. We must therefore be very careful not to follow slavishly anything that has been taught in the past. We are as responsible to God as the Reformers were, or as any Puritans were, and it is our business to interpret Scripture, as much as it was their duty to do so. We are not merely to be gramophone records of anyone who has lived in the past however august he may have been. That seems to me to be another inevitable conclusion.

Perhaps the thing that stands out most prominently is that what has bedevilled this whole question, and caused the greatest confusion throughout the centuries, has been the idea of a state church. That has been the greatest curse in the history of the church and of the world! This of course is seen especially in Roman Catholicism, in Eastern Orthodoxy in its various branches, and in Anglicanism – chiefly Anglicanism in this country. I suggest that this association between church and state has been responsible for many of the greatest calamities, directly, and also because of the violent reactions they have produced. We have seen how it produced such a violent reaction in France. It is very difficult to disentangle the antagonism to the king from the antagonism to the church. That was because they were one; and so when people revolt against the king they revolt against the church. That is what happened in France, and in Russia. The Russians had not only suffered under the tyranny of the Tsars – those dissolute men – but also under the tyranny of a foul creature like Rasputin, a priest, and the whole power of Russian Orthodoxy. So when they got rid of the one they got rid of the other also, because the two belonged together. And this is surely an acute problem both in Spain and in Portugal at the present time, and is likely to be an acute problem in Italy also and in various other countries.

## III

Those are some of the very broad general conclusions at which we can arrive. Let me next suggest that there are certain dangers confronting us in this revolutionary situation, as they have confronted all who have been in it before us. There are three main dangers of which we have to be very wary. The first is that we must never allow ourselves as Christians to be thought of as mere defenders of the status quo. I put that first because historically it has been the greatest danger. Christianity has been equated with what has been termed the Establishment – king and church, king and bishop. This is the danger therefore of which we have to be very wary. Let me illustrate what I mean, because this has done grave harm to the Christian cause. Take the famous stanza written by Cecil Frances Alexander, the lady who wrote hymns such as 'There is a green hill far away.' It reads thus –

*The rich man in his castle,*
*The poor man at his gate;*
*God made them high or lowly*
*And ordered their estate.*

We have given the impression far too often, as Christians, that that is our standpoint. But were Luther and Calvin guilty of this? It was surely their danger because of their belief in law and order. Wesley and Whitefield were certainly guilty of this. They were both horrified at the possibility of rebellion in America, and we have to confess that the record of Whitefield as regards slavery was very poor indeed. How human and how fallible we are! Many also in America who from 1773 to 1776 and after spoke and fought so strongly for their own liberty as against England and the oppression that England was guilty of, did not seem to see that the same applied to the poor black slaves whom they continued to buy and sell and to employ for nearly a hundred years afterwards. This shows us the limits of human understanding. The same was true in Wales of some of the great religious leaders and preachers. We were celebrating in 1974 the bicentenary of the birth of John Elias. John Elias was a thoroughgoing Tory. He stood, as did most of the Welsh Calvinistic Methodists, for conservatism; and they opposed what was then called liberalism.

But this has been especially true of the Roman Catholic Church. Throughout history you have had this alliance between Roman Catholicism and the king. It is interesting to observe how the Roman church, in a typical manner, changes her point of view from time to time according to changing circumstances. When the kings were in authority, they supported the kings and condemned revolutions; but when a revolution took place and another government came into power they justified rebellion against that government. The principle of 'the just war' could be manipulated to suit the exigencies of any particular situation! That has been prominent in the long story of Roman Catholicism; and that is what makes this new movement of 'the theology of liberation' so interesting. The same has been true of Orthodoxy, and also of Anglicanism. Is it not true that Anglicanism in the last century not only gave the impression, as has been said, of being 'the Tory Party at prayer,' but was also guilty of supporting the whole notion of colonialism? What is still more tragic is that the missionary enterprise was so often linked with colonialism and colonial ideas.

Whether you agree with the recent pronouncement of the General Secretary of the World Council of Churches or not, his assertion is true that this whole outlook, based upon the church-state idea, has been more productive of the problems of racialism confronting the new nations in Africa today than perhaps anything else. So we must be very careful not to give the impression that we are always on the side of the Establishment and the existing authorities. The Plymouth Brethren are by no means innocent in this respect. By regarding any participation in politics in any form as being the height of sin they inevitably landed themselves on the side of the status quo. The first Member of Parliament from among the Brethren told me and many others that he was more or less ostracised in his Brethren meeting because he had committed the terrible sin of taking part in politics. This shows how defective and contradictory our thinking can be. While they denounced a man for going into politics they never denounced men for going into the army. They gloried in the fact that certain of their members were generals and had had very high promotion. Are Evangelicals in the United States clear in this respect in their attitude to the coloured people? I have met some who base their whole attitude toward the coloured people on the fact that the latter are the descendants of Ham.

These are serious matters in a revolutionary age. Without our desiring to do so we can be jockeyed into a position in which we are regarded as mere defenders and advocates of the status quo. It is not insignificant, surely, that certain well-known evangelists are supported by numbers of millionaires, and that some of them in a recent presidential election even went so far as to propose that a certain evangelist might be put up as presidential candidate! They did this because of their political and economic interests. So, the impression has gained currency that to be a Christian, and more especially an evangelical, means that we are traditionalists, and advocates of the status quo.

I believe that this largely accounts for our failure in this country to make contact with the so-called working classes. Christianity in this country has become a middle-class movement; and I suggest that that is so because of this very thing. Nonconformity is by no means clear on this question. In the last century, and in this present century, far too often, as nonconformist men have got on in the world, and made money, and become managers and owners, they have become opponents of the working classes who were agitating for their rights. So it is as true of the nonconformists in this country as it is of the Anglicans and Roman Catholics and others. For some strange reason one of the greatest temptations to a man who becomes a Christian is to become respectable. When he becomes a Christian he also tends to make money; and if he makes money, he wants to keep that money, and resents the suggestion that he should share that money with others by means of taxation, etc. Looking at history it seems to me that one of the greatest dangers confronting the Christian is to become a political conservative, and an opponent of legitimate reform, and the legitimate rights of people.

We must now turn to the second danger, which is the exact opposite. We always tend to go from one extreme to the other. In this conference, which has had to be selective, we have not considered the Levellers; but they were important people in the seventeenth century. The Levellers were not an accident. They played a prominent part in the debates held in Putney under the auspices of the army, and then in the later discussions that took place on these very matters in Whitehall as to how the country was to be governed, and what was to be done with the church. There were also the Fifth Monarchy Men, the Millenarians and many groups such as the Diggers in the seventeenth century. They did not belong to the mainline Puritans, but Cromwell – who was perhaps the most honest man in the seventeenth century, a man who strove to be true to his conscience above all others that I know of in political history – was ready to listen to them. He was torn between these various ideas, and his sympathies were on both sides. These men objected to the whole hierarchical view of life. They actually anticipated most of what is being demanded at the present time. They said that God was over all, even over kings and bishops. The individual soul and personal experience were of vital interest to them, and they claimed their right to express their opinions. The Methodist Awakening of the next century emphasised this also and stressed the importance of personal experience, and assurance of salvation – man and his standing before God. They taught a new notion of humanity and of the common people. They realised that they had brains; that is why they wanted to be taught to read and write. All this is inevitable, it is a natural outworking of true Christianity. So when you come to the nineteenth century you find that these Christian men were concerned about reform. In Sheffield the poet Ebenezer Elliott wrote in his moving manner –

*When wilt thou save the people,*
*O God of mercy, when?*
*The people, Lord, the people,*
*Not thrones and crowns, but men.*

This was the spirit. Throughout the centuries the talk had been about thrones and crowns and kings; but it is men that matter, so these men were concerned about reform. The result was that nonconformity in the nineteenth century became very interested in reform.

It is vital, however, that we should realise that it was mainly political reform that interested them. What they agitated for, and fought for, was political equality. Macaulay understood this. He was a very astute thinker. At the time of the Reform Bill, as I told you, he was very fearful that there might be a revolution. But the Reform Bill was passed, and he saw that the danger had gone, but he realised that it was but a temporary respite. He said that the agitators were satisfied for the time being because they had the vote. They were being given more political equality. But he saw, and said, that the real problem, the ultimate problem would arise when the masses asked for economic equality and complete economic freedom. I suggest that we have already reached that particular point.

So nonconformity, on the whole, in this country was content during the nineteenth century with political reform and political freedom. Today this concern is represented partly by the recent movement which emphasises 'The cultural mandate,' and teaches that it is our primary duty as Christians to see that the lordship of Christ is exercised in every realm and department of life – in drama, art, literature, politics, in Trade Unions, and in every other respect. Finally, there is this movement teaching the 'theology of liberation or revolution.' In practice in most countries, including ours, the latter is showing itself as a spirit of lawlessness. It is a defiance even of laws passed by the majority, and at times defiance of the guidance and instruction given by their own appointed leaders. The legitimate desire for reform has tended to give way to a spirit of revolution and lawlessness.

The third danger is to advocate complete other-worldliness. I have already dealt with that by emphasising that it is the duty of the Christian always to be concerned about these matters and to have a world view.

## IV

What, then, are we to do in the light of all this? What has this conference taught us? It was designed to help us to face the revolutionary position in which we find ourselves. The first and most obvious lesson must be that there is no blueprint in this matter. We have been hearing how great men, men of God, men who were concerned above all else about exposition of Scripture, exegesis and interpretation, differed and disagreed. We have heard of the different points of view, and disagreements; and we are left to face the position for ourselves, very much as they were. We have the advantage of knowing what they thought and said, whether we think it was right or wrong; but we certainly do not have any ready-made solution.

So, we must go back to the Scripture and attempt to summarise its teaching. The first is, that the New Testament never advocates revolution, but rather the reverse. Take the attitude to slavery for instance. Surely it is of importance at this point. Notice that the New Testament when dealing with this did not denounce slavery as such, or try to put an end to it. Its approach is illustrated in the Epistle to Philemon, for instance, where the apostle Paul makes a spiritual appeal and urges that the slave, though still remaining a slave, should now be regarded as a brother and a brother beloved. There is no broadside attack upon institutions such as slavery. Still more significant, surely, is the symbolical character of the Apocalypse, the book of Revelation, where the situation is dealt with quite deliberately in a symbolic manner in order that the Christians might receive comfort and help and enlightenment, but without aggravating the position, or adding to their sufferings, by a denunciation of the worldly and religious powers that were opposed to them and persecuting them. A fair reading of the New Testament leaves us with that impression, that Christianity is not a revolutionary movement in the sense that this new theology of revolution or liberation would have us believe. That is entirely contrary to the New Testament teaching. On the other hand, the Christian is represented as 'salt' in society and 'leaven,' and surely the whole point of those comparisons is that Christian influence is to be a quiet influence and a slow process of influencing society.

In the light of that principle it seems to me that we can justify the attitude of Luther and Calvin at the time of the Reformation as over and against that of the Anabaptists. Is it not true to say that, in the situation that obtained at that time, and remembering especially the views of the state, and the relation between the church and the state then held commonly, that Luther and Calvin probably saved the Protestant Reformation? That was surely the motive that governed their attitude to the Anabaptists and to the Peasants' Revolt.

The seventeenth century, I would suggest, was mainly a political revolution. While the ministers, the preachers, were involved for spiritual reasons, it was essentially, and mainly a political revolution. It can be argued that the ideas entered the minds of the politicians through the preachers and their teaching. I would accept that, but I would still maintain that the revolution itself was primarily political. I would venture to say that the American War of Independence was mainly political also. The great influx in the population of which we heard had a great deal to do with it, and in spite of the influences on the part of the preachers the whole outlook leading to the war was essentially a political one.

Nothing is clearer from the history than that there is tension always between liberty and order. This is the great problem. Am I right when I suggest that the danger of Calvinism is always to over-stress order? Order has to be stressed, the danger is to over-stress it. Arminianism over-stresses liberty. It produced the laissez-faire view of economics, and it always introduces inequalities – some people becoming enormously wealthy, and others languishing in poverty and in destitution. That outlook, which is essentially Arminian, always leads to a reaction – chaos first, then a violent reaction ending in a dictatorship on either the right or the left.

Another general remark at this point is that a lack of political and social concern on the part of Christians can very definitely alienate people from the gospel and the church. I hasten to add, on the other hand, that a demonstration of great interest in political and social matters never succeeds in attracting people to Christianity. The history of the past proves that conclusively. Christopher Hill says that there were two revolutions in the seventeenth century. The one he is most interested in, the political and social, he says failed. The Restoration of Charles II proves that. At the same time it is clear that the attempt to reform people by Acts of Parliament has always failed; and the state of the world today proves that that cannot succeed. It is pathetic, not to say ludicrous, to notice the way in which certain modern Evangelicals, who seem to have started reading some ten or twelve years ago, after having spent their time exclusively in evangelistic activities, are now rushing their ill-digested reading into print, and seem to think that they are innovators in saying that we should all be taking an interest in politics and social matters. They do not seem to have heard of the 'social gospel' craze of the earlier part of this century. All this has been tried with great thoroughness. I well remember certain men who were concerned about social and political matters, and who constantly preached on such themes, and packed their chapels for a while, but only as long as they preached politics. The moment they began to preach the gospel truly the crowds left them. Politically-minded people are always ready to make use of the church, but they always abandon and shun her when she ceases to be of any value to them.

We must always remember these two aspects. If we give the impression that we have no concern about political and social matters we shall alienate people; and I suggest that we have done so, and so the masses are outside the church. On the other hand, if we think we are going to fill our churches and solve our problems by preaching politics and taking an interest in social matters we are harbouring a very great delusion.

## V

What then is our position? We start from the position that the Christian citizen is a man who says that his citizenship is in heaven. 'Our citizenship is in heaven' (Phil. 3:20). Christ said, 'My kingdom is not of this world.' The Christian's primary concern must always be the kingdom of God, and then, because of that, the salvation of men's souls. The Christian is a 'pilgrim and a stranger.' He is a traveller and a sojourner in this world. Those are preliminary assumptions.

At this point I ask a question: Does eschatology come in at this point? I believe it does. The Christian, if he is at all instructed must have a view of history. The Bible has a view of history. There is a Christian view of history, and surely it is that everything is leading to an end. There is a development and a progress in history, and it is all leading up to 'that one far off divine event to which the whole creation moves' – our Lord's Second Coming. This is basic to the whole of the New Testament teaching. It ends with, 'Even so, come, Lord Jesus.' The main function of government and of culture and of all these agencies is mainly to restrain evil, to make life possible, and indeed to introduce an element of enjoyment into life. That all comes under common grace, but that ultimate great event dominates everything. And I believe that if we are to face our particular age truly we have to face that question. Remembering all the warnings against being concerned about the 'times and seasons,' and as one who has been emphasising that for nearly fifty years, I ask whether there are not indications that we may be in 'the end of time.' Are we reaching the ultimate stage? The sign of being in that 'time,' I would suggest, is the worship of man. The number of man, 666! Are we reaching that? Is not democracy bound of necessity to lead to that ultimately? The moment democracy loses any kind of biblical sanction it is bound to lead to the worship of men and the setting up of men as the ultimate power over against God, and indeed as god. We are in an age when man is being worshipped. 'Man come of age,' 'Man come into his own,' Man claiming even to be now in the position to exercise the 'powers of the Creator' as a Cambridge professor put it a year or two back. These are the characteristic phrases of today. And we are witnessing anti-God movements and a whole world attitude of anti-God. Not only so, the Turkish Empire has been destroyed, and the Jews are in Palestine. How difficult it is for us to understand how the Puritans could think that England was the elect nation. England is not the elect nation. God's ancient people are the elect nation. That nation because of its disobedience was put on one side, and Christ said that God was going to give the kingdom to 'a nation that bringeth forth the fruits thereof' – the church. But he has not abandoned his ancient people. So, it seems to me, there are certain signs which should at least make us think. I find them to be of great comfort as we face the confusion and the chaos of the present time. Are we not also perhaps beginning to witness a crumbling and a final destruction of the Roman Catholic Church? I do not know. But it is our business as Christians to keep our eyes open. We are exhorted to do so. We are exhorted to expect certain signs by our Lord in his last great addresses.

## VI

So I come to my final conclusion. I suggest we are back in New Testament times again. A whole era began to come to an end with the French Revolution in 1789. We are now back to the New Testament position; we are like the New Testament Christians. The world can never be reformed. Never! That is absolutely certain. A Christian state is impossible. All the experiments have failed. They had to fail. They must fail. The Apocalypse alone can cure the world's ills. Man even at his best, even as a Christian, can never do so. You can never make people Christians by Acts of Parliament. You can never christianise society. It is folly to attempt to do so. I would even suggest that it is heresy to do so. Men must be 'born again.' How can they live the Christian life if they have not become Christians? Good fruit can only come from a good tree, a good root; and the idea that you can impose a Christian life or culture upon non-Christian people is a contradiction of Christian teaching. Nevertheless, government and law and order are essential because man is in sin; and the Christian should be the best citizen in the country. But as all are sinful, reform is legitimate and desirable. The Christian must act as a citizen, and play his part in politics and other matters in order to get the best possible conditions. But we must always remember that politics is 'the art of the possible'; and so the Christian must remember as he begins that he can only get the possible. Because he is a Christian he must work for the best possible and be content with that which is less than fully Christian. That is what Abraham Kuyper seems to me to have done. I have recently read the life of Kuyper again and it is clear that his enactments as Prime Minister and head of the government were almost identical with the radicalism of Lloyd George. They were two very different men in many ways but their practical enactments were almost identical. The chief respect in which they differed was in their view of education.

I now come to what, to me, in many ways is the most important matter of all. I suggest that this is the main conclusion at which the conference should arrive. The Christian must never get excited about reform, or about political action. That raises for me a problem with respect to the men of the seventeenth century and other times. It is that they should have become so excited about these matters. I would argue that the Christian must of necessity have a profoundly pessimistic view of life in this world. Man is 'in sin' and therefore you will never have a perfect society. The coming of Christ alone is going to produce that. The Christian not only does not get excited, he never pins his hopes to Acts of Parliament, or any reform or any improvement. He believes in improvement, but he never pins his hopes to it, he never gets excited or over-enthusiastic; still less does he become fanatical or bigoted about these matters.

Another principle of great importance at a time such as this is that there is no point in changing one form of tyranny for another. There is also no point in fighting against impossible odds. So in many countries today the Christian can do nothing but indulge in passive resistance, and he must continue in that until a point arrives that his government tries to interfere with his relationship to God, or his worship of God. His resistance must then become an active resistance. But should he live in a country where a large number of people are agreed about reform and improvement, and that seems possible, I would say that it is his duty to join them and to belong to them. But he must never be foolish or foolhardy. He must be passive in his resistance until he feels that it is possible to produce the desirable form.

So the Christian is left with this profound pessimism with regard to the present, but with a glorious optimism with regard to the ultimate and the eternal future.

How does he live in the meantime? He must heed the great exhortations of the Scripture, and at a time such as this our Lord's exhortation is – 'Take heed to yourselves, lest at any time your hearts be overcharged with surfeiting, and drunkenness, and cares of this life, and so that day come upon you unawares. For as a snare shall it come on all them that dwell on the face of the whole earth. Watch ye therefore, and pray always, that ye may be accounted worthy to escape all these things that shall come to pass, and to stand before the Son of man' (Luke 21:34-36). That is our supreme duty, and I suggest that the primary function of preachers at the present time is to constantly urge that exhortation upon their people. We are not to get excited about the 'christianising' of art or politics or anything else, imagining that you can do so. Exhort people to be ready and prepared; warn them. This surely is the primary business of the preacher at a time like this.

As for the people, they are to act according to their consciences at all times. Ultimately we cannot dictate to another man as to what he is to do. Niemoller in Germany defied Hitler and was sent to prison. Another Christian, Erich Sauer, did not do so, and was able to continue with his ministry. We get this difference constantly. A man like Hromodka, a Czechoslovakian, was able to justify himself as a Christian preacher and professor in a communist country, whereas other people spend most of their time in denouncing communism. I suggest that our overriding concern should always be our relationship to God, and our looking for, and longing for the coming of Christ. That is the only answer. Man has reached the ultimate. He can no longer be persuaded. He has gone beyond that and worships himself. I can see nothing beyond the present position. Democracy is the ultimate and highest human idea of government but because of man's fallen sinful nature it must lead to lawlessness and chaos.

Little can be done to arrest this or prevent it; so we look to this 'glorious appearing of our great God and Saviour,' and in the meantime we do our utmost to open the eyes of our fellow men and women to what is coming to them. They are entitled to liberty and freedom; but, still more important, they have to meet God and stand before him in judgment.

So I end by saying that we must live as the early Christians did. In the final analysis, to the Christian what do all these things matter? What is your life, the life about which we get so excited and are ready to fight, and to agitate, and to quarrel and to divide? 'What is your life? It is but a vapour.' 'In this tabernacle we do groan being burdened,' and we shall continue to do so until the King comes, and 'the kingdoms of this world become the kingdoms of our Lord and of his Christ.'

# 1976

## *Jonathan Edwards and the Crucial Importance of Revival*

In dealing with Jonathan Edwards and the crucial importance of revival, we are really but continuing and concluding what has been the general theme of this conference from the beginning – the Puritan experiment in New England.[1] Why have we considered this theme? We have done so primarily because we wanted to pay tribute to our friends in America who are celebrating the bi-centenary of their liberation from the yoke of England, and the celebration of their independence. But we had a subsidiary reason or motive, and that was that we might learn from what happened in that new land in the seventeenth century. In other words what we have been considering in this conference has pinpointed once more, or underlined, what constitutes the essence of Puritanism.

There is much debate at the present time as to what Puritanism really is; and I believe that that experiment in New England has reminded us, and shown us clearly what Puritanism is in its essence. It is concerned with the nature of the Christian church. Some would have us believe that Puritanism is essentially an interest in pastoral theology; but that was incidental. The essence of Puritanism was the desire to carry the reform, which had already happened in the matter of doctrine, further into the nature and the life and polity of the Christian church. The theme of this conference demonstrates that in this way. Here were a number of men who for a number of reasons – the main one being persecution – crossed the Atlantic and went to live in this new country. They had all been Anglicans, but the moment they had the freedom to

[1] 'The Puritan Experiment in the New World' was the general title for 1976.

do what they really believed they ceased to be Anglicans. They dropped episcopacy and they introduced the Congregational idea of the church. That is the lesson which stands out very clearly. The same happened later in this country to most of the Puritans; but these men, with the opportunity and the liberty to do what they wanted to do, and what they believed, did immediately what was only done some 30 years later in this country at the time of the war, the rebellion, against Charles I, and then during the Commonwealth, and eventually in the Great Ejection of 1662. I argue therefore that what happened in New England is one of the most vital bits of evidence with regard to the true character and nature of Puritanism.

However, I am to deal with Jonathan Edwards in particular. I take for granted the main facts concerning him. He was born in 1703 and died in 1758. Curiously enough he died as a result of being vaccinated against smallpox. He was a man who had a very curious and active mind. He was interested in scientific matters as well as theology, and that was the immediate cause of his death. He received the education that was available in New England at that time, and went to Yale University. In 1727 he was ordained as assistant pastor to his grandfather, Solomon Stoddard, in the town of Northampton, Massachusetts. Within a year or so the old man died and Jonathan Edwards became the sole pastor. There he remained until 1750 when he was literally turned out of his church. That was one of the most amazing things that ever happened, and it should come as a word of encouragement to ministers and preachers. Here was this towering genius, this mighty preacher, this man at the centre of a great revival – yet he was literally voted out of his church by 230 votes against 23 in 1750. Do not be surprised then, brethren, as to what may happen to you in your churches!

Having been driven from his church in Northampton in that way, he went to a place that was on the frontier in those days, amongst Indians, called Stockbridge. I believe that in the providence of God he was sent there; because he wrote some of his greatest masterpieces while he was there. In the same way as the imprisonment of John Bunyan for twelve years in Bedford gave us his classics, so, I believe, this isolation of Jonathan Edwards was the means of giving us some of his classics. From there he was called to be the president of the then College of New Jersey, now known as the Princeton University, and after having been there a very short time he died in the way I have described.

However, the thing that stands out in the life of this man was the remarkable revival that broke out under his ministry in Northampton, beginning at the end of 1734, and in 1735, and then later his participation with others in the so-called Great Awakening in connection with the visit of George Whitefield and others in 1740. Those are the salient facts in the life of this great man.

There are certain points of difference between him and those of whom we have heard hitherto in the conference. He was an eighteenth-century man, not a seventeenth-century man. He was born in America. Most of those of whom we have been hearing were born in this country and then went over to America. I believe also that we are entitled to say that with Jonathan Edwards a new element or a new factor can be seen in Puritanism. Most of the great Puritans had a strain or a strand of what one is compelled to describe as scholasticism in them. That led to the involved character of their style, and the divisions and sub-divisions which characterise their works. Edwards is comparatively free from that, and the result is that his method is more direct, more living. Furthermore, I am going to suggest that the element of the Holy Spirit is more prominent in Edwards than in any other of the Puritans.

Yet he belongs to the tradition which we have been considering. He believed in the Covenant theology, but he rejected the Halfway Covenant idea completely. In a sense that was indirectly the cause of his being turned out of his church in 1750. He would not baptize the children of certain people, and he insisted upon a certain standard of behaviour and conduct in those who were to be admitted to the Communion table. In addition Jonathan Edwards would have nothing to do with the teaching of preparationism. He belongs here to John Cotton rather than to Thomas Hooker. He puts his view in this way, 'Everything in the Christian scheme argues, that man's title to, and fitness for heaven, depends on some great divine influence, at once causing a vast change, and not any such gradual change as is supposed to be brought to pass by men themselves in the exercise of their own power. The exceeding diversity of the states of men in another world argues it' (*Works* vol. 2, 557). As I am going to show he believed in a direct and immediate influence of the Spirit, and in sudden and dramatic conversion. But, like the other men, he was fond of reading the works of William Ames and was indebted to them, and adopted much of Ames' teaching, as did the others, in his preaching. He, of course, as they were, was a Calvinist and a Congregationalist, and he put great emphasis, as they all did, on the moral and the ethical elements in the Christian faith and Christian living. However, I venture to make the assertion that in Edwards we come to the very zenith or acme of Puritanism, for in him we have what we find in all the others, but in addition, this spirit, this life, this additional vitality. Not that the others were entirely lacking in that, but it is such an outstanding characteristic in him that I would assert that Puritanism reached its fullest bloom in the life and ministry of Jonathan Edwards.

He came upon the scene after a period of considerable lifelessness in the churches. It is very important that we should realise this. It is most comforting for us because we live in a very similar period. Here is a description of the period immediately preceding this great revival, as given by the Rev W. Cooper, one of the ministers at that time, in his preface to Edwards' *Distinguishing Marks of a Work of the Spirit of God:* 'But what a dead and barren time has it now been, for a great while, with all the churches of the Reformation. The golden showers have been restrained; the influences of the Spirit suspended; and the consequence has been, that the gospel has not had any eminent success. Conversions have been rare and dubious; few sons and daughters have been born to God and the hearts of Christians not so quickened, warmed, and refreshed under the ordinances, as they have been. That this has been the sad state of religion among us in this land, for many years (except one or two distinguished places which have at times been visited with a shower of mercy while other towns and churches have not been rained upon) will be acknowledged by all who have spiritual senses exercised, as it has been lamented by faithful ministers and serious Christians' (vol. 2, 257).

As Mr Cooper says, there had been some touches here and there, and particularly in the church of which Jonathan Edwards became minister, under the ministry of his grandfather, old Mr Stoddard. But they had not spread, and they had been periodic, and had more or less finished altogether. So there had been this lifeless condition of the church; but now something new happened. After the drought, came showers; life began to make itself manifest once more. Something happened which continued to affect the life of America most profoundly for at least a hundred years, and indeed even until today. It is quite astonishing to notice the new interest in Jonathan Edwards during the last forty years or so. I can illustrate this from my own experience. Just before I entered the ministry in 1927 I sought help as regards reading from a friend of mine who not long before had taken first class Honours in Divinity in the University of Oxford. He recommended a large number of books which he had been reading himself for his degree. Among the books was one called *Protestant Thought before Kant* by a man called McGiffert. The only thing that impressed me in that book was a chapter on a man called Jonathan Edwards, though he was dealt with mainly as a philosopher. But my interest was aroused immediately. The next time I met my friend I asked, 'Could you tell me where I can find out something further about this man Jonathan Edwards?' 'Who is he?' he said! He knew nothing about him, and although I made many enquiries I could not find anybody who could tell me anything about Edwards or about his works. It was not until some two years later, quite by accident, that I found the two volumes of the complete works of Jonathan Edwards which I then purchased for five shillings. I was like the man in our Lord's parable who found a pearl of great price. Their influence upon me I cannot put into words.

However, since then, and beginning in the early 1930s there has been a revival of interest in Edwards in a most astonishing manner. Professor Perry Miller is largely responsible for this, but he is not the only one. Every year several books seem to appear on Jonathan Edwards. There are two men who spend their vacations in the library of Yale University going through manuscript sermons by Jonathan Edwards. In other words, they are reprinting the complete works of Edwards – a definitive edition. I had the privilege of meeting these two men in 1967 and of handling some of the manuscripts of the sermons of this great man. The two volumes recently republished by the Banner of Truth Trust have often been regarded as the Complete Works, but they are not. A man published a book in the 1860s consisting of numerous other things which are not in these two volumes, and there are still more – sermons, letters, occasional remarks, miscellanies, and so on. They are all going to be reprinted in the definitive edition.

The explanation of this astounding fact is, of course, that Jonathan Edwards, amongst other things, is America's greatest philosopher. Everyone seems to grant that, and so they are interested in him. I would issue a word of warning at this point. You must be careful and discriminating as you read some of these newer books on Jonathan Edwards. Several of them are written by professors of English literature, others by philosophers; and they are interested in him chiefly as a great thinker, as a great writer, as a man who had a dominating influence even upon the literature of the United States, and who in a sense, was a precursor of the Romantic Movement in English literature. But as many of these men are not Christians they tend unconsciously, and unwittingly, to misinterpret him and to misrepresent him. So they must be read with discrimination. But I am calling attention to the fact that this amazing man who died more than two hundred years ago is still exerting this powerful influence upon the thought life of America as he continued to do through last century as well. Of course, he divided opinion. He has been denounced without measure. For instance, Oliver Wendell Holmes writes about Jonathan Edwards, thus: 'Edwards had a theology rooted in the deepest depths of hell,' and he wrote in 'a language which shocks the sensibilities of a later generation.' He goes on to say, 'Had Edwards lived longer I have no doubt his creed would have softened into a kindly, humanised belief.' In other words Edwards would have written the kind of literature written by 'The Autocrat at the Breakfast Table.' Thank God, we have Edwards as he is, not as Oliver Wendell Holmes, the humanist, who never understood Edwards at all, would like him to be.

Clarence Darrow, the man who defended that schoolmaster, Scopes, who was prosecuted for teaching evolution in the early 1920s and who stood against William Jennings Bryan in the famous 'monkey trial' wrote, 'It is not surprising that Edwards' main business in the world was to scare silly women and little children, and blaspheming the God he professed to adore … Nothing but a disturbed or a diseased mind could have produced his "Sinners in the Hands of an Angry God."' I quoted that because of that reference to the sermon preached by Edwards under that title, 'Sinners in the Hands of an Angry God.' You can hear references to that sermon not infrequently on the television and elsewhere. The fact is that all most people seem to know of Edwards is that he once preached a sermon bearing that title. That is all they know about him, and they probably have not even read that sermon. They just go on repeating what others have said about it, and it is regarded, as you see from the words of Oliver Wendell Holmes, as just an assault, a ranting assault upon the sensibilities, and as violence done to reason, and so on. This is, of course, quite ridiculous.

Anyone who knows anything about Jonathan Edwards knows that he was as far removed from being a ranter as it is possible for a man to be. But he did say some very strong and very alarming things which are liable to be misunderstood. Edwards himself has answered this particular criticism. He says: 'Another thing that some ministers have been greatly blamed for, and I think unjustly, is speaking terror to them who are already under great terrors, instead of comforting them. Indeed if ministers in such a case go about to terrify persons with that which is not true, or to affright them by representing their case worse than it is, or in any respect otherwise than it is, they are to be condemned; but if they terrify them only by still holding forth more light to them, and giving them to understand more of the truth of their case, they are altogether to be justified. When consciences are greatly awakened by the Spirit of God, it is but light imparted, enabling men to see their case, in some measure, as it is; and, if more light be let in, it will terrify them still more. But ministers are not therefore to be blamed that they endeavour to hold forth more light to the conscience, and do not rather alleviate the pain they are under, by intercepting and obstructing the light that shines already. To say any thing to those who have never believed in the Lord Jesus Christ, to represent their case any otherwise than exceeding terrible, is not to preach the word of God to them; for the word of God reveals nothing but truth; but this is to delude them' (vol. 1, 392). In other words, Edwards believed the Bible which says terrifying things about any man who dies in his sins. That is all Edwards did. It was pure reasoning from the words of Scripture. It was not what Edwards said, it was what the Scriptures said; and he felt it to be his duty to warn people. But he qualifies that, saying, 'I know of but one case, wherein the truth ought to be withheld from sinners in distress of conscience, and that is the case of melancholy; and it is not to be withheld from them, as if the truth tends to do them hurt; but because, if we speak the truth to them, sometimes they will be deceived, and led into error by it, through that strange disposition there is in them to take things wrong' (vol. 1, 392). In other words, no man was further removed from the violence of a ranting travelling evangelist than Jonathan Edwards. That is the defence which one should make when one hears people referring to him as that terrible man who preached the sermon on 'Sinners in the Hands of an Angry God.'

Now let us look at this man who has had such a lasting influence, and who seems to be becoming again almost a dominating influence in religious thought in America. I confess freely that this is one of the most difficult tasks I have ever attempted. The theme is almost impossible, and very largely for the reason that I have already given, namely the influence of Edwards upon me. I am afraid, and I say it with much regret, that I have to put him ahead even of Daniel Rowland and George Whitefield. Indeed I am tempted, perhaps foolishly, to compare the Puritans to the Alps, Luther and Calvin to the Himalayas, and Jonathan Edwards to Mount Everest! He has always seemed to me to be the man most like the apostle Paul. Of course, Whitefield was a great and mighty preacher, as was Daniel Rowland, but so was Edwards. Neither of them had the mind, neither of them had the intellect, neither of them had the grasp of theology that Edwards had; neither of them was the philosopher he was. He stands out, it seems to me, quite on his own amongst men. So the task confronting me, if I may follow my analogy of Mount Everest, is to decide whether to approach him by the south Col or by the north Col. There are so many approaches to this great summit; but not only so, the atmosphere is so spiritually rarified, and there is this blazing whiteness of the holiness of the man himself, and his great emphasis upon the holiness and the glory of God; and above all the weakness of the little climber as he faces this great peak pointing up to heaven. All I can hope to do is to give some glimpses of this man and his life, and what he did, with the ultimate end and object of persuading every one to buy these two volumes of his works, and to read them!

Let us start with the man himself. The first thing that must be said is that he was a phenomenon. Here is a man brought up in that, as yet, undeveloped country. Of course, there were able men there, and colleges had come into being – Harvard and Yale were in existence. But they do not explain him. He was born in a comparatively isolated area, and yet he stands out as a sheer genius, ridiculing any notions of evolution, or the theory of acquired characteristics and so on. Unlike most of the other men we have been hearing about in this conference, he had been neither to Oxford nor Cambridge. He was an original, suddenly shot forth, a mighty intellect, accompanied by a brilliant imagination, amazing originality, but above all by honesty. He is one of the most honest expositors I have ever read. He never evades a problem; he faces them all. He does not skirt round a difficulty; he had this curious interest in truth in all its aspects, and then with all those scintillating gifts there is his humility and modesty, and added to that his exceptional spirituality. He knew more about experimental religion than most men; and he placed great emphasis upon the heart. In other words, what strikes one about Edwards as one looks at the man as a whole is the completeness, the balance. He was a mighty theologian and a great evangelist at the same time. How foolish we have become! This man was both, as was the apostle Paul. He was also a great pastor; he dealt with the souls and their problems. He was equally expert with adults as with children; and he was a great defender of conversion in children, and paid great attention to children, even allowing them to have meetings on their own. He seems to be everything and to be perfectly balanced. He opposed hyper-Calvinism and was equally opposed to Arminianism. This element of balance in his teaching, and in his position, is shown in the following statement: 'In efficacious grace we are not merely passive, nor yet does God do some, and we do the rest. But God does all, and we do all. God produces all, and we act all. For that is what he produces, viz. our own acts. God is the only proper author and fountain; we only are the proper actors. We are in different respects, wholly passive and wholly active' (vol. 2, 557, para. 64).

Now that was Edwards' position, and we note this element of balance which I am emphasising. There is no contradiction there: the ultimate antinomy is presented perfectly.

What then was the secret of this man? I have no hesitation in saying this: the spiritual always controlled the intellectual in him. I believe he must have had a great struggle with his towering intellect, and his original thinking. Moreover he was a voracious reader, and it would have been the simplest thing in the world for such a man to have become a pure intellectual such as Oliver Wendell Holmes, Perry Miller, and many others wished he had become. But as they put it, theology kept breaking in. But that constitutes the special glory of this man – and this is what explains him – that he always kept his philosophy and his speculations subservient to the Bible and regarded them as mere servants. Whatever he might be tempted to think, the Bible was supreme: everything was subordinate to the word of God. All his rich and brilliant gifts were not only held to be subservient, but were used as servants. In other words he was God-dominated.

Someone has said of him that 'he combined passionate devotion and a profoundly integrated mind.'

Let us now look at him for a moment as a preacher, for he was pre-eminently a preacher. This is what he wanted to be, and this is what he continued to be until that very short time at Princeton. Had he had his way I believe he would have continued always as a preacher, an evangelist, and a teacher. Let us start by looking at his view of religion. What is true religion? Here is a question we need to ask ourselves; and in the case of Edwards the answer is perfectly clear. It is what is called today an existential meeting with God. It is a living meeting with God. God and myself, these 'two only realities.' Religion is something, to Edwards, that belongs essentially to the heart. It is essentially experimental, essentially practical. This is made clear in the famous account he gives of an experience he once had. Do not forget that we are dealing with one of the greatest geniuses the world has ever known and the greatest American philosopher of all times. This is what he tells us:

'Once, as I rode out into the woods for my health, in 1737, having alighted from my horse in a retired place, as my manner commonly has been, to walk for divine contemplation and prayer, I had a view, that for me was extraordinary, of the glory of the Son of God, as Mediator between God and man, and his wonderful, great, full, pure, and sweet grace and love, and meek and gentle condescension. This grace that appeared so calm and sweet, appeared also great above the heavens. The person of Christ appeared ineffably excellent, with an excellency great enough to swallow up all thought and conception – which continued, as near as I can judge, about an hour; which kept me the greater part of the time in a flood of tears, and weeping aloud. I felt an ardency of soul to be, what I know not otherwise how to express, emptied and annihilated; to lie in the dust, and to be full of Christ alone; to love him with a holy and pure love; to trust in him; to live upon him; to serve and follow him; and to be perfectly sanctified and made pure, with a divine and heavenly purity. I have several other times had views very much of the same nature, and which have had the same effects.

'I have, many times, had a sense of the glory of the Third Person in the Trinity, and his office as Sanctifier; in his holy operations, communicating divine light and life to the soul. God in the communications of his Holy Spirit, has appeared as an infinite fountain of divine glory and sweetness; being full, and sufficient to fill and satisfy the soul; pouring forth itself in secret communications; like the sun in its glory, sweetly and pleasantly diffusing light and life. And I have sometimes an affecting sense of the excellency of the word of God as a word of life; as the light of life; a sweet, excellent, life-giving word; accompanied with a thirsting after that word, that it might dwell richly in my heart' (vol. 1, 47).

Now that represents his essential view of religion.

Another quotation also helps to bring out the same emphasis:

'All will allow that true virtue or holiness has its seat chiefly in the heart, rather than in the head. It therefore follows, from what has been said already, that it consists chiefly in holy affections. The things of religion take place in men's hearts, no further than they are affected with them. The informing of the understanding is all vain, any farther than it affects the heart, or, which is the same thing, has influence on the affections. Those gentlemen, who make light of these raised affections in religion, will doubtless allow that true religion and holiness, as it has its seat in the heart, is capable of very high degrees, and high exercises in the soul' (vol. 1, 367).

There we have his essential view of religion; it is mainly a matter of the heart, and unless it affects the heart it is of no value, whatever it may do in the head. One further quotation helps to emphasise this matter. It is out of one of Edwards' greatest sermons which bears the title: 'A Divine and Supernatural Light, immediately imparted to the soul by the Spirit of God, shown to be both a Scriptural and Rational Doctrine.' I tend to agree here with Professor Perry Miller. He says that in this one sermon – and it is a comparatively short one – you have a synopsis of the whole of Edwards' teaching. He defines positively what this spiritual and divine light is:

'A true sense of the divine and superlative glory in these things; an excellency that is of vastly higher kind, and more sublime nature, than in other things; a glory greatly distinguishing them from all that is earthly and temporal. He that is spiritually enlightened truly apprehends and sees it, or has a sense of it. He does not merely rationally believe that God is glorious, but he has a sense of the gloriousness of God in his heart. There is not only a rational belief that God is holy, and that holiness is a good thing, but there is a sense of the loveliness of God's holiness. There is not only a speculatively judging that God is gracious, but a sense how amiable God is on account of the beauty of this divine attribute' (vol. 2, 14).

There, then, we have some idea of Edwards' view of religion. That is what religion is, and this is the test by which we should examine ourselves.

Let us now turn to Edwards' method of preaching. We note at once that he preached sermons, and that he did not deliver lectures. Edwards did not lecture about Christian truths. I am told frequently these days that many preachers seem to be lecturers rather than preachers. Preaching is not lecturing. Neither did Edwards just give a running commentary on a passage. That is not preaching either; though many today seem to think that it is. That was not Edwards' idea of preaching; and it has never been the classical idea of preaching.

He started with a text. He was always scriptural. He did not merely take a theme and speak on it, except when he was expounding some doctrine, but even then he chose a text. He was always expository. He was also invariably analytical. He had an analytical mind. He divides up his text, his statement; he wants to get at the essence of the message; so the critical, analytical element in his wonderful mind comes into play. He does this in order that he may arrive at the doctrine taught in the verse or section; and then he reasons about this doctrine, shows how it is to be found elsewhere in Scripture, and its relationship to other doctrines, and then establishes its truth. But he never stops at that. There is always the application. He was preaching to people and not giving a dissertation, not giving expression in public to his private thoughts in the study. He was always concerned to bring home the truth to the listeners, to show the relevance of it. But, above all, and I quote him, he believed that preaching should always be 'warm and earnest.' I remind you again that we are dealing here with a giant intellect and brilliant philosopher; and yet this is the man who places all this emphasis upon warmth and upon feeling. This is how he states this principle:

'The frequent preaching that has lately obtained, has in a particular manner been objected against as being unprofitable and prejudicial. It is objected that, when sermons are heard so very often, one sermon tends to thrust out another; so that persons lose the benefit of all. They say, two or three sermons in a week is as much as they can remember and digest. Such objections against frequent preaching, if they be not from an enmity against religion, are for want of duly considering the way that sermons usually profit an auditory. The main benefit obtained by preaching is by impression made upon the mind at the time, and not by an effect that arises afterwards by a remembrance of what was delivered. And though an after-remembrance of what was heard in a sermon is oftentimes very profitable; yet, for the most part, that remembrance is from an impression the words made on the heart at the time; and the memory profits, as it renews and increases that impression' (vol. 1, 394).

I would add that I have often discouraged the taking of notes while I am preaching. It is becoming a custom among evangelical people; but it is not, as many seem to think, the hallmark of spirituality!

The first and primary object of preaching is not only to give information. It is, as Edwards says, to produce an impression. It is the impression at the time that matters, even more than what you can remember subsequently. In this respect Edwards is, in a sense, critical of what was a prominent Puritan custom and practice. The Puritan father would catechise and question the children as to what the preacher had said. Edwards, in my opinion, has the true notion of preaching. It is not primarily to impart information; and while you are writing your notes you may be missing something of the impact of the Spirit. As preachers we must not forget this. We are not merely imparters of information. We should tell our people to read certain books themselves and get the information there. The business of preaching is to make such knowledge live. The same applies to lecturers in colleges. The tragedy is that many lecturers simply dictate notes and the wretched students take them down. That is not the business of a lecturer or a professor. The students can read the books for themselves; the business of the professor is to put that on fire, to enthuse, to stimulate, to enliven. And that is the primary business of preaching. Let us take this to heart. Edwards laid great emphasis upon this; and what we need above everything else today is moving, passionate, powerful preaching. It must be 'warm' and it must be 'earnest.' Edwards sometimes wrote out his manuscript sermon in full, and then read it to the congregation; but not always. He sometimes preached from notes.

Now look at Edwards the theologian! I can but glance at this; but it is all to be found in the two volumes of his Works. In those two volumes, if you have no more, you have a compendium of theology. Remember that he was teaching this to people like ourselves; indeed to people who had not had the education that most have had today. He deals with all the major themes, Original Sin, the Freedom of the Will, Justification by Faith, a History of the Work of Redemption. He lays down the principles of evangelism in sermons; he has Five Discourses on the Soul's Eternal Redemption. He paid much attention to eschatology, the doctrine of the last things, and the ultimate glory that awaits us as children of God. He was, as I say, a mighty theologian; and if you really want to know something about these various themes turn to Edwards. You will find the doctrine in a form which you can easily follow, and you will be greatly benefited as a result of so doing.

But we must leave that and come to what, after all, is the most remarkable thing of all about Jonathan Edwards. He was pre-eminently the theologian of revival, the theologian of experience, or as some have put it 'the theologian of the heart.' The most astonishing thing about this phenomenon, this mighty intellect, was that no man knew more about the workings of the human heart, regenerate and unregenerate, than Jonathan Edwards. If you want to know anything about the psychology of religion, conversion, revivals, read Jonathan Edwards. When you have read him you will find that William James' *Varieties of Religious Experience* is like turning from a solid book to a paper-back. The same applies to Starbuck, and, of course, still more so to the idle vapourings of William Sargant who refers to the famous sermon on 'Sinners in the Hands of an Angry God.' You will find the complete answer to all that if you read the works of Edwards. These men are mere tyros, merely paddling at the edge of the ocean, whereas Edwards takes you out into the depths where you begin to see man face to face with his Maker.

In this field Edwards stands out supremely and without a peer. An American of the name of Hofstadter published a book in the 1960s entitled *Anti-Intellectualism in American Life*. Some English Evangelicals seem to have discovered this recently, and reversing their previous practice, are now telling us to put great emphasis upon the intellect. The answer to that, once more, is to read Jonathan Edwards. It is not anti-intellectualism. You cannot use the term anti-intellectual when you are talking about Jonathan Edwards! It is quite the reverse; in him you have an intellect fired by, and filled with, the Holy Spirit. That is what should be true of all of us. My contention is that what Edwards wrote in this connection is a unique literature; and that there is nothing anywhere that I know of, or have heard referred to, which is in any way comparable to what he has written. He did this in various ways. He gives personal accounts of people's experiences; and I have already quoted something of his own experience. There is more in his Personal Narrative, in his diaries. He gives us an extended account of some of the amazing experiences that came to his wife. Jonathan Edwards' wife was as great a saint as Jonathan Edwards himself, and she had some almost incredible experiences. He gives an account of them and examines them. One of the treatises in the two volumes is called 'A Narrative of Surprising Conversions.' It is the most exciting, thrilling reading you can ever find. Have you read them? Well, read them! You will not be able to stop once you start.

Another most important group of his writings consists of his accounts of revivals. He was asked to do this. One of his treatises was on the Revival of Religion in New England. It was sent to friends in Boston and then to this country, and it was read with great avidity by men in England and Scotland. There are references to revivals, and what happened in them, in many of his letters, and also frequently in his sermons. But what is unique and superlative is the way in which he analyses experiences – both individual experiences and revival in general. It is here that he is pre-eminently the expert. If you want to know anything about true revival, Edwards is the man to consult. His knowledge of the human heart, and the psychology of human nature, is quite incomparable.

Edwards wrote these things because in a sense he was compelled to do so, because of criticisms and misunderstandings. He was always fighting on two fronts right through his life. A movement of the Spirit took place in his own church, and spread to other churches in quite an extensive area, and then came the Great Awakening in 1740 associated with his name and also Whitefield and others. All this divided the people and the churches into two groups. There were some who were totally opposed to the revival. They were orthodox men who held the same theology as Edwards. They were Calvinists, but they disliked revival. They disliked the emotional element, they disliked the novelty. They had many objections to what was happening; and Edwards had to defend the revival against these critics. But then there were men at the other extreme, the wild men; and with them the wild fire came in that always tends to come in during a revival. These were the enthusiasts, the men who went to extremes, the men who were guilty of folly. Edwards had to deal with them also; so here he was, fighting on the two fronts. But, of course, his one interest was the glory of God and the benefit of the church. He had no desire to be a controversialist, but he had to write for and defend the truth.

The main works containing these analyses of experiences and these justifications of experiences and revivals are found in works like *A Treatise concerning the Religious Affections*. That is one of his most famous books. It really consisted of a series of sermons on one verse – 1 Peter 1:8: 'Whom having not seen ye love, in whom though now ye see him not, yet believing, ye rejoice with joy unspeakable and full of glory.' What he does in these books is to show the difference between the true and the false in the realm of experience. That is the theme of all these different treatises and it is worked out on the two sides in order to deal with the opponents and the enthusiasts at the same time. Here is the way in which he divides up the subject in the *Treatise concerning the Religious Affections*. He divides it into three parts. Here are his headings: Part 1, 'Concerning the nature of the affections and their importance in religion.' He has to establish that they are legitimate. The opponents of revival preached their great doctrinal sermons but they were cold, and any emotion or any fervour was automatically taboo. Edwards therefore has to justify them and to show that there is a place for them. Then he goes on to show that 'True religion lies much in affections,' then 'Inferences from this.' Then Part 2, 'Showing that there are no certain signs that religious affections are truly gracious or that they are not.' That is typical Edwards – the negative and the positive. He goes on to show that the fact that affections 'are raised very high is no sign' that they are true; the fact that there are 'great effects on the body is no sign,' 'fluency and fervour are no sign,' 'that they are not excited by us is no sign,' 'that they come with texts of Scripture is no proof that they are real,' 'that there is an appearance of love is no sign,' 'religious affections of many kinds are no sign,' 'joys following in a certain order are no sign,' 'much time and zeal in duty,' 'many expressions of praise, great confidence, affecting relations are no sign.' None of these are true signs of necessity either that they are or that they are not genuine. Then Part 3 shows what are distinguishing signs of truly gracious and holy affections. 'Gracious affections are from divine influence.' 'Their object is the excellence of divine things ...' 'Christian practice is the chief sign to others and to ourselves.'

That was Edwards. He is not credulous, and he is not hypercritical. He examines the two sides always. He had to defend a number of unusual and remarkable phenomena that occurred in the revival of the 1740s. He had to defend, and does defend, the fact that even the body may be affected. Edwards' wife, on one occasion, exhibited the phenomenon which is known as levitation. She was literally carried from one part of the room to another without making any effort or exertion herself. Sometimes people would swoon and become unconscious in meetings. Edwards did not teach that such phenomena were of the devil. He has some striking things to say about this. He was always warning on both sides, warning against quenching the Spirit, warning also against being carried away by the flesh and being deluded by Satan through the flesh. He warned everybody. On one occasion Edwards even warned George Whitefield, who was staying with him. Whitefield had a tendency to obey and to listen to 'impulses' and he would act on them. Edwards ventured to criticise Whitefield on that score, and to warn him against possible dangers.

Here are some illustrations of the way in which Edwards does this wonderful work. They will show how he warned some people against the danger of rejecting the revival as a whole in terms of philosophy or history, and the danger of looking at particular aspects of revival only and not regarding it as a whole and its remarkable results. But nothing is more important than the way in which he warned people against the terrible danger of judging in these matters in terms of their own personal experiences, instead of in terms of the teaching of the Scriptures. One of our greatest dangers in the Christian church, and particularly in evangelical churches, today, is the habit of reducing some of the great statements of the Scripture to the level of our own experiences. Take for example that verse on which Edwards preached in connection with his *Treatise concerning the Religious Affections,* 'Whom having not seen ye love: in whom, though now ye see him not, yet believing ye rejoice with joy unspeakable and full of glory' (1 Pet. 1:8). There are many today who interpret that in terms of their own experience and who know nothing about a joy which is 'unspeakable and full of glory.' They say that that is experienced by every Christian. This is how Edwards warns against that danger:

'I would propose it to be considered, whether or no some, instead of making the Scriptures their only rule to judge of this work, do not make their own *experience* the rule, and reject such and such things as are now professed and experienced, because they themselves never felt them. Are there not many, who, chiefly on this ground, have entertained and vented suspicions, if not peremptory condemnations, of those extreme terrors, and those great, sudden, and extraordinary discoveries of the glorious perfections of God, and of the beauty and love of Christ? Have they not condemned such vehement affections, such high transports of love and joy, such pity and distress for the souls of others, and exercises of mind that have such great effects, merely, or chiefly, because they knew nothing about them by experience? Persons are very ready to be suspicious of what they have not felt themselves. It is to be feared that many good men have been guilty of this error; which however does not make it the less unreasonable. And perhaps there are some who upon this ground do not only reject these extraordinary things, but all such conviction of sin, discoveries of the glory of God, excellency of Christ, and inward conviction of the truth of the gospel, by the immediate influence of the Spirit of God, now supposed to be necessary to salvation. These persons who thus make their own experiences their rule of judgment, instead of bowing to the wisdom of God, and yielding to his word as an infallible rule, are guilty of casting a great reflection upon the understanding of the Most High' (vol. 1, 371).

Or take again his defence of unusual or high experiences of God and the work of the Spirit. He writes:

'It is no argument that a work is not of the Spirit of God, that some who are the subjects of it have been in a kind of ecstasy, wherein they have been carried beyond themselves, and have had their minds transported into a train of strong and pleasing imaginations, and a kind of visions, as though they were rapt up even to heaven, and there saw glorious sights. I have been acquainted with some such instances, and I see no need of bringing in the help of the devil into the account that we give of these things, nor yet of supposing them to be of the same nature with the visions of the prophets, or St Paul's rapture into paradise. Human nature, under these intense exercises and affections, is all that need be brought into the account' (vol. 2, 263).

Look now at what he says about the witness of the Spirit with our spirits. There is much confusion about this at the present time. How do you interpret Romans 8:15, 16? This is how Jonathan Edwards deals with the witness of the Spirit:

'There have been instances before now, of persons crying out in transports of divine joy in *New England*. We have an instance in Captain Clap's memoirs (published by the Rev. Mr Prince), not of a silly woman or child, but a man of solid understanding, that, in a high transport of spiritual joy, was made to cry out aloud on his bed. His words, p. 9, are "God's Holy Spirit did witness (I do believe) together with my spirit, that I was a child of God; and did fill my heart and soul with such full assurance that Christ was mine, that it did so transport me, as to make me cry out upon my bed, with a loud voice, *he is come, he is come*"' (vol. 1, 370).

Does every Christian feel and know this witness of the Spirit? God forbid that we should reduce these glorious statements to the level of our poor and puny experiences. In the same paragraph he refers to that never-to-be-forgotten experience that John Flavel had on a certain occasion when he was travelling on a journey.

Here is his defence of the astonishing experiences which were given to his wife. Having given an extensive account of her experiences he analyses them and evaluates them. There were many then, and there are many still, who would dismiss it all as ecstasy, fancy, an over-wrought imagination, and so on. This is how Edwards comments on it:

'Now if such things are enthusiasm, or the offspring of a distempered brain, let my brain be possessed evermore of that happy distemper! If this be distraction, I pray God that the world of mankind may be all seized with this benign, meek, beneficent, beatific, glorious distraction! What notion have they of true religion, who reject what has here been described! What shall we find to correspond with these expressions of Scripture. The peace of God that passeth all understanding: Rejoicing with joy unspeakable, and full of glory: God's shining into our hearts, to give the light of the knowledge of the glory of God, in the face of Jesus Christ: with open face, beholding as in a glass the glory of God, and being changed into the same image, from glory to glory, even as by the Spirit of the Lord: Being called out of darkness into marvellous light: and having the day-star arise in our hearts? What, let me ask, if these things that have been mentioned do not correspond with these expressions, what else can we find that does correspond with them?' (vol. 1, 69).

In that way Edwards defended the unusual and exceptional experiences that were being vouchsafed to certain people at that particular time. Yet, with all his analysis, negative and positive, and his examination and questioning and querying, he never leaves us confused and despondent as Thomas Shepard does in his study of the *Parable of the Ten Virgins*. Edwards always elevates, always stimulates, and does not make us feel hopeless. He creates within us a desire to know something of these things.

Let me conclude with a word of application. To end without application would be false to the memory of this great man of God. What are the lessons for today from Jonathan Edwards? No man is more relevant to the present condition of Christianity than Jonathan Edwards. None is more needed. Take all we have been considering, and on top of that take the treatise he wrote in 1748 with the title *An Humble Attempt to Promote Explicit Agreement and Visible Union of God's People in Extraordinary Prayer for the Revival of Religion and for the Advancement of Christ's Kingdom on Earth*. Some friends in Scotland had been meeting together to pray in this way, and they wrote to Edwards and told him about this. They asked whether he agreed with this and whether he would write about it. So he wrote this great treatise pleading with people to join together, and to agree to do so once a month and in various other ways. He argues and pleads very specially in terms of what he and they regarded then as the nearness of the second coming of Christ and the glory that was to be revealed. It is a mighty and a glorious statement. Surely revival is the only answer to the present need and condition of the church. I would state it thus. An apologetic which fails to put supreme emphasis on the work of the Holy Spirit is doomed to be a complete failure. But that is what we have been doing. We have brought out an apologetic which is highly philosophical and argumentative. We have argued about modern art, modern literature, modern drama, politics and social views as if this is what is needed. What is needed is an effusion, an outpouring of the Spirit; and any apologetic which does not finally bring us to the need of such an outpouring will ultimately be useless. I believe we are again in much the same position as that which obtained before those great things happened in the '30s of the eighteenth century. The Boyle Lectures had been instituted in the previous century to provide an apologetic, and to defend religion and the gospel. And we have been doing the same with much assiduity. Not only so, Bishop Butler's famous *Analogy* had appeared in defence of the gospel in a different manner. But these were not the factors that changed the entire situation. It was revival; and our only hope is revival. We have tried everything else. Edwards reminds us once more of the supreme need of revival.

Let us be clear as to what he said about this. We must know what revival means. We must know the difference between an evangelistic campaign and revival. They are not to be compared. We must realise the difference between experiencing the power of the Spirit in revival and the calling of people to make a decision. Some years ago a certain well-known and prominent evangelical leader at the time was urging me to attend a certain evangelistic campaign, and full of enthusiasm said, 'You must go. It's marvellous. Wonderful! People go streaming forward. No emotion. No emotion!' He kept on repeating 'No emotion.' He had not read Jonathan Edwards! We should be seriously concerned if there is no emotion. If people can take some supposed decision for Christ with no emotion, what is it that really happens? Is it conceivable that a soul may realise the danger of spending eternity in hell, know something about the holiness of God, and believe that the Son of God came into the world and even died on a cruel cross and rose again from the dead that he might be saved, and yet feel no emotion?

Read Edwards on revival. The term he used always is 'an outpouring of the Spirit.' Today, we are hearing much about what is called 'renewal.' They dislike the term revival; they prefer 'renewal.' What they mean by that is that we have all been baptized with the Spirit at the moment of regeneration, and that all we have to do therefore is to realise what we already have and yield ourselves to it. That is not revival! You can do all they teach and derive many benefits; but you still have not had revival. Revival is an outpouring of the Spirit. It is something that comes upon us, that happens to us. We are not the agents, we are just aware that something has happened. So Edwards reminds us again of what revival really is.

That leads to a warning to those who are quenching the Spirit; and there are many who are guilty of that at the present time. A book by the late Ronald Knox on Enthusiasm has become popular among certain Evangelicals. He was an intellectual Roman Catholic ignorant of these things. He, of course, mentions Edwards and the famous sermon. The New Testament warns us against 'quenching the Spirit.' We can be guilty of doing so in many ways. We can quench the Spirit by being exclusively interested in theology. We can do so also by being concerned only about the application of Christianity to industry, to education, to art, to politics, etc. At the same time Edwards gives similar warnings to those who emphasise experience only. Nothing is more striking than the balance of this man. You must have the theology; but it must be theology on fire. There must be warmth and heat as well as light. In Edwards we find the ideal combination – the great doctrines with the fire of the Spirit upon them.

I close with two special words of application. The first is to preachers. What Edwards said to preachers in his own day is urgently needed by us at this present time:

'I should think myself in the way of my duty, to raise the affections of my hearers as high as possibly I can, provided that they are affected with nothing but truth, and with affections that are not disagreeable to the nature of the subject. I know it has long been fashionable to despise a very earnest and pathetical way of preaching; and they only have been valued as preachers, who have shown the greatest extent of learning, strength of reason, and correctness of method and language. But I humbly conceive it has been for want of understanding or duly considering human nature, that such preaching has been thought to have the greatest tendency to answer the ends of preaching; and the experience of the present and past ages abundantly confirms the same. Though, as I said before, clearness of distinction, illustration, and strength of reason, and a good method in the doctrinal handling of the truths of religion, is in many ways needful and profitable, and not to be neglected; yet an increase in speculative knowledge in divinity is not what is so much needed by our people as something else. Men may abound in this sort of light and have no heat. How much has there been of this sort of knowledge, in the Christian world, in this age! Was there ever an age, wherein strength and penetration of reason, extent of learning, exactness of distinction, correctness of style, and clearness of expression, did so abound? And yet, was there ever an age, wherein there has been so little sense of the evil of sin, so little love to God, heavenly-mindedness, and holiness of life, among the professors of the true religion? Our people do not so much need to have their heads stored, as to have their hearts touched; and they stand in the greatest need of that sort of preaching which has the greatest tendency to do this' (vol. 1, 391).

Then a word to church members. Does all I have said make you feel that you are hopeless? Does it make you doubt perhaps whether you are Christian? My advice to you is: Read Jonathan Edwards. Stop going to so many meetings; stop craving for the various forms of entertainment which are so popular in evangelical circles at the present time. Learn to stay at home. Learn to read again, and do not merely read the exciting stories of certain modern people. Go back to something solid and deep and real. Are we losing the art of reading? Revivals have often started as the result of people reading volumes such as these two volumes of Edwards' works. So read this man. Decide to do so. Read his sermons; read his practical treatises, and then go on to the great discourses on theological subjects.

But above all, let all of us, preachers and listeners, having read this man, try to capture and to lay hold upon his greatest emphasis of all – the glory of God. Let us not stop at any benefit we may have had, and not even with the highest experiences we may have enjoyed. Let us seek to know more and more of the glory of God. That is what leads always to a true experience. We need to know the majesty of God, the sovereignty of God, and to feel a sense of awe, and of wonder. Do we know this? Is there in our churches a sense of wonder and of amazement? This is the impression Jonathan Edwards always conveys and creates. He teaches that these things are possible for the humblest Christian. He was preaching and ministering to most ordinary people, and yet he tells them that these things are possible to all of them. Then, beyond all, and at a time of crisis and uncertainty like the present, I know nothing more wonderful than his emphasis on the 'blessed hope.' Read the sermon which he preached at the funeral of David Brainerd. It is an account of heaven and of the glory that awaits us as God's children. In a collapsing world with everything dissolving before our eyes, is it not time that we lifted up our heads and our eyes, and looked to the glory that is coming. Let the financial position of this country collapse, let everything collapse, God's purposes are sure and certain. Nothing 'can make him his purpose forego'; and there is a glory awaiting us which baffles description. It has been prepared for us, and there it awaits all who truly look to these things, and 'the blessed appearing of our great God and Saviour.'

So, let us leave Jonathan Edwards by quoting what he himself said of David Brainerd. I cannot think of anything better to say about Edwards himself:

'How much is there, in particular, in the things that have been observed of this eminent minister of Christ, to excite us, who are called to the same great work of the gospel-ministry, to earnest care and endeavours, that we may be in like manner faithful in our work; that we may be filled with the same spirit, animated with the like pure and fervent flame of love to God, and the like earnest concern to advance the kingdom and glory of our Lord and Master, and the prosperity of Zion! How amiable did these principles render this servant of Christ in his life, and how blessed in his end! The time will soon come, when we also must leave our earthly tabernacles, and go to our Lord that sent us to labour in his harvest, to render an account of ourselves to him. O how does it concern us so to run as not uncertainly; so to fight, not as those that beat the air! And should not what we have heard excite us to depend on God for his help and assistance in our great work, and to be much in seeking the influences of his Spirit, and success in our labours, by fasting and prayer; in which the person spoken of was abundant? This practice he earnestly recommended on his deathbed, from his own experience of its great benefits, to some candidates for the ministry that stood by his bedside. He was often speaking of the great need ministers have of much of the Spirit of Christ in their work, and how little good they are like to do without it; and how, "when ministers were under the special influences of the Spirit of God, it assisted them to come at the consciences of men, and (as he expressed it) as it were to handle them with hands: whereas, without the Spirit of God, said he, whatever reason and oratory we make use of, we do but make use of stumps, instead of hands."

'Oh that the things that were seen and heard in this extraordinary person, his holiness, heavenliness, labour, and self-denial in his life, his so remarkably devoting himself and his all, in heart and practice to the glory of God, and the wonderful frame of mind manifested in so steadfast a manner, under the expectation of death, and the pains and agonies that brought it on, may excite in us all, both ministers and people, a due sense of the greatness of the work we have to do in the world, the excellency and amiableness of thorough religion in experience and practice, and the blessedness of the end of such a life, and the infinite value of their eternal reward, when absent from the body and present with the Lord; and effectually stir us up to endeavours that, in the way of such a holy life, we may at last come to so blessed an end' (vol. 2, 35-6).

# 1977
## *Preaching*

THE general subject of this conference is not an academic matter. We are dealing with contemporary problems and the most urgent matters facing the Christian church at the present time. Should there be any doubt about that let me quote some words recently written by Dr Charles Smyth, a contemporary church historian, in reviewing the book *Reformation, Conformity and Dissent*. He writes, 'The problems forced upon the consciousness of the Puritans in the seventeenth century are still uncomfortably present with all of us today.' That is a true statement, and we can therefore rejoice that we have been able to meet together and discuss them in this way.

Our object has been to show that the differences between Anglican thinking and Puritan thinking are not superficial.[1] The differences between these two bodies of people revealed themselves not with respect to certain trivial matters but concerning fundamental questions. Reference has been made more than once to a book by Dr John F. H. New on *Anglican and Puritan* which, in spite of certain limitations, emphasises the fact that the differences between the Anglicans and the Puritans were not odd, peripheral differences, but really fundamental differences resulting from fundamentally differing viewpoints.

We come now to this difference in the matter of preaching. This is, of course, in a sense the inevitable conclusion to which everything that has gone before leads. The whole question of authority, the view of the church and the business and function of the church, the view of the government of the church, the very shape and size of the buildings favoured by the two sides, the use

[1] Addresses for 1977 followed the general theme, 'Anglican and Puritan Thinking.'

of liturgies – all these matters in a sense are preparatory to this great question of preaching. The subject of preaching comes as a climax in any consideration of the Puritan view of worship and of the conduct of the Christian church. It is pathetic to notice that in New's book, which is otherwise so good, he only devotes two pages to preaching. It is almost incredible that this should be so, but that is exactly what he has done. Just two pages devoted to this all-important question of preaching in a book dealing with the Puritans! I am concerned to show that it is an extremely important subject at this present time. We are living in an age which is querying everything, and among these things it is querying the place and the value and the purpose of preaching. In increasing numbers people seem to be depreciating the value of preaching, and they are turning more and more to singing of various types and kinds, accompanied with various kinds of instruments. They are going back also to dramatic representations or recitals of the Scripture, and some are going back even to dancing and various other forms of external manifestations of the act of worship. All this is having the effect of depreciating the place and value of preaching.

Now we know that the Reformation – even before you come to the particular Puritan emphasis – swept away all such things. It swept away the medieval 'mystery plays' as they are called, and dramatic performances in the church. The Reformation got rid of all that and it is very sad to observe that people who claim an unusual degree of spirituality should be trying to lead us back to that which the Reformers saw so clearly had been concealing the gospel and the truth from the people. If you mime the Scriptures, or give a dramatic representation of them, you are distracting the attention of people from the truth that is conveyed in the Scriptures; whereas preaching, as I am going to show, is essentially concerned with bringing out the truth of the Scriptures. It is essential that we should realise the all-importance of preaching, which is at a discount today, not only for the reasons already given, but also because of the idea of increasing participation on the part of the people. What is becoming an increasing demand in the running of industry is found also in the realm of the Christian church.

I believe that there should be a place in the church for the exercise of any gift that any individual church member may chance to have; but I am certain that all Christians are not given the gift of expounding the Scriptures. All are not called or meant to preach. This is something peculiar and special, and we must get rid of the idea which opposes the preaching of one man who is called to the work, or two or three if you like, and would replace it by some kind of discussion or the expression of so-called 'beautiful thoughts.'

With the Puritans we stand for preaching. Their view of preaching, with which we are going to deal, was governed by theology. One's view of preaching is ultimately not a matter of taste, but is an expression of one's theological standpoint, and ultimately, indeed, one's view of the gospel. This is something that I could demonstrate in history even before the Protestant Reformation. There were certain movements of the Spirit within the body of the Roman Catholic Church before the Reformation. A man like John Tauler in Germany was awakened by the Spirit in a new way and, I believe, filled with the Spirit. The effect it had upon him was to turn him into a great preacher, a very popular preacher; and people crowded to hear his preaching. The same had happened in this country in the case of John Wycliffe and the Lollards in the fourteenth century. John Wycliffe was a great preacher, and his followers, the Lollards, used to travel up and down this country preaching to the people in the open air and elsewhere. In other words, if you regard John Wycliffe as 'the morning star' of the Reformation, you see that in his case also his awakening by the Spirit led to a great emphasis on preaching. This has always been the chief characteristic of a time of reformation and revival. When you come to the Reformation itself this proposition needs no demonstration. Martin Luther was pre-eminently a great preacher. So was John Calvin. Let us not forget this. These men were, first and foremost, regular preachers and great preachers. You cannot think of John Knox in Scotland for a moment without thinking of his great preaching and of the way in which Mary Queen of Scots would tremble as she listened to him. She was more afraid of his preaching than of the troops which the English sent to take her captive. The same was true of Zwingli in Switzerland. These men became great preachers. And in this country there is no question but that Hugh Latimer was first and foremost a great and popular preacher, whose preaching at St Paul's Cross used to attract large crowds of people. He was in a sense a typical Puritan preacher. Though he was not a Puritan in the technical sense he had the same spirit in him.

I am simply demonstrating the point that the basis of our view of preaching is always theological. All these men claimed, and the Puritans claimed, and all who believe in the supremacy of preaching have always claimed, that this was our Lord's own method of teaching the truth. Our Lord was a preacher. John the Baptist, the forerunner, was also a preacher primarily. In the book of Acts we find the same: Peter on the Day of Pentecost got up and preached, and he continued to do so. The apostle Paul was pre-eminently a great preacher. We see him preaching in Athens, as he *declares* the truth to the Athenians. That was the essential view of preaching held by the Puritans.

As we proceed to consider this subject I want to demonstrate that the Anglican and the Puritan views were different, and that this was clearly shown on both sides. Let us first look at the Anglicans. The Anglican view of preaching is seen in this fact, that in the Book of Common Prayer no sermon is required for the offices of Morning and Evening Prayer. That is a most significant fact, which tells us a great deal. Here was the book which was introduced in order to regulate these matters; so the very idea that you can have morning and evening prayers without any insistence upon preaching is of supreme significance. Secondly, Queen Elizabeth and her bishops came out very strongly against what were called 'prophesyings,' which were essentially preaching occasions. The queen and the bishops with few exceptions were opposed to this and they finally put an end to it in 1576. This is typical Anglicanism. The queen was the Supreme Governor of the Church of England and it was her word that counted, and so she had the right through her bishops to put an end to prophesying. In the same way Richard Hooker, pre-eminently the representative and definer of the spirit and outlook of Anglicanism, preferred, and argued for, the reading of the Scriptures privately and in the church, and the reading of the Homilies which were prepared sermons on various subjects, to the Puritan type of preaching which he disliked and attacked. He was fundamentally opposed to it temperamentally as well as intellectually. And when we turn to the seventeenth century we find that Archbishop Laud, and later a popular preacher Robert South, were constantly making fun of, and ridiculing and caricaturing, Puritan preaching. In other words, the whole ethos of Anglicanism was against the Puritan idea of preaching.

Turning to the Puritan view, we find at once that to them preaching was central, and the most important thing of all. The Elizabethan Archbishop Grindal – a very great man who deserves our study and attention – was a great believer in preaching. He had been on the continent during the Marian persecutions. He said that 'exhortations, reprehensions, and persuasions are uttered with more affection to the moving of the hearers in sermons than in Homilies.' I agree with those who say that he was only a partial Puritan. He had been a wholehearted Puritan, but he became less and less of a Puritan as time went on. But even after he had been made Archbishop of Canterbury he wrote a letter to Queen Elizabeth – a very plain and direct letter – in which he defended prophesyings and said, 'With regard to preaching, nothing is more evident from Scripture than that it was a great blessing to have the gospel preached, and to have plenty of labourers sent into the Lord's harvest. That this was the ordinary means of salvation, and that hereby men were taught their duty to God and their civil governors; that though reading of homilies was good, yet it was not comparable to preaching, which might be suited to the diversity of times, places, and hearers, and be delivered with more efficacy and affection. The homilies were devised only to supply the want of preachers, and were, by the statute of King Edward VI, to give place to sermons whenever they might be had. He hoped therefore that Her Majesty would not discountenance an ordinance so useful, and of divine appointment.' He, further, went on to tell the queen that in his opinion she should not interfere in this kind of subject connected with ecclesiastical matters, because she was not competent to do so; and for his pains he was degraded and was no longer allowed to function as Archbishop of Canterbury. Such a notable statement, and especially the fact that it comes from Grindal, is of very great significance.

Turning to Thomas Cartwright, Puritan and the real father of Presbyterianism in England, we find that he said that 'the word of God is vital in its operation only when applied to hearts and consciences of believers by way of consolation and rebuke.' To illustrate this point he said, 'As the fire stirred giveth more heat, so the word, as it were, blown by preaching, flameth more in the hearers than when it is read.' That is, to me, a very striking and most valuable statement. It tells us, incidentally, something of the purpose of preaching. The real function of preaching is not to give information, it is to do what Cartwright says; it is to give it more heat, to give life to it, to give power to it, to bring it home to the hearers. The preacher is not in the pulpit merely to give knowledge and information to people. He is to inspire them, he is to enthuse them, he is to enliven them and send them out glorying in the Spirit.

William Bradshaw, the man who wrote the first book on Puritanism in the early years of the seventeenth century, said this – 'they (Puritans) hold that the highest and supreme office and authority of the pastor is to preach the gospel solemnly and publicly to the congregation by interpreting the written word of God, and applying the same by exhortations and reproof unto them.' When we come in the 1640s to the Westminster Directory drawn up by the Westminster Assembly we find that it says, 'Preaching of the word, being the power of God unto salvation, and one of the greatest and most excellent works belonging unto the ministry of the gospel, should be so performed that the workman need not be ashamed, but may save himself and those that hear him.'

So we find when we look at this question of preaching in general, and in terms of general statements, that there was an obvious radically different view of the place of preaching as between the Anglican and the Puritan.

But let us go on to see how the Puritans showed this difference also in their practice. This again is most interesting. In definitions of the church and the nature of the church, among the Puritans you will find always that at first two things were mentioned, and soon they became three. But, invariably the first 'mark' or 'note' is preaching, the true preaching of the word. This is followed by the regular administration of the sacraments, and thirdly by the exercise of discipline. But always, in these definitions, the preaching of the word comes first, before the administration of the sacraments.

Then, secondly, I must say more about the 'prophesying' which I have already mentioned and which was quite a feature of early Puritanism in the reign of Queen Elizabeth from about 1563 until it was prohibited in 1576. It was a very interesting procedure in which a number of preachers and others would come together. Sometimes only preachers were present, sometimes the public was allowed to listen. Each preacher was given the same text and each one had to expound this text. The younger preachers came first and there might have been four or five men preaching on the same text in the same meeting. It was a kind of school of the prophets, the idea being to train men to preach. Under Roman Catholicism preaching had been at such a discount that there were very few preachers left in this country. All the emphasis was put on the sacraments, and on the priests, and on the various things to which I have referred – various plays, etc. The result was that there were very few preachers indeed. Grindal, as we have seen, reminded Queen Elizabeth that the Homilies came into being because the men who should have been preaching were unable to preach, and so had to be given something to read to the people; but that was only meant to be a temporary measure. The Puritans realised the need of preachers, and the way to train preachers, they felt, was to adopt this method of getting a number of men to deliver sermons on the same text followed by a discussion and questions. That was the method, the excellent method they adopted, and it did good work; but the queen objected to it. She was undoubtedly afraid of it. Her bishops, partly to please her, and partly to maintain discipline, and their own position, were also afraid of it and the tendencies to which it was leading, and so in the end it was prohibited, as I say, in 1576. But the very fact that the Puritans introduced these 'prophesyings' is striking evidence of the view taken by them of preaching.

Later when that was stopped, they introduced another expedient which was greatly used. It was what were known as 'lectures,' given by godly preachers. In a parish there was a vicar and perhaps one curate or more. The lecturer was a man who had no parochial duties, whose business was to expound the Scriptures, and to preach. Very often the lecturer was supported, not by the parish, but by some wealthy man or by a town council. There were a number of noblemen in that century, in the time of Elizabeth, who were partial to the viewpoint of the Puritans. The Earl of Leicester, a great favourite of Queen Elizabeth's, was very favourable towards the Puritans and he shielded them many times with the authority and influence he possessed. He was very much interested in these lectureships. The result was that in many of the market towns of the country you would have found such a man attached to the church. Walter Travers was a lecturer in the Temple Church. The Master of the Temple was Richard Hooker, but Walter Travers was the lecturer. The Puritans by this device, and this was allowed, were able to safeguard the preaching of the gospel.

Another way in which the Puritans emphasised preaching was that when they began to put up their own buildings they put their pulpits in the centre. What attracted the attention of the worshippers was not the altar, so-called, but a pulpit with an open Bible on it. It is regrettable to find increasingly that there is no pulpit Bible in many nonconformist churches at the present time and there are too many pulpits placed in a corner! I think that has some significance. But the Puritans had a central pulpit; and the Bible was there on it.

Moreover some of these men preached large numbers of sermons. Some preached every day of the week, and on Sundays more than once. Calvin himself had done this in Geneva. We are liable to forget that Calvin was pre-eminently a great preacher.

He preached at times every day and twice on a Sunday; and the Puritans perpetuated this idea. There was constant and systematic preaching, and people would travel considerable distances in order to hear such preaching. Nothing was so characteristic of the Puritans as their belief in preaching and their delight in listening to preaching. Then the number of sermons printed by them was remarkable. This raises a very interesting point, which we tend to forget, namely, that so much of the theological teaching of the Puritans was given in the form of preaching and sermons. I suggest in passing that we must consider once more whether the best way of teaching theology is not through preaching, through exposition of the word. If you keep to the word you will preserve a balance, and be constantly reminded of the importance of applying it as you go along.

Let us now turn to the question, as to why the Puritans made preaching so central? There are a number of answers. The first is that true preaching is the exposition of the word of God. It is not a mere exposition of the dogma or the teaching of the church. That is an important contrast. The Roman Catholics, to the extent that they did any preaching, simply expounded and expanded the dogma of their church. That was not the Puritan idea of preaching. Preaching, they said, is the exposition of the word of God; and therefore it must control everything. Some went so far as to say that, in faithful exposition of the word, God himself is preaching, and that if a man is giving a true exposition of Scripture, God is speaking; because it is God's word, and not the word of man. So they urged that this must come first; this must be supreme. We surely need to think about and to ponder this matter also. If I were asked to state the main difference between religion and Christianity, I would say that religion always puts its emphasis on what man does in his attempt to worship and to please and placate his God. That is what is found in all the so-called great religions of the world. With all the ceremonial and ritual and the emphasis on worship found in Mohammedanism, Hinduism, Buddhism, the emphasis is on man doing something and rendering his service. Religion always puts emphasis on that. Christianity on the other hand is primarily a listening to God. God is speaking! Religion is man searching for God; Christianity is God seeking man, manifesting himself to him, drawing himself unto him. This, I believe, is at the back of the Puritan idea of placing in the central position the exposition of the word in preaching.

The Puritans also asserted that the sermon is more important than the sacraments or any ceremonies. They claimed that it is as much an act of worship as the Eucharist and more central in the church service. The sacraments, they taught, seal the word preached and are therefore subordinate to it. This is a most important point. That was their view of the sacraments. Let us remember that some of them, and Calvin in particular, held a very high view of the Lord's Supper. He did not agree with Zwingli that it was merely a memorial service. He believed in a spiritual Real Presence in the Lord's Supper; but he said that 'the communion without a sermon is but a dumb show.' In other words, the Puritan view was that the sacraments sealed the word. They did not convey it: they sealed it. It is the preaching that conveys the word to us, and the sacraments seal it, confirm it to us, certify it to us. So we must give supremacy to the preaching over against a sacrament.

Likewise they said that preaching is much more important than liturgy and long liturgical services because preaching teaches the people how to pray for themselves. They regarded church members as 'a royal priesthood,' so if you have a long liturgical service which leaves not time for exposition of the word, for preaching, you are not training your people to pray for themselves. But they are meant to pray because the Bible teaches 'the universal priesthood of all believers.' Everyone who is a member of a church is a member of a royal priesthood, and each one should be praying. So they need to be taught how to pray; and you must give more time to the preaching and exposition of the word, and the teaching, than to a liturgical service.

Furthermore, they argued that preaching is the biblical way of promoting holiness; and they were very much concerned about this. They were appalled at the unworthy life that was lived by many who were regarded by Hooker and others as Christians because they regarded the church and the State as being coterminous. Every man in the parish according to that Anglican view was not only a citizen of the country but also a member of the church. Yet many lived sinful lives; and to the Puritans this was quite contrary to the teaching of the New Testament where the teaching is, 'Be ye holy for I am holy' and where the church is 'a holy nation.' The way to promote holiness, they said, is not to believe in some kind of sacramental grace, or to be going to make confessions to the priest; the way to promote holiness is to teach people the word of God and to bring the impact of this teaching forcibly upon the minds of people. Patrick Collinson in his book on Elizabethan Puritanism quotes someone as saying, 'Anglicans make the chiefest, which is preaching, but an accessory, i.e. a thing without which their office may and doth consist.' To the Anglicans the service and the sacraments were the great thing; preaching was nothing but an 'accessory.'

On the other hand, the Puritans frequently indulged in exposition of the word apart from any sacramental or liturgical action. There was this fundamental difference; and the Puritans were concerned to emphasise that it is only by preaching that holiness can be promoted among the people. In preaching you are taking the word to them, and applying it to them in the way that Thomas Cartwright had indicated.

William Perkins defines the business of preaching thus: 'It is to collect the church and to accomplish the number of the elect.' That is the primary business of the church. Its other function is 'to drive the wolves away from the folds of the Lord.' It is to build up the people in knowledge, so that as the various spiritual wolves come with their heresies, their errors, their false teaching, and all their insinuations, they may drive them away with the word. Preaching makes up the number of the elect, and then proceeds to protect them by the word of God.

Let me turn to consider the method of preaching for here, again, we find the same contrast. On the whole, the Anglican method was to take a subject, sometimes a theological subject or an ethical subject, or some general theme, and then to preach a disquisition on this particular subject. That is what is found in the Homilies, and other places. The Puritan idea on the other hand was most concerned about exact exegesis of a text. You start with a word, with a verse or paragraph, and your first business is to discover its exact meaning. Then, having discovered the exact meaning of your text, you find the doctrine in that text. This is essential in their view of preaching. They were always out to find a doctrine, and doctrine is to be found in the word. You do not impose doctrine on the word. You do not start with doctrine and then find a text to fit it. You start with the word and then find the doctrine in the text. You then produced reasons which justified your finding this doctrine and then you referred to other Scriptures which taught the same doctrine and confirmed the idea, the doctrine, that you claimed to discover in your text. Thus, by comparing Scripture with Scripture you adduced your proofs and so you established your doctrine. Having thus stated it and established it, you went on to the 'use' or the application. They never failed to do this. They did not stop at a mere exposition; there was always this *use*. There were often a number of 'uses.' Then they considered and discussed *objections,* and gave their *answers,* and so on. They insisted upon this particular form to the sermon.

William Perkins in his book *The Art of Prophesying,* one of the first books written on this whole business of preaching, said that there were four great principles which should guide and govern the preacher:

'1. To read the text distinctly out of the canonical Scriptures.

'2. To give the sense and understanding of it, being read, by the Scripture itself. (In other words, your exposition must be scriptural. You must compare scripture with scripture.)

'3. To collect a few and profitable points of doctrine out of the natural sense.

'4. To apply (if he have the gift) the doctrines, rightly collected, to the life and manner of men in a simple and plain speech.'

There we have a very good description not only of Puritan preaching but of any true authentic preaching. As preachers we are not out just to give an essay or disquisition on a subject. It is always a bad sign when men read a text and then shut the Bible and put it on one side, and proceed to preach their prepared sermon. From the beginning to the end what the preacher says should be coming out of the word. What matters is not the man or his ideas: it should always be this word, for it alone is the source of the preacher's authority. So we find that there was obviously a clear difference between the Anglican idea of a sermon, and of preaching, and that of the Puritans.

But now let us turn to something that brings out the difference still more clearly, namely, the style of preaching. Perhaps it is at this point that the greatest difference of all becomes obvious and evident. As we look at the Anglicans let me say quite clearly that, judged from one standpoint, there were some very great Anglican preachers at the beginning of the seventeenth century. Bishop Andrewes was undoubtedly a great preacher. John Donne, Dean of St Paul's, was a remarkable preacher as was also Bishop Jeremy Taylor. I am not now referring to preachers in the Puritan sense of the term. I am using it in the sense in which our Victorian grandfathers tended to use it. They talked about 'great pulpiteers' or 'popular preachers.' John Donne was one of the most popular preachers London has ever known. He was a remarkable man. He was over forty years of age, if I remember correctly, when he was converted from a very worldly life. He was a great poet also; but he underwent a remarkable conversion. He was clearly a natural speaker and a man of great eloquence. He preached his amazing sermons, quite often on the theme of death, and people crowded to hear him. This was largely because of the style of the preaching. It was not so much the content as the style. The style was ornate and eloquent and oratorical. Sermons were full of classical allusions, often studded with lengthy quotations in Latin or Greek. This display of classical learning was considered to be an essential part of a sermon. In other words it was a kind of performance. Preachers generally read their sermons; obviously you either had to read them or commit them to memory and recite in a kind of dramatic recital. As people in past days would go to a political meeting to hear a political orator, so people went to hear and to listen to preachers because they were interested in oratory and eloquence and ornate balanced sentences and cadences and beautiful illustrations.

That was the kind of sermon preached by Anglican Caroline divines. Richard Baxter once heard Bishop Andrewes and his comment was: 'When I read such a book as Bishop Andrewes' sermons or heard any such kind of preaching, I felt no life in it; methought they did but play with holy things.' That is a very good criticism of what they did. It was a performance. It is interesting to note that during that selfsame seventeenth century there were also remarkable preachers in France. Jacques Bossuet was undoubtedly one of the greatest orators the world has ever known and he was a Roman Catholic preacher. Another was Massillon; Archbishop Fénélon was also a great preacher. The prime characteristic of the preaching of these 'oratorians,' as they were called, was that it was a great performance, an oratorical performance. The truth was subordinate. They did not deny it, but it was concealed by these externals. Samuel Taylor Coleridge passed this judgment on the sermons of Jeremy Taylor. He described him as a 'ghost in marble.' There was something ethereal, not very real, and as cold as marble about them. This is the result of putting emphasis on the style and the ornate character of the sermon, and on the language and the diction rather than on the truth itself.

It is most interesting and instructive in this connection to note the attitude of the great Puritan Thomas Goodwin who was himself a great preacher – one of the greatest of them all. Thomas Goodwin tells us that as a young man he greatly admired the preaching of a certain Dr Senhouse in Cambridge; but he found it to be 'distinguished rather for its ostentatious display of rhetoric than for its clear statement of evangelical truth.' He said it was characterised primarily by 'literary distinction.' It was 'eloquent and popular rather than an evangelical and useful sermon.' He (Thomas Goodwin) contrasted the 'solemnity of preaching' with these 'fine sermons' and this 'vainglorious eloquence.' Poor Thomas Goodwin! He was a man born with a gift of natural eloquence, and in his early days he greatly admired these oratorical eloquent preachers in Cambridge. It was his ambition to emulate them and to become such a preacher himself. He said that the greatest fight of his life was to conquer this 'master lust.' His 'master lust' was nothing physical or moral; it was the desire to obtain distinction and honour by eloquent preaching. There is a story in this connection of how he was asked on one occasion to preach the University sermon in Cambridge. He had prepared a most eloquent sermon with wonderful purple patches in it; and he knew that he would win much praise for it. But he was convicted quite suddenly in his conscience by the Holy Spirit as to the wrongness of this. There followed a kind of intellectual suicide. He had to excise the purple patches because as a spiritually-minded man he wanted his sermon to be understood by the most humble member of the congregation.

In other words the Puritans reprobated and avoided that which was the chief characteristic of Anglican preaching, not only then but later also in people like Tillotson and Stillingfleet and Robert South and their imitators up to the present century. They believed in 'plain, direct, experimental, saving preaching.' Preaching was to be 'simple, earnest, faithful.' They were called to preach salvation through grace by faith in our Lord Jesus Christ.

We must be careful at this point not to gather the impression that, because they were opposed to this ornate, artificial, oratorical kind of preaching, their preaching was dull or pedestrian. They were often caricatured as being such; but these men, many of them, were very learned men. What they insisted on was that human wisdom should be concealed because the preacher is declaring a divine and not a human message. This was well expressed by William Perkins, who held to the views I am illustrating. Perkins, it has been said, argued that 'the preacher must understand that he may, yea he must, privately use his liberty in the arts and philosophy and variety of reading whilst he is forming his sermon.' The preacher while preparing his sermon may and indeed should make use of the arts, philosophy, and a wide variety of reading. The preacher is to be a cultured man and the wider his reading the better preacher he is likely to be. Do not think of the Puritans as anti-intellectuals because they denounced the ornate kind of preaching, or that they did not believe in any kind of learning. But Perkins does not stop at that. He says that, while this is right in the framing of the sermon, the preacher ought in public to conceal all these aids from the people, and not to make the least ostentation.

That excellent statement reminds us that wide reading is good and furnishes the mind of the preacher; and that while he may make use of his reading, he must not parade it, or make a display of it. A preacher whose sermon consists of a mass of quotations is simply displaying his learning, often his pseudo-learning! Perkins believed in learning; but that the preacher should conceal it. The essence of art is to conceal art. Furnish your mind, but do not parade your learning.

Thomas Fuller, a church historian of the seventeenth century, and a quaint writer, writing in this connection about William Perkins, whom I have just quoted, wrote, 'But this may be said of Master Perkins, that as physicians order infusions to be made by steeping ingredients in them and taking them out again, so that all their strength and virtue remains (in the liquid) yet none of the bulk or mass is visible therein, he [the preacher], in like manner [referring to Perkins] did distil and soak much deep scholarship into his preaching, yet so insensibly that nothing but familiar expressions did appear. In a word, his church [in Cambridge] consisting of the university and town, the scholar could hear no learneder and the townsman no plainer sermons.'

There was this great man with his knowledge and erudition and learning. Like an apothecary he steeped it all into the liquid base of his sermon. He gets all the value out of it, and it is there in the liquid; but as the chemist throws away the herbs and what the people get is the distilled essence of the herbs in the liquid, so the preacher should only present the distilled essence of his learning. This is the standard by which our preaching should always be judged. The most learned man who comes to listen to us should find that he is receiving something, and that he is listening to a man who can address him on his own level; but the most ignorant man who comes should equally obtain a blessing on his level. A preacher who only appeals to one or the other is not fit to be in a pulpit.

While they insisted upon that, it needs to be emphasised that the Puritans were not dull preachers, not heavy preachers. They were lively preachers; some of them, apparently, were almost violent in their gesticulations. The liveliness was true of Calvin. These men used illustrations to illustrate and not merely to adorn the sermon. Nothing so prostitutes preaching as to use illustrations merely to call attentions to illustrations. We should abominate that. The Puritans in their preaching were intimate, direct, clear, and urgent. Some of them were guilty of shouting! We must get rid of the notion that theirs was dull, drab, solemn, boring preaching. Far from it! In the criticisms of Puritan preaching by Hooker and South and others, you will find that they concentrated on this and made fun of gesticulating preachers in the pulpit.

In general they did not read their sermons, and quite often they did not even have notes. It is interesting to observe that Calvin either preached from notes or in an entirely extempore manner. He did not read his sermons, and his preaching as a result was lively. I came across something recently which I had not realised before; and I mention it in order to stimulate further investigation of it. It is that some of the early Baptists in this country not only did not believe in reading sermons or reciting them; after having read the Scriptures they would shut the Bible as they began to preach. Their view of preaching was that it was a kind of exhortation, something similar or comparable to the idea conveyed by 'prophecy' in 1 Corinthians 14. Thomas Helwys, one of the first Baptists in this country, in contrasting the worship he believed in and that of Johnson, one of the Independents, not Baptist, said this: 'They, as partes or means of worship, read chapters, texts to preach on, and Psalms out of the translation; we already in praying, so in prophesying and singing psalms, lay aside the translation, and we suppose that will prove the truth that all books, even the originals themselves, must be laid aside in the time of spiritual worship, yet still retaining the reading and interpreting of Scriptures in the church for the preparing to worship, judging of doctrine, deciding of contraries as the ground of faith and of the whole profession.'

I interpret that as meaning that when they read the Scriptures in a public service they would give a brief exposition of it verse by verse. But when they came to the preaching they seemed to leave that on one side and turn to some kind of prophetic utterance. The same is to be found later in Wales in the case of the Methodist Father, Howell Harris of Trevecca. It is a well-known fact that he rarely took a text when preaching. He addressed the people directly in what he called 'exhorting' which we would call preaching. He had been living in the Scriptures and meditating on them and praying, and he would thus have a message out of the Scriptures; but he conveyed this to the people directly and not by means of exposition. In doing so he was departing from the general practice of the Puritans. Some of the Baptists apparently did the same, and some of the other Separatists had done so even before the Baptists. In other words, they seem to have been carrying the prophetic element in preaching to bounds which some of us might question. At any rate it is surely something that should make us consider again whether our preaching should not contain more of this prophetic element.

Have you ever thought of how the early Christians preached – how the apostles and the early preachers preached? We can be quite certain that it was not what has become traditional among us. The reports in the book of Acts of Paul's sermons indicate that he had, as it were, the whole of the Old Testament message in his mind, and delivered this to the people in a manner showing how it leads up to what had happened in the Lord Jesus Christ. This is seen clearly in his sermon on Mars Hill in Athens, and his sermon in Antioch in Pisidia. We have so tended to forget this and have become so tied to exegesis and exposition, pure and simple, that we think that when we have expounded a verse or a passage then we have truly preached. But true preaching always emphasises a message, and such a message is not always directly upon some particular piece of exegesis. I mention that in passing, in connection with the fact that the preaching of the Puritans was characterised by freedom, fervour, and passion.

Richard Baxter summed it up in the famous words, 'I preached as never like to preach again, and as a dying man to dying men.' That sums up Puritan preaching in its very essence. Thomas Goodwin, after he was truly converted, we are told by his biographer, began to preach 'from the fulness of his heart.' 'He preached earnestly, for he preached a full and free salvation which had been the life and joy of his own soul. He preached experimentally, for he preached as he had felt and tasted and handled of the good word of life. His great desire was to convert sinners to Christ. He thought no more of the applause, reputation, or honour which had been so precious to him. He desired to know nothing among men save Jesus Christ and him crucified. God gave testimony to the word of his grace.'

Let me sum it all up by quoting Isaac Watts, an inheritor of the Puritan tradition, who lived in the latter years of the seventeenth century and the first half of the eighteenth century. He said to preachers: 'Let me recommend to you, to do your part, that that plain practical preaching, that was begun by our good old Puritans, and by keeping up which the modern nonconformists, as much as they have been despised, have been so useful, may not be lost among us.' That is, surely, the word that comes to us. Let us make sure that that 'plain practical preaching' which was begun by the good old Puritans may not be lost among us. Baxter likewise exhorts us, 'Let the awful and important thoughts of souls being saved by my preaching, or left to perish and be condemned to hell by negligency, I say let this awful and tremendous thought dwell ever upon your spirit.'

Let us close with the words of the master of all preachers, the greatest preacher of them all, and the greatest evangelist and builder up of churches and teacher, the apostle Paul: 'Now thanks be unto God, which always causeth us to triumph in Christ, and maketh manifest the savour of his knowledge by us in every place. For we are unto God a sweet savour of Christ, in them that are saved, and in them that perish: to the one we are the savour of death unto death; and to the other the savour of life unto life. And who is sufficient for these things? For we are not as many, which corrupt the word of God: but as of sincerity, but as of God, in the sight of God speak we in Christ.' That is the Puritan idea of preaching.

The Puritans were men who were God-conscious, dominated by a sense of the presence of God. They were not men-pleasers. They did everything, to use the words of John Milton, 'as in my great taskmaster's eye,' knowing that we shall have to render up an account of our ministry. To us it has been given to stand between God and man and to be either 'a savour of life unto life' or 'a savour of death unto death.' What a tremendous task! God grant that it may be our idea, and that every time we ascend a pulpit we shall realise we are in the sight of God, and that we are speaking 'in Christ' and for him! God grant that we may learn – to use the words of Isaac Watts – 'from the good old Puritans' and realise that the supreme need of our day and generation is the declaration of the word of God in the power of the Holy Spirit.

# 1978

# *John Bunyan: Church Union – 'Light from John Bunyan and Other Puritans'*

In preparing the programme for this conference we felt that we must pick out the most important aspects of John Bunyan's work, his labours and his contribution to the life of the Christian church. The first two aspects are quite obvious to all and well-known, but I want to show that this third aspect – church union – should be equally obvious because of the part it played in the life and thinking of John Bunyan. I would like to emphasise the fact that the programme for this conference was drawn up at the beginning of the year and so my subject was not chosen as the result of a controversy that has arisen during the past six months or so. You can apply it to that if you choose, but that is your business, not mine. My business therefore is to draw attention to the attitude of John Bunyan himself to the question of the nature of the church and of the consequent relationship of different churches and points of view to one another. We are dealing with it, I emphasise, because it played a big part in Bunyan's life and thinking. It caused him much pain, and it led him into grievous controversy.

Why was he interested in it? It was because he was primarily a preacher. We have been thinking about him so far mainly as a writer; but John Bunyan thought of himself essentially as a preacher and as a pastor. He wrote his books because he was a pastor and because he wanted to help the poor people who were members of his church in Bedford. This was the source of his great concern about this whole question of the relationship of Christians to one another; I trust that it is also our concern. One of the chief reasons for our interest in these seventeenth-century men, as we have been reminded several times already, is that our world is strangely similar to theirs. I, for one, am interested in them mainly for that reason, that we may learn from them, and watch them, as they battled with the same problems and difficulties which confront us.

As we consider what determined John Bunyan's views on this subject I believe the first answer is his personality – the man he was. He was not an academic man. He had had very little education. He was not without education, but it was not much. Certainly he had had no university education such as so many of his contemporaries had received. He was comparatively an uneducated man; and he was very conscious of this, and conscious of his limitations in an intellectual sense. But in addition he was a man who did not like 'to meddle with things' which were, as he put it, 'controverted and in dispute among the saints.' He was not a controversialist by nature. There are such people, but he was not one of them. Neither was he 'a party man.' John Bunyan was a big-natured man, a generous man, a loving man, a man whose interest was not in truth in an academic sense. His great concern for souls animated him and was the mainspring of most of his activity. He actually disliked controversy. He said so many times. Nevertheless, when provoked into it, he could acquit himself well and could give as well as receive, and he could give in an almost violent manner now and again. But it is interesting to note that afterwards he was ashamed of himself, and ashamed of the strong language he had used and the measure of abuse in which he had indulged with regard to his opponents. We must think of him, then, a preacher, a pastor, a man who, because of the terrible experiences through which he had passed, had a profound concern of soul for the ordinary man and woman, and Christian people in particular.

The second element, I would say, that governed his view on this subject was his view of faith and belief. This can be illustrated by my quoting what he puts into the mouth of Faithful as he speaks to Talkative in *Pilgrim's Progress*. This is what he says: 'There is therefore knowledge and knowledge; knowledge that resteth in the bare speculation of things, and knowledge that is accompanied with the grace of faith and love.' To Bunyan it was very important to distinguish between intellectual knowledge and knowledge that is accompanied by faith and love also. 'Faith,' he said, 'is not a notional and historical assent in the head; it is a principle of life, a principle of strength.' That was his view and this, I believe, governed his attitude towards some of these controversial questions.

The third factor that determined his attitude toward this question was the influence of others upon him; and there can be no question at all about this. First, there was the history of the disputes and controversies of the seventeenth century; and it was of course a century of great disputes and controversies. I have been tempted to go into this fairly thoroughly but I must refrain from doing so. There had been considerable argument about all these matters, and there were the different groupings and sects – Anglicans, Puritans, Independents, Baptists, and the various sub-divisions of each, the Sectarians and so on. It was an age of great turmoil, and endless divisions and differences of opinion. This had led to many conferences and discussions, particularly concerning this matter which, as we shall see, was the main controversy in his life, namely, that of the question of the place of baptism by immersion in the life of the believer, and in the whole attitude towards the nature of the church. This question had really become vocal somewhere about 1641. There had been a Baptist church since about 1612, and others had come into being; but they were very small. It was about 1641 that the question of baptism by immersion really became a matter of interest and discussion. It is important to remember that prior to 1640 people who had become Baptists in their theory had not been immersed. They were not re-baptized by immersion but by affusion, so that for that period of time there was no immersion; but from 1641 and onwards numbers became convinced that they should be 'dipped' as they put it, that the body should be dipped into water in order to symbolize burial and rising again with Christ; and this led to many disputes.

The principal dispute was in a church here in London. In 1966 I gave a paper in this conference on a man called Henry Jacob and his church.[1] It was the first Congregational or Independent chapel in London and it was founded in 1616. After his death other men followed him, and eventually there came a man into the pastorate of that church named Henry Jessey. Jessey was undoubtedly a very great man, and he greatly influenced Bunyan's thinking as we shall see. There was much dispute about this whole question of baptism in his church. There were those who felt that they must be re-baptized. The problem arose very largely over their view of the Church of England. The question was whether the baptism administered by the Church of England was valid at all. Having come to doubt the whole position of that church obviously the question of the validity of its baptismal procedure arose at the same time; and so this was frequently discussed. In 1644 a conference was held at which Thomas Goodwin, Philip Nye, and others of the Independent leaders and some Separatist leaders met together to discuss their attitude to this whole matter and especially as to what should be done with respect to those members who had been re-baptized. They decided that a man called Kiffin – who was the leader amongst these Baptists – and his friends were 'motivated by tender conscience and holiness rather than obstinacy,' and that therefore 'they should not be excommunicated or admonished.' You may remember that in America, John Cotton, who had gone from this country to America in the interest of religious liberty, not only persecuted Baptists but he and other leaders excommunicated Roger Williams who had become a convinced Baptist. But these men, Goodwin, Nye, Jessey, and others did not take that position. They said that this was a matter of tender conscience and holiness and that convinced Baptists should not be excommunicated or admonished, and that in the church of Jessey they should regard these dissidents as members and desire to converse together so far as their principles permit them, 'unless they grew giddy and scandalous.' That was the limit! As long as they stopped short of becoming 'giddy' on the subject and 'scandalous,' they were to be indulged in this particular manner. But soon after that the problem became yet greater. Jessey himself became convinced that

[1] See above p. 171.

he should become a Baptist; but at first he was not re-baptized. However in a very short time he was re-baptized, but still remained pastor of that Congregational church. Eventually some of the more zealous Baptists went right away and formed a church on their own – a separate Baptist Independent church. However in Jessey's own church, liberty was still given. Whether you believed in infant baptism, or adult baptism by immersion – whatever your view, you were allowed to hold it, and there was no break in the fellowship. That continued to be the view and the rule in Jessey's church until his death in 1663. Incidentally it is interesting to note that in one of the oldest and most famous Baptist churches in this country, the Broadmead Baptist Church, Bristol, the same applied for many years. The members were given complete liberty to hold whatever view they liked. Thomas Goodwin felt in 1646 that he could not refuse as members, or censure, those members who turned to Anabaptism. Independent pastors refrained from baptising the children of church members who were opposed to infant baptism, and they would not give believer's baptism to any except those who remained in the church. The particular Baptists co-operated by baptising believers as individuals rather than as church members.

That in general outline is some of the history. Another great influence on John Bunyan was a man called John Gifford, to whom reference has been made in previous papers. He was an extraordinary man and had undergone an astonishing conversion. He had been a major in the Royalist army and had been what we would call a quack doctor at the present time. But after his conversion he became minister of a small gathered church in Bedford. Bunyan was introduced to him and his church largely through the three or four old women whom he heard talking together one afternoon as they were sitting in the sun – talking about some 're-birth' and some wonderful experiences they had had. He discovered that they were members of this little church and so he began to attend there, with the result that Gifford, as we shall see, had a great influence upon him. Another man who had much influence upon Bunyan's thinking was William Dell, a curate in the neighbouring village of Yeldon. He was a very able man who eventually held a very high position in the Anglican church. He wrote very clearly and so his views had much influence.

Another most important factor in determining Bunyan's views was what happened during the Commonwealth under Cromwell. That great period during Cromwell's Protectorate from 1649–60 was one of the most amazing epochs in the whole history of this country. To me it was certainly one of the most glorious. Many fail to realise what the situation was in this country at that time. Of course, they were not clear about everything, but they were clear about certain things. A man was allowed to preach as long as he had a certificate from some respectable person. No articles of faith were prescribed. No subscription was enforced. No mention was made by name of episcopacy, presbyterianism, congregationalism, or the question of baptism. None of these things was mentioned at all. It was a time of great religious liberty. Oliver Cromwell is a man whom we do not honour as we should. Cromwell's establishment, as John Brown of Bedford (John Bunyan's chief biographer) puts it, recognised no one form of ecclesiastical organisation. It had no church courts, no church assemblies, no church laws, no church ordinances. Nothing was said about rites and ceremonies, nothing even about the sacraments; the mode of administering the Lord's Supper and baptism was left an open question to be determined by each congregation for itself. All that the commissioners (the men appointed to handle this whole matter) dealt with was the personal piety and intellectual fitness of the man presented to the living. If in these respects he was shown to be worthy he was at once installed. The church buildings were regarded as the property of the parish, and in one there was to be found a Presbyterian community, and in another an Independent, and in a third a Baptist church. Almost complete freedom was accorded; but this great liberty was not extended to popery or prelacy. That was the limit: no bishops! Neither did this liberty extend to 'such as under the profession of Christ, held forth and practised licentiousness.' It is most important that we should bear that in mind as a part of the background to the thinking of Bunyan. This is what had been in vogue for much of the eleven years, indeed up to the time when Bunyan was imprisoned.

The fourth factor that determined Bunyan's view on this whole matter of church order and baptism was of course his imprisonment; and this he expressed very clearly and plainly. He said, when he wrote his Confession of Faith and the rules of his practice: 'What governed me was to "weigh and pause, and pause again, the grounds and foundation of those principles for which I have suffered."' In his imprisonment for nearly twelve years he was detached from everything that was secondary. There were intermissions, but roughly those twelve years led him to think that he was to be detached from everything that was secondary, and only emphasise and insist upon things that were primary and essential. I am reminded of the remark that was made by Dr Samuel Johnson on one occasion to his friend Boswell (it certainly worked in the case of Bunyan), 'Depend upon it, sir, when a man knows he is to be hanged in a fortnight it concentrates his mind wonderfully.' It would do no harm to some of us just to pause and consider, now and again, whether we shall be as concerned on our deathbed as we are now about some of the subjects over which we get so excited at the present time! It is good to recall also what Edmund Burke said at Bristol on a famous occasion when he was fighting a parliamentary election. A large crowd of people had gathered to hear the great orator who had gone there to make one of his important pronouncements on politics. As he stepped forward to the desk a man handed him a bit of paper on which was written the message that the man who was opposing him in the election had suddenly dropped dead. The great orator Burke read out the message to the people and then, instead of delivering the masterly oration which he had prepared, he looked at them and said, 'What phantoms we are; and what phantoms we pursue.' God grant that we may be animated by that spirit as we take part in these discussions!

## I

Such then, were the factors that determined Bunyan's point of view. That view he stated many times. Let us start with his general position which he stated in a treatise which he wrote in 1684 called *A Holy Life: The Beauty of Christianity*. Observe that 'a holy life' not 'opinions' is 'the beauty of Christianity.' He writes: 'It is strange to see at this day how notwithstanding all the threatenings of God [remember it was James II who was on the throne at the time], men are wedded to their own opinions, beyond what the law of grace and love will admit. Here is a Presbyter, here is an Independent, and a Baptist, so joined each man to his own opinion that they cannot have that communion one with another, as by the testament of the Lord Jesus they are commanded and enjoined. What is the cause? Is the truth? No! God is the author of no confusion in the church of God (1 Cor. 14:33). It is, then, because every man makes too much of his own opinion, abounds too much in his own sense, and takes not care to separate his opinion from the iniquity that cleaveth thereto. That this confusion is in the church of Christ, I am of Paul, I am of Apollos, I am of Cephas, I am of Christ, is too manifest. But what unbecoming language is this for the children of the same Father, members of the same body, and heirs of the same glory, to be accustomed to? Whether it is pride, or hypocrisy, or ignorance, or self, or the devil, or the Jesuit, or all these jointly working with the church, it makes and maintains these names of distinction. This distance and want of love, this contempt of one another, these base and under-valuing thoughts of brethren, will be better seen, to the shame and confusion of some, in the Judgment.' That is a clear statement of Bunyan's general position.

What this means, then, is that Bunyan was a Separatist. He believed that the church consisted of visible saints. This being his view, he obviously had no interest in Roman Catholicism, nor in Anglicanism, nor in Presbyterianism. In this respect he was clearly influenced by the opinion of William Dell the Anglican rector of Yeldon, about ten miles north of Bedford. What Dell had written very clearly on this matter is worth quoting. He wrote:

'God hath not set up any company of men or synod in the world to shine to a whole nation so that all people shall be constrained to follow their judgment and to walk in their light. If two or three Christians in the country, being met in the name of Christ, have

Christ himself with his word and Spirit among them, they need not ride many miles to London to know what to do. What wild and woeful work do men make when they will have the church of God thus and thus, and get the power of the magistrate to back theirs, as if the new heavens wherein the Lord will dwell must be the work of their own fingers, as if the New Jerusalem must of necessity come out of the Assembly of Divines at Westminster. It is a great dishonour done to God and his word when we cannot trust his word to do his work, but must be calling in the power of the world. But if the power of the word will not reform men, all the power of the world will never do it. Luther said well when he said "I will preach and teach and write, but I will not constrain anybody."'

Dell wrote, further, that he could not see what was gained by knocking down an establishment of Episcopacy only to set up an establishment of Presbyterianism. 'For what,' asked Dell, 'is a national assembly but an archbishop multiplied, and what a provincial assembly but a bishop multiplied? And a classical but a dean and archdeacon multiplied? Thus, the former lords being removed, the church would swarm with other lords, and Christ's own kingdom would never be suffered to return to Christ's own lordship and dominion.' That was the position of William Dell, and he goes on to quote the apostle Peter about 'a chosen generation, and a royal priesthood, etc.' He continues, 'Presbyters and bishops differ only in office, not in character, from the rest of the church, and that office they receive from the church, as an alderman or common councilman, differs from the rest of the citizens, not in themselves, but only by the city's choice. And all churches are equal as well as all Christians, all being sisters of one mother, beams of one sun, branches of one vine, streams of one fountain, members of one body, branches of one golden candlestick, and so equal in all things.' It seems to be beyond doubt that this teaching of Dell, whom Bunyan used to visit and to whom he listened carefully, helped to determine his view.

Bunyan's view of the use of the Book of Common Prayer was expressed in no uncertain terms. He objected to it root and branch, and he expressed himself concerning it in his book *A Discourse concerning Prayer* thus: 'A good sense of sin and the wrath of God, and some encouragement from God to come unto him is a better Common Prayer book than that which is taken out of the papistical mass-book, being the scraps and fragments of the devices of some popes, some friars, and I know not what.' He goes on to say, 'But here now the wise men of our days are so well skilled as that they have both the matter and manner of their prayers at their finger ends; setting such a prayer for such a day, and that twenty years before it comes. One for Christmas, another for Easter and six days after that. They have also bounded how many syllables must be said in every one of them at their public exercises. For each saint's day, also, they have them ready for the generations yet unborn to say. They can tell you also when you shall kneel, when you shall stand, when you should abide in your seats, when you should go up into the chancel, and what you should do when you come there. All which the apostles came short of, as not being able to compose so profound a manner.' Obviously, therefore, he could not continue as an Anglican. He had been baptized in the Anglican church, but he left it, and joined the Independent church in Bedford.

Bunyan was also very much opposed to the Quakers who were a kind of radical party among the Puritans. Some would not even count them as Puritans at all, and Bunyan disliked them intensely. He disliked their teaching of what they called the Christ within, and the 'inner light' and so on. He felt that this threatened the whole of God's kingdom, and also his own personal faith. In other words Bunyan was not a mystic. He even disliked mysticism. He taught that 'historical certainties' are absolutely essential to faith. The Quakers tended to say that the historical element did not matter very much; it was the 'inner light' that counted. Bunyan contended that if faith does not rest on certain essential certainties, there was no true faith. Likewise, the Bible, he said, was equally essential; whereas the Quakers tended to undervalue the Bible. Bunyan did not want to be 'lost in God.' He wanted to have 'a person to person dialogue with the Father or with the Son.' He sought objective truth and he desired to speak to a 'person outside himself.' He also disliked asceticism. Bunyan enjoyed his food and singing, and disliked a false asceticism. He also abominated the excesses of the Ranters.

## II

That was his general position. He was a Separatist, but not a Quaker. But, more particularly, we are concerned about his attitude to the whole question of baptism. This led to his great controversy with the Strict and Particular Baptists. There were four main divisions of Baptists at that time. There were the Strict and Particular Baptists who were Calvinists and who would not communicate with anyone whatsoever outside the members of their churches, that is with anyone who had not been baptized by immersion. The Open and Particular Baptists were also Calvinistic. These were the people to whom Bunyan belonged. They denied the absolute necessity of baptism and were much more liberal in their communion with others. There were also the Seventh-day and Particular Baptists, and, finally there were the General Baptists who were not Calvinists. Bunyan's controversy was with the Strict and Particular Baptists. His general position has been very well stated by George Offor who produced and edited the three-volume edition of the *Works of John Bunyan* in 1859. It is good to keep this in our minds as the background to Bunyan's teaching. Offor writes: 'Bunyan saw all the difficulties of this question: he was satisfied that baptism is a personal duty, in respect of which every individual must be satisfied in his own mind, and over which no church had any control; and that the only enquiry as to the fitness of a candidate for church fellowship should be, whether the regenerating powers of the Holy Ghost had baptized the spirit of the proposed member into newness of life. This is the only *livery* by which a Christian can be known. Bunyan very justly condemns the idea of water baptism being either the Christian's livery or his marriage to the Saviour.' Offor goes on to say: 'Bunyan had no doubt upon this subject: he deemed water baptism an important personal duty; and that a death to sin and resurrection to newness of life – a different tint, or dye, given to the character – was best figured by immersion in water: still he left it to every individual to be satisfied in his own mind as to this outward sign of the invisible grace. "Strange," he says, "take two Christians equal on all points but this; nay, let one go far beyond the other for grace and holiness; yet this circumstance of water shall frown and sweep away all his excellencies; not counting him worthy of that reception that with hand and heart shall be given to a novice in religion because he consents to water."' Those were the catholic opinions that were held in general by John Bunyan.

But as I have said earlier he was influenced by the opinion of his pastor John Gifford, the minister of the gathered church in Bedford for a few years. This good man made his opinion quite clear on the subject. It is to be found in the church book of what has come to be known as the Bunyan Meeting in Bedford until the present time. Gifford had written as follows in the church book: 'Faith in Christ and holiness of life, without respect of this or that circumstance, or opinion in outward and circumstantial things. By which means grace and faith was encouraged, love and amity maintained; disputings and occasion to janglings and unprofitable questions avoided and many that were weak in the faith confirmed in the blessing of eternal life.' He wrote further, 'In your assemblies avoid all disputes which gender to strifes; as questions about externals and all doubtful disputations.' Writing from his deathbed John Gifford said: 'Concerning separation from the church about baptism, laying on of hands, anointing with oil, psalms or any externals, I charge every one of you respectively, as you will give an account for it to our Lord Jesus Christ, who shall judge both the quick and dead at his coming, that none of you be found guilty of this great evil, which, while some have committed – and that through zeal for God, yet not according to knowledge – they have erred from the law of the love of Christ, and have made a rent from the true church, which is but one.' This godly man John Gifford wrote that to the members of his church as he was actually dying. It was his last letter to the church. All this quite clearly influenced

Bunyan as he entered into this controversy. He did so most reluctantly and with much heart-searching and grief. The controversy arose in the following manner. Bunyan was released from prison in 1672 having been there more or less continuously since 1660. Soon after his release he wrote a book called *A Confession of my Faith and a Reason of my Practice in Worship*. During his years in prison he had been meditating about these matters, and as he was resuming his ministry he thought he would make his position quite clear to his people. So he drew up a statement of his faith. That was quite clear, and there was no difficulty about it. The trouble arose when he came to give 'the reason for his practice in worship.' This he divided into two main sections. First he defined those 'with whom I dare not have communion.' He was quite clear and explicit about this. He would not have communion with certain people, with those who 'did not profess faith and holiness,' those who were not visible saints. His reason for this was that 'a little leaven leaveneth the whole lump.' He goes on to elaborate that in detail; but that is his position in principle.

In the second section he deals with 'those with whom I dare have communion'; and it is this section that got him into trouble. He wrote: 'Thus have I shewed you with whom I dare not have communion: and now to show you with whom I dare. But in order thereto, I desire you, First, to take notice; that touching shadowish or figurative ordinances, I believe that Christ hath ordained but two in his church, viz., Water baptism and the Supper of the Lord; both which are of excellent use to the church in this world; they being to us representations of the death and resurrection of Christ; and are, as God shall make them, helps to our faith therein. But I count them not the fundamentals of our Christianity, nor grounds or rule to communion with saints: servants they are, and our mystical ministers to teach and instruct us in the most weighty matters of the kingdom of God: I therefore here declare my reverent esteem of them; yet dare not remove them, as some do, from the place and end, where by God they are set and appointed; nor ascribe unto them more than they were ordered to have in their first and primitive institution. It is possible to commit idolatry even with God's own appointments: but I pass this, and come to the thing propounded.' Another statement he made was in reply to the question: 'Do you not count that by water baptism, and not otherwise, that being the initiating and entering ordinance, they ought to be received into fellowship?' He answered: 'No; but tarry, and take my sense with my word. For herein lies the mistake, To think that because in time past baptism was administered upon conversion, that therefore it is the initiating and entering ordinance into church communion, when by the word no such thing is testified of it. Besides, that it is not so will be manifest, if we consider the nature and power of such an ordinance.'

Bunyan's position, clearly, was that he believed in the two sacraments. He believed in baptism by immersion but he would not put it into a primary position. It is not essential. It is not at the centre, so he goes on to make statements such as this: 'Again; if water baptism, as the circumstances with which the church were pestered of old, trouble their peace, wound the consciences of the godly, dismember and break their fellowship, it is, although an ordinance, for the present to be prudently shunned; for the edification of the church, as I shall show anon, is to be preferred before it.' Then he quotes Ephesians 4:1-6, 'One Spirit, one Lord, one faith, one baptism (not of water, for by one Spirit are we all baptized into one body), one God and Father of all, who is above all, and through all, and in you all.'

Bunyan proceeds, 'This is a sufficient rule for us to hold communion by, and also to endeavour the maintaining of that communion, and to keep it in unity, within the bond of peace against all attempts whatsoever. I am bold therefore to have communion with such, because they also have the doctrine of baptisms: I say the doctrine of them. For here you must note, I distinguish between the doctrine and practice of water baptism; the doctrine being that which by the outward sign is presented to us, or which by the outward circumstance of the act is preached to the believer: namely, the death of Christ; my death with Christ; also his resurrection from the dead, and mine with him to newness of life. This is the doctrine which baptism preacheth, or that which by the outward action is signified to the believing receiver. Now I say, he that believeth in Jesus Christ hath richer and better than that (of baptism in water), namely, is dead to sin, and that lives to God by him, he hath the heart, power, and doctrine of baptism: all then that he wanteth, is but the sign, the shadow, or the outward circumstance thereof; nor yet is *that* despised but forborne for want of light. The best of baptisms he hath.' Bunyan is referring to a man, you see, who is born again, who as he puts it, is 'baptized with the Spirit' and who is regenerate, but who has not been baptized in water. Of such, he says, 'The best of baptisms he hath. He is baptized by that one Spirit; he hath the heart of water baptism, he wanteth only the outward show, which, if he had, would not prove him a truly visible saint; it would not tell me he had grace in his heart. It is no characteristical note to another of my sonship with God. Indeed, it is a sign to the person baptized, and a help to his own faith [that is the essence of Bunyan's view of the purpose of baptism. Baptism is a sign to the person himself and a help to his faith]. He should know by that circumstance that he hath received remission 'of sins; if his faith be as true, as his being baptized is felt by him. But if, for want of light, he partake not of that sign, his faith can see it in other things, exceeding great and precious promises. Yea, as I have also hinted already, if he appear not a brother before, he appeareth not a brother by that: And those that shall content themselves to make that the note of visible church membership, I doubt make things not much better, the note of their sonship with God.'

There, we have a particularly clear statement of Bunyan's position. But let him continue to speak to us: 'Vain man! Think not by the straitness of thine order, in outward and bodily conformity, to outward and shadowish circumstances, that thy peace is maintained with God, for peace with God is by faith in the blood of his cross; who hath borne the reproaches of you both. Wherefore he that hath communion with God for Christ's sake, is as good and as worthy of the communion of saints as thyself. He erreth in a circumstance, thou errest in a substance; who must bear these errors? Upon whom must these reproaches fall? Some of the things of God that are excellent have not been approved by some of the saints: What then? Must these for this be cast out of the church? No, these reproaches by which the wisdom of heaven is reproached hath fallen upon me, says Christ. But to return; God hath received him, Christ hath received him, therefore do you receive him. There is more solidity in this argument, than if all the churches of God had received him. This receiving them, because it is set as an example to the church, is such as must needs be visible to them; and is best described by that word which discovereth the visible saint. Whoso, therefore, you can by the word judge a visible saint, one that walketh with God, you may judge by the selfsame word that God hath received him. Now him that God receiveth and holdeth communion with, him you should receive and hold communion with. Will any say we cannot believe that God hath received any but such as are baptized (in water)? I will not suppose a brother so stupefied; and therefore to that I will not answer.'

Thus Bunyan continues at length. It is very difficult to know what to omit of these extraordinary statements which he made. Let me quote one more found at the end of this particular book in which he gives 'a reason of my practice in worship.'

'I return now to those that are visible saints by calling, that stand at a distance from one another, upon the accounts before specified. Brethren, *Close, close;* be one, as the Father in Christ is one. This is the way to convince the world that you are Christ's, and the subjects of one Lord; whereas the contrary makes them doubt it. This is the way to increase love, that grace so much desired by some, and so little enjoyed by others. This is the way to savour and taste the Spirit of God in each other's experience; for which if you find it in truth you cannot but bless, if you be saints, the name of our Lord Jesus Christ. This is the way to increase knowledge, or to see more in the word of God; for that may be known by two, that is not seen by one. This is the way to remove secret jealousies and murmurings one against the other. Yea, this is the way to prevent much sin, and greatly to frustrate that design of hell. This is the way to bring them out of the world into fellowship that now stand off from our gospel privileges, for the sake of our vain janglings. This is the way to make Anti-Christ shake, totter, and tremble. This is the way to leave Babylon as an habitation for devils only; and to make it a hold for foul spirits, and a cage only for every unclean and hateful bird. This is the way to hasten the work of Christ's kingdom in the world, and to forward his coming to the eternal judgment. And this is the way to obtain much of that, "Well done, good and faithful servant," when you stand before his face. (In the words of Paul), "I beseech you, brethren, suffer the word of exhortation: for I have written a letter unto you in few words."'

## III

When this book was published it produced an immediate reaction. There were, in particular, three men – much more learned than John Bunyan – here in London, William Kiffin and two others, who belonged to the Strict and Particular Baptist church, who having read it immediately attacked John Bunyan violently. They did so in several ways. They published a book against him, and they then invited him to come up to London to have a public debate on the whole question. Bunyan refused to do so. He felt that he lacked the learning of these three men, but he also felt that such a debate would be unprofitable, and that it would only cause yet greater confusion in the church. So he decided that he would publish a reply to them; and he did so in a book called *Differences in judgment about water baptism no bar to communion*. As the very title shews he took the view that these differences do not constitute a bar to communion. That is what he had been saying in his book; but they took the opposite view. They would not allow into the membership of their church any man who had not been baptized by immersion. So Bunyan wrote this book in reply to them.

Let us begin by quoting from the preface which he wrote to this book. 'Courteous reader, Be entreated to believe me, I had not set pen to paper about this controversy, had we been let alone at quiet in our Christian communion. But being assaulted for more than sixteen years, wherein the brethren of the baptized way, as they had their opportunity, have sought to break us in pieces merely because we are not, in their way, all baptized first, I could not, I durst not, forbear to do a little, if it might be, to settle the brethren, and to arm them against the attempts which also of late they begin to revive upon us. That I deny the ordinance of baptism, or that I have placed one piece of an argument against it, though they feign it, is quite without colour of truth.' [They were misrepresenting him. They were maligning him. They were saying that he did not believe in the ordinance of baptism. He denies that completely.] He continues, 'All I say is, that the church of Christ hath not warrant to keep out of their communion the Christian that is discovered to be a visible saint by the word, the Christian that walketh according to his light with God. I will not make reflections upon those unhandsome brands that my brethren have laid upon me for this, as that I am a Machiavellian, a man devilish, proud, insolent, presumptuous, and the like; neither will I say as they, The Lord rebuke thee – words fitter to be spoken to the devil than a brother. But reader, read and compare; lay aside prejudice and judge. What Mr Kiffin hath done in the matter I forgive, and love him never the worse, but must stand by my principles because they are peaceable, godly, profitable, and such as tend to the edification of my brother, and as I believe will be justified in the day of judgment. I have also here presented thee [he is writing to the reader] with the opinion of Mr Henry Jessey, in the case, which providentially I met with as I was coming to London to put my papers to the press; and that it was his judgment is asserted to me, known many years since to some of the Baptists, to whom it was sent, but never yet answered; and will yet be attested if need shall require. Farewell. Thine in all Christian service according to my light and power.'

After that preface Bunyan goes on to answer them in detail. It is very much a re-statement of what he had already said in the book that had caused the offence. But there are one or two statements which we must quote. Here is one which helps to bring out his position yet more clearly. He argues, 'But, say you, "He that despiseth his birthright of ordinances, our church privileges, will be found to be a profane person, as Esau in God's account." Baptism is not the privilege of a church as such. But what? Are they all Esau's indeed? Must we go to hell, and be damned, for want of faith in water baptism? And take notice, I do not plead for a despising of baptism, but a bearing with our brother, that cannot do it for want of light.'

Bunyan treats this matter very largely in terms of the weaker brother – a man who is a true Christian but who does not see this question of being baptized by immersion. Bunyan himself was clear about this. He believed in it, but there were weaker brethren. He calls them such for the sake of argument, and his argument is, that though they may be weak at this point, yet because they are brothers they should be received into the church. He does not plead for a despising of baptism, but a bearing with the brother that cannot submit to it for want of light. He says, 'The best of baptism he hath, namely, the signification thereof; he wanteth only the outward show, which if he had, would not prove him a truly visible saint. It would not tell me that he had the grace of God in his heart; it is no characteristical note to another of my Sonship with God. But why did you not answer these parts of my argument? Why did you only cavil at words? Which if they had been left out, the argument yet stands good. "He that is not baptized (in water), if yet a true believer, hath the doctrine of baptism. Yea, he ought to have it before he be convicted; it is his duty to be baptized or else he playeth the hypocrite. There is, therefore, no difference between that believer that is and he that is not yet baptized with water; but only his going down into the water, there to perform an outward ceremony the substance of which he hath already; which yet he is not commanded to do with respect to membership with the church; but to obtain by that, further understanding of his privilege by Christ, which before he had made profession of, and that as a visible believer."'

Here are yet further examples and illustrations of Bunyan's argumentation. 'But that I practise instituted worship, upon the same account as Paul did circumcision, and shaving, is too bold for you to presume to imagine. What? because I will not suffer water to carry away the Epistles from the Christians; and because I will not let water baptism be the rule, the door, the bolt, the bar, the wall of division between the righteous and the righteous, must I therefore be judged to be a man without conscience to the worship of Jesus Christ? The Lord deliver me from superstitious and idolatrous thoughts about any of the ordinances of Christ and of God.'

Yet more pertinently Bunyan argues, 'Now why did you not take this argument in pieces, and answer those scriptures, on which the strength thereof depends; but if to contest, and fall out about water baptism, be better than to edify the house of God, produce the texts that we may be informed.' Bunyan, it is clear, was a very clever controversialist when he was forced to be so. But he disliked it. Here is another example of his controversial skill. He was asked the question: 'Whether your principle and practice is not equally against others as well as [against] us, viz. Episcopal, Presbyterians, and Independents, who are also of our side, for our practice, though they differ with us about the subject of baptism. Do you delight to have your hand against every man?' He answers, 'I own water baptism to be God's ordinance, but I make no idol of it. Where you call now the Episcopal to side with you, and also the Presbyterian etc. you will not find them easily persuaded to conclude with you against me. They are against your manner of dipping, as well as the subject of water baptism; neither do you, for all you flatter them, agree together in all but the subject. Do you allow their sprinkling? Do you allow their signing with the cross? Why then have you so stoutly, an hundred times over, condemned these things as anti-Christian? I am not against every man, though by your abusive language you would set every one against me; but am for union, concord, and communion with saints, as saints, and for that cause I write my book.'

'To conclude, In all I have said, I have put a difference between my brethren of the baptized way; I know some are more moderate than some. When I plead for the unbaptized, I chiefly intend those that are not so baptized as my brethren judge right, according to the first pattern. But if any shall count my papers worth the scribbling against, let him deal with my arguments, and things immediately depending upon them, and not conclude that he hath confuted a book, when he hath only quarrelled at words. I have done when

I have told you, that I strive not for mastery, nor to show myself singular; but, if it might be, for union and communion among the godly. And count me not as an enemy, because I tell you the truth. And now, dissenting brethren, I commend you to God, who can pardon your sin, and give you more grace, and an inheritance among them that are sanctified by faith in Jesus Christ.'

He appends to all this a statement which had been made by Henry Jessey, the minister of the Independent church which had been founded here in London by Henry Jacob in 1616. It supports the position taken by Bunyan. Henry Jessey bases his statement on an exposition of Romans 14:1-6 in particular, but really on the whole of that particular chapter. Here are some extracts from it. '"The like figure whereunto even baptism doth also now save us [he is quoting from 1 Pet. 3:21), not the putting away of the filth of the flesh but the answer of a good conscience toward God, by the resurrection of Jesus Christ"; not excluding water baptism; but showing, that the spiritual part is chiefly to be looked at: though such as slight water baptism, as the Pharisees and lawyers did (Luke 7:30) reject the counsel of God against themselves, not being baptized. And such as would set water baptism in the Spirit's place exalt a duty against the deity and dignity of the Spirit, and do give the glory due unto him, as God blessed for ever, unto a duty. By which mistake of setting up water baptism in the Spirit's place, and assigning it a work, which was never appointed unto it; of forming the body of Christ, either in general, as in 1 Corinthians 12:13 and Ephesians 4:5, or as to particular churches of Christ, we may see the fruit; that instead of being the means of uniting as the Spirit doth; that it hath not only rent his seamless coat, but divided his body which he hath purchased with his own blood, and opposed that great design of Father, Son, and Spirit, in uniting poor saints, thereby pulling in pieces what the Spirit hath put together.'

## IV

That is a good summary of John Bunyan's position. In confirmation of that, there are certain facts which show how he adhered to that position. To confirm the fact that he disliked this controversy, it is a simple fact of history, that having written that reply and one other which I am going to quote, he never mentioned the subject again. He had expressed his view; there was nothing to add. If men rejected it and separated, well, it was for them to do so. He believed in liberty. It is an interesting fact, also, that though he himself believed in adult baptism by immersion, he had three of his children baptized in infancy in the church at Elstow, one in 1650, one in 1654, and the third in 1672, he himself having joined the church in Bedford in 1653. It was not central or vital to him. Another interesting fact is that the two successors to John Bunyan in the pastorate of the church in Bedford were paedo-baptists. In other words, he had convinced his people concerning this matter, and so they chose these men because of what they were spiritually and because of their general soundness in the faith. Another fact that must be borne in mind is that the dispute on this subject was the cause of many leaving the Separatists altogether and becoming Quakers who did not believe in sacraments at all. They had become so disgusted and upset by this controversy and quarrel that they took up the Quaker position. Another very interesting fact which has frequently been pointed out, and my reading confirms it, is that anyone reading *Pilgrim's Progress* without knowing any of the history of John Bunyan, would have no idea as to which particular denomination he belonged. That is surely most significant.

In other words, as we have seen in the quotations, John Bunyan's position was quite clear. He believed in adult baptism by immersion and he says in one place, 'I am called an Anabaptist' and does not object to that. He did, incidentally, object to many of the excesses of the Anabaptists on the Continent, but that was a minor issue. He would not refuse admission to his church to a believer who did not agree with his view. He would accept into the church those who had been baptized as infants, or those who may have been baptized by affusion on confession of faith. He granted complete liberty in this matter; and as we have seen, the subsequent history of the church confirms that the members had been convinced by him.

Let me close with a quotation from one other book which he wrote called *An Exhortation to Peace and Unity*. John Bunyan was concerned about 'peace' and 'unity.' He could see and was deeply concerned about the unbelievers in the world. He emphasised that the divisions in the church were a hindrance to the outsider to believe. This was his great concern. These divisions also confused and disturbed and upset weak believers within the church, so he wrote *An Exhortation to Peace and Unity;* and this is how he ends his exhortation: 'Shall the Papists agree and unite to carry on their interest, notwithstanding the multitudes of order, degrees, and differences that are among them, and shall not those that call themselves reformed churches unite to carry on the common interest of Christ in the world, notwithstanding some petty and disputable differences that are among them?' You see his argument. The Roman Catholics are divided endlessly among themselves, but they present a common front against all Protestants. Are we, he says, that belong to the reformed churches, are we not going to unite to carry on the common interest of Christ in the world? He did not want all to belong to the same denomination, but he desired all to have this liberty. The local church is to be at entire liberty in this matter. This was his position, and so he makes this great appeal: 'Quarrels about religion, as one observes, were sins not named among the Gentiles. What a shame is it, then, for Christians to abound in them, especially considering the nature of the Christian religion, and what large provisions the author of it hath made to keep the professors of it in peace; insomuch, as one well observes, it is next to a miracle that ever any, especially the professors of it, should fall out about it. Consider and remember' [here is his final argument and appeal once more] 'that the Judge stands at the door; let this moderate our spirits, that the Lord is at hand. What a sad account will they have to make when he comes, that shall be found to smite their fellow servants, and to make the way to his kingdom more narrow than he ever made it? Let me close all in the words of that great Apostle, 2 Corinthians 13:11: "Finally, brethren, farewell. Be perfect, be of good comfort, be of one mind, live in peace; and the God of love and peace shall be with you."'

## V

Such was Bunyan's view of the nature of the church and church unity. Quite explicitly he defined it yet more clearly in a treatise called *Peaceable Principles and True* thus: 'And since you would know by what name I would be distinguished from others, I tell you, I would be, and hope I am, a Christian; and choose, if God should count me worthy to be called a *Christian,* a Believer, or other such name which is approved by the Holy Ghost, Acts 11:26. And as for those factious titles of Anabaptists, Independents, Presbyterians or the like, I conclude, that they came neither from Jerusalem, nor Antioch, but rather from hell and Babylon; for they naturally tend to divisions; "you may know them by their fruits." '

I ask again, Have we ears to hear? Bunyan reminds us that every one of us will have to give an account of our stewardship. There is only one foundation. 'Other foundation can no man lay than that which is laid, which is Jesus Christ.' 'Let every man be careful how he builds on it.' 'Every man's work is going to be judged.' 'The Day will declare it.' John Bunyan keeps on saying and repeating that! This dread thought obviously gripped him when he was in the prison and afterwards. 'The Day will declare it.' 'The Judge standeth at the door.' Every man's work is going to be tried! It is a very serious thing to refuse membership in the church of God to anyone who is born of the Spirit, who is a visible saint. But every man shall bear his own burden. Bunyan gave complete liberty in the matter of baptism to all believers. He himself was open; he would receive any true visible saint to the communion.

'Let every man examine himself'; let us all do so as realising that we who are truly born again will be ultimately together in the same heaven, basking in the sunshine of the same glorious face. Brethren, we are again in a day of uncertainty. Everything is in a state of confusion. Re-alignments are taking place in the church; those who hold lightly to the truth, and those who even deny it, are tending to come together, and they will undoubtedly end in a so-called 'great world church' which is no church at all. The question we must face urgently is: How are we going to confront them? What are we going to present over and against them? This is not a plea for uniformity. It is not a plea for not discussing or considering this question, or as it is sometimes expressed, 'sweeping it under the carpet.' Not at all! Let us discuss it as brethren; but what we must never do, surely, is to divide and separate and to make that which John Bunyan regarded as secondary, central and all important and a cause for breaking or refusing communion. John Bunyan 'being dead yet speaketh.' May God give us grace to listen to, and to consider deeply, profoundly in the presence of God, what he said with such blazing sincerity and eloquence.

# Appendix

## 1662–1962

## *From Puritanism to Nonconformity*[1]

WE meet together to commemorate and to consider that notable event which took place in 1662 when roughly 2,000 ministers of the Church of England were ejected from the Church of England. We do so, also, in order to pay our tribute to the memory of those great and remarkable men of God.

I have chosen as the title of my remarks, '1662–1962,' and I have done so for a number of reasons. One is that we may safeguard ourselves from taking a merely historical, still less a merely antiquarian interest in this great event. The real value of looking to the past and to history is that it should help us and guide us to face the problems and difficulties of our own age and generation. I am not interested in that which is merely antiquarian and historical; we turn to these men in order that we may learn from them.

Let me, at the same time, make it quite clear that we are not doing this in any controversial spirit. This has been a matter of great controversy, of course and inevitably, during the past three centuries. But I can say quite honestly that as far as I am concerned at any rate, my interest is not controversial. I am not concerned to revive 'old forgotten far-off things and battles long ago' merely for the sake of controversy or of delighting in a fight and a skirmish. The times are too desperate and too serious for any of us to indulge

[1] The Annual Lecture of the Evangelical Library, 1962. Reproduced courtesy of the Evangelical Library, 5/6 Gateway Mews, Ringway, Bounds Green, N11 2UT.

ourselves in the mere enjoyment of ecclesiastical or theological skirmishes and battles. We turn to this great story, rather, for this reason – and that is why I coupled together 1962 and 1662 – that we may observe, up to a point at any rate, the contrast between those times and our times, trusting that in the goodness of God our doing so will serve to stimulate us and rouse us out of our lethargy, and, perhaps, under the mighty hand of God, may be the means of reviving us again.

1662–1962! There has never been a time, perhaps, since 1662 when conditions, and the whole atmosphere and climate of thought and of opinion, were more inimical to what we are doing tonight than this very period in which we live. We are living in an age which seems to me to be an exact reproduction of what we are told about the children of Israel in Judges 2:10, '... And there arose another generation after them, which knew not the Lord, nor yet the works which he had done for Israel.' Now that is a very significant statement. You observe that they not only did not know the Lord, they did not even know their history – they did not know what the Lord had done for Israel before their time. That is a perfect description of this age. It is an age which does not really know the Lord as the fathers knew him, and the result is that it is not interested in the fathers either; it is not interested in what God has done in past ages and generations.

It is an age that is self-centred and very proud of itself, proud of the twentieth century, proud of its knowledge, proud of its learning, and especially proud of its superiority over every preceding age. But its particular source of pride is its 'rediscovery,' as it likes to put it, of the importance of the principle of unity in the life of the church. The great word of this age is the word 'ecumenicity.' This is something which is being exalted at the expense of everything else, and anything which seems contrary to this whole notion of unity and comprehension and ecumenicity is derided.

The result is that the whole climate of opinion today is as adverse as is possible to a true consideration of what happened in 1662. This shows itself in the books and pamphlets that have been published already, where one finds nothing but a certain amount of lip service and of praise paid to these men. They are praised in terms of their concern about political and religious liberty; but as to the motives which animated them, and the reasons which led them to take the stand they took, those are not only criticised, they are actually condemned. At the very best they are but excused in a patronizing manner. The argument is that we are in such an entirely different position today because of our 'advance,' and our greatly increased knowledge and understanding as contrasted with the people of three hundred years ago, that we can no longer possibly hold the views which they held.

Let me give but one illustration of this from a recent address by the present chairman of the Congregational Union of England and Wales. 'Next,' he says, 'we must reckon with a different attitude to the Bible. Part of our fathers' security was in the Bible; and here we confront another revolution. They handled the Bible in a way no longer possible. I doubt whether John Calvin was what is now crudely called a "Fundamentalist"; but those parts of his writings which have given rise to this modern heresy had great influence over our fathers.' He goes on to say: 'The atmosphere of their meeting-houses was much more like that of a modern Gospel Hall than we should find congenial.' That is the voice of modern Congregationalism expressing what it thinks of the glories of the conventicles! He goes on, 'The confidence with which the writers of that period assumed that in the Old and New Testaments alike there was a pattern of church order laid down, which it was their duty to discover and reproduce rested upon presuppositions which we no longer make.' Later on he says, 'We believe the decision was right.' It seems to come to this, that they were right in what they did, but entirely and completely wrong in their reasons for doing so!

That is typical of the attitude of members even of the free churches today to what happened in 1662. I feel sorry for them, for they are in a very real difficulty. Believing as they do in what is almost a religion of ecumenicity how can they be happy about 1662? So they find themselves in this curious position of feeling compelled to praise these men, but, at the same time, compelled to indicate quite clearly that their motives and ideas and reasons were altogether wrong, and quite impossible for us with our new and greater understanding of the Scriptures. 1662 and New Delhi[1] do not make good bedfellows!

The more I read these modern references to 1662 the more I am reminded of what our Lord says in Matthew 23:29-31: 'Woe unto you, scribes and Pharisees, hypocrites! because ye build the tombs of the prophets, and garnish the sepulchres of the righteous, and say, If we had been in the days of our fathers, we would not have been partakers with them in the blood of the prophets. Wherefore ye be witnesses unto yourselves that ye are the children of them which killed the prophets.' What is the point of praising the fathers of 1662 if you say that they were essentially wrong in their teaching and outlook? That is to put yourself into the position of enemies of the men whose glorious memory we are commemorating this evening. In the same way they refer to what happened in 1662 as 'schism.' But it was not schism! Time does not allow us to enter into that on this occasion, but it is certainly not schism. There is a difference between schism and separation. Schism is always a grievous sin, but separation is sometimes a Christian's duty.

The question, then, that we are forced by our contemporaries to ask ourselves is this: Should we be commemorating what happened in 1662 at all? Had we not better forget all about it? Must we not regard it as a regrettable incident in the history of the church, as so many today regard even the Protestant Reformation as a regrettable incident in the history of the Christian church? Would it not be better, therefore, to forget all about 1662 and proceed to implement our modern ideas and notions concerning the unity of the Christian church? In other words, how do we justify what we are doing this evening?

I would return the following answers. The Evangelical Library, in particular, is justified in doing this, because were it not for what happened in 1662 and all that led up to it, there most certainly

[1] The reference is to the Third Assembly of the World Council of Churches, held in New Delhi, India, 19 November – 5 December 1961, which produced a much-heralded 'Statement on Unity.'

would never have been such a thing as an Evangelical Library. I mean by that, not only that evangelicalism as such would never have been what it has been, but also and in a very literal sense, that if you took all the books written by the Puritans themselves, and those that derive from them, out of the Evangelical Library, you would find but a small collection remaining. So it is right that the Evangelical Library in particular should be commemorating this great and notable event in the history of the Christian church.

But that is not our only reason. The period, roughly, from 1560 to 1660 is beyond any question – and this is granted by most secular historians – the most remarkable period in the entire history of this country, judged from every standpoint and by every standard. Merely from the standpoint of culture, or from the standpoint of the greatness of this country politically in the counsels of the nations, it is an outstanding century. Indeed, some of the most important things in the world tonight not only would never have arisen but certainly could not be understood, were it not for this great history. What gave origin and being to the United States of America? We all know that it was the result of the action of the 'Pilgrim Fathers' – the forefathers and forerunners of the people we are talking about – who crossed the Atlantic and settled in the western hemisphere for precisely the same reasons as drove these others out of the church in 1662. There, they founded that new democracy, the greatest and the most important country in the world today. Surely it is a right and a wise thing to consider that great period of history which, in a sense, made the modern world.

Then consider certain other facts. Look at the next century, the eighteenth century, and the great revival, the great Evangelical Awakening, associated in this country with people like Whitefield and the Wesleys, Daniel Rowland and Howell Harris, and others, and in America with Jonathan Edwards. These men really lived on the works and writings of the men whose memory we are commemorating this evening. They read them, they studied them; and, sometimes, it is rather amusing to notice in some of their journals, they record not only that they read the works of these Puritans, but even charged one another with actually preaching the sermons of the Puritans without acknowledgment! If you are to understand the Evangelical Awakening of the eighteenth century it is essential that you should know something about the history of 1662. It undoubtedly was the mainspring behind that great revival or, at least, it helped to sustain it.

When you come to the nineteenth century you find the same thing. The man who, beyond any question, must be regarded as the greatest preacher of the last century – Charles Haddon Spurgeon – literally lived upon the Puritans. No man knew the works of these people better than Charles Haddon Spurgeon. And those who have read Bishop Ryle will know how he constantly pays tribute to them. The best in evangelicalism in the Church of England is as indebted to these men as was a man like Spurgeon.

But over and above these reasons, the very greatness of the men themselves as men of God demands our attention. We turn to them for the same reason as we are exhorted in Hebrews 11 to consider those mighty heroes of the faith in Old Testament times. Here are men made in the same mould, living in the seventeenth century. Nothing is more stimulating and invigorating to a man's faith than to look at spiritual giants and to see how they lived and conducted themselves in this cruel, sinful, and gainsaying world.

Those are some of our reasons for considering this great event at such a degenerate time in the history of the church as this. We are not concerned primarily to express our own opinions, but to set forth the facts and to allow them to speak for themselves. It is generally agreed that there is no such thing as impartial or unbiased history; nevertheless that should always be our objective.

## I

The first question that arises is, What happened in 1662? – what was this great event; why do we pay attention to it; what gave origin to it; what brought it to pass? The answer to that question, in the first place, is that it is something that can only be understood as the end of an era, the end of a story. You cannot consider 1662 and hope to understand it, if you approach it directly, immediately, and in and of itself. 1662 is like the estuary of a river; and if you want to understand that you have to go back and trace the source of the river. You have to go back up into the hills and the mountains and the springs out of which the little trickle first came. That is particularly true with regard to this matter. It is only understood as we go right back. Indeed, we must go back over a hundred years if we are to understand precisely what took place in 1662. To what am I referring? It is to the origin and the rise of Puritanism. 1662 is, in a sense, the end of Puritanism; thereafter it was called nonconformity. But until then it had been called Puritanism. Without knowing something about the story of Puritanism we cannot hope to understand what happened in that year 1662. It is essential, therefore, that we should make a hurried review of the history.

The story goes back, as I am indicating, well over a hundred years before 1662. The Protestant Reformation in England took place in the reign of Henry VIII, but immediately there were certain people in the Reformed English church who began to feel that the Reformation was incomplete, and had not gone far enough. They are the people who came to be known as 'Puritans.' If we are to understand 1662 we must understand the real and essential nature of Puritanism. Here is one definition of it: 'It was a purification, an effort, wise or unwise, to rid the Christianity of England from all adhesions foreign to its nature, or obstructive to its power; an endeavour to remove everything in doctrine, discipline, ceremonial, which during the Middle Ages had been added to the gospel of Christ.' That is essential Puritanism. We can add something to that, namely, that Puritanism was not primarily a preference for one form of church government rather than another; but it was that outlook and teaching which put its emphasis upon a life of spiritual, personal religion, an intense realisation of the presence of God, a devotion of the entire being to him.

That is essential Puritanism. People think of Puritanism as just a narrow view of ethics, and of morality, and of conduct. They think of it as just a negative protest against pleasures. But that is not Puritanism. The essence of Puritanism was a desire that the Reformation in the Church of England should be completed. Now in the matter of doctrine all were agreed that there was a true reformation. In that respect the fathers very rightly and wisely had said that we must judge all teaching and all doctrine by the teaching of the Scripture. The Puritans argued that you should follow that out, not merely with regard to doctrine, but also with regard to the practice of the church, with regard to worship, with regard to everything. 'Why stop short at doctrine?' they asked. 'Why not be logical and consistent and apply the same canon of judgment to the practice of the church as you do to the belief of the church?'

That was the essential point about this Puritan movement which began, actually, in the reign of Henry VIII. Many of these men had been in contact with the reformers on the continent. This refers particularly to the Swiss reformers; not so much with Luther as with Calvin and Bullinger and others. We must get rid of the notion that what happened in 1662 was primarily just a political matter, or a matter of church and state, or a desire for political liberty. The mainspring of Puritanism, from the beginning to the end, was the desire for a pure church, pure in practice as well as in doctrine, pure in life as well as in belief.

Certain people, then, began to contend for this. One of the first – and in many ways he can be called the father of Puritanism – was a great man, John Hooper, who became Bishop of Gloucester, and who was martyred in the reign of Queen Mary.[1] He got into trouble over his puritanical views in the reign of Henry VIII and had to flee to Switzerland. There he came into contact with Bullinger and others. It is important that we should know something about this man because all the lineaments and characteristics of the men of 1662 were to be found in him. Here are some illustrations of his views and teaching. 'The Scriptures,' said Hooper, 'are the law of God; none may set aside their commands nor add to their injunctions. Christ's kingdom is a spiritual one. In this neither pope nor king may govern. Christ alone is the Governor of his church and the only Lawgiver.' Why did he say that? The answer is, that Henry VIII never really ceased to be a Catholic. All he ceased to be was a Roman Catholic. He did not change his doctrine. All he demanded

[1] See, for example, J. C. Ryle, *Five English Reformers* (Edinburgh: Banner of Truth Trust, 2014 reprint), pp. 45-96.

was that instead of the Pope being the head of the Church of England he, the king, should be the head of the church. He remained, in his doctrine, a Roman Catholic to the end of his life. That is what Hooper had in his mind when he said that. He goes on: 'Christ binds the apostles and all the church unto the things he hath taught. No law at all should be spoken of concerning the conscience but only the word of God, unto which law the conscience of men in matters of faith is bound only. God give thee grace to read the Holy Bible and have a little understanding of it. God hath given thee the Scriptures to judge thy bishop, doctor, preacher, and curate, whether he preach gall or honey, his own laws or God's laws. The church of Christ the more it is burdened by men's laws the further it is from the true and sincere verity of God's word. The Scripture and the apostles' churches are solely to be followed, and no man's authority, or even cherubim or seraphim.' That is typical of what the men of 1662 believed and taught.

But let me quote a little more of Hooper. Here he is preaching before King Edward VI: 'Yet do I much marvel that in the same book it is appointed that he that will be admitted to the ministry of God's work or his sacraments must come in white vestments [he is criticising the Prayer Book, and the instructions laid down] which seemeth to repugn[1] plainly with the former doctrine that confessed the only word of God to be sufficient; and sure I am they have not in the word of God that thus a minister should be apparelled nor yet in the primitive and best church.' And further, 'Why should the candidate for the ministry hold the bread and chalice in the one hand and the Bible in the other? Why should he not also hold in his hand the baptismal font and the water, or at least the basin with water? But it is not meet however much these unscriptural things may be borne with for a while on account of the weak, that the king and council should halt in any part. Let the primitive church be restored [that is it!] which never yet had nor shall have any match or like. Let all the movements and tokens of idolatry and superstition be removed, and the true religion of God be set in their place.'

[1] Repugn = oppose, conflict with.

Then he goes on still more strongly and says this: 'Great shame it is for a noble king, emperor, or magistrate contrary unto God's word to detain and keep from the devil, or his minister, any of their goods or treasures as the candles, vestments, crosses, altars! For if they be kept in the church as things indifferent, at length they will be maintained as things necessary.' What a prophetic word! And what a word to this age and generation in 1962! If you just keep them as 'things indifferent' for the while, the time will soon come, says Hooper, when they will be 'maintained as things necessary.'

Let us hear just another word from him. He eventually, after much pressure was brought to bear upon him, accepted the bishopric of Gloucester, and the time came for him to be consecrated into that position. But he strongly objected to being called 'My lord,' and he was eventually released from giving a promise that he would diligently observe, without any alteration whatsoever, the Book of Prayer set forth by the bishops. He declined at first to take the oath which bishops were called upon to take which he deemed 'a shameful and impious form,' or to put on the habits which the bishops were expected to wear. Both, he said, were without the sanction of the word of God.

Here, in Hooper, we have a clear expression of the principles that animated the minds of the men of 1662 and which led them to take the action which they eventually took. We can put it like this. There were two parties. First there was this Puritan party that felt that reformation was incomplete and that it must be carried further so that the life and practice of the church in its entirety should be consistent with biblical teaching. 'It affirmed that nothing may be imposed on the church of Christ, or on the consciences of its members, as an article of faith, or as an observance, whether in itself indifferent or not, which is not commanded by the word of God.' The other party maintained 'that things indifferent, which are neither contrary to Scripture, nor forbidden by it, may be imposed by the authority of the church or by some lawful power.' The fight that went on in the church for the hundred years up to 1662 was the fight between those two opposing views of what was right and wrong in the life of the church. Permit me a final quotation from

Hooper. This is what he says with regard to the 'vestments' worn by ministers in the church. 'The doctrine of Paul is this (Gal. 3) that whosoever recalls things abrogated in Christ transgresses the will of God. And the same Paul openly teaches that the priesthood of Aaron has been abolished in the priesthood of Christ (Heb. 7, 8, 9, 10) with all its rites, vestments, unctions, consecrations and the like. If, therefore, the shadows of the Aaronic priesthood cannot consist with the priesthood of Christ, much less that Popish priesthood, which even by the testimony of their own books has been derived from Aaron, or from the Gentiles.' 'There is nothing,' he says again, 'to be done in the church, but is commanded or forbidden by the word of God, though not expressly, yet by necessary collation.'

## II

There, we have been looking at what is really meant by Puritanism. During the reign of the woman rightly called 'Bloody Mary,' many of the leading reformers were put to death. Others escaped to the continent, but after her death they came back. In the meantime, on the continent they had come into contact with Calvin and Bullinger and other mighty men of God.

What, then, was the position when Elizabeth came to the throne in 1558? It was that many, if not most, of the leading men in the church were men who had been deeply influenced by what they had learned in the Reformed Church on the continent. Let me quote from Lord Macaulay on this subject. 'The reformers of England,' he says, 'wished to go as far as their continental brethren. They unanimously condemned, as anti-Christian, numerous dogmas and practices which Henry VIII retained, and which Elizabeth approved.' He confirms that Bishop Hooper had the strongest aversion to the episcopal vestments, that Bishop Ridley pulled down the altars of his diocese, and 'ordered the eucharist to be administered in the middle of churches at tables, which the Papists irreverently termed "oyster boards"'; that 'Bishop Jewell pronounced the clerical garb as "stage dress, a fool's coat, a relic of the Amorites"'; that 'Archbishop Grindall "long hesitated about accepting a mitre, from dislike of what he regarded as the mummery of consecration."' The last two, remember, were the great leaders of the church at the beginning of Elizabeth's reign. Macaulay adds 'that Bishop Parker prayed that the Church of England might model herself on the Church of Zurich, and that Bishop Ponet thought the word "bishop" should be exchanged for "superintendent."' 'When it is considered,' says Macaulay, 'that none of these prelates belonged to the extreme section of the Protestant party, it cannot be doubted that if the general sense of that party had been followed, the work of reform would have been carried on as unsparingly in England as in Scotland.'

But listen to what another authority has to say. Hallam, who has been called 'the Lord Chief Justice of our historical literature,' in exposing the fallacy that Puritan scruples were confined to but a few writers, writes, 'Except Archbishop Parker, who had remained in England during the late reign (of Mary), and Cox, Bishop of Ely, who had taken a strong part at Frankfurt against innovation, all the most eminent churchmen, such as Jewell, Grindall, Sandys, Nowell, were in favour of leaving off the surplice and what were called "the popish ceremonies." Whether their objections are to be deemed narrow and frivolous or otherwise, it is inconsistent with veracity to dissemble that the queen alone was the cause of retaining those observances to which the great separation from the Anglican establishment is ascribed.'

All that is of extreme importance. The Puritans, in other words, and these leading reformers were in essential agreement. They were in agreement with that school of reformers on the continent who had made the breach with Rome complete in practice as well as in doctrine.

From the very beginning, and even among some of the most notable leaders, there was this feeling that reformation was incomplete, that it must be completed.

That is essential Puritanism – that the church must be purged of all these things that had been introduced by Rome in the Middle Ages and before that, that the church must be pure in every respect. Furthermore, we can say that the principle of adherence to

Scripture was acknowledged on all hands to be the principle of the Reformation in all matters, not only of doctrine but also of practice. Protestantism, these men asserted, was essentially a spiritual, moral, and intellectual religion. A rectification of the belief of Christians by the test of God's word was its primary, its distinctive work. A rejection of those symbols in which Romanism expressed its character appeared to be the next step in advance.

All this was recognised by the Reformed communions of Germany, of Switzerland, and of Scotland. These had passed on from the rejection of Roman doctrine to a rejection equally complete of Romish ritual. It was not unreasonable, therefore, that the Puritans should argue that the same should be done in the Church of England, and that 'having emptied the cup of the Romish enchantress of its sorceries, she should cast away the glittering chalice in which they had shown their witching colours.' But although this was the view of some of the greatest leaders in the Church of England, Queen Elizabeth not only opposed them but insisted upon having her own way. She asserted her authority and overruled the bishops and the leaders in the church.

There is no question but that this whole trouble and dispute, which lasted for the hundred years ending in 1662, is mainly to be attributed to that headstrong woman, Queen Elizabeth I. She caused an Act of Uniformity to be passed in the year of her accession to the throne, 1558, and in that, assent to the Prayer Book and its teaching was made obligatory. But – and this is an important point – at first this was not rigidly enforced, so the Puritans felt that they could honestly and conscientiously still stay in the Church of England. They felt that they had but to bide their time, and that the inevitable logic of their teaching would eventually become evident to all. So there was no thought in their minds of leaving the church; they remained within, determined to develop their teaching and to influence others. It cannot be emphasised too frequently that the main body of the Puritans persisted in that attitude right down to 1662.

As the story continues in the reign of Elizabeth we find that gradually the Puritans divided into three main groups. The

Puritans proper were those who were quite conscientiously Anglicans and believed in its system of government and, in general, in its prayer book and formularies. That was one group. But another group arose which believed in Presbyterianism. This was led by a man called Thomas Cartwright who eventually had to leave the Church of England about 1570, though he was Lady Margaret's Professor of Divinity in Cambridge. The Presbyterians were in line, of course, with the Protestants in Scotland and in Switzerland. Among other things they did not believe in bishops, or in the Book of Common Prayer. Their idea was that the Church of England should be turned into a Presbyterian church. After that, a third group arose who became known, after their founder, Robert Browne, as 'Brownists' or Separatists. These believed in immediate withdrawal from the Church of England – 'reformation without tarrying for any.' They said that there was no purpose in staying inside, that none would ever succeed in changing the state church, and that therefore they should go out at once and do that which they believed to be right.

As the reign of Elizabeth went on, she became more and more severe in her treatment of the Puritans, especially the Separatists. Her trouble was that she felt that her power and that of the bishops went more or less together, and that if the power of the bishops diminished, her power would also probably suffer. She was a brilliant politician, but much of the trouble in the church of God can be laid at her door. Men such as Burleigh, and even the favourite Leicester, were sympathetic to the Puritans, but Elizabeth was not to be persuaded. Doubtless she had her problems and her difficulties, not least of which was her fear of offending Spain, but her real trouble was that she resembled her headstrong father rather than her brother, Edward VI.

But we must hurry on. James I came to the throne in 1603, and with his coming the Puritans, of all types, began to feel that a new day had dawned and that a great hope was opening before them. Here was a man who had come from Scotland, from the Presbyterian Church of Scotland, and who was a Calvinist in his doctrine. So they thought that they had but to appeal to him and state their case and all would be well. So they presented him with what has become known as 'The Millenary Petition.' They presented it to him at Hampton Court. What were the terms of the petition? They were very moderate. They asked for the abolition of popish ceremonies from worship, and they asked for the providing of adequate preachers. Those were the two main things. They asked not to be forced to use the Prayer Book, that tender consciences be respected, that popish ceremonies should be got rid of, and that the king and the government should make certain that there was a good and regular and adequate ministry in the churches. James decided, as the result of this petition, to call what became known as the Hampton Court Conference. Very few of the Puritans were invited, but many of the opposing party were present.

Very little came out of this conference because the leaders in the Anglican church, who were by now becoming Arminian in doctrine in spite of the Thirty-Nine Articles, were utterly opposed to the Puritans and their teaching. Indeed, the main thing that came out of that Hampton Court Conference was the Authorised Version of the Bible, published in 1611. The king prevaricated. He became concerned about himself and his power above everything else. His slogan was, 'No bishop, no king,' and he saw in the Puritans a real danger to his throne. He was a petty man, though he was in some senses a well read and a learned man – 'the wisest fool in Christendom.' The result of his policy was that by 1605 it is said that some three hundred Puritan ministers had left the Church of England. Some went to Holland, and others to various other countries. In 1620 the famous voyage of the Pilgrim Fathers in the *Mayflower* to America took place. Many of these men had been living in Holland having found life impossible in England; others joined them, and off they went to start a new life of religious freedom in New England. These figures are important as there is a tendency today to say that the Puritans were happy and content until the advent of Laud. The facts are that many left the country, and those who remained were discouraged and disappointed but, nevertheless, continued to protest.

Charles I came to the throne in 1625, and soon the power in matters ecclesiastical passed into the hands of Archbishop Laud. From that time the acute trouble began. Laud enforced Queen Elizabeth's Act of Uniformity in a way that Elizabeth herself had never done. Not only that, he compelled the clergy to read what was called the *Book of Sports* from the pulpit on a particular Sunday. That meant that they had to read a book in which the people were urged and encouraged to set up a Maypole and to have games around it on Sundays, and to indulge in various other practices. Not only were they not to condemn these sports, they were to encourage the people to practise them and to indulge in them. He proscribed Calvinistic preaching, and persecuted some of the best preachers. He was determined to extirpate Puritanism and so he began to persecute its adherents with great cruelty.

Here are some instances of the kind of thing which Charles I, through Laud, became guilty of doing. Many will know of the saintly Archbishop Leighton and his devotional commentary on the First Epistle of Peter. Well, his father was prosecuted in 1630 in the Star Chamber. He was deprived of his holy orders and committed to prison for publishing a book called *Zion's Plea Against Prelacy* after the Puritan fashion. He escaped and was recaptured. His age at the time was somewhere between forty and fifty, 'his complexion fair, his forehead lofty.' He writes to his wife and says, 'I mean to come over (from Utrecht) upon Jehovah's protection, under whose wings if we walk, nothing can hurt us.' He was first severely whipped; next he was set in the pillory and had one of his ears cut off, his nose was then slit, and he was branded on the cheek with a red-hot iron. This was the first half of his punishment. He was taken back to the Fleet prison, kept there for a week, and then 'his sores upon his back, ears, nose, and face being not cured, he was whipped again in the pillory in Cheapside, and there had the remainder of his sentence executed upon him, by cutting off the other ear, slitting the other side of the nose, and branding the other cheek.' Even worse treatment was meted out to the famous William Prynne.

These are but typical specimens of what took place. The results to which it led are not surprising. In twelve years, under Laud's administration, 4,000 Puritans became planters in America. They left this country, faced the terrible hazards of crossing the Atlantic, and went to live in the New World. Neal, in his *History of the Puritans,* affirms that he had a list of seventy-seven divines ordained in the Church of England who became pastors of emigrant churches in America before the year 1640. That is how things were going.

But now we come to the crucial point at which Charles I and Laud over-reached themselves. Not satisfied with what they were doing in England they tried to impose bishops and a liturgy upon the Church of Scotland. That produced an immediate crisis. The Scots reacted with their characteristic vigour and thoroughness and almost violence. They brought into being what is known as 'The Solemn League and Covenant,' which in its essence was an assertion that nothing would suffice but the introduction of Presbyterianism and the abolition of prelacy, and a pledge to implement this. This eventually led to the outbreak of the Civil War, the first Civil War. Things became so desperate that all parties could see that something must be done. So the famous Westminster Assembly of Divines was set up and given the task of trying to produce some kind of religious settlement. It met in Westminster Abbey – hence its name. The people taking part in it were Anglicans, Presbyterians (some from Scotland, and others who were of Presbyterian sympathy in the Church of England), and six Independents. These Independents were not direct successors of Robert Browne and the first Separatists, because there had been a kind of lapse. But a certain number of men, such as Thomas Goodwin and others, from a study of the Scriptures had come to the conclusion that bishops and the hierarchical form of church government, and liturgies, were wrong, and that the true form of church government was congregational, each church being autonomous and therefore independent. That explains how, in the Westminster Assembly, there were Independents taking part. The Assembly produced the famous Westminster Confession of Faith and the Directory of Public Worship and the Larger and Shorter Catechisms, etc.

I am trying very hurriedly to summarise the history because it is essential as a background. Roughly speaking, from 1645 to

1653, the Presbyterians were in the ascendancy. They were certainly controlling parliament, and they were very powerful in the realm of the church. But from about 1653 to the end of the Commonwealth the Independents gained control. Cromwell himself was an Independent, and he soon realised that the 'new presbyter,' as he put it, was as dangerous as the 'old priest.' So he came out strongly on the side of the Independents, and the Presbyterians lost their power.

From the beginning of the Presbyterian ascendancy and during the whole of the Commonwealth, the religious condition of England was confused, and it is difficult, therefore, for us to understand it. The church was still established but the bishops and deans and canons had been abolished. The Prayer Book was not allowed to be read in church services, but if a minister knew it by heart, and could recite it, they did not stop him. At the same time they brought in the book produced by the Westminster Assembly called a Directory of Public Worship, and suggested that it should be used instead of the Book of Common Prayer.

At this point I quote the introduction to this Directory of Public Worship of God because it summarises very well the attitude of these men to the Book of Common Prayer. This is how they put it: 'In the beginning of the blessed Reformation, our wise and pious ancestors took care to set forth an order for redress of many things, which they then, by the word, discovered to be vain, erroneous, superstitious, and idolatrous, in the public worship of God. This occasioned many godly and learned men to rejoice much in the Book of Common Prayer, at that time set forth; because the mass, and the rest of the Latin service being removed, the public worship was celebrated in our own tongue: many of the common people also received benefit by hearing the scriptures read in their own language, which formerly were unto them as a book that is sealed.

'Howbeit, long and sad experience hath made it manifest, that the Liturgy used in the Church of England (notwithstanding all the pains and religious intentions of the Compilers of it), hath proved an offence, not only to many of the godly at home, but also to the reformed churches abroad. For, not to speak of urging the reading of all the prayers, which very greatly increased the burden of it, the many unprofitable and burdensome ceremonies contained in it have occasioned much mischief, as well by disquieting the consciences of many godly ministers and people, who could not yield unto them, as by depriving them of the ordinances of God, which they might not enjoy without conforming or subscribing to those ceremonies. Sundry good Christians have been, by means thereof, kept from the Lord's table; and divers able and faithful ministers debarred from the exercise of their ministry (to the endangering of many thousand souls, in a time of such scarcity of faithful pastors), and spoiled of their livelihood, to the undoing of them and their families. Prelates, and their faction, have laboured to raise the estimation of it to such a height, as if there were no other worship, or way of worship of God, amongst us, but only the Service-book; to the great hindrance of the preaching of the word, and (in some places, especially of late) to the justling[1] of it out as unnecessary, or at best, as far inferior to the reading of common prayer; which was made no better than an idol of many ignorant and superstitious people, who, pleasing themselves in their presence at that service, and their lip-labour in bearing a part in it, have thereby hardened themselves in their ignorance and carelessness of saving knowledge and true piety.

'In the meantime, Papists boasted that the book was a compliance with them in a great part of their service; and so were not a little confirmed in their superstition and idolatry, expecting rather our return to them, than endeavouring the reformation of themselves: in which expectation they were of late very much encouraged, when, upon the pretended warrantableness of imposing of the former ceremonies, new ones were daily obtruded upon the Church.

'Add hereunto (which was not foreseen, but since hath come to pass), that the Liturgy hath been a great means, as on the one hand to make and increase an idle and unedifying ministry, which contented itself with set forms made to their hands by others,

[1] Justling = jostling, pushing forcefully.

without putting forth themselves to exercise the gift of prayer, with which our Lord Jesus Christ pleaseth to furnish all his servants whom he calls to that office: so on the other side, it hath been (and ever would be, if continued) a matter of endless strife and contention in the Church, and a snare both to many godly and faithful ministers, who have been persecuted and silenced upon that occasion, and to others of hopeful parts, many of which have been, and more still would be, diverted from all thoughts of the ministry to other studies; especially in these latter times, wherein God vouchsafeth to his people more and better means for the discovery of error and superstition, and for attaining of knowledge in the mysteries of godliness, and gifts in preaching and prayer.

'Upon these, and many the like weighty considerations in reference to the whole book in general, and because of divers particulars contained in it; not from any love to novelty, or intention to disparage our first reformers (of whom we are persuaded, that, were they now alive, they would join with us in this work, and whom we acknowledge as excellent instruments, raised by God, to begin the purging and building of his house, and desire they may be had of us and posterity in everlasting remembrance, with thankfulness and honour), but that we may in some measure answer the gracious provision of God, which at this time calleth upon us for further reformation, and may satisfy our own consciences, and answer the expectation of other reformed churches, and the desires of many godly among ourselves, and withal give some public testimony of our endeavours for uniformity in divine worship, which we have promised in our Solemn League and Covenant; we have, after earnest and frequent calling upon the name of God, and after much consultation, not with flesh and blood, but with his holy word, resolved to lay aside the former Liturgy, with the many rites and ceremonies formerly used in the worship of God; and have agreed upon this following Directory for all the parts of public worship, at ordinary and extraordinary times.'

That was the attitude of the Puritans in general, and so it continued until the death of Oliver Cromwell.

## III

There is one other matter that I must mention here before we come right on to 1660. It has often been said in defence of what happened in 1662 that the Puritans, when they were in power from about 1643 to 1660, did exactly the same thing to their opponents, and turned a number of excellent Episcopalians out of the church because they would not be Presbyterian or Independent or Puritanical or pledge themselves to 'The Solemn League and Covenant.' Is that a true charge? It is a fact that a number of genuine Episcopalians were turned out. The exact number is not certain; again it may have been anything up to 2,000. But why were they turned out? Why did the Puritans eject some of these Episcopalians? The answer is most interesting and most important. It was not because any religious test was imposed upon their consciences. When we come to 1662 we shall see that that was the sole reason for the ejectment – a religious test was imposed upon the consciences of the Puritans. The Puritans, however, did not do that. Indeed, they did not even force men to subscribe to 'The Solemn League and Covenant.' Richard Baxter, one of the leading Puritans, never subscribed to it at all, and no one was compelled to do so. In the same way they were not compelled to subscribe to the Westminster Confession of Faith.

Why, then, were they turned out? The vast majority were turned out because they were living scandalous lives or because they were inefficient ministers. I say the vast majority. There were notable and shining exceptions – people such as Jeremy Taylor, the author of *Rules for Holy Living* and *Rules for Holy Dying,* and people like Archbishop Ussher, Bishop Hall, and Chillingworth. In their case the reason was mainly political. They were Royalists and they were acting as Royalists, and they were ejected for that reason. Unfortunately the political element came in too prominently in all parties and confused the purely religious issues.

But something else is still more important. When the Puritans did eject these men they dealt with them in a tender manner. Undoubtedly there were exceptions to this, but speaking generally this is true. Jeremy Taylor himself uses the following words in this connection, and his testimony is crucial in this matter. He talks about 'the gentleness and mercy of a noble enemy.' That can never be said of the people who ejected the Puritans in 1662, but Jeremy Taylor, as an honest man, had to pay his opponents that great tribute. Not only so, the money that was raised by the sale of cathedral lands was used in part to support the bishops and the deans and the clergy who had been deprived of their offices. Furthermore, one fifth of the income that was derived from the parishes and the livings of the men who were turned out, was devoted to the relief of these very clergymen who had been ejected. So the Puritans, in power, and speaking generally, were magnanimous and generous, and tried thus to mitigate the sufferings of the men whom they had turned out. They were not perfect, any more than we are, and they were a mixed company, some of whom in their bigotry and bitterness were guilty of treating their opponents with cruelty and brutality.

We must add this, that the real father of true religious tolerance was none other than Oliver Cromwell. In this matter, and in spite of what he did to Roman Catholics in Ireland, he towers above everybody else. There was intolerance shown by the Presbyterians; still more was found amongst the people who were known as the Fifth Monarchy Men, and other sects. Each man was fighting for his particular view. Oliver Cromwell withstood them all in turn and stands out above them all. He said that there must be liberty for all apart from Roman Catholics. He even gave asylum to the Jews in this country. Oliver Cromwell is undoubtedly the father of religious tolerance in this country. He suffered endless abuse from Presbyterians, Fifth Monarchy Men, Levellers, Quakers, and also Episcopalians, because of this.

That completes our very rapid review and survey of what happened up until 1660. We shall see the vital importance of our being aware of this background. My one concern in this lecture is to present the facts. Unlike those, to whom I referred at the beginning, who do not give the facts but merely make their comments and express their opinions, I want the facts concerning the men of 1662 to speak for themselves in order that we may know what happened then and why it happened. I am not concerned about what has happened since then. We are met to do honour to the memory of the men of 1662.

## IV

We come now to 1660. Oliver Cromwell had died in 1658; his son, Richard, had been in control for a while but proved unsatisfactory. There was great confusion, and the majority of the people began to feel that the king must be brought back. So they decided to bring back Charles II. He returned to London in May 1660. The position at this time was something like this. The Presbyterians were in control once more. The Parliament was a Presbyterian parliament in the main, and as regards the church, the Presbyterian party amongst the Puritans was in the ascendancy. The Independents held aloof, because they had already seen that they must go out. The Presbyterian party had remained within the church, still hoping that the Church of England could be turned into a Presbyterian church. That had been their hope throughout the years, so they still remained inside.

During the Commonwealth, I must remind you again, there was a most extraordinary position. There was still a kind of state religion, but occupying the offices in this Church of England were some men who were Presbyterian, others who were Independents, and others who held yet other views, in addition to those who were genuinely Episcopalian in their attitude. For instance, John Owen, who had become, in the 1640s, a convinced Independent as the result of reading a book by an American Puritan of the name of John Cotton, was still an official minister of the Church of England out in Essex at Coggeshall. He had become the Dean of Christ Church, Oxford, and Vice-Chancellor of Oxford University during the Commonwealth. Thomas Goodwin, also Independent as we have seen, became the President of Magdalen College in Oxford, and so on. Now that was an extraordinary situation – it was still called the Church of England but there was that curious admixture within the body.

So when we arrive at 1660 the position was that the Puritan Presbyterians were still in the Church of England and still hopeful. Indeed, they now became very hopeful. It was the Presbyterians who, in large measure, were responsible for the bringing back of Charles II. General Monck belonged to them, and the Scots – largely because the Stuarts happened to be Scots, and Charles had made certain promises to them – were great Royalists at this point, and said that the king must be brought back. So all the Presbyterians acted together while the Independents held aloof.

All the latter asked for was that they might be given a certain amount of liberty to worship in their own way. They did not take part in the negotiations, they simply made it known that they wanted liberty. Baxter puts it like this: 'I have credibly heard that Dr Thomas Goodwin, Philip Nye, and Dr Owen, the leaders of the Independents, did tell the king that as the Pope allowed orders of religious parties in mere dependence on himself, without subjection to the bishops, all that they desired was (not to be the masters of others), but to hold their own liberty of worship and discipline, in sole dependence on the king, as the Dutch and French churches do, so they may be saved from the bishops and ecclesiastical courts.' That is all they asked for.

The Episcopalians, who had been ejected between 1648 and 1660, now saw their opportunity of coming back. The remainder of the clergy was in a most extraordinary position. During the Commonwealth large numbers of them had remained in the church and had even subscribed to the Solemn League and Covenant, though they did not believe in it. But, of course, the moment Charles came back they began to show their true colours and to turn from the position they had adopted during the time of the Commonwealth and Cromwell. What many of the common people, as well as the nonconformists, felt about them is expressed in the lines about the famous Vicar of Bray.[1]

[1] *The Vicar of Bray* was a satirical eighteenth-century song depicting the political expediency and hypocrisy of some clergy in maintaining their positions during the seventeenth-century upheavals. Its chorus ran:

The Presbyterians were feeling really hopeful. Their leaders were Richard Baxter, Reynolds, who became the Bishop of Norwich, Thomas Manton, and one of the famous men bearing the name of Calamy. They got into touch with Charles II before he came back, and Charles, on May 1st, 1660, made his famous Declaration of Breda. What did he say? He promised 'a liberty to tender consciences, and that no man shall be disquieted or called in question for differences of opinion in matters of religion which do not disturb the peace of the kingdom.' He gave that solemn promise. Baxter and others were in ecstasies. The time to which they had looked forward had almost come. Charles was promising a 'liberty to tender consciences'; they were sure that all was going to be well. So when Charles returned to London, Baxter and others went to meet him and put before him a plea for tolerance.

What was their plea? There were a number of items. 'The king would require only,' they said – this was their advice to him – 'The king would require only, first, to make "things necessary" the terms of union; secondly, to enforce discipline against sin; and thirdly, to abstain from casting out faithful ministers, and obtruding unworthy men upon the people.' I am making this point for the reason that many people think of these men, ejected in 1662, as ignorant and wild fanatics and hopeless bigots who were so unreasonable that nothing could be done with them. They were, on the contrary, most reasonable men, Baxter in particular. Indeed, if any charge is to be brought against Baxter it is that he was much too reasonable and much too ready to make concessions and to compromise.

They told Charles that he had but to observe those three things and all would be well. Baxter, while addressing Charles, was quite convinced that he was influencing him and was expecting Charles, when he had finished, to say, 'I will announce that I will do this.' But he did not know his man. Charles refused to commit himself, but decided that, instead, he would call a

---

*And this is law, I will maintain*
*Unto my dying day, Sir*
*That whatsoever king may reign,*
*I will be the Vicar of Bray, Sir!*

conference, to which he would invite Baxter and his friends as representing the Presbyterians to meet the bishops and the leaders of the Episcopalians. Baxter was delighted and went to the conference full of hope. In the conference, Baxter and his friends produced a statement which they had prepared. In it they said that they believed a firm agreement to subsist between both parties as to the doctrinal truths of the reformed religion, and in the substantial parts of divine worship, the differences being only with respect to church government, and in some particulars relating to liturgy and ceremonies. Further, they were prepared to accept a compromise. The famous Archbishop Ussher had produced a compromise scheme between Presbyterianism and Episcopacy. It is sometimes called Presbyterian Episcopacy, and sometimes Episcopalian Presbytery. In other words, it was an attempt to combine what they regarded as the benefits of Episcopacy with the excellences of Presbyterianism. We need not enter into details.

Now this is most important. It demonstrates how utterly reasonable these men were in their proposals. With reference to the Liturgy, these Presbyterians declared themselves satisfied as to the lawfulness of liturgical forms of worship provided they were agreeable to the word of God, convenient to the worshipper, consonant with the liturgies of other Reformed churches, not too rigorously imposed, and did not exclude extempore prayer. They believed that a certain number of 'learned, godly, and moderate divines' might revise the Book of Common Prayer so as to bring it into harmony with these conditions.

Men like John Owen and Thomas Goodwin would never have agreed with that, neither would the Scottish Presbyterians; but Baxter was prepared to say that. Then, secondly, as regards ceremonies, they repeated those objections which had been brought against them by the Puritans for a hundred years. The worship of God, they said, is in itself perfect without addition of ceremonies. 'God is a jealous God, and his worship is certainly then most pure, and most agreeable to the simplicity of the gospel, and to his holy and jealous eyes when it is strictly conformable to the perfect rule of faith and worship contained in the word of God.' The ceremonies had, along with popery, been rejected 'by many of the Reformed churches abroad,' had occasioned endless contention and dispute, and caused separation from the church, prejudicing rather than promoting her unity. That was their attitude. Above all, they besought His Majesty not to render 'unnecessary things' by human command 'necessary and penal,' nor to 'impose' kneeling at the sacrament and observance of holidays of human institution. Further, they proposed to abolish the use of the surplice, and of the cross in baptism, and the practice of bowing at the name of Christ – 'these things being, in the judgment of the imposers themselves, but indifferent and mutable; in the judgment of others a rock of offence; and, in the judgment of all, not to be valued with the peace of the church.'

In the fourth place, and this is a most astounding concession on their part, which again the Independents and the Scots would never have made, they went on to say that they acknowledged the king 'to be supreme governor over all persons and in all things and causes as well ecclesiastical as civil.' John Knox would never have dreamt of saying that, neither would John Calvin; but Baxter, with his genius for compromise, was ready to go even as far as that.

But though these proposals were so reasonable and conciliatory, the bishops rejected them. Thus, there developed an impasse which Charles II tried to resolve in October of that year, 1660. He then issued what was called his famous 'Declaration concerning Ecclesiastical affairs.' It was Charles' attempt to solve the problem and to relieve this impasse. In this Declaration he acknowledged the loyalty of the Presbyterians and their zeal for peace in church and state. He repeated his promise given at Breda. He declared that Presbyterians and Episcopalians approved Episcopacy and a set form of Liturgy, disliked sacrilege and the alienation of church revenues, and were anxious to advance piety and true godliness. The ceremonies, he said, would not be peremptorily insisted upon. Episcopacy would be maintained, but moderated. Care would be taken that the Lord's day should be applied to holy exercises 'without unnecessary divertizements' and that insufficient, negligent, and scandalous ministers should not be permitted in the church. None, he said, were to be admitted to the Lord's Supper till they had made a credible profession of faith, and all possible diligence was to be used in the instruction and reformation of scandalous offenders. No bishop was to exercise arbitrary power or impose anything beyond the law of the land. The Book of Common Prayer was to be preserved but 'an equal number of learned divines of both persuasions' were to review the same, making such alterations as should be thought necessary, and adding certain forms, couched, as much as might be, in scriptural phrases, which ministers, who preferred them to others, might use. As for the ceremonies, they were not to be abolished, but those who found them galling to conscience, were to be indulged in their omission. The matters of kneeling at the sacrament, the use of the cross in baptism, the wearing of the surplice were left as open questions, for the time being, to be decided and determined upon by a national synod. The oath of canonical obedience, and the subscription required by the canon, were to be dispensed with in the 'ordination, institution, and induction' of clergymen, and in the taking of university degrees. Lastly, and to sum up the whole matter, no minister was to forfeit his benefice in virtue of the Elizabethan Act of Uniformity, who 'read and declared his assent to all the Articles of religion, which only concern the confession of the true Christian faith, and the doctrine of the sacraments comprised in the Book of Articles.'

That was Charles' Declaration in October, 1660. The Presbyterians were now elated. Reynolds, one of their leaders, actually became Bishop of Norwich, and Baxter and Calamy promised that if this Declaration was made law they would also become bishops, in this modified sense, in the Church of England. All seemed to be well, and settlement seemed to be at hand. But, as the result of the efforts and the influence of the bishops, especially Sheldon, who was then Bishop of London, and afterwards Archbishop, this Declaration of King Charles II was turned down by the House of Commons by a majority of twenty-six, and was never allowed to become law and to be put into practice.

In the early part of 1661 there was a general election in which a new House of Commons was elected which was intensely Royalist and no longer mainly Presbyterian. Something had to be done about the religious impasse. It was decided, therefore, to call what became known as the Savoy Conference to try and settle this whole matter of worship. It had its first meeting on April 15th, 1661. Twelve bishops were present and twelve Presbyterians. Each party was supported by nine assistant divines. It was intended to be a conference to arrive at a compromise, an understanding. But Sheldon, Bishop of London, was determined from the outset that it should not succeed. He did not desire comprehension. He was intent upon one thing only, and that was the elimination of the Puritans *in toto*. The main matter before the conference was the Prayer Book. Let us remember that from the very beginning over a hundred years before, the main bone of contention was always the Book of Common Prayer. That was the main matter before this conference, and the Presbyterians, the Puritans, put forward suggested modifications which they thought would help. They presented a paper called 'Exceptions to the Prayer Book,' together with a reformed liturgy drawn up by Baxter. It has been said that the Puritans insisted upon the adoption of the latter as the condition of their remaining in the church. This is not so; it was merely meant to show their position, and to serve as a basis for discussion in order to arrive at a compromise. In the very first sentence of their document there is an emphatic disclaimer of all wish to substitute a uniformity of their own for the uniformity of the Prayer Book. But the bishops rejected them briefly and peremptorily saying, 'For preserving of the church's peace, we know no better nor more efficacious way than our set Liturgy.' They were determined to do so from the beginning. Parliament met on May 8th, 1661. It was decided as one of its first acts that a copy of 'The Solemn League and Covenant' should be burned by the public hangman. Bishops were recalled to the House of Lords, from which they had been excluded since the days of Cromwell, Puritans were turned out of municipal corporations, and the Episcopalian form of church government was fully restored.

Worse was to come. On June 19th, 1661, a first reading was given to a bill known as the Bill for the 'Uniformity of Public Prayers.' It was a bill that had been drawn up by the Royalists, aided and assisted by the bishops, and particularly Sheldon. Their motive when they drew and drafted this bill was to make it impossible for the Puritans to agree and to conform. Sheldon said so quite openly. He said, 'Now that we know their minds, we shall make them all knaves if they conform.' He said later, 'If we thought so many would have conformed we would have made the Act stricter.' A man on the Royalist side, the Earl of Bedford, said to some of the Puritans, 'I wish it had been otherwise, but they were resolved either to reproach you or to undo you.' The Bill was so unfair and so extreme that even Charles II tried to moderate its terms and demands. But the Commons and the bishops would not listen to him. Even the House of Lords tried to moderate it, but they would not listen to them either. The bishops were adamant, and determined to oust the Puritans altogether from the church.

Having thus refused the suggested compromises with regard to the Prayer Book put forward by the Presbyterians, they held a convocation of their own in November, 1661, and in a very short time produced their modifications of the old Prayer Book. In other words, they produced the Prayer Book which is still in use in the Church of England. Instead of modifying it in a manner that would please and placate, and make it easier for the Puritans, they modified it in the other direction, and introduced innovations which made it still more difficult for the latter. This is true in spite of the fact that the rubric explaining the reason for kneeling at the sacrament was restored, that 'till death us depart' in the Marriage Service was changed into 'till death us do part,' and that the word 'the' was added before 'resurrection' in the phrase in the burial service – 'in sure and certain hope of resurrection to eternal life.' Dr McCrie says, in summing it up, 'Though they made about six hundred trifling alterations in the Liturgy not a single change was made in favour of the Puritans.' Here are illustrations of this. The word in the old Prayer Book before the Convocation of November, 1661, for the minister in the church was 'minister.'

They deliberately changed that into 'priest.' Various other things that had always been offensive to the Puritans they deliberately brought back again, things that had been left out of the Prayer Book of Edward VI. As Bishop Burnet frankly admits, 'care was taken that nothing should be altered so as it had been moved by the Presbyterians, for it was resolved to gratify them in nothing.' And again, 'And now, all the concern that seemed to employ the bishops' thoughts was, not only to make no alteration on their account, but to make the terms of conformity stricter than they had been before the war.'

They also insisted, between the introduction of the Bill of Uniformity and this Convocation, that 'The Solemn League and Covenant' should be renounced, and that there should be re-ordination of all men who had never been ordained by bishops. The latter is a very important point. That had never been said before. Until this Act of Uniformity of 1662 the Church of England had always acknowledged the ordination of other churches, other Reformed churches, which were sound in doctrine. Never until 1662 did the Church of England lay down by law that a man must be ordained by a bishop before he is a fit and a proper person to administer the things of God. In addition they insisted that any man applying for ordination had to say that it was always unlawful to take up arms against the king.

The demands of this Bill of Uniformity were given royal assent on May 19th, 1662, and so became the Act of Uniformity. It had been introduced the previous May. It had had its third reading in July 1661, and it received the royal assent on May 19th, 1662. It laid down that 'all ministers in the Church of England must conform to the demands of this Act by St Bartholomew's Day, August 24th, 1662.' I emphasise the date for this reason. They deliberately put the final date on St Bartholomew's Day, August 24th, and not as was expected on Michaelmas Day, which is in September, for this cruel reason. The clergymen received their annual tithes on Michaelmas Day. By fixing the final date for conformity, therefore, on August 24th, they saw to it that those who did not conform would lose a year's tithes – payment for services which they had already rendered to the church. Observe the difference between the treatment they meted out to their opponents and the treatment meted out to them by the Puritans during the time of the Commonwealth.

What were the demands of an Act of Uniformity? They were not all new, of course, but consisted mainly of the things to which the Puritans had always objected, as well as certain additions. The Act crystallised and brought to a head the points at issue between the two parties. A crisis was precipitated and all ministers in the Church of England had to decide one way or the other.

What was it that was demanded of the clergy? Here are the main things to which the authorities said that they must subscribe and to which the Puritans objected. A man desiring to enter the office of a deacon (that is the first office that a clergyman has) has to conform in the following way. As a prerequisite to this office, the following three Articles are placed before the candidate and he has to subscribe to them. This subscription was first introduced in 1583, and made legally binding by the Canons of 1604. It is still in force.

1. 'That the Queen's Majesty [that was Queen Elizabeth I, of course], under God, is the only supreme governor of this realm, and of all other of Her Highness's dominions and countries, as well in all spiritual or ecclesiastical things or causes, as temporal; and that no foreign prince, person, prelate, state, or potentate hath, or ought to have, any jurisdiction, power, superiority, pre-eminence, or authority, ecclesiastical or spiritual, within Her Majesty's said realms, dominions, and countries.' (You notice that she is 'supreme' authority not only in things temporal but also in things spiritual and ecclesiastical.)

2. 'That the Book of Common Prayer, and of ordering of bishops, priests, and deacons, containeth in it nothing contrary to the word of God, and that it may lawfully be used, and that he himself will use the form in the said book prescribed in public prayer, and administration of the sacraments, and none other.'

3. 'That he alloweth the Book of Articles of religion, agreed upon by the archbishops and bishops of both Provinces, and the

whole clergy, in the Convocation holden at London in the year of our Lord one thousand, five hundred and sixty-two; and that he acknowledgeth all and every the Articles therein contained, being in number Nine and Thirty, besides the ratification, to be agreeable to the word of God.'

To these Articles the candidate is to subscribe in the following terms: 'I, N.N., do willingly and *ex animo* subscribe to these three Articles above mentioned, and to all things that are contained in them.' Besides the subscription, there is required of the young man aspiring to be a deacon the Oath of Supremacy, the latter part of which runs thus: 'And I do declare that no foreign person, prelate, state, or potentate, hath, or ought to have, any jurisdiction, power, superiority, pre-eminence, or authority, ecclesiastical or spiritual, within this realm, so help me God.'

The man who is to be a deacon has to subscribe to those three Articles. He has to subscribe to them not conditionally but in an absolute manner. The deacon is bound by words as explicit as human language admits of to receive from his very soul every iota of the Prayer Book, the Ordination Services, and the Thirty-Nine Articles. Some men tried to say that they could make subscription in principle but that they could have their own mental reservations. There was a lawsuit over a clergyman of the name of Smith who said that he subscribed to the Thirty-Nine Articles so far forth as the same were agreeable to the word of God. But the judges trying the case said that this was insufficient and that the subscription must be not conditional but absolute.

Then when this deacon, in about a year's time, becomes a priest he has to do very much the same thing. He has to subscribe again to three Articles, he has to say: 'I, A.B., do declare that I will conform to the Liturgy of the Church of England as it is now by law established.' This done, he kneels before the Ordinary, and is instituted, and after induction – that is, after being put into actual possession – he is, within a short time, to read on a Sunday, openly and publicly, this profession: 'I, A.B., do hereby declare my unfeigned assent and consent to all and everything contained and prescribed in and by the book entitled the Book of Common Prayer and admission of the Sacraments and other rights and ceremonies of the Church according to the use of the Church of England; together with the Psalter and Psalms of David, pointed as they are to be sung or said in churches; and the form or manner of making, ordaining, and consecrating of Bishops, Priests, and Deacons.' He is also bound publicly to read the Thirty-Nine Articles and declare his 'unfeigned assent thereunto.'

These were the demands that were made, and as I am pointing out, they are absolute demands. Strangely enough, I read in this morning's *Guardian*[1] a report of the Church Assembly yesterday in which Dr Mortimer, the Bishop of Exeter, introducing a new Bill said this – that not only the Act of Uniformity of Elizabeth and of 1662 but also the Act of Uniformity of 1871 'requires scrupulous observance down to the last comma of the Book of Common Prayer.'

The Act of Uniformity re-affirmed that no man could be a minister in the Church of England unless he subscribed to those three special Articles. Why did the Puritans object to this? What was it that offended them? Why did the ejectment of 1662 ever take place? What were the things that these reasonable Presbyterians objected to in particular? The answer to that, very fortunately, has been summarised for us. During the Savoy Conference, after much argument and disputation and waste of time, Bishop Cosin asked the Presbyterians to state what parts of the Liturgy they regarded as sinful, leaving the other alterations which were merely expedient to be settled again. They gave their reply to him under eight headings. The following, they said, were 'flatly sinful.'

1. 'That no minister be admitted to baptize without using the sign of the cross.' The service in the Prayer Book says that when a child is baptized the sign of the cross must be made. They said that was sinful.

2. 'That no minister be admitted to officiate without wearing a surplice.'

3. 'That none be admitted to the Lord's Supper without he receive it kneeling.'

[1] 3rd July, 1962.

4. 'That ministers be obliged to pronounce all baptized persons regenerated by the Holy Ghost, whether they be the children of Christians or not.' The phrase in the Prayer Book Collect is this: 'We yield thee humble thanks, most merciful Father, that it hath pleased thee to regenerate this infant with thy Holy Spirit, to receive him for thine own child by adoption, and to incorporate him into thy holy church.' The Prayer Book says that that has to be said whenever an infant is baptized. These men regarded it as sinful to have to say that, and equally so if they were baptizing an adult.

5. 'That ministers be obliged to deliver the Sacrament of the body and blood of Christ to the unfit, both in health and sickness, and that by personal application, putting it into their hands, even those who are found to receive it against their wills through consciousness of their impenitency.'

6. 'That ministers are obliged to absolve the unfit, and that in absolute expressions.' In the Prayer Book there is a service giving the 'priest,' as he is called, power to give absolution of sins which is absolute. They objected to that and felt it was sinful.

7. 'That ministers are forced to give thanks for all whom they bury as brethren whom God has taken to himself' – 'This our dear brother here departed ...' Regarding the state and the church as co-extensive it follows that everyone who is buried is a Christian brother whose soul, of course, is going to God. They objected to having to say that.

8. 'That none may be preachers who do not subscribe that there is nothing in the Common Prayer Book, Book of Ordination, and the Thirty-Nine Articles contrary to the word of God.'

Those were the points which Baxter and his friends made in reply to the question and the request of Bishop Cosin at the Savoy Conference.

But those were not their only objections to the Book of Common Prayer. There were others such as:

The Puritans had always objected to the use of the Apocryphal books in the church services; but now it was determined to add to the calendar of lessons a few more passages from the Apocrypha. The stories of Bel and the Dragon, and Susanna and the Elders, and Tobit and his Dog, were selected, apparently because they were the most offensive that could be found.

Secondly, the Puritans had always objected to the number of Saints' days. Now the bishops introduced a few more, such as 'the Conversion of St Paul,' and 'St Barnabas.' Two new offices were also drawn up for two new days: January 30th, called 'King Charles the Martyr,' in memory of Charles I, and May 29th, the day of the birth and restoration of Charles II who was styled, 'our most religious king'!

Thirdly, the Puritans asserted that none but parents ought to exercise sponsorial functions in baptism, but now a rubric was inserted requiring that in all cases there should be three godparents to the child, and the use of the cross was made imperative in the private, as well as the public, administration of baptism. The parents, indeed, are put on one side and the godparents take their place.

Fourthly, they denied that the salvation of baptized infants dying in infancy could be proved from Scripture. And some of them even declared that the rubric which affirmed this dogma was sufficient of itself to prevent their conforming. But now this rubric was made still more emphatic and prominent than before, by being placed at the end of the Baptismal Service, and printed not in red, but in black, 'so as to have,' says a clergyman of the Church of England, 'the force of a deliberate dogmatical statement, and not a mere rubrical injunction.'

Fifthly, these Puritans regarded the ordination which some of them had received at the hands of a presbytery as altogether valid, and not only felt it to be an insult, but doubted if it were not sinful, to repeat the solemn rite. But now the necessity of Episcopal ordination was expressly asserted, and a repetition of the rite was exacted of all who had been ordained by other than by Episcopal hands.

It was at this same time, also, that the Collect was introduced which prays for the Sovereign as 'most religious.' Remember that the monarch at the time was the dissolute and dissipated Charles II!

There is one other further thing which must be mentioned. There is a statement made in the Catechism, which also belongs to these formularies of the Church of England, which the Puritans had always found to be equally repulsive. Here it is. In the answer to the second question in the Catechism the child is taught to say this: 'In my baptism I was made a member of Christ, a child of God, and an inheritor of the kingdom of heaven.'

## V

Those, then, were the main grounds on which these men objected to what was being enforced upon them by the Act of Uniformity and on which they refused to conform. How many of them did so? We cannot be exact in the number; it was roughly round about 1,909. This includes many who had been ejected immediately on the return of Charles II in 1660. They were chiefly the men who had been placed in the livings of the Episcopalians ejected by the Puritans. It includes, also, others ejected during 1661, and also some who themselves had withdrawn in the light of what was happening. Our real concern, however, is with those ejected in 1662. It involved men who were in positions in the universities and schools as well as officiating clergymen in the church as such. At Oxford, eleven heads of colleges and halls, thirty-nine fellows, and three fellows who were serving as ministers elsewhere, and three college chaplains were removed in 1660. At Cambridge, five heads of colleges, eighteen fellows, two college chaplains and so on. At Eton there were ejected, in 1660, five fellows, the headmaster, and the chaplain; twenty-nine other schoolmasters were also ejected.

Why were these men ejected? What were the reasons they gave in addition to the ones that have been mentioned already? Here are some of the answers: Mrs Alleine, the wife of the saintly Joseph Alleine, of Taunton, author of *An Alarm to the Unconverted,*[1] says: 'Before the Act of Uniformity came out, my husband was very earnest day and night with God, that his way might be made

[1] Published by the Trust as *A Sure Guide to Heaven* (Puritan Paperbacks series).

plain to him, and that he might not desist from such advantages of saving souls with any scruple upon his spirit. He seemed so moderate, that both myself and others thought he would have conformed, he often saying, that he would not leave his work for small and dubious matters; but when he saw those clauses of assent and consent, and renouncing the covenant, he was satisfied.'

Another, Samuel Birch, who had been a friend of Alleine's at Oxford, puts it like this: 'My Lord and Master ... I am at thy footstool; I may not do evil that good may come. I may not do this great sin against my God and the dictates of my conscience. I therefore surrender myself, my soul, my ministry, my people, my place, my wife, my children, and whatsoever else is herein concerned, into thy hand, from whom I received them. Lord have mercy on me, and assist me for ever and ever to keep faith and a good conscience.'

Another, Edward Bury, rector of Great Bolas, in Shropshire, puts it like this: 'I solemnly profess, in the presence of the great God, before whom I must shortly give an account of my words and actions, that in my most impartial judgment, after all the light I can get by reading, praying, thinking, and discoursing with above twenty judicious and solid divines of both persuasions, I look upon it as my duty not to conform; and whatever becomes either of myself or my family, as I cannot force my judgment, so I cannot force my conscience.'

A certain Mr Lawrence, of Baschurch, gives his reason thus: 'I have eleven arguments for conformity,' pointing to his wife and ten children, 'but Christ hath said, "Whoso loveth wife or children more than me, is not worthy of me."' This one argument weighed with him more than the eleven arguments on the other side. Another, Mr John Hicks, of Saltash, put it like this, when asked how he should provide for his family: 'Had I as many children as that hen,' pointing to one with a numerous brood, 'I should not question that God will provide for them all.' Another said: 'God feeds the young ravens and he will feed my children.'

Richard Baxter cast himself in verse upon Providence in these words:

*Must I be driven from my books?*
*From house, and goods, and dearest friends?*
*One of Thy sweet and gracious looks*
*For more than this will make amends.*

*My Lord hath taught me how to want*
*A place wherein to lay my head;*
*While He is mine, I'll be content*
*To beg, or lack, my daily bread.*

## VI

Those were the reasons these men gave for their refusal to subscribe and to conform to the Act of Uniformity. But what kind of men were they? I have already answered the question. These were not ignorant fanatics, blinded bigots, or men with a kind of morbid scrupulosity of conscience.

What were they? They were great scholars, some of the greatest scholars that the Church of England has ever produced, outstanding scholars, godly, righteous, and holy men. Here is a description of them in the words of the Rev. Robert Halley, D.D. He says: 'To praise the preaching of Baxter, the theology of Owen, the genius of Howe, the learning of Goodwin, the reasoning of Charnock, the sermons of Bates, the devotion of Flavel, the meditations of Isaac Ambrose, the expositions of Matthew Poole, the labours of Oliver Heywood, the life of Joseph Alleine! No, indeed! It is not for me to praise the men who have done much to make old England what it is: a great, a free, a glorious, a strong, a religious, a Protestant country. They have left their deep and indelible impressions upon the history of our land, and upon all its institutions; while their influence is felt, perhaps more powerfully than at home, in our free colonies growing rapidly into great nations. They have given to their country and its dependencies, in a language which, more than any other, promises to become universal, a religious literature, so thoughtful, so devout, and so practical, that pious conformists as well as nonconformists acknowledge it, as subordinate to Scripture, to be the wealth of our churches, the strength of our preachers, and our best defence against the progress of Popery on the one hand and of Rationalism on the other.'

Such were these men, great and mighty scholars, mighty preachers, men of character and of strength of conviction, men of courage. They proved that. When so many of the Episcopalians fled for safety, and for their lives, from the Plague and the Fire of London some three years later, these were the men who remained and preached to the people and gathered congregations round themselves, proving what wonderful and noble men they were.

## VII

How did they face it all? How did they face the ejection? Here, again, we are in the fortunate position of being able to give examples of how they left their dear congregations and people and went out and faced the unknown future. This is the kind of thing they said when they preached their Farewell sermons.

Here is part of a sermon by Richard Alleine, the father-in-law of the famous Joseph Alleine, the Taunton evangelist. This is how he preached in his last sermon before having to go out after twenty years' ministry at Batcombe: 'The sun is setting upon not a few of the prophets; the shadows of evening are stretched forth upon us; our work seems to be at an end; our pulpits and our places must know us no more. This is the Lord's doing; let all the earth keep silence before him. It is not a light thing for me, brethren, to be laid aside from the work, and cast out from the vineyard of the Lord … I know that some will add to the affliction of the afflicted by telling the world it is their own fault, and that they might prevent it if they would. Whether this be so or no, God knoweth; and let the Lord be the judge. Blessed be God, whatever be laid to our charge, this is not – that we are secluded from insufficiency or scandal. You are not ignorant what things there are imposed upon us as the condition of continuing our ministration; which, however lawful or expedient, they may be in the judgment of many, yet have the most specious arguments in their favour left me utterly dissatisfied with them. I must profess before God, and angels, and men, that my non-submission is not from any disloyalty to authority, nor from pride, humour, nor factious disposition; but because I dare not contradict my light, or do anything concerning which my heart tells me the Lord says, "Do it not." After all my most impartial enquiries, after all my seeking counsel of the Lord, I find that I am plainly put to this choice – to part with my ministry or my conscience. I dare not lie before God and the world, nor tell you that I approve, I allow, I heartily consent to what I neither do nor can; but must choose rather that my ministry be sealed up by my sufferings than lengthened out by a lie. Through the grace of God, though men reproach me, my heart shall not reproach me while I live. "If our hearts condemn us, God is greater than our hearts, and knoweth all things." … Since matters stand so that I must either lose my place or my peace, I cheerfully suffer myself to be thrust off the stage. And now, welcome the cross of Christ; welcome reproach; welcome poverty, scorn, and contempt, or whatever else may befall me on this account. This morning I had a flock, and you a pastor; now, behold a pastor without a flock, a flock without a shepherd; this morning I had a house, but now I have none; this morning I had a living, but now I have none. "The Lord hath given, the Lord hath taken away; blessed be the name of the Lord." Beloved, I am sensible of many weaknesses and disadvantages I am under, which may render a suffering state the harder to be borne; help me by your prayers, and not me only, but my brethren also, with whom my lot must fall. "Pray for us; for we trust that we have a good conscience, in all things willing to live honestly." Pray for us, that God may make our silence speak, and preach the same holy doctrine that we have preached with our lips; pray for us that He would give us supports answerable to our sufferings, and that, "according to our earnest expectation and our hope, Christ may be magnified in us, whether it be by life or by death."

'And thus, brethren, I bid you farewell in the words of the apostle: "Finally, brethren, farewell; Be perfect, be of good comfort, be of one mind, live in peace, and the God of love and peace shall be with you." And that "God of peace that brought again from the dead our Lord Jesus, that great Shepherd of the sheep, through the blood of the everlasting covenant, make you perfect in every good work to do his will, working in you that which is well-pleasing in his sight, through Jesus Christ, to whom be glory for ever and ever. Amen."' That is a typical example of the way in which they parted with their beloved flocks.[1]

## VIII

Time does not permit our telling you something of what they had to suffer. These learned, godly men were not only turned out of their livings and churches, they were not allowed to be tutors, they were not allowed to be schoolmasters, and they had to leave their houses as well as their stipends and their tithes. Their followers in the main were very poor people with the result that most of them were left utterly destitute.

But, to add to the trouble, a Conventicle Act was passed which prohibited the gathering together of more than five persons in addition to the household to listen to the exposition of the word of God. And then, on top of that, the Five Mile Act was passed prohibiting these men to go within five miles of where they had formerly ministered. Later, many of them were thrown into prisons because they persisted in preaching in spite of all these Acts. John Bunyan was in jail in Bedford for twelve years for doing so, and many others were treated in the same manner. Let me sum up the kind of suffering they had to endure by quoting the words of Richard Baxter. 'The jails are filled with nonconformists: nine ministers are now in Newgate and many more in other places. And almost all of them mulct[2] and fined in far more than ever they were worth. Their goods and their books taken by distress: they are fain to fly or abscond that are not in prison: their wives and children in distress and want: they are judged by the justices unworthy, so much as to be summoned to answer for themselves before they are judged, or to be heard plead their own cause, or to know and witness their accusers and witnesses; but as I myself was distrained of all my

[1] Further 'Farewell Sermons' can be found in *Sermons of the Great Ejection* (Banner of Truth Trust, 1962, 2012).

[2] Mulct = punished or penalized (usually by fining).

goods and books on five convictions before ever I heard of any accusation, or saw a judge, so it is with many others, and more. In a word, lords, knights, and clergymen, take us for insufferable persons in the land, unfit for human society, enemies to monarchy, obedience, and peace, and corporations promise to choose such Parliament men as are for our extirpation.'

That was the kind of suffering to which they were subjected. But they met it in a glorious manner. One of them, Thomas Browning, quoted by R. Tudur Jones in his recent book, *Congregationalism in England 1662–1962,*[1] faced it like this. Writing to his flock from Northampton prison, he says: 'Our tender Father has an handkerchief in his hand to wipe away our tears ... The cup of afflictions for the Gospel is sweeter, the deeper; a stronger cordial, the nearer the Bottom: I mean death itself.' Bunyan, as is well known, wrote his immortal classic, *Pilgrim's Progress,*[2] while in jail in Bedford. They had learned with Paul to say, 'I have learned in whatsoever state I am therewith to be content ... I can do all things through Christ which strengtheneth me.'

## IX

Why did they suffer all this? Why did they refuse to subscribe? These seem to me to have been their reasons. It was: First: that they regarded Jesus Christ as the sole Head of the church, and nobody else. Secondly: that to them the word of God was supreme, and the sole judge in all matters in connection with the life of the church. Thirdly: that they put life and spirit and spirituality before institutions and organisations and tradition. Fourthly: that they put conscience before comfort and all else; and freedom, and the right of private judgment, as being more important than any kind of suffering they might have to endure. Fifthly: that they lived consciously as under the eye of God, regarding life in this world as but a journey and a pilgrimage. Like Moses they kept their eyes fixed on 'the recompense of the reward.'

[1] London: Independent Press, 1962.

[2] Edinburgh: Banner of Truth Trust, 2017.

## X

What good came out of it all? In spite of the suffering and the injustice, has any special good come out of it all? Part of the answer to that question was given at the beginning. Let me note some further answers. There is time merely for headings.

Here is the first good that came out of it. Someone wrote these words: 'Had all the ministers conformed' – and this was a man of rank writing at the time – 'Had all the ministers conformed, people would have thought that there was nothing in religion, that it was only a thing to be talked of in the pulpit or serve a state design. But these men, giving up their livings, and exposing themselves and their families to outward evils rather than they would conform to things not agreeable as they apprehended to the gospel they preach, have convinced men that there is a reality in religion, and have thereby given a check to Atheism.' By doing what they did and suffering all this, they proved to men that religion is something real, that they meant what they said, and that they were ready to suffer for it. That great good came out of it. Religion would have been regarded as a farce if they had conformed after all they had preached.

The second good – their incomparable writings. In the Evangelical Library we have those massive tomes – books by John Owen and Thomas Goodwin, John Flavel, Thomas Brooks, John Howe, and the rest of them – very largely for this reason, that as they were forbidden to preach they occupied their time in writing books. If they had not been ejected, and if those other Acts had not been passed, possibly they would have preached so much that they would have had no time for writing. Thus the tables were turned upon the subtle enemy, and these ejected Puritans have continued to preach for three centuries in a way that they could never have done had they not been ejected. God brings good out of evil. He reigns: 'He ruleth over all.' We have this rich legacy from these men.

What have we got from the men who conformed? There are but two that I can think of that have left anything – William

Gurnall and his *Christian in Complete Armour,*[1] and John Trapp the commentator. They conformed. But these men who went out have given us this rich and abiding heritage.

But, above all, they have left us this noble, glorious, wonderful example of holy living, patient endurance in suffering, and loyalty to the word of God and its message, even at the cost of being 'fools for Christ's sake' and being regarded as 'the offscourings of all things.'

## XI

What, then, are the questions these men compel us to face in 1962?

There is one general question: What do we think of the Protestant Reformation? These men, as we have seen, were ejected from the church because they not only believed in the Protestant Reformation but believed, further, that it had not gone far enough in the Church of England. What is our view of the Protestant Reformation? There are many in all sections of the Christian church today who are saying loudly that the Protestant Reformation was a disaster. Do we join them and go back to Rome, or do we join the men of 1662 and at all costs go back to the New Testament and the pattern found there of a gospel church?

But they compel us to face certain particular questions also.

1. Which comes first: Is it the position in which we find ourselves as a result of the accident of birth and upbringing and tradition? Or is it the truth of God? Am I to be influenced primarily by the fact that I happen to have been brought up in a certain denomination, or am I to be influenced primarily by the teaching of the word of God?

2. Is it right and honest to make mental reservations, or to give my private interpretation, to articles or confessions of faith to which I am asked to subscribe? They compel us to face that question. Whatever may be said against them, the Puritans were honest men. They could not prevaricate, they could not indulge in mental reservations. Has that always been true? Is it true of us?

[1] First published by the Trust in 1964; reprinted many times.

3. Are we always to abide by majority decisions, and to say when we are out-voted, that though we think the majority is quite wrong, it is still our business to stay inside and bear our witness to the truth and try to influence the others in that direction? The Puritans, as I have shown, tried to do that for a hundred years and more. In 1662 they came to the conclusion that it was impossible, that it could not be done. So they were ejected. Their story compels all who hold their evangelical views to face this question. When do we come to the position of 1662? At what point do we feel that we are compromising the truth and violating conscience?

4. Should we not be ever vigilant to observe all authoritarian tendencies, and all tendencies to ecclesiasticism and the hierarchical principle in the life and activities of churches, or groups, or councils of churches, and above all as churches look more and more to, and fraternise increasingly with, Rome?

5. Should we not always be extremely suspicious of increasing liturgical tendencies in worship, and the tendency to exalt the 'service' at the expense of the sermon?

I ask these questions very deliberately because I notice an increasing tendency to ecclesiasticism, to ceremonial as expressed in the wearing of gowns and robes, and in procession – in free churches as well as in the Anglican church – and likewise a tendency to elevate and exalt offices, and to develop a bureaucracy which exercises increasing control over the local church and the individual Christian.

My last question is this: If these men of 1662 were prepared to go to this extreme length, and to suffer such untold sufferings, concerning the matters which divided them from their contemporaries – the things to which I have been referring, and which they said themselves were not primarily matters of doctrine – if they were prepared to go to such lengths concerning those matters, what should be our attitude towards flagrant denials of the very foundations and first principles of the Christian faith, or the widespread indifference to doctrine which are to be found in the churches in 1962? As in 1662, the choice before us today is – conformity or purity?

There, it seems to me, are the questions which these men put before us in our age and generation. As we take our leave of them, those noble souls, I find echoing in my ears the words written by Wordsworth with respect to Milton. But instead of Milton put John Owen, put Thomas Goodwin, put Thomas Manton, put John Howe – put any one of them you like, and say this:

*. . . ! thou shouldst be living at this hour:*
*England hath need of thee: she is a fen*
*Of stagnant waters: altar, sword, and pen,*
*Fireside, the heroic wealth of hall and bower,*
*Have forfeited their ancient English dower*
*Of inward happiness. We are selfish men;*
*O! raise us up, return to us again;*
*And give us manners, virtue, freedom, power.*
*Thy soul was like a Star, and dwelt apart;*
*Thou hadst a voice whose sound was like the sea:*
*Pure as the naked heavens, majestic, free.*

Oh, for such a voice! The voice of any one of those mighty men of whom, as the author to the Epistle to the Hebrews so rightly says, 'the world was not worthy.'

Shall we leave it then at that? No, let us go beyond Wordsworth, let us quote a hymn:

*A noble army – men and boys,*
*The matron and the maid,*
*Around the Saviour's throne rejoice,*
*In robes of light arrayed;*
*They climbed the steep ascent of heaven,*
*Through peril, toil, and pain:*
*O God, to us may grace be given*
*To follow in their train!*

Let us go beyond even the hymn-writer to the word of God: 'Wherefore seeing we also are compassed about with so great a cloud of witnesses, let us lay aside every weight, and the sin which doth so easily beset us, and let us run with patience the race that is set before us, looking unto Jesus the author and finisher of our faith; who for the joy that was set before him endured the cross, despising the shame.' These men did look to him, and followed him, and were made more than conquerors. 'God of our fathers! be the God of their succeeding race.'

# Index